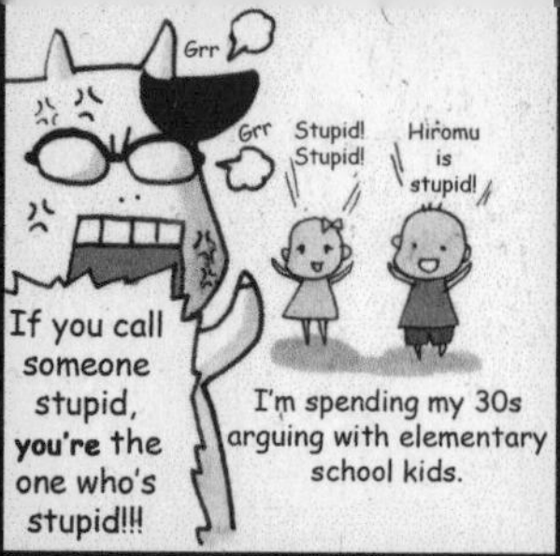
Hiromu is stupid!
Stupid! Stupid!
Grr
Grr
If you call someone stupid, **you're** the one who's stupid!!!
I'm spending my 30s arguing with elementary school kids.

My niece and nephew call me "stupid" so often that one day I just had to reply, "I am stupid, and that's why I don't have a real job and spend all my time drawing manga." To which they immediately responded, "You're right!"

—Hiromu Arakawa, 2008

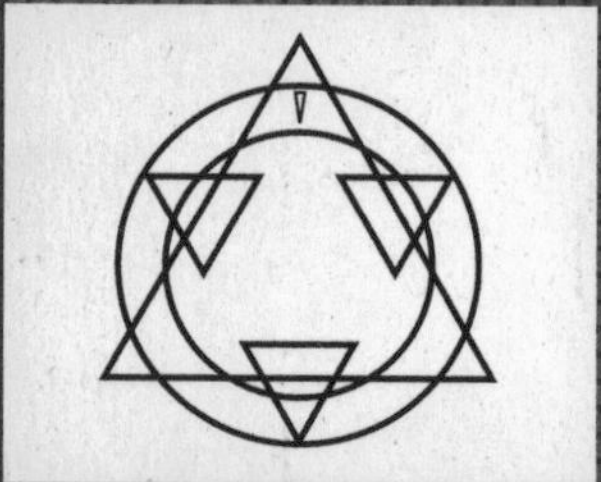

Born in Hokkaido (northern Japan), Hiromu Arakawa first attracted national attention in 1999 with her award-winning manga *Stray Dog*. Her series *Fullmetal Alchemist* debuted in 2001 in Square Enix's monthly manga anthology *Shonen Gangan*.

FULLMETAL ALCHEMIST
VOL. 18

Story and Art by Hiromu Arakawa

Translation/Akira Watanabe
English Adaptation/Jake Forbes
Touch-up Art & Lettering/Wayne Truman
Design/Julie Behn
Editor/Annette Roman

Editor in Chief, Books/Alvin Lu
Editor in Chief, Magazines/Marc Weidenbaum
VP, Publishing Licensing/Rika Inouye
VP, Sales & Product Marketing/Gonzalo Ferreyra
VP, Creative/Linda Espinosa
Publisher/Hyoe Narita

Printed in the U.S.A.

Published by VIZ Media, LLC
P.O. Box 77010
San Francisco, CA 94107

10 9 8 7 6 5 4 3 2 1
First printing, May 2009

www.viz.com

store.viz.com

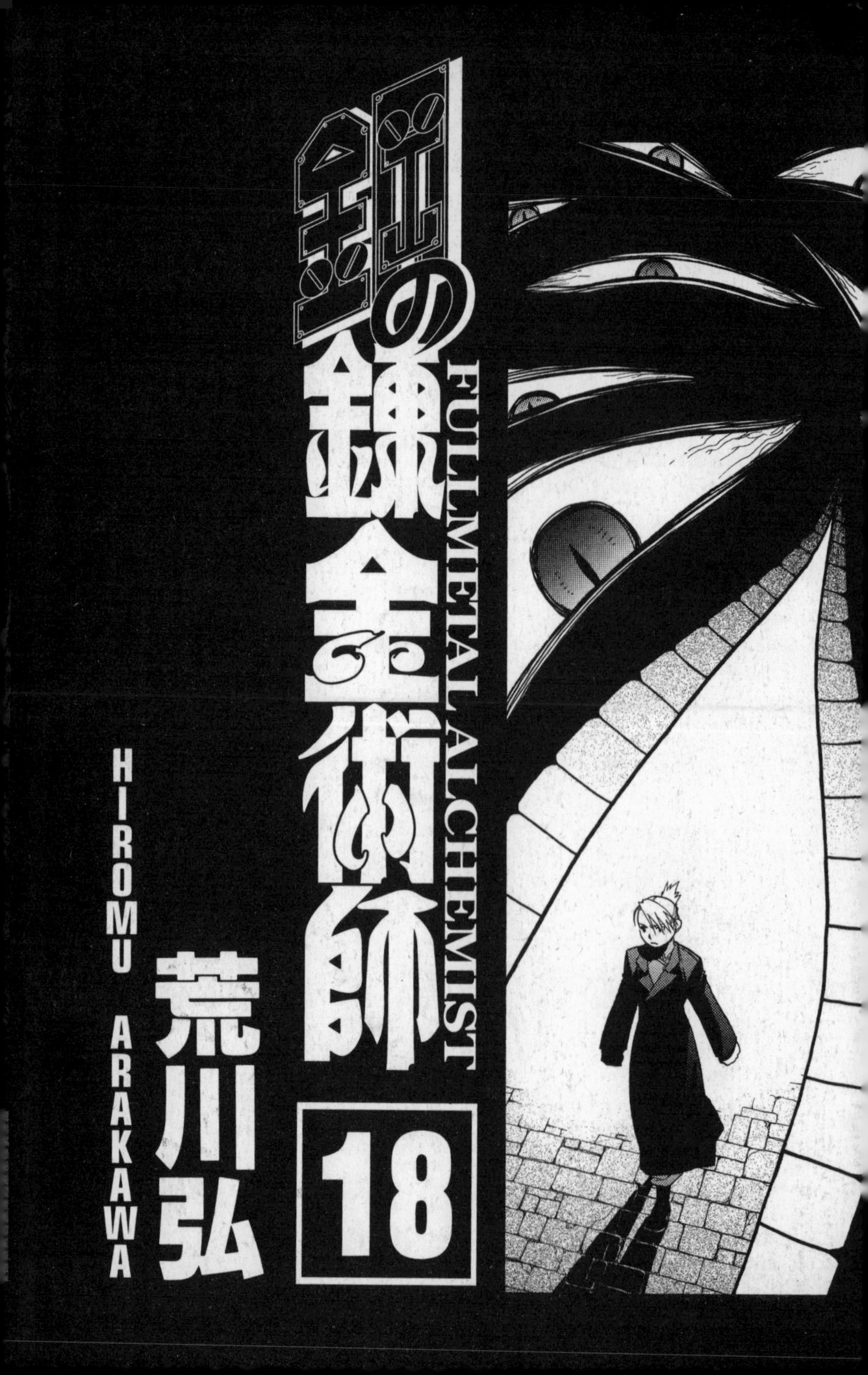

鋼の錬金術師

FULLMETAL ALCHEMIST

18

荒川弘

HIROMU ARAKAWA

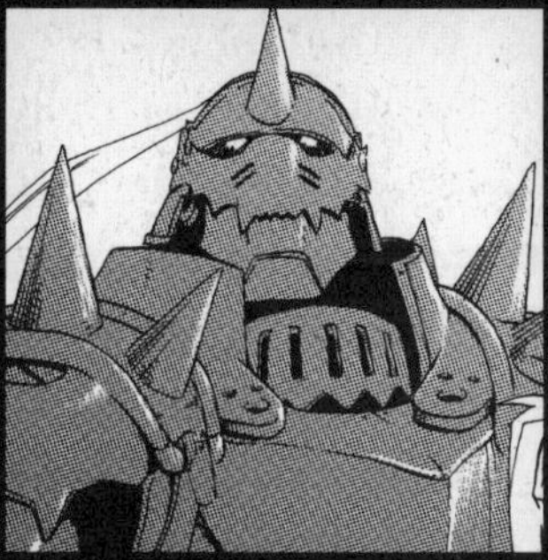

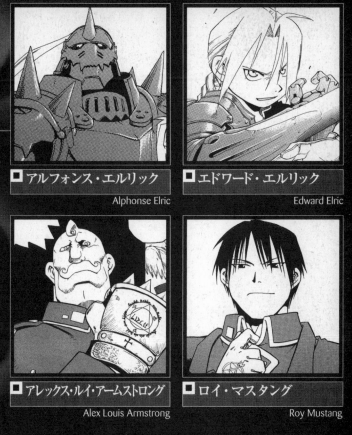

アルフォンス・エルリック

Alphonse Elric

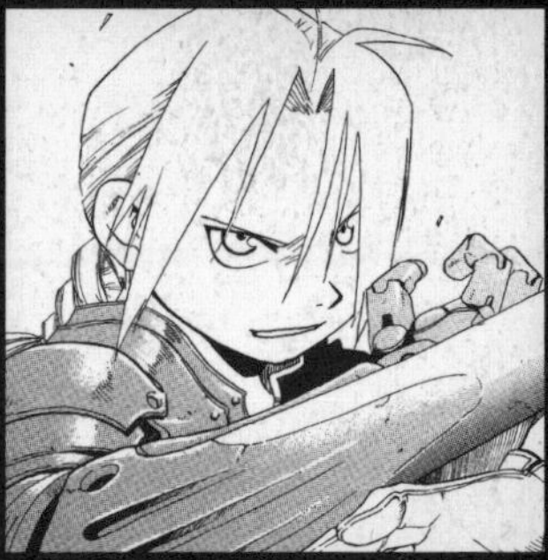

エドワード・エルリック

Edward Elric

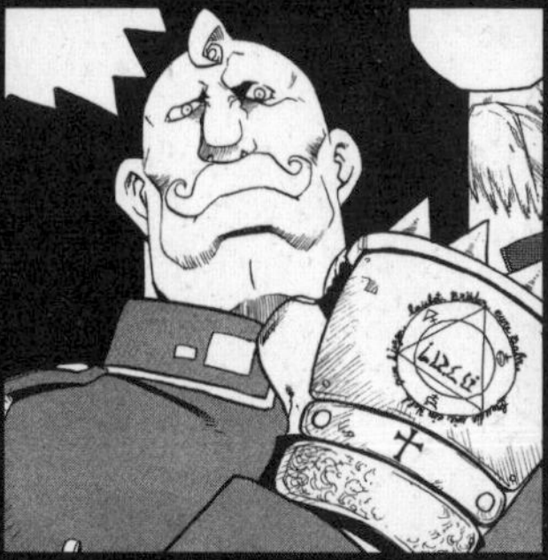

アレックス・ルイ・アームストロング

Alex Louis Armstrong

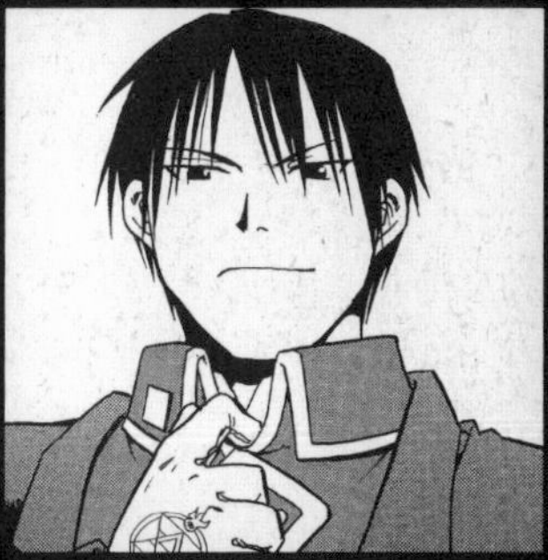

ロイ・マスタング

Roy Mustang

OUTLINE
FULLMETAL ALCHEMIST

Using a forbidden alchemical ritual, the Elric brothers attempted to bring their dead mother back to life. But the ritual went wrong, consuming Edward Elric's leg and Alphonse Elric's enti body. At the cost of his arm, Edward was able to graft his brother's soul into a suit of armor. Equipped with mechanical "auto-mail" to replace his missing limbs, Edward becomes a state alchemist in hopes of finding a way to restore their bodies. Their search embroils them in a deadly conspiracy that threatens to take the innocence, if not the lives, of everyone involved.

At Fort Briggs, on the snowbound northern border, the Brothers Elric make a shocking discovery. The bloody history of Amestris, dotted with wars and annexations along every border, has been carefully orchestrated by the Homonculi and their military pawns to achieve a single goal: turning the entire nation into one giant Transmutation Circle! While Major General Armstrong and her loyal soldiers investigate the Homonculi's tunnels beneath Briggs, Ed and Al are stuck behind bars as part of an elaborate ruse to trick Military High Command. While temperatures plummet, the cat-and-mouse game heats up!

鋼の錬金術師
FULLMETAL ALCHEMIST

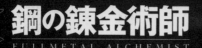

CHARACTERS
FULLMETAL ALCHEMIST

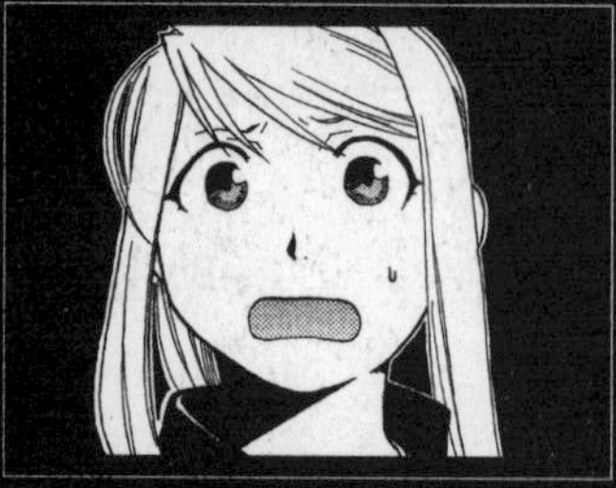

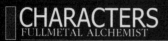

ウィンリィ・ロックベル

Winry Rockbell

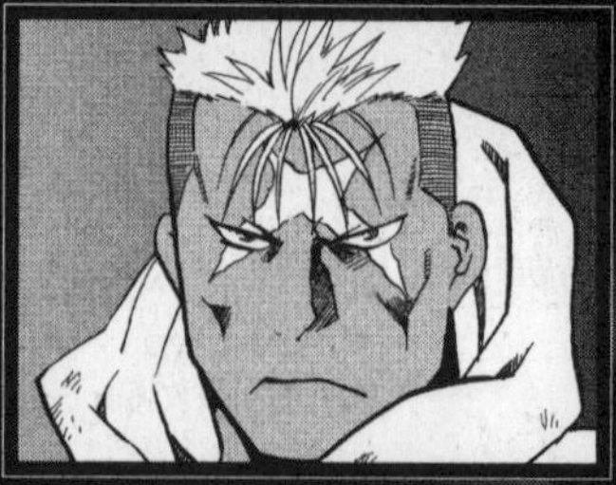

スカー

Scar

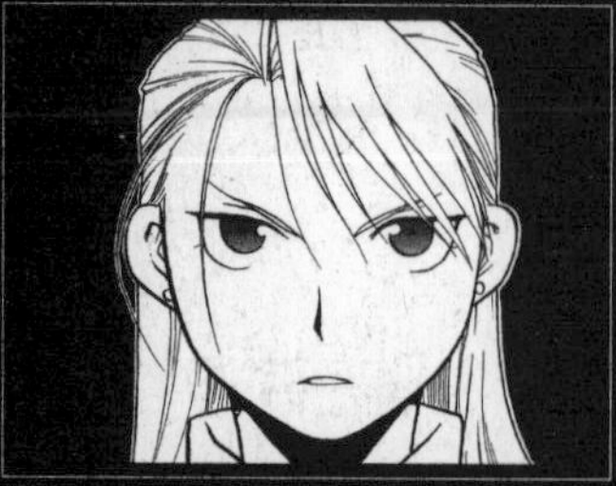

リザ・ホークアイ

Riza Hawkeye

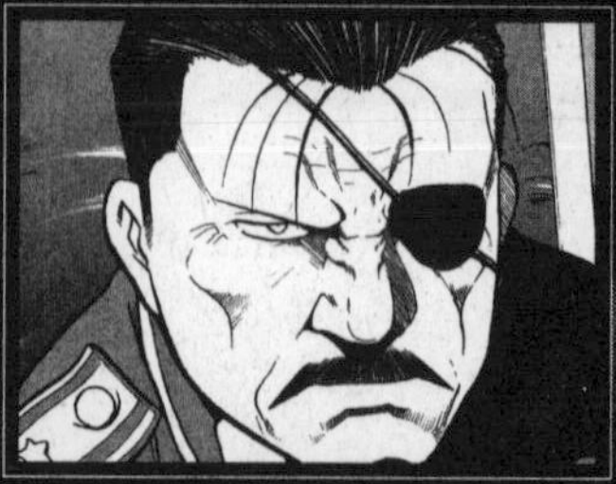

キング・ブラッドレイ

King Bradley

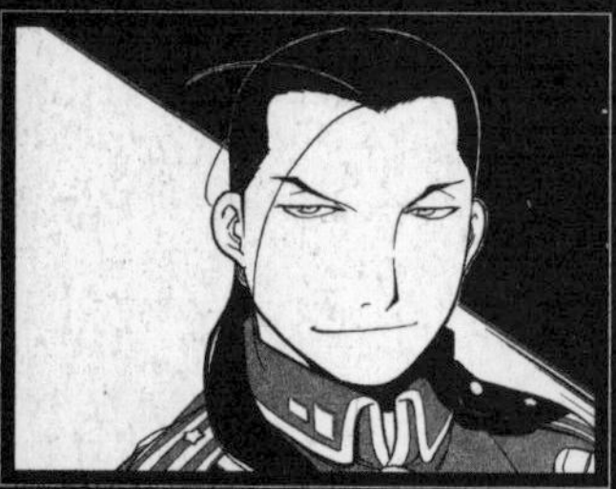

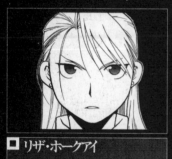

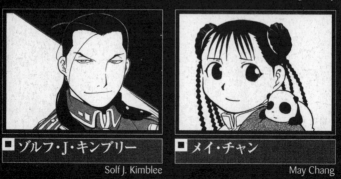

ゾルフ・J・キンブリー

Solf J. Kimblee

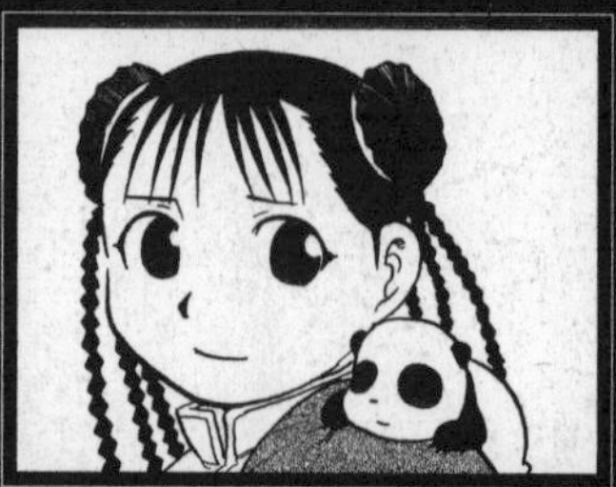

メイ・チャン

May Chang

CONTENTS

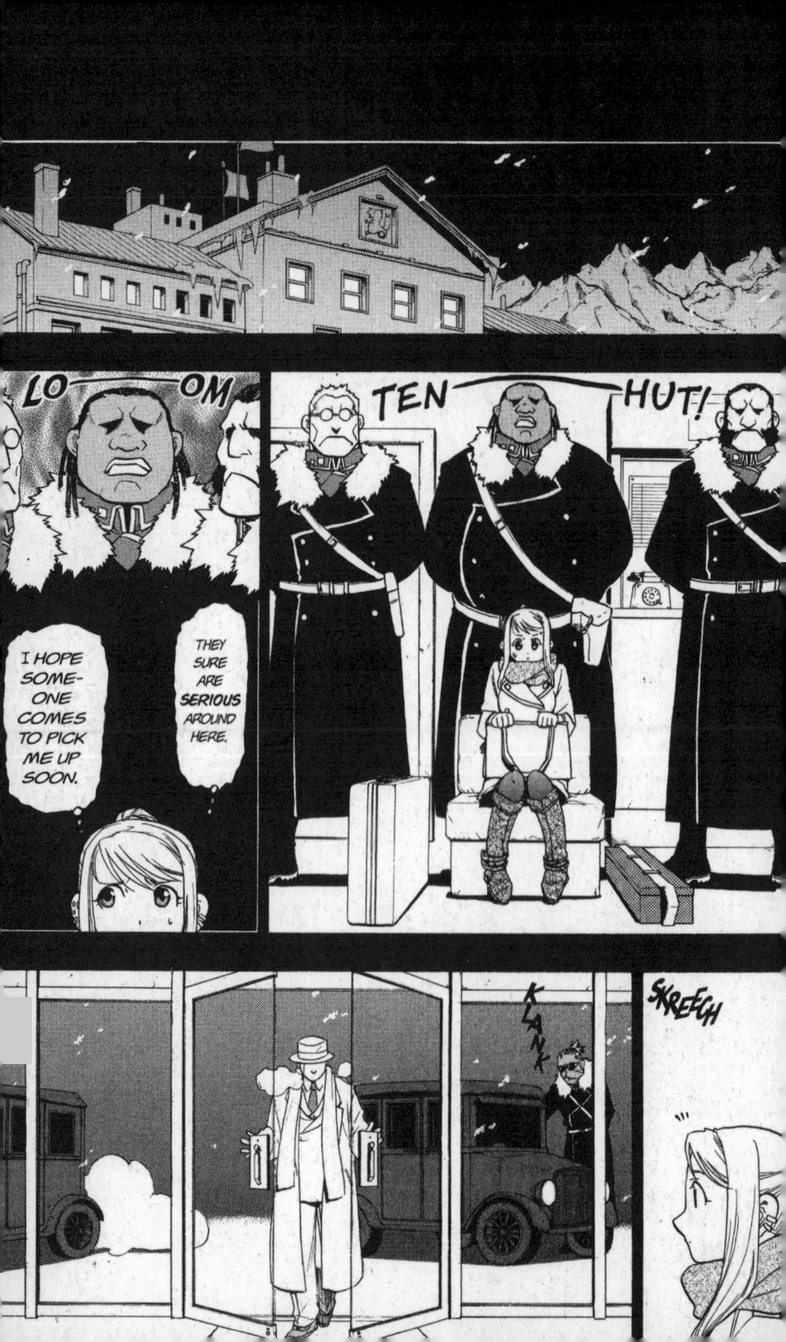
TEN—HUT!
LO—OM
THEY SURE ARE SERIOUS AROUND HERE.
I HOPE SOMEONE COMES TO PICK ME UP SOON.
SKREECH
KLANK

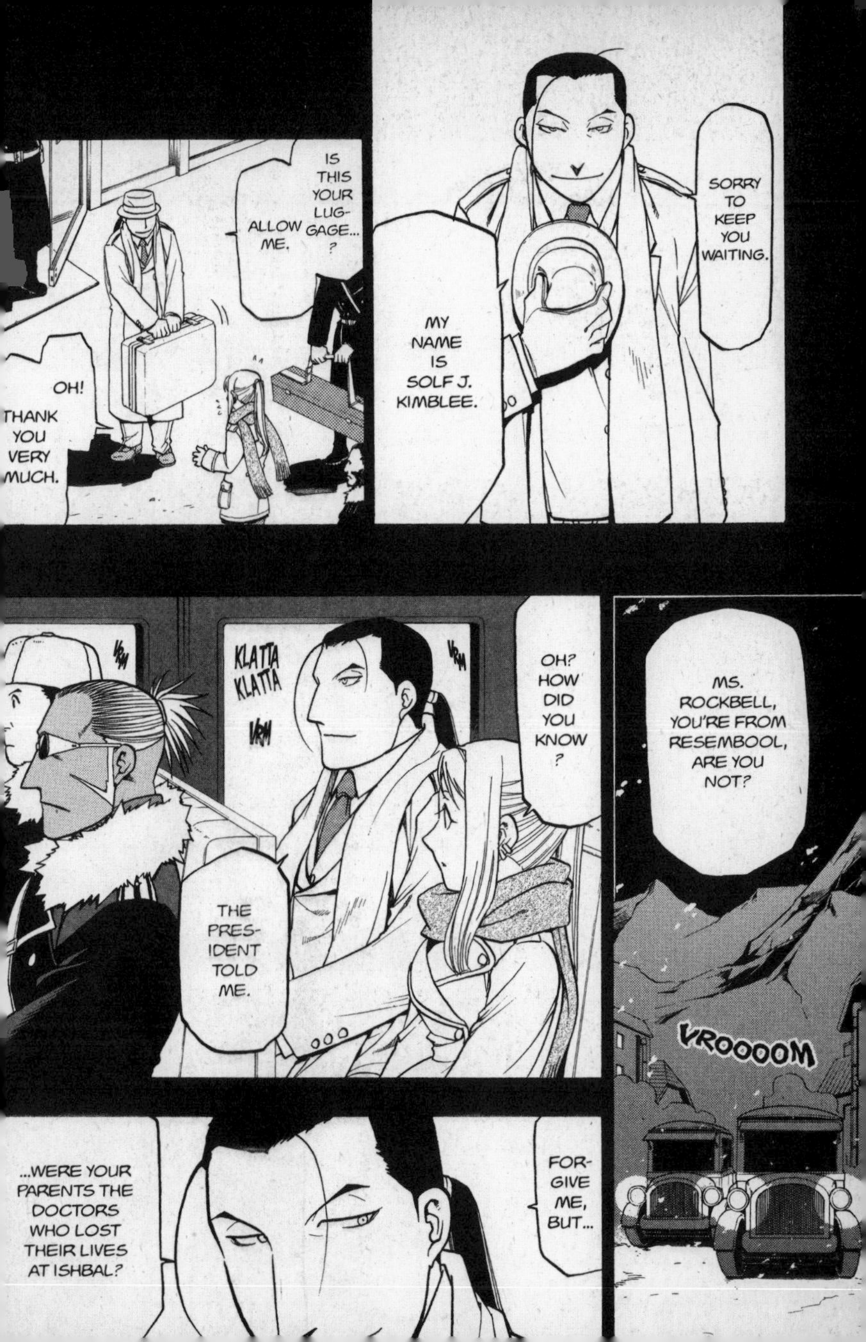
SORRY TO KEEP YOU WAITING.
MY NAME IS SOLF J. KIMBLEE.
IS THIS YOUR LUG-GAGE...?
ALLOW ME.
OH!
THANK YOU VERY MUCH.
MS. ROCKBELL, YOU'RE FROM RESEMBOOL, ARE YOU NOT?
VROOOOM
OH? HOW DID YOU KNOW?
VRM
KLATTA KLATTA
VRM
THE PRES-IDENT TOLD ME.
FOR-GIVE ME, BUT...
...WERE YOUR PARENTS THE DOCTORS WHO LOST THEIR LIVES AT ISHBAL?

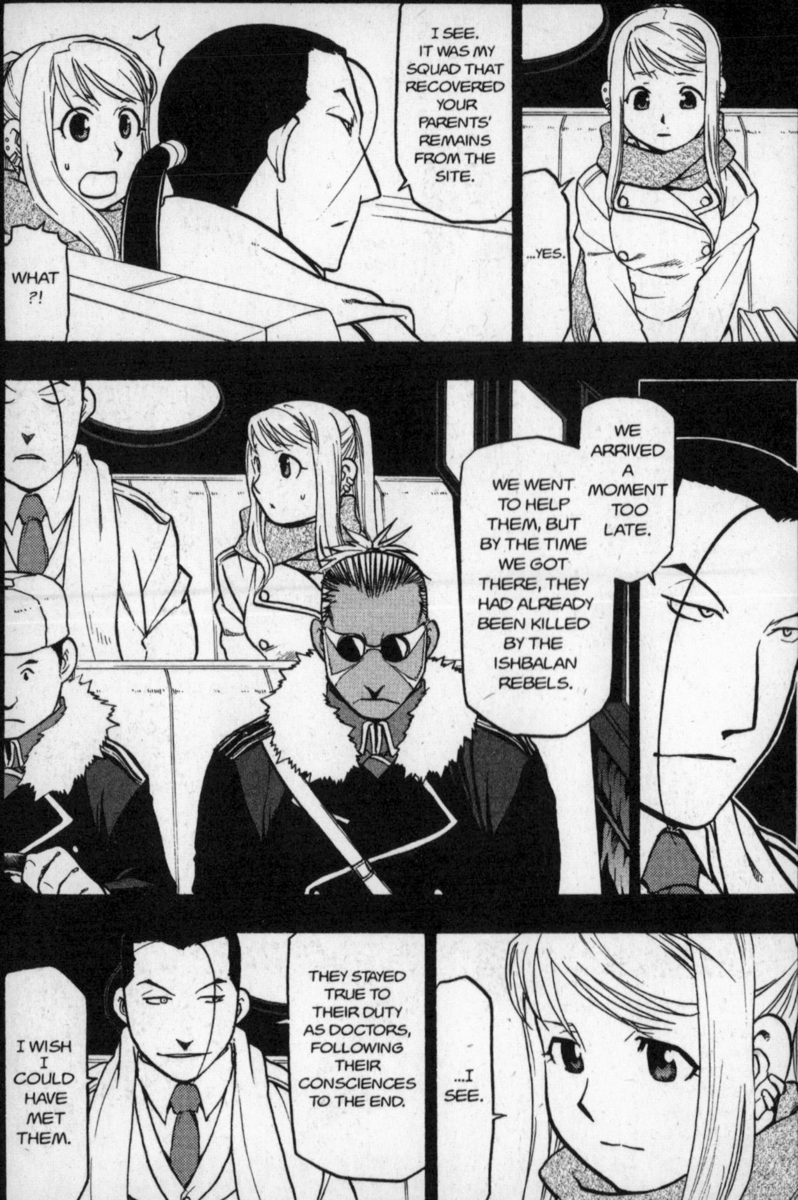
...YES.
I SEE. IT WAS MY SQUAD THAT RECOVERED YOUR PARENTS' REMAINS FROM THE SITE.
WHAT ?!
WE ARRIVED A MOMENT TOO LATE.
WE WENT TO HELP THEM, BUT BY THE TIME WE GOT THERE, THEY HAD ALREADY BEEN KILLED BY THE ISHBALAN REBELS.
...I SEE.
THEY STAYED TRUE TO THEIR DUTY AS DOCTORS, FOLLOWING THEIR CONSCIENCES TO THE END.
I WISH I COULD HAVE MET THEM.

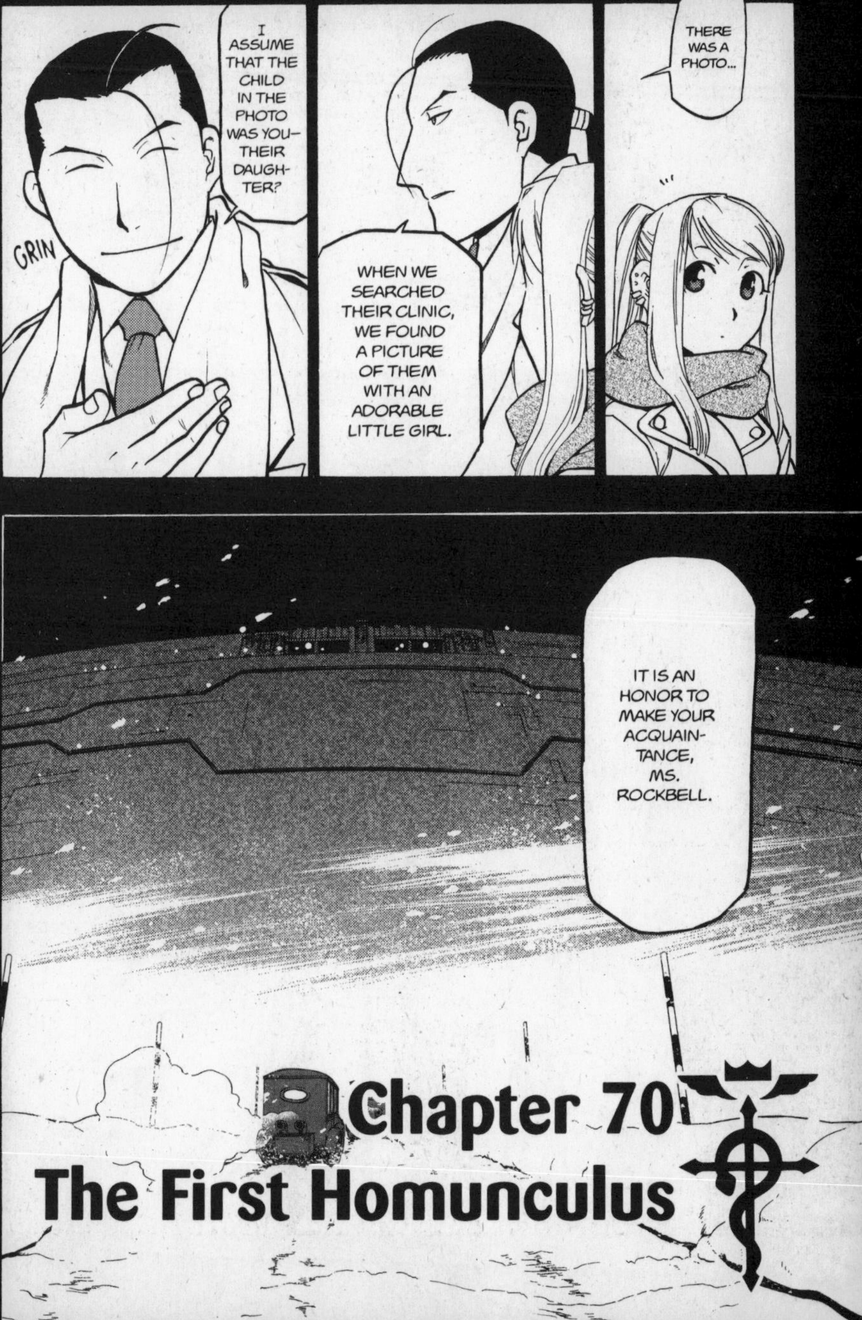
THERE WAS A PHOTO...
WHEN WE SEARCHED THEIR CLINIC, WE FOUND A PICTURE OF THEM WITH AN ADORABLE LITTLE GIRL.
I ASSUME THAT THE CHILD IN THE PHOTO WAS YOU—THEIR DAUGHTER?
GRIN
IT IS AN HONOR TO MAKE YOUR ACQUAINTANCE, MS. ROCKBELL.
Chapter 70
The First Homunculus

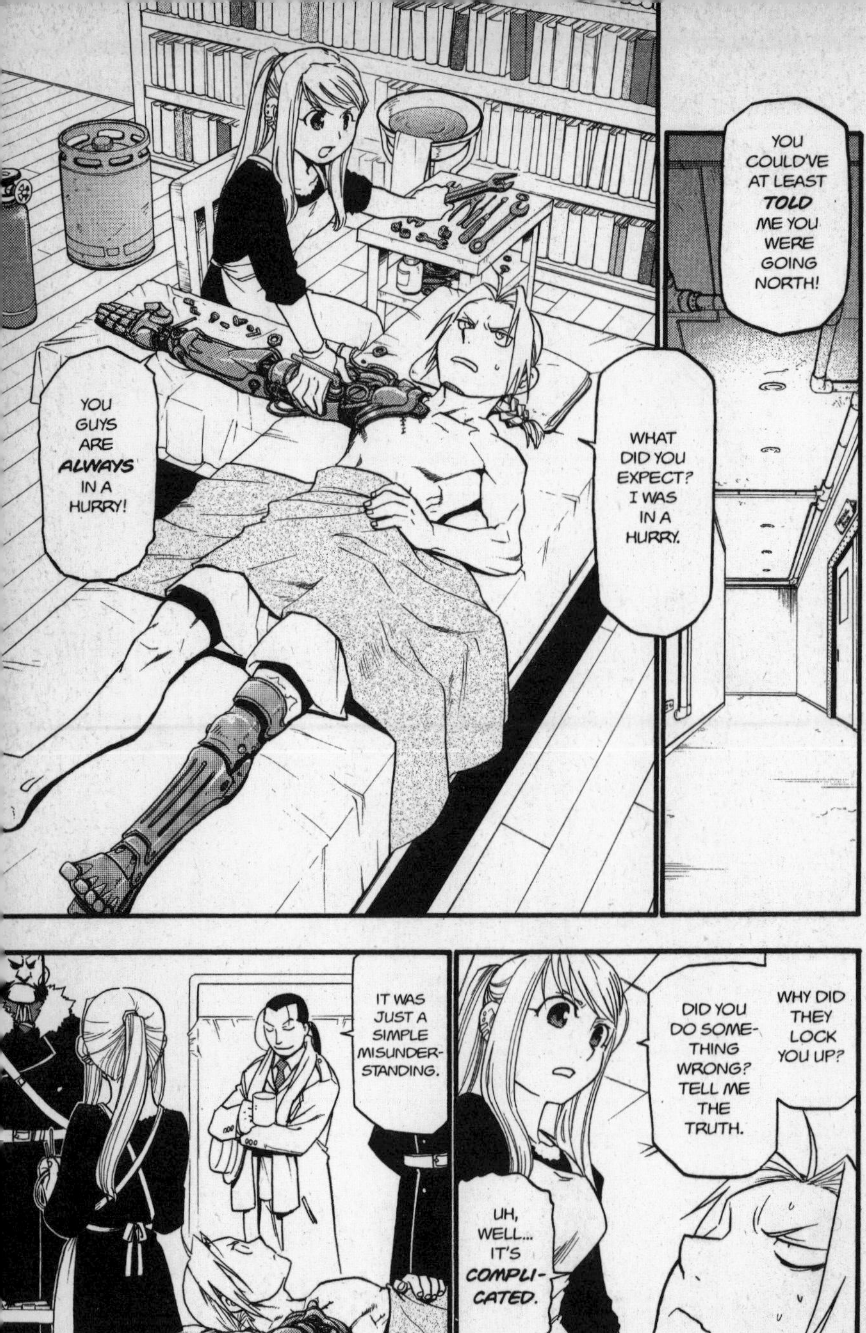
YOU COULD'VE AT LEAST **TOLD** ME YOU WERE GOING NORTH!
WHAT DID YOU EXPECT? I WAS IN A HURRY.
YOU GUYS ARE **ALWAYS** IN A HURRY!
WHY DID THEY LOCK YOU UP?
DID YOU DO SOME-THING WRONG? TELL ME THE TRUTH.
UH, WELL... IT'S **COMPLI-CATED.**
IT WAS JUST A SIMPLE MISUNDER-STANDING.

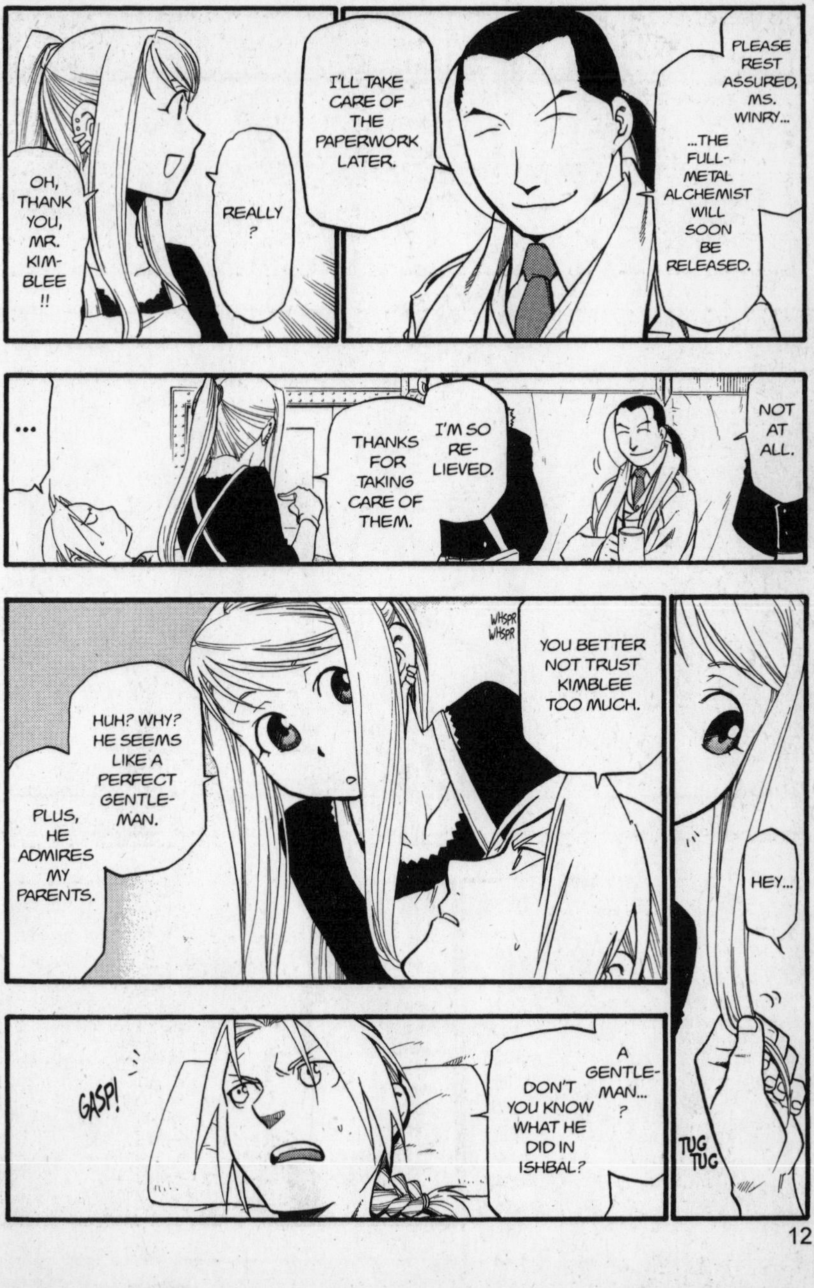
PLEASE REST ASSURED, MS. WINRY...
...THE FULL-METAL ALCHEMIST WILL SOON BE RELEASED.
I'LL TAKE CARE OF THE PAPERWORK LATER.
REALLY?
OH, THANK YOU, MR. KIM-BLEE!!
NOT AT ALL.
I'M SO RE-LIEVED.
THANKS FOR TAKING CARE OF THEM.
...
HEY...
TUG TUG
WHSPR WHSPR
YOU BETTER NOT TRUST KIMBLEE TOO MUCH.
HUH? WHY? HE SEEMS LIKE A PERFECT GENTLE-MAN.
PLUS, HE ADMIRES MY PARENTS.
A GENTLE-MAN...?
DON'T YOU KNOW WHAT HE DID IN ISHBAL?
GASP!

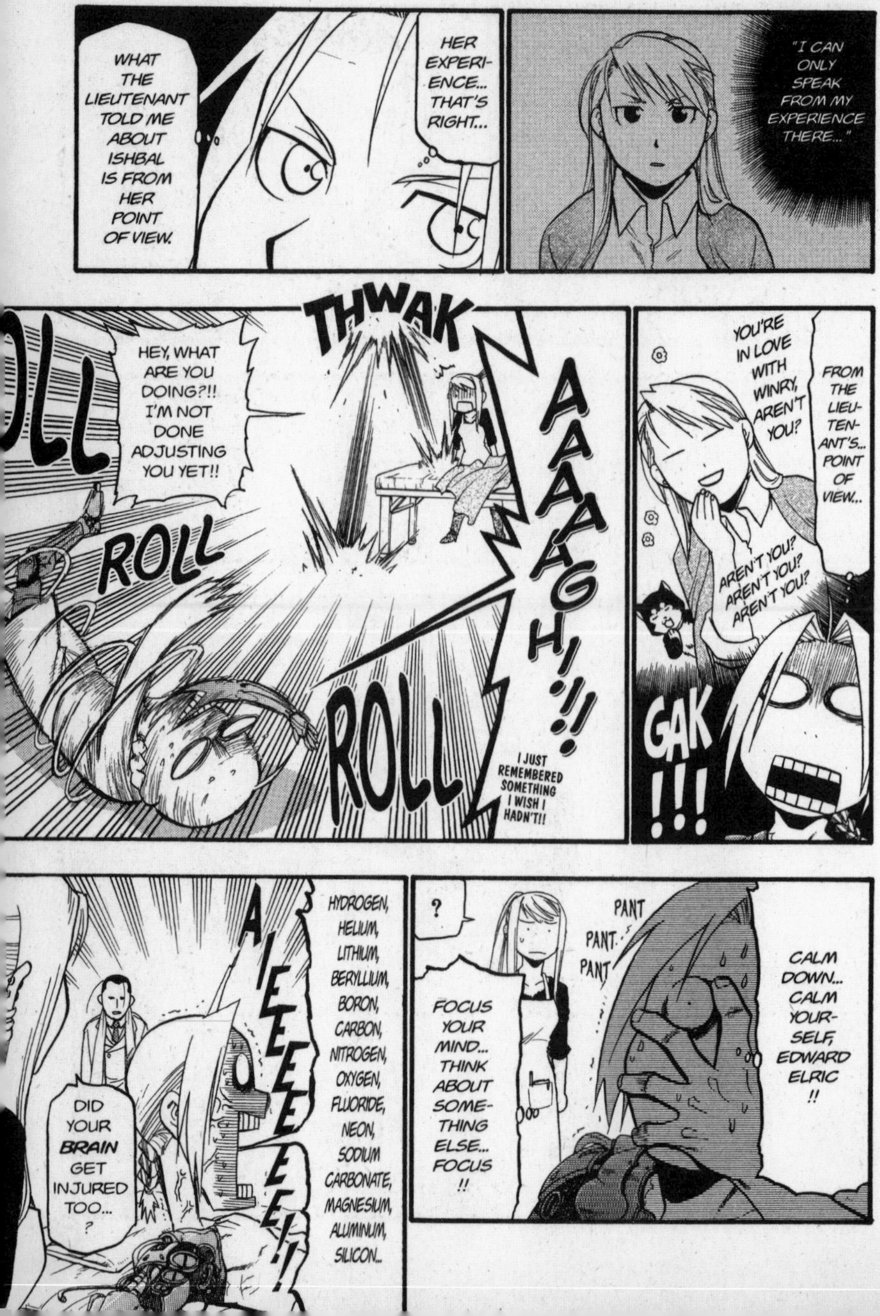
"I CAN ONLY SPEAK FROM MY EXPERIENCE THERE..."
HER EXPERIENCE... THAT'S RIGHT...
WHAT THE LIEUTENANT TOLD ME ABOUT ISHBAL IS FROM HER POINT OF VIEW.
FROM THE LIEUTENANT'S... POINT OF VIEW...
YOU'RE IN LOVE WITH WINRY, AREN'T YOU?
AREN'T YOU? AREN'T YOU? AREN'T YOU?
GAK!!!
AAAAGH!!!
THWAK
I JUST REMEMBERED SOMETHING I WISH I HADN'T!!
HEY, WHAT ARE YOU DOING?!! I'M NOT DONE ADJUSTING YOU YET!!
ROLL
ROLL
ROLL
CALM DOWN... CALM YOURSELF, EDWARD ELRIC!!
PANT
PANT
PANT
?
FOCUS YOUR MIND... THINK ABOUT SOMETHING ELSE... FOCUS!!
HYDROGEN, HELIUM, LITHIUM, BERYLLIUM, BORON, CARBON, NITROGEN, OXYGEN, FLUORIDE, NEON, SODIUM CARBONATE, MAGNESIUM, ALUMINUM, SILICON...
AIEEEEEE!!
DID YOUR BRAIN GET INJURED TOO...?

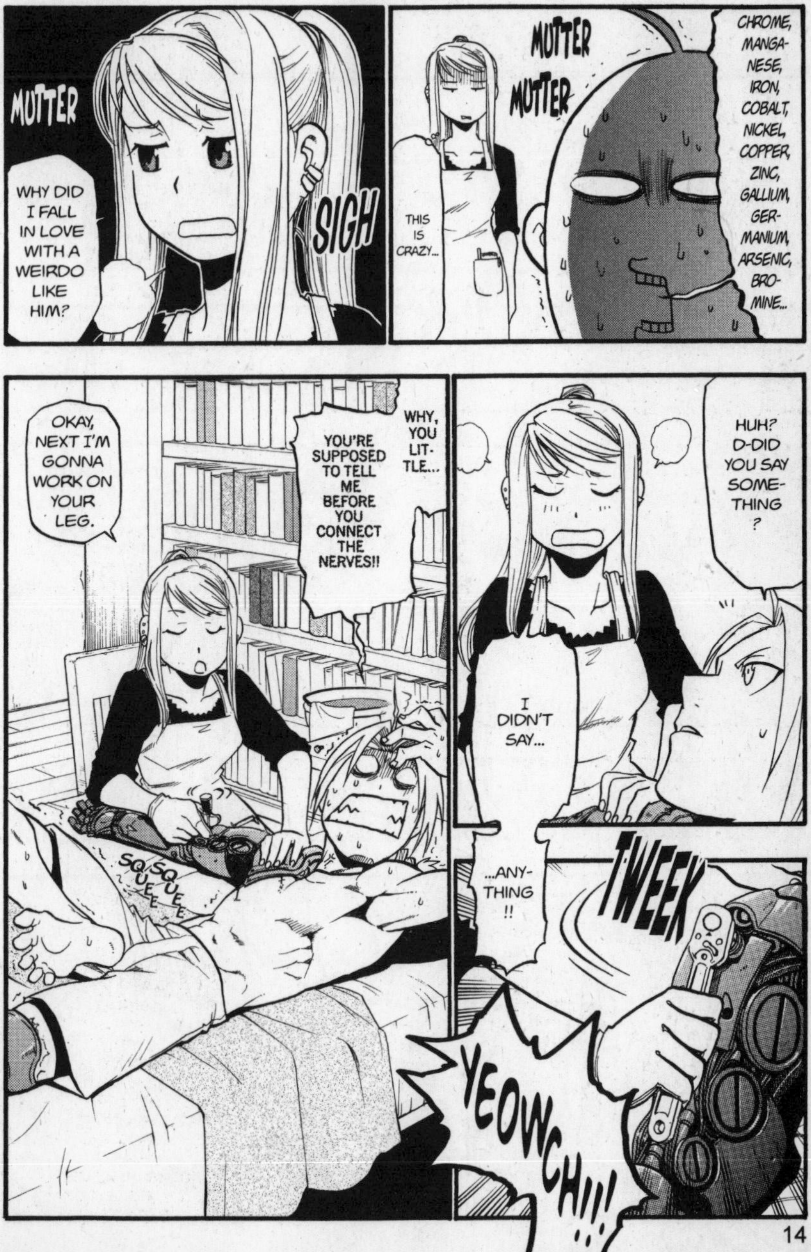
CHROME, MANGANESE, IRON, COBALT, NICKEL, COPPER, ZINC, GALLIUM, GERMANIUM, ARSENIC, BROMINE...
MUTTER MUTTER
THIS IS CRAZY...
MUTTER
SIGH
WHY DID I FALL IN LOVE WITH A WEIRDO LIKE HIM?
HUH? D-DID YOU SAY SOMETHING?
I DIDN'T SAY...
...ANYTHING!!
TWEEK
OKAY, NEXT I'M GONNA WORK ON YOUR LEG.
WHY, YOU LITTLE...
YOU'RE SUPPOSED TO TELL ME BEFORE YOU CONNECT THE NERVES!!
SQUEEE SQUEEE
YEOWCH!!!

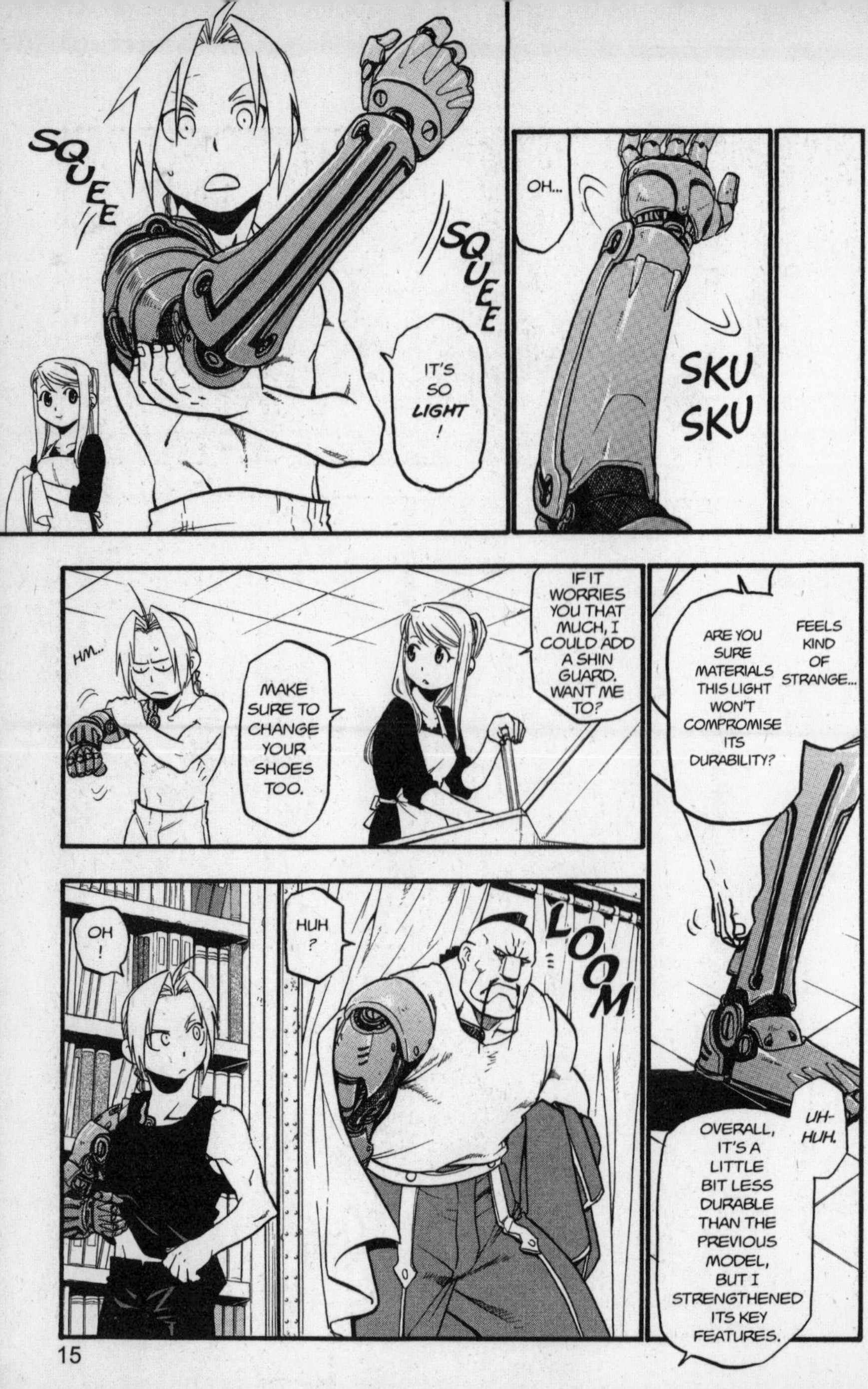
OH...
SKU SKU
SQUEEE
SQUEEE
IT'S SO LIGHT!
FEELS KIND OF STRANGE...
ARE YOU SURE MATERIALS THIS LIGHT WON'T COMPROMISE ITS DURABILITY?
UH-HUH.
OVERALL, IT'S A LITTLE BIT LESS DURABLE THAN THE PREVIOUS MODEL, BUT I STRENGTHENED ITS KEY FEATURES.
IF IT WORRIES YOU THAT MUCH, I COULD ADD A SHIN GUARD. WANT ME TO?
MAKE SURE TO CHANGE YOUR SHOES TOO.
HM...
HUH?
LOOM
OH!

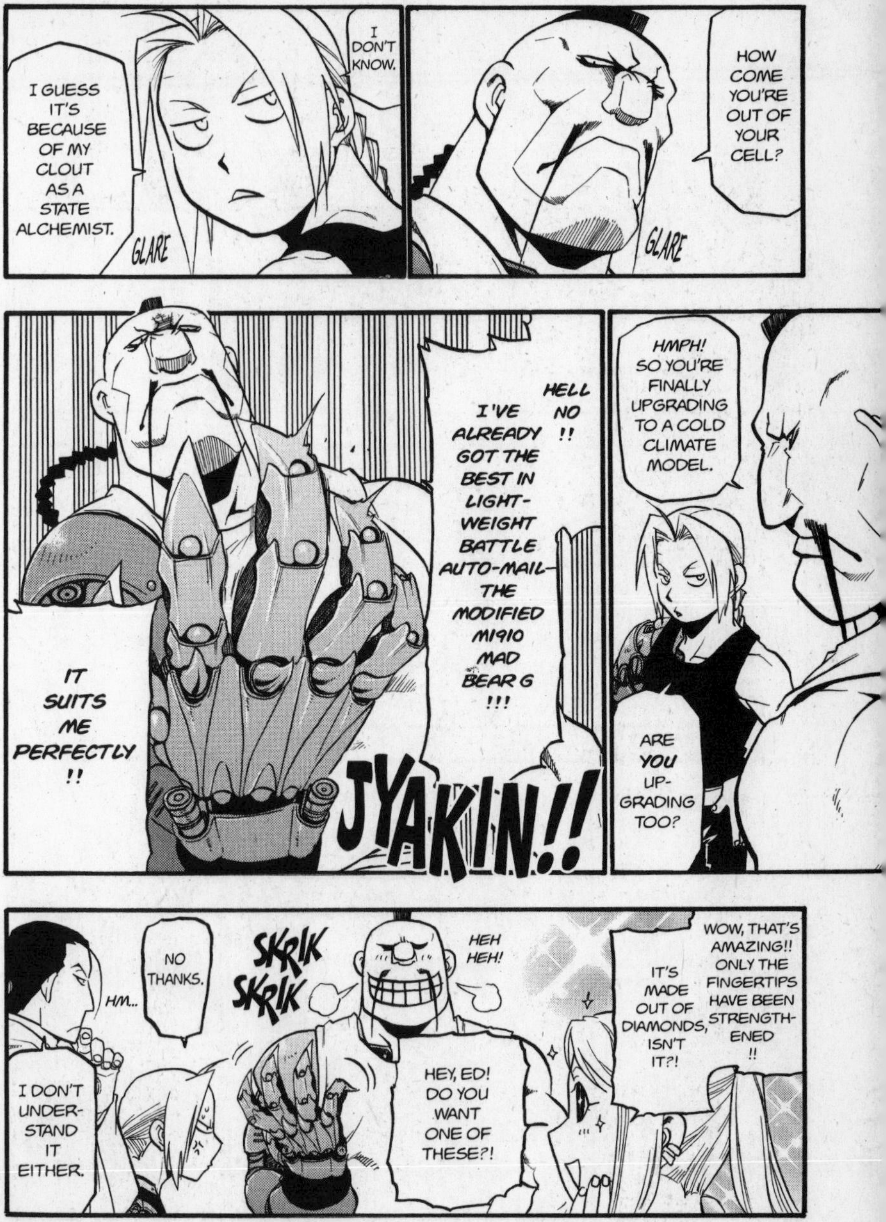
HOW COME YOU'RE OUT OF YOUR CELL?
GLARE
I DON'T KNOW.
I GUESS IT'S BECAUSE OF MY CLOUT AS A STATE ALCHEMIST.
GLARE
HMPH! SO YOU'RE FINALLY UPGRADING TO A COLD CLIMATE MODEL.
ARE YOU UPGRADING TOO?
HELL NO!!
I'VE ALREADY GOT THE BEST IN LIGHT-WEIGHT BATTLE AUTO-MAIL—THE MODIFIED M1910 MAD BEAR G!!!
JYAKIN!!
IT SUITS ME PERFECTLY!!
WOW, THAT'S AMAZING!! ONLY THE FINGERTIPS HAVE BEEN STRENGTH-ENED!!
IT'S MADE OUT OF DIAMONDS, ISN'T IT?!
HEH HEH!
SKRIK SKRIK
HEY, ED! DO YOU WANT ONE OF THESE?!
NO THANKS.
HM...
I DON'T UNDER-STAND IT EITHER.

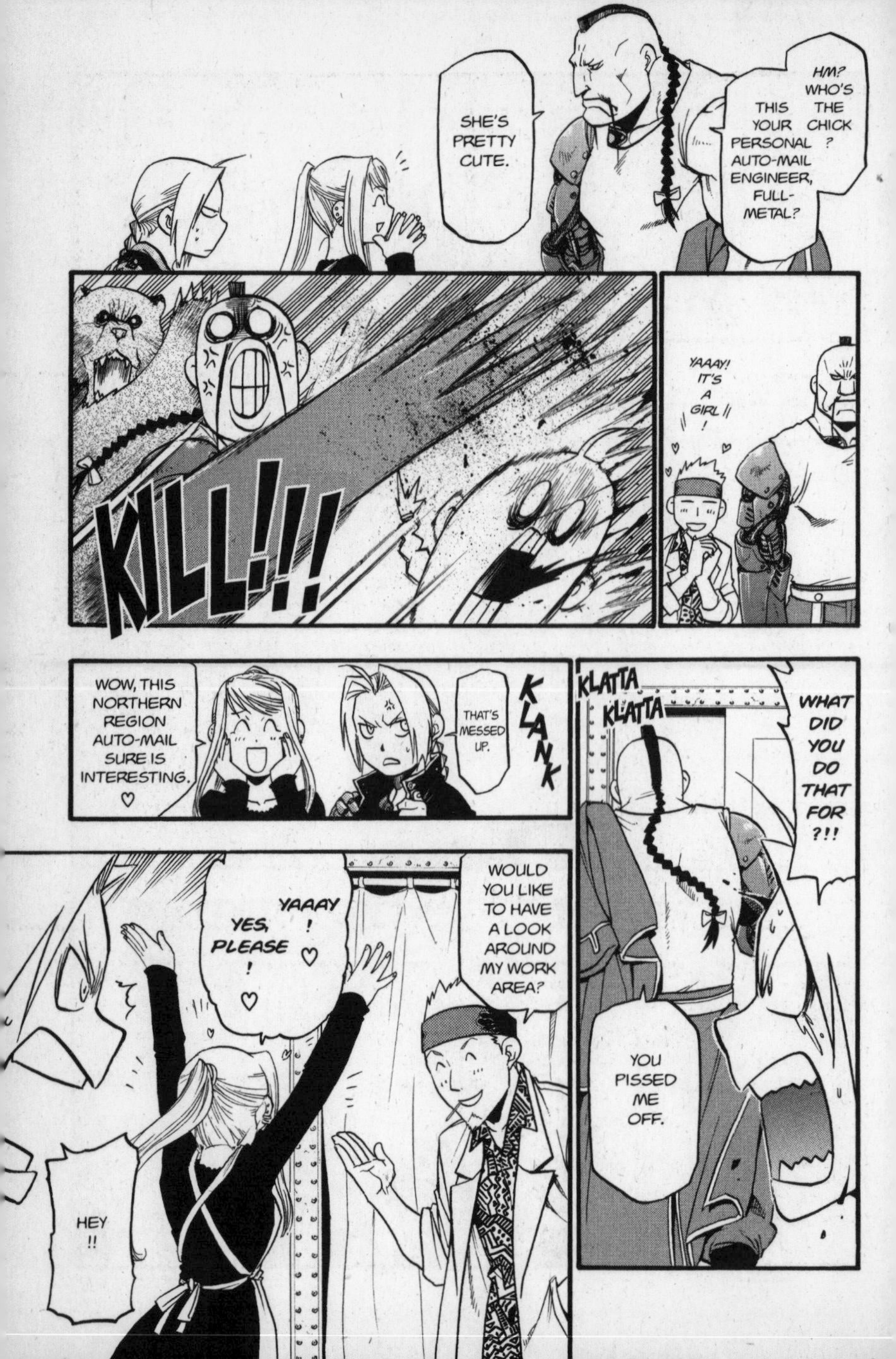
HM? WHO'S THE CHICK? THIS YOUR PERSONAL AUTO-MAIL ENGINEER, FULL-METAL?
SHE'S PRETTY CUTE.
YAAAY! IT'S A GIRL!!
KILL!!!
KLATTA KLATTA
WHAT DID YOU DO THAT FOR?!!
YOU PISSED ME OFF.
KLANK
THAT'S MESSED UP.
WOW, THIS NORTHERN REGION AUTO-MAIL SURE IS INTERESTING. ♡
WOULD YOU LIKE TO HAVE A LOOK AROUND MY WORK AREA?
YAAAY! ♡
YES, PLEASE! ♡
HEY!!

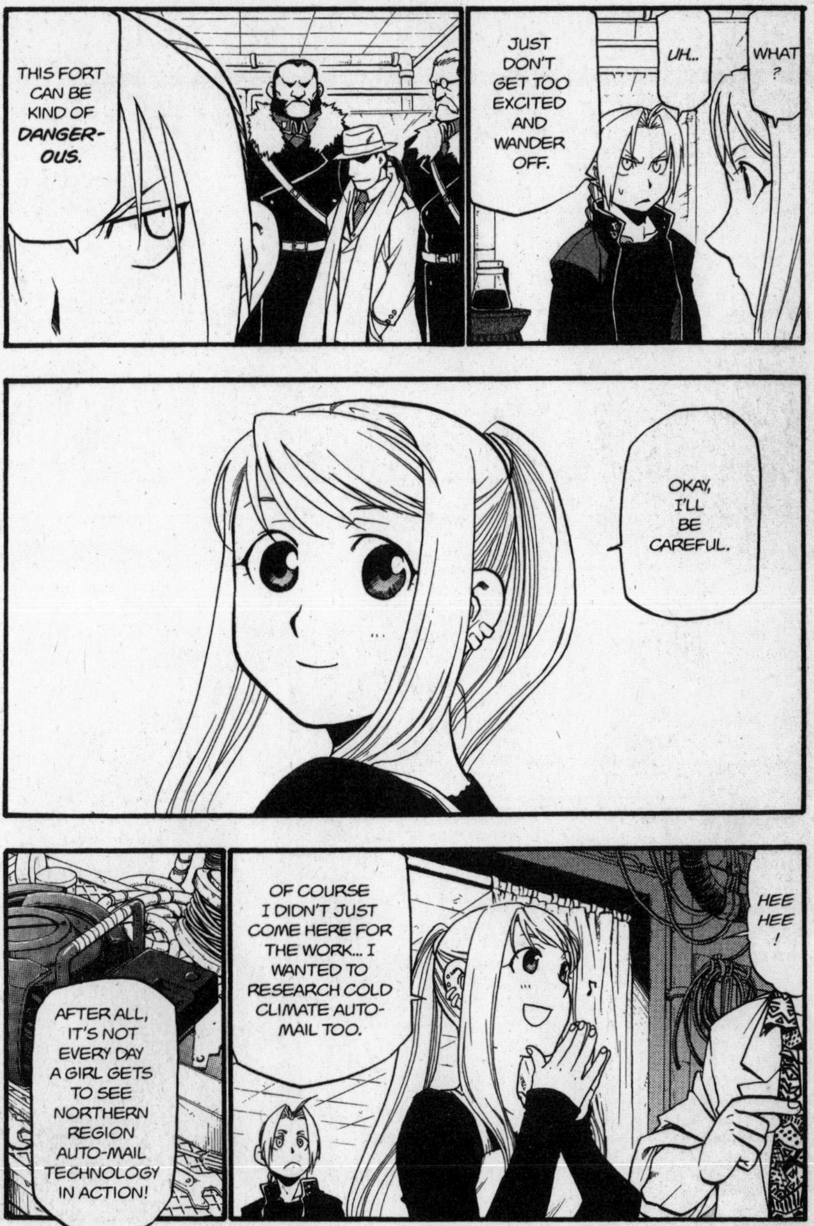
WHAT?
UH...
JUST DON'T GET TOO EXCITED AND WANDER OFF.
THIS FORT CAN BE KIND OF DANGER-OUS.
OKAY, I'LL BE CAREFUL.
HEE HEE!
OF COURSE I DIDN'T JUST COME HERE FOR THE WORK... I WANTED TO RESEARCH COLD CLIMATE AUTO-MAIL TOO.
AFTER ALL, IT'S NOT EVERY DAY A GIRL GETS TO SEE NORTHERN REGION AUTO-MAIL TECHNOLOGY IN ACTION!

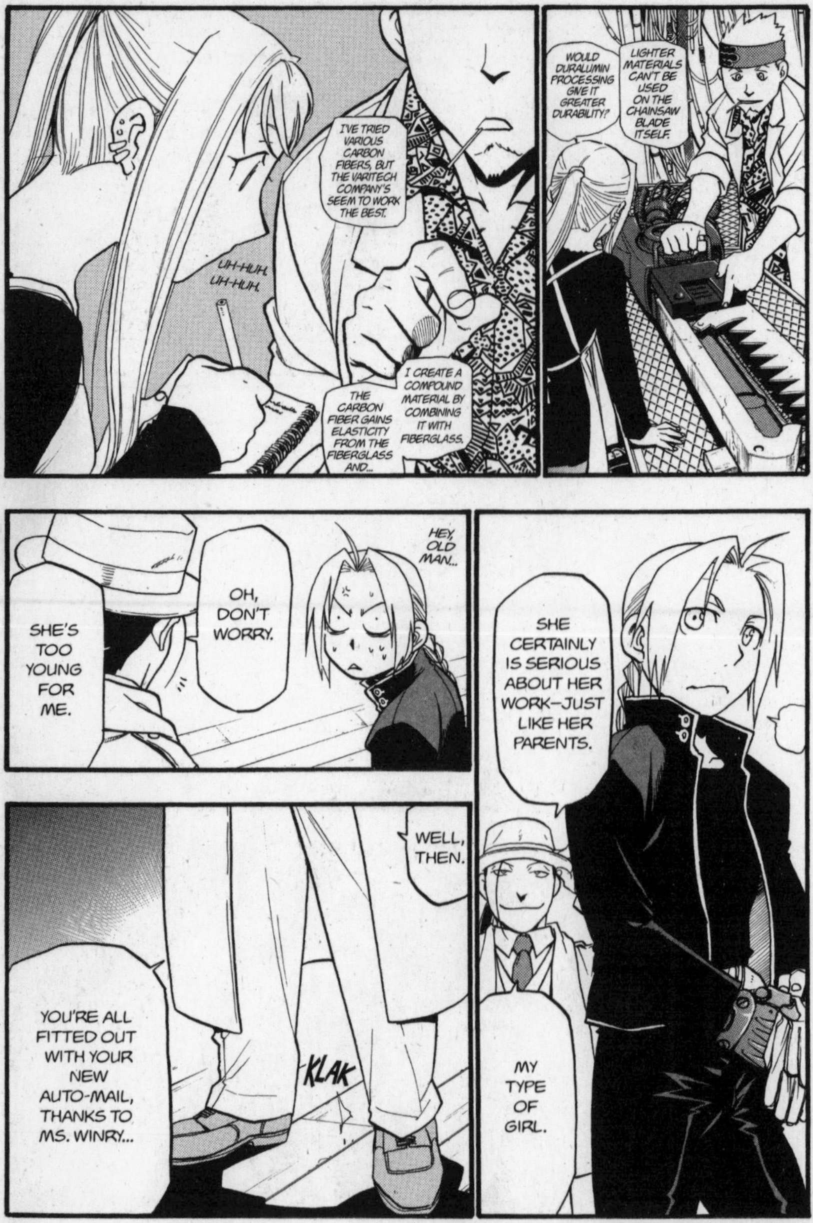
LIGHTER MATERIALS CAN'T BE USED ON THE CHAINSAW BLADE ITSELF.
WOULD DURALUMIN PROCESSING GIVE IT GREATER DURABILITY?
I'VE TRIED VARIOUS CARBON FIBERS, BUT THE VARITECH COMPANY'S SEEM TO WORK THE BEST.
UH-HUH. UH-HUH.
I CREATE A COMPOUND MATERIAL BY COMBINING IT WITH FIBERGLASS.
THE CARBON FIBER GAINS ELASTICITY FROM THE FIBERGLASS AND...
SHE CERTAINLY IS SERIOUS ABOUT HER WORK—JUST LIKE HER PARENTS.
MY TYPE OF GIRL.
HEY, OLD MAN...
OH, DON'T WORRY.
SHE'S TOO YOUNG FOR ME.
WELL, THEN.
KLAK
YOU'RE ALL FITTED OUT WITH YOUR NEW AUTO-MAIL, THANKS TO MS. WINRY...

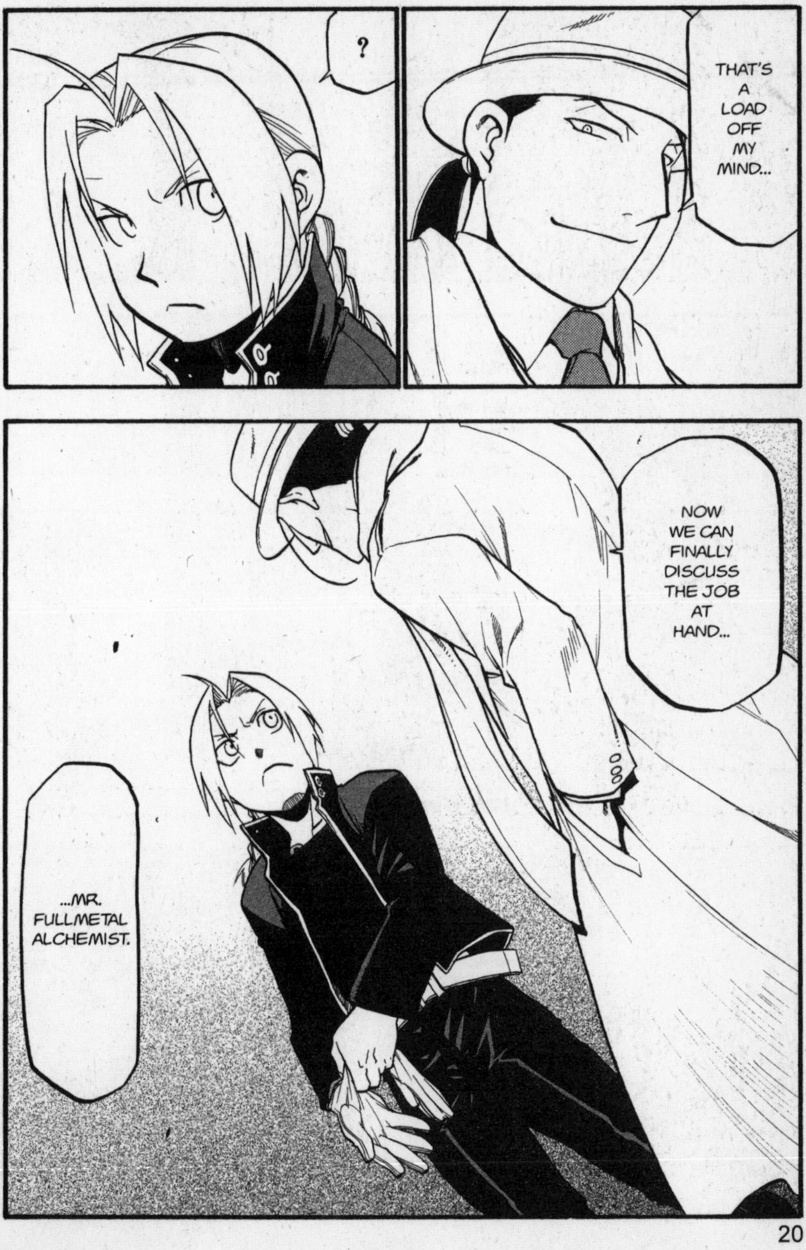
THAT'S A LOAD OFF MY MIND...
?
NOW WE CAN FINALLY DISCUSS THE JOB AT HAND...
...MR. FULLMETAL ALCHEMIST.

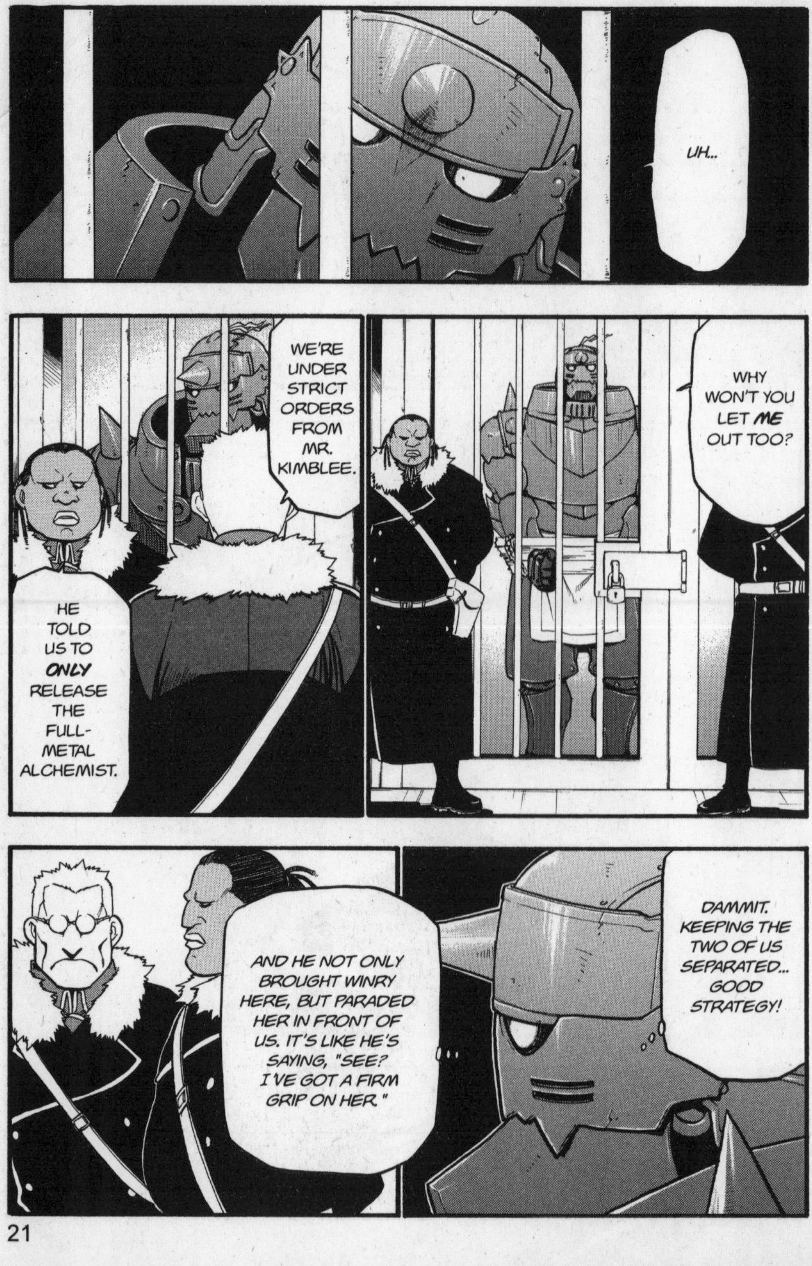
UH...
WHY WON'T YOU LET ME OUT TOO?
WE'RE UNDER STRICT ORDERS FROM MR. KIMBLEE.
HE TOLD US TO ONLY RELEASE THE FULL-METAL ALCHEMIST.
DAMMIT. KEEPING THE TWO OF US SEPARATED... GOOD STRATEGY!
AND HE NOT ONLY BROUGHT WINRY HERE, BUT PARADED HER IN FRONT OF US. IT'S LIKE HE'S SAYING, "SEE? I'VE GOT A FIRM GRIP ON HER."

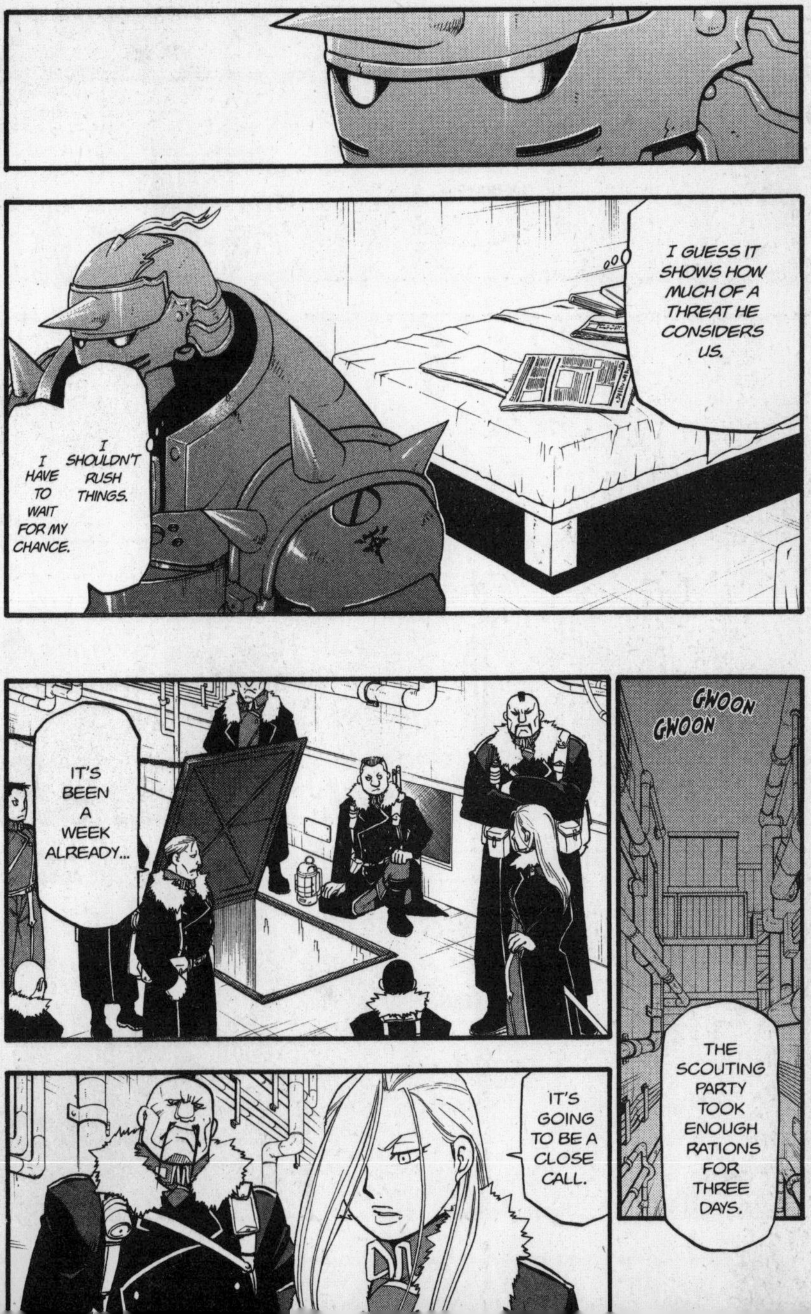
I GUESS IT SHOWS HOW MUCH OF A THREAT HE CONSIDERS US.
I SHOULDN'T RUSH THINGS.
I HAVE TO WAIT FOR MY CHANCE.
GWOON
GWOON
THE SCOUTING PARTY TOOK ENOUGH RATIONS FOR THREE DAYS.
IT'S BEEN A WEEK ALREADY...
IT'S GOING TO BE A CLOSE CALL.

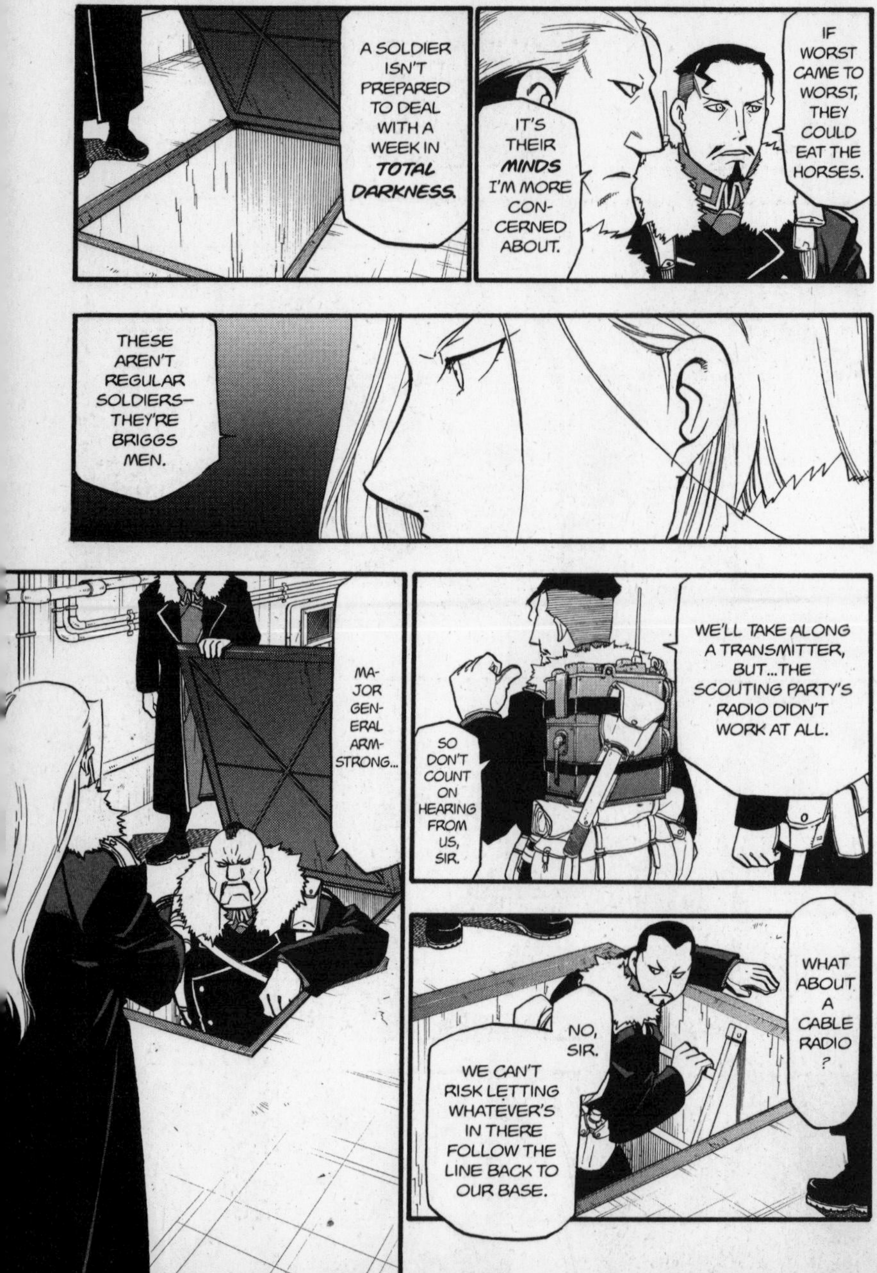
IF WORST CAME TO WORST, THEY COULD EAT THE HORSES.
IT'S THEIR MINDS I'M MORE CONCERNED ABOUT.
A SOLDIER ISN'T PREPARED TO DEAL WITH A WEEK IN TOTAL DARKNESS.
THESE AREN'T REGULAR SOLDIERS— THEY'RE BRIGGS MEN.
WE'LL TAKE ALONG A TRANSMITTER, BUT...THE SCOUTING PARTY'S RADIO DIDN'T WORK AT ALL.
SO DON'T COUNT ON HEARING FROM US, SIR.
WHAT ABOUT A CABLE RADIO?
NO, SIR.
WE CAN'T RISK LETTING WHATEVER'S IN THERE FOLLOW THE LINE BACK TO OUR BASE.
MAJOR GENERAL ARMSTRONG...

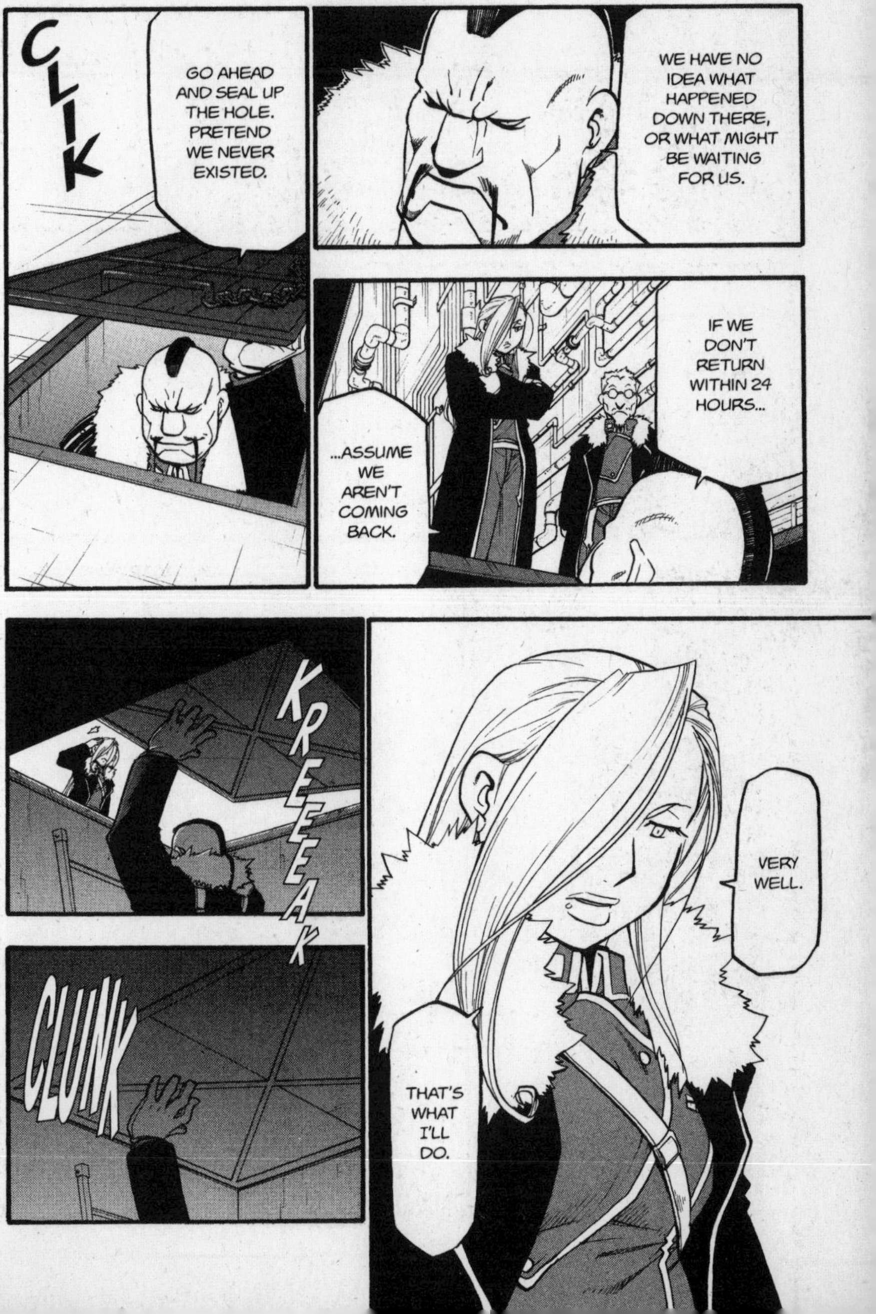
WE HAVE NO IDEA WHAT HAPPENED DOWN THERE, OR WHAT MIGHT BE WAITING FOR US.
IF WE DON'T RETURN WITHIN 24 HOURS...
...ASSUME WE AREN'T COMING BACK.
GO AHEAD AND SEAL UP THE HOLE. PRETEND WE NEVER EXISTED.
CLIK
VERY WELL.
THAT'S WHAT I'LL DO.
KREEEAK
CLUNK

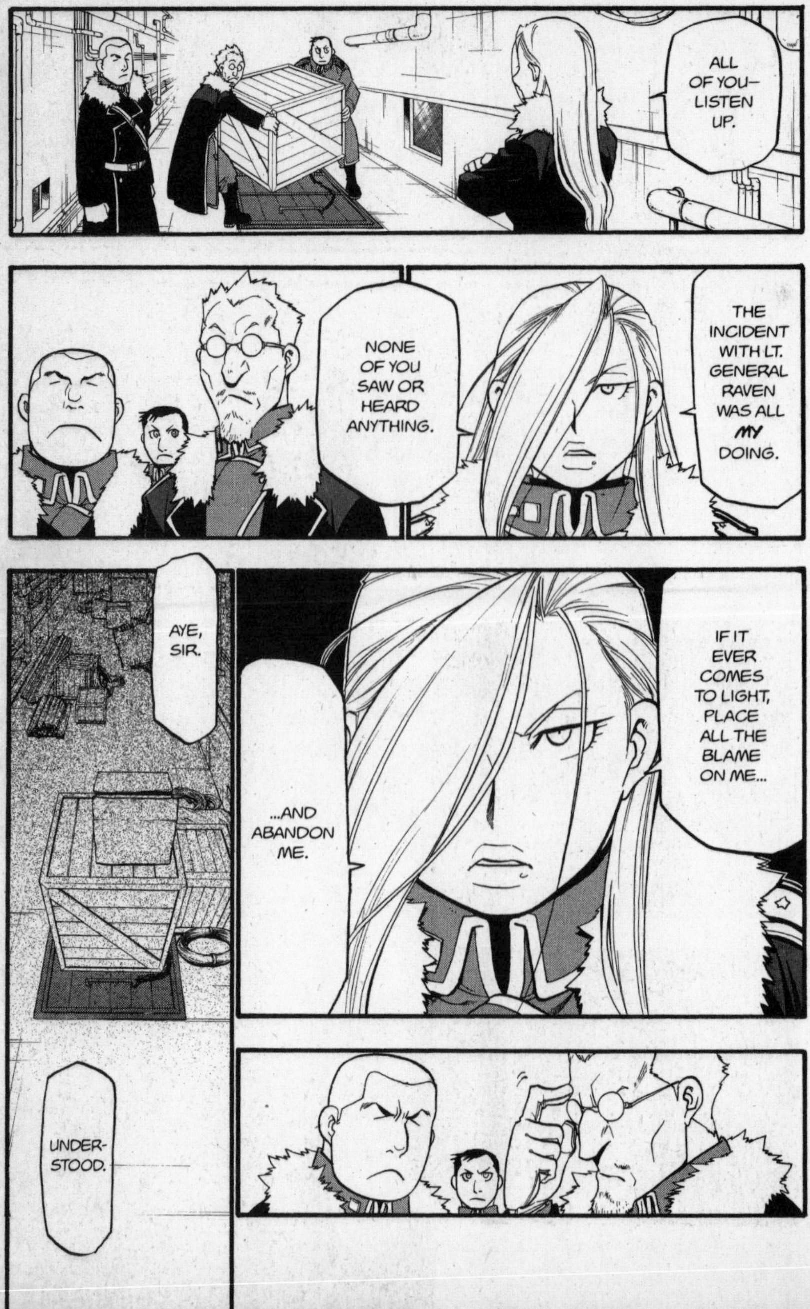
ALL OF YOU— LISTEN UP.
THE INCIDENT WITH LT. GENERAL RAVEN WAS ALL MY DOING.
NONE OF YOU SAW OR HEARD ANYTHING.
IF IT EVER COMES TO LIGHT, PLACE ALL THE BLAME ON ME...
...AND ABANDON ME.
AYE, SIR.
UNDER-STOOD.

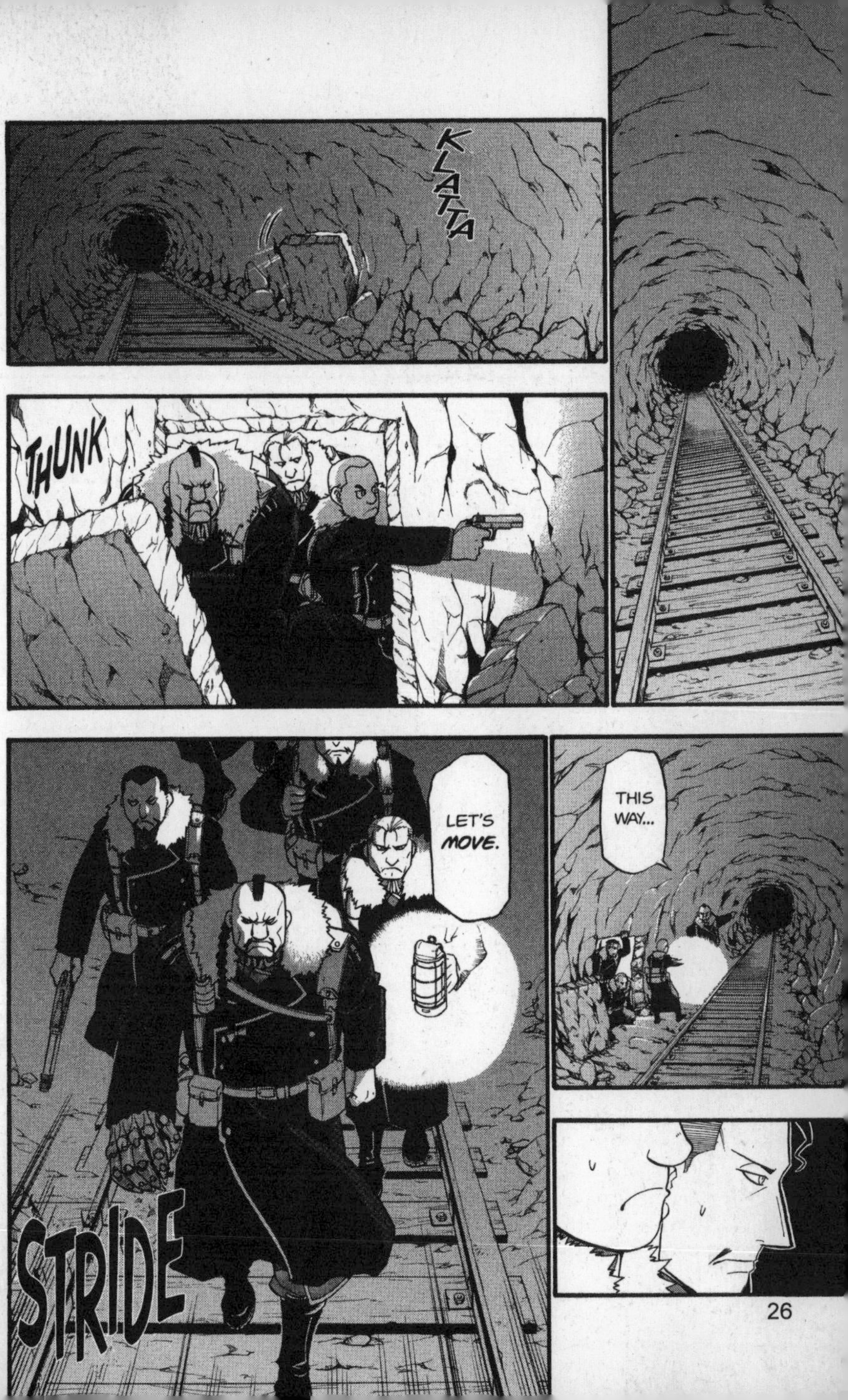
KLATTA
THUNK
THIS WAY...
LET'S MOVE.
STRIDE

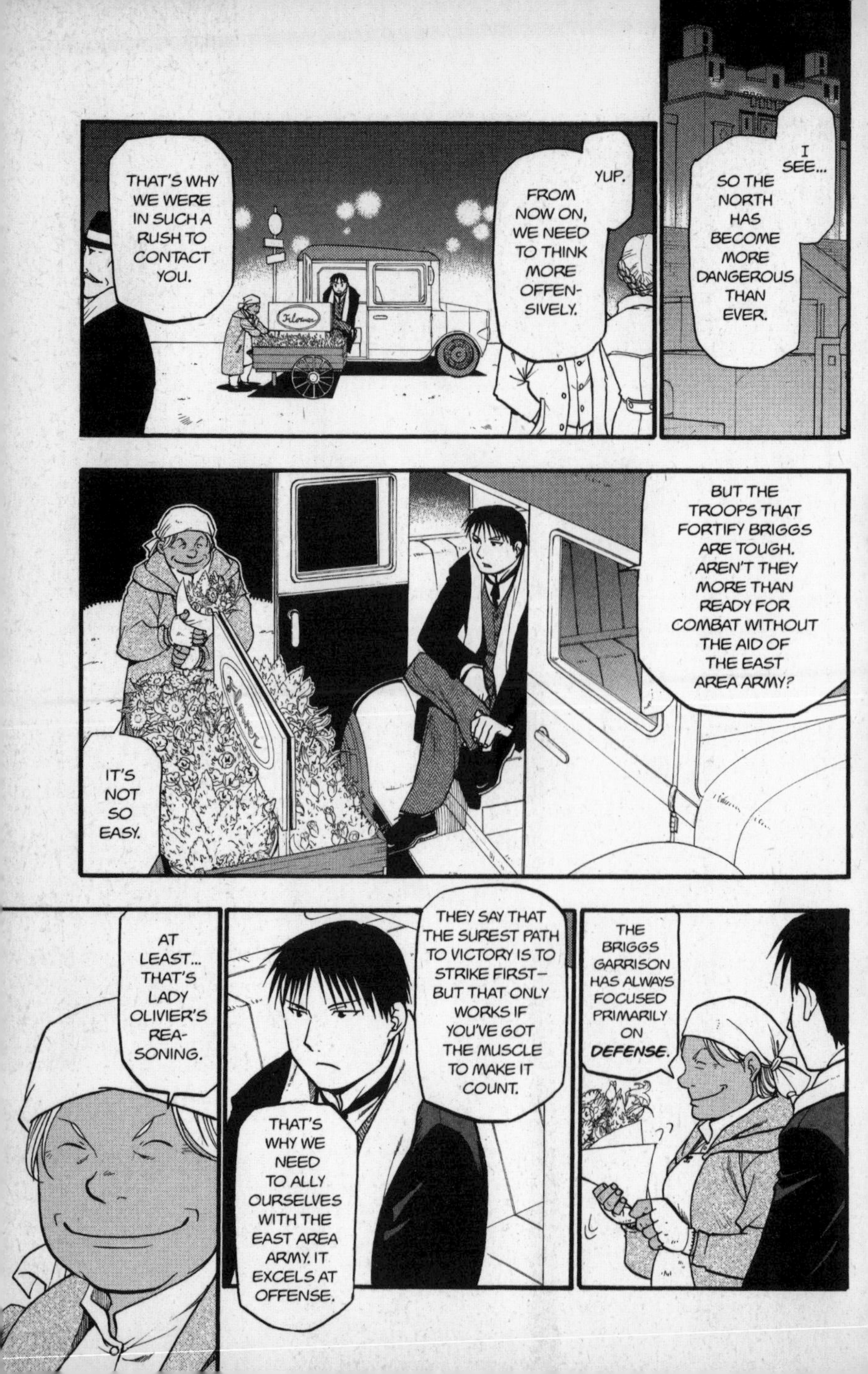
I SEE...
SO THE NORTH HAS BECOME MORE DANGEROUS THAN EVER.
YUP.
FROM NOW ON, WE NEED TO THINK MORE OFFEN-SIVELY.
THAT'S WHY WE WERE IN SUCH A RUSH TO CONTACT YOU.
BUT THE TROOPS THAT FORTIFY BRIGGS ARE TOUGH. AREN'T THEY MORE THAN READY FOR COMBAT WITHOUT THE AID OF THE EAST AREA ARMY?
IT'S NOT SO EASY.
THE BRIGGS GARRISON HAS ALWAYS FOCUSED PRIMARILY ON DEFENSE.
THEY SAY THAT THE SUREST PATH TO VICTORY IS TO STRIKE FIRST— BUT THAT ONLY WORKS IF YOU'VE GOT THE MUSCLE TO MAKE IT COUNT.
THAT'S WHY WE NEED TO ALLY OURSELVES WITH THE EAST AREA ARMY. IT EXCELS AT OFFENSE.
AT LEAST... THAT'S LADY OLIVIER'S REA-SONING.

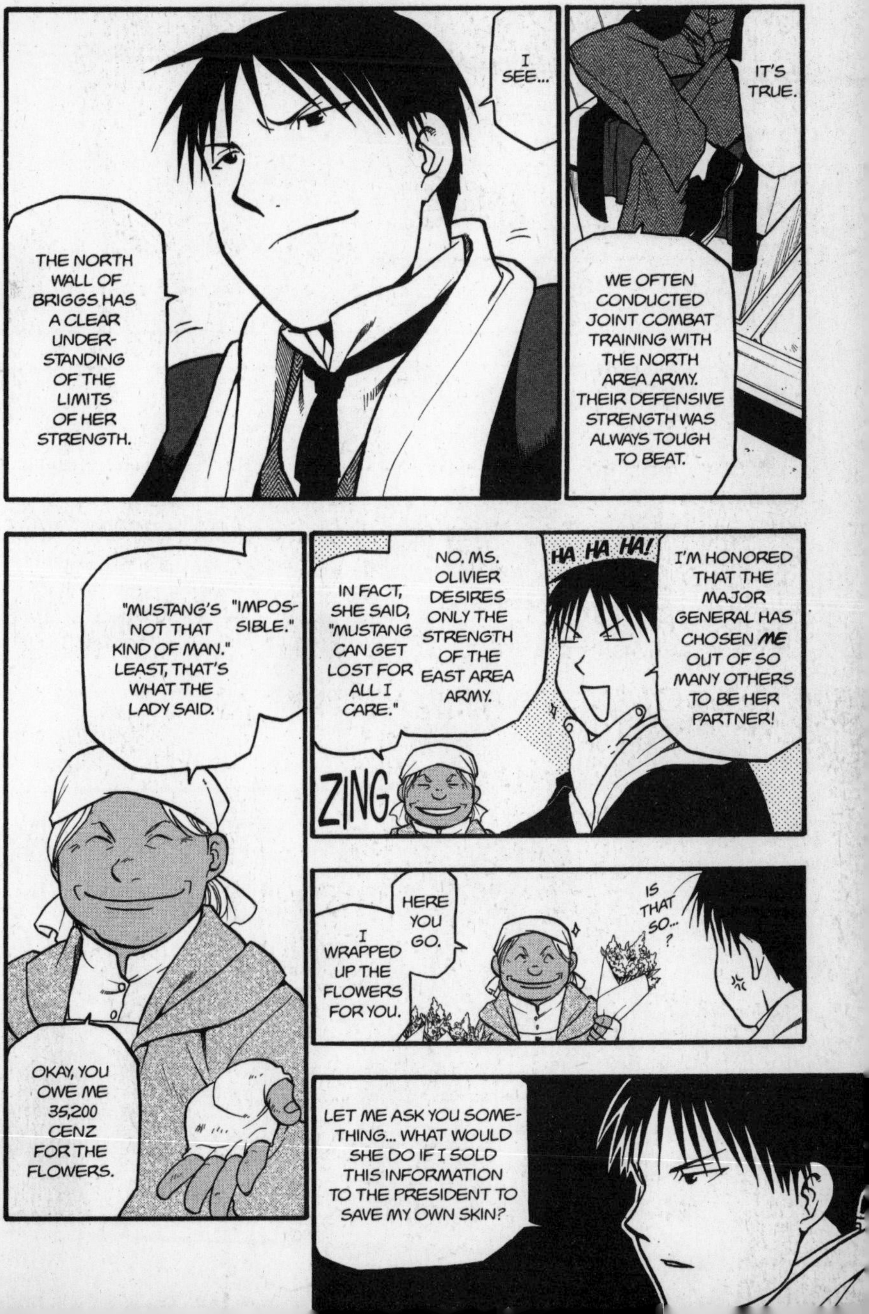

IT'S TRUE.
WE OFTEN CONDUCTED JOINT COMBAT TRAINING WITH THE NORTH AREA ARMY. THEIR DEFENSIVE STRENGTH WAS ALWAYS TOUGH TO BEAT.
I SEE...
THE NORTH WALL OF BRIGGS HAS A CLEAR UNDER-STANDING OF THE LIMITS OF HER STRENGTH.
I'M HONORED THAT THE MAJOR GENERAL HAS CHOSEN *ME* OUT OF SO MANY OTHERS TO BE HER PARTNER!
HA HA HA!
NO. MS. OLIVIER DESIRES ONLY THE STRENGTH OF THE EAST AREA ARMY.
IN FACT, SHE SAID, "MUSTANG CAN GET LOST FOR ALL I CARE."
ZING
IS THAT SO...?
HERE YOU GO.
I WRAPPED UP THE FLOWERS FOR YOU.
LET ME ASK YOU SOME-THING... WHAT WOULD SHE DO IF I SOLD THIS INFORMATION TO THE PRESIDENT TO SAVE MY OWN SKIN?
"IMPOS-SIBLE."
"MUSTANG'S NOT THAT KIND OF MAN." LEAST, THAT'S WHAT THE LADY SAID.
OKAY, YOU OWE ME 35,200 CENZ FOR THE FLOWERS.

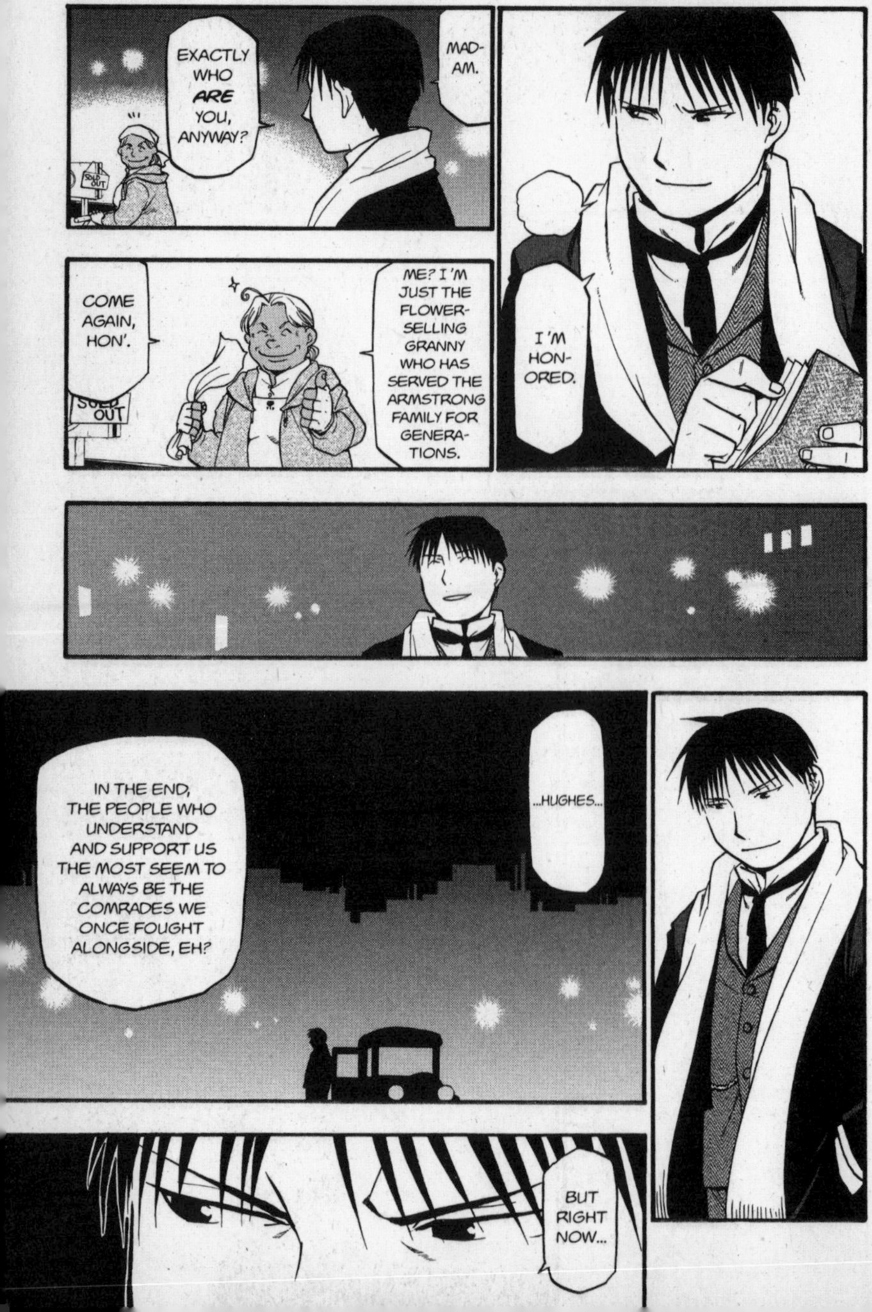
I'M HONORED.
MADAM.
EXACTLY WHO ARE YOU, ANYWAY?
ME? I'M JUST THE FLOWER-SELLING GRANNY WHO HAS SERVED THE ARMSTRONG FAMILY FOR GENERATIONS.
COME AGAIN, HON'.
SOLD OUT
...HUGHES...
IN THE END, THE PEOPLE WHO UNDERSTAND AND SUPPORT US THE MOST SEEM TO ALWAYS BE THE COMRADES WE ONCE FOUGHT ALONGSIDE, EH?
BUT RIGHT NOW...

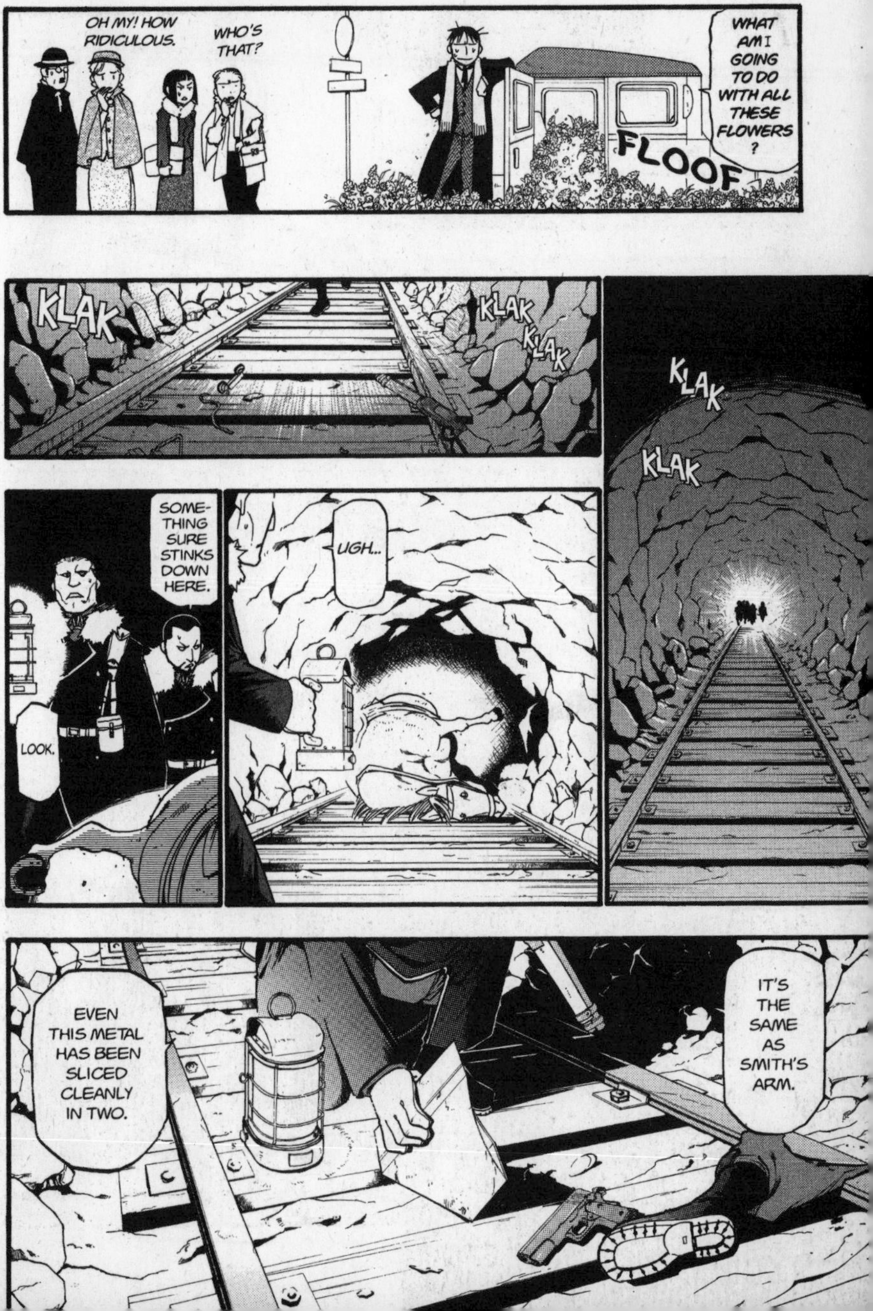
WHAT AM I GOING TO DO WITH ALL THESE FLOWERS?
FLOOF
WHO'S THAT?
OH MY! HOW RIDICULOUS.
KLAK
KLAK
KLAK
KLAK
KLAK
KLAK
UGH...
SOME-THING SURE STINKS DOWN HERE.
LOOK.
IT'S THE SAME AS SMITH'S ARM.
EVEN THIS METAL HAS BEEN SLICED CLEANLY IN TWO.

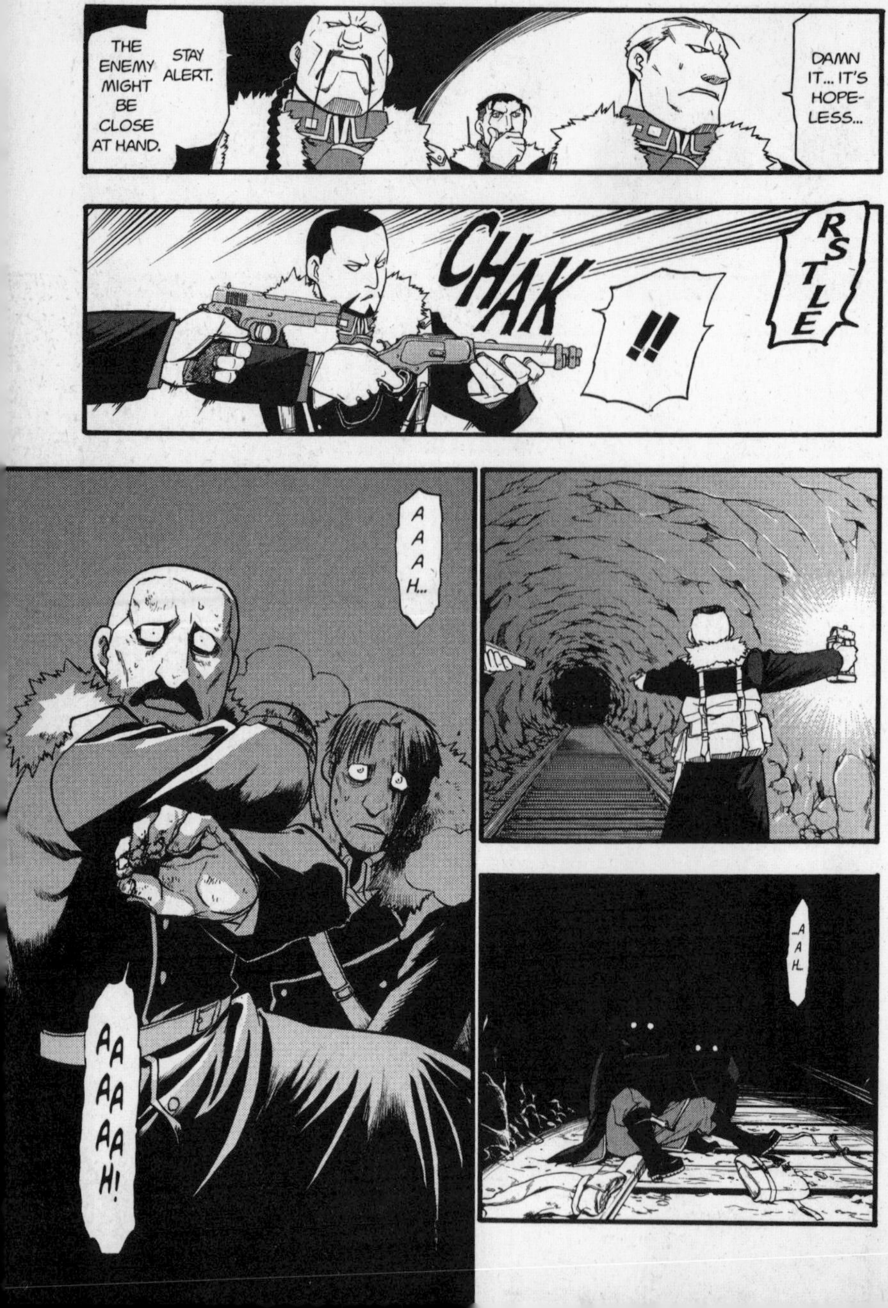
DAMN IT... IT'S HOPELESS...
STAY ALERT.
THE ENEMY MIGHT BE CLOSE AT HAND.
RSTLE
!!
CHAK
...AAH...
AAAH...
AAAAAAH!

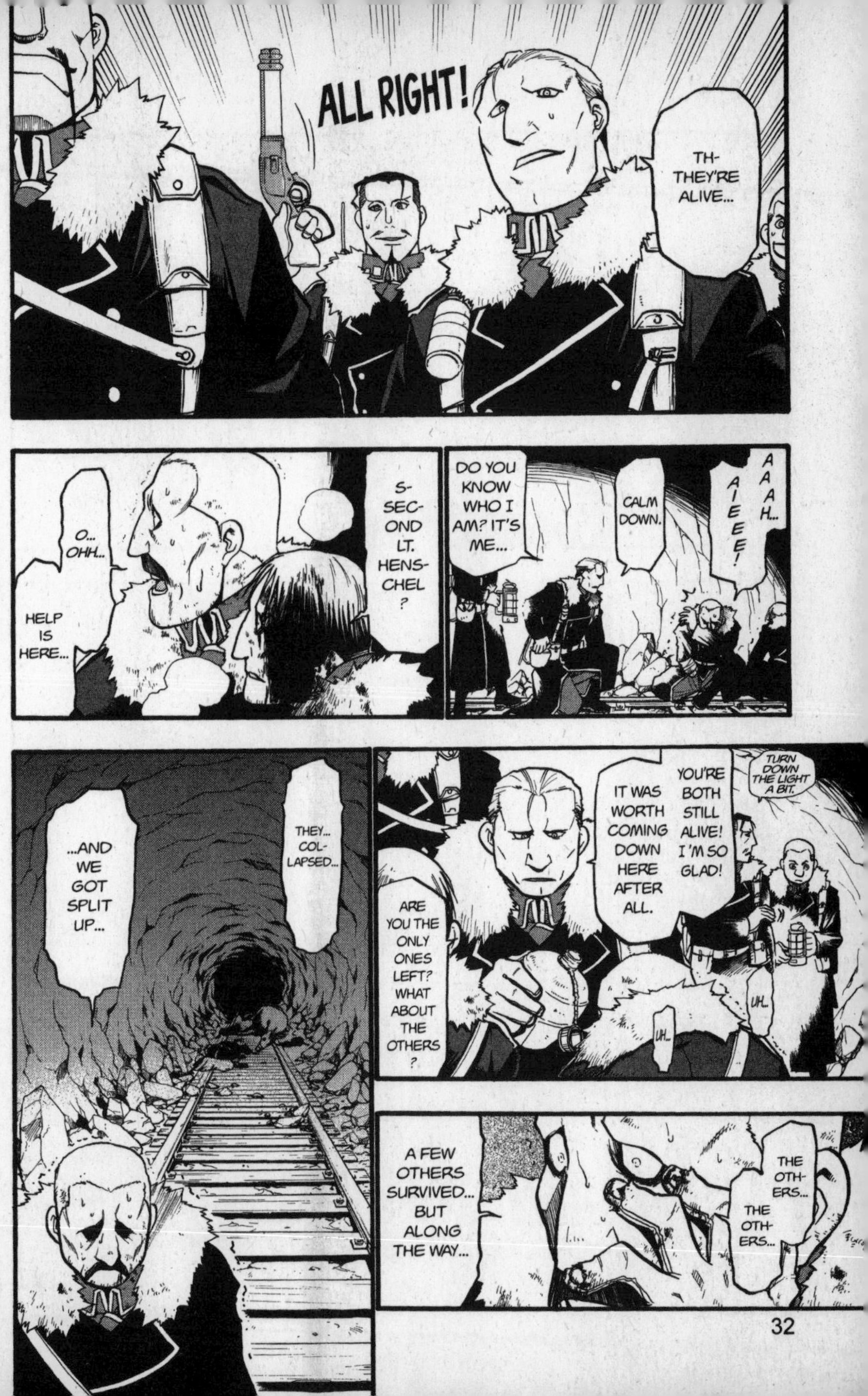
TH- THEY'RE ALIVE...
ALL RIGHT!
AAAH...
AIEEEE!
CALM DOWN.
DO YOU KNOW WHO I AM? IT'S ME...
S-SECOND LT. HENSCHEL?
O... OHH...
HELP IS HERE...
TURN DOWN THE LIGHT A BIT.
YOU'RE BOTH STILL ALIVE! I'M SO GLAD!
IT WAS WORTH COMING DOWN HERE AFTER ALL.
UH...
ARE YOU THE ONLY ONES LEFT? WHAT ABOUT THE OTHERS?
UH...
THE OTHERS...
THE OTHERS...
A FEW OTHERS SURVIVED... BUT ALONG THE WAY...
THEY... COLLAPSED...
...AND WE GOT SPLIT UP...

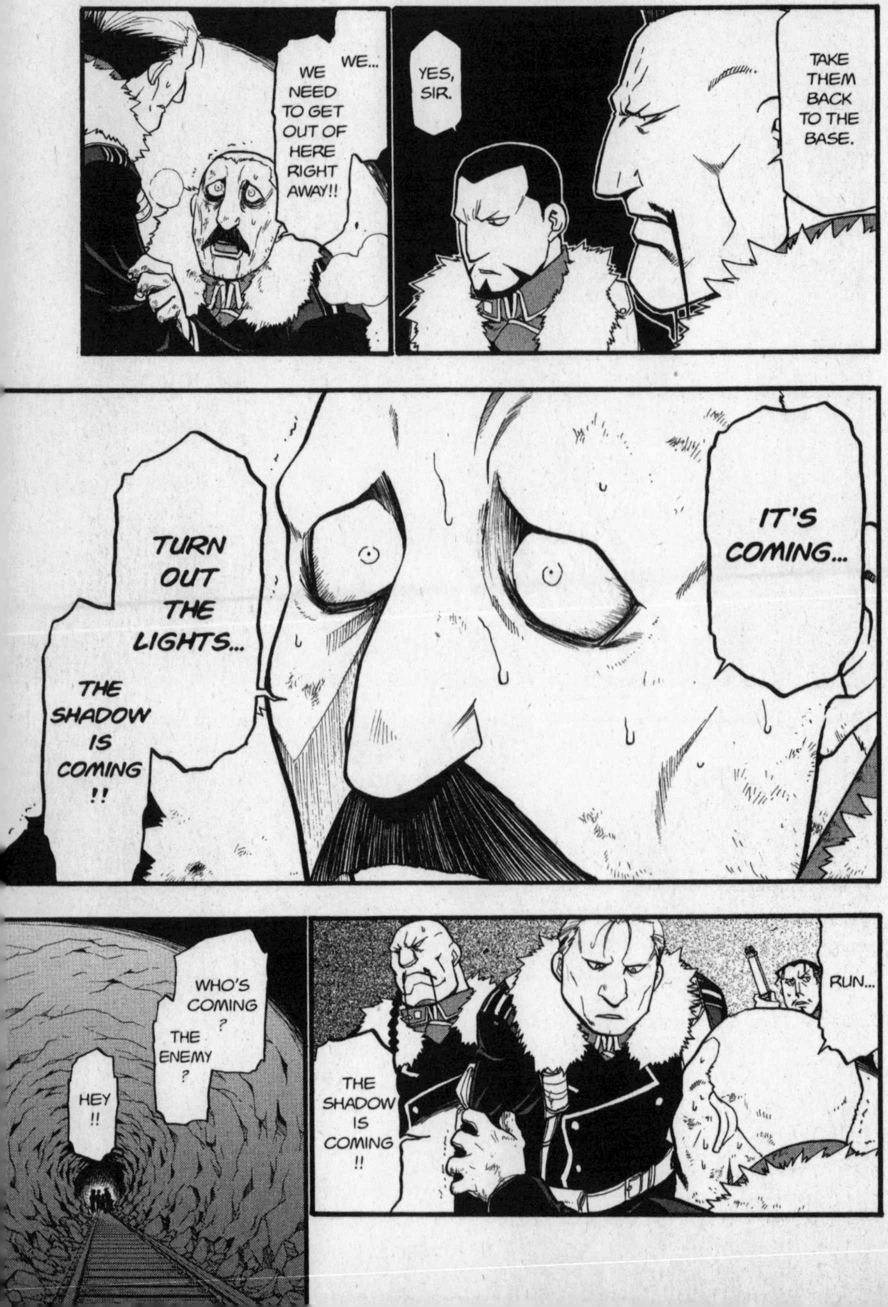
TAKE THEM BACK TO THE BASE.
YES, SIR.
WE...
WE NEED TO GET OUT OF HERE RIGHT AWAY!!
IT'S COMING...
TURN OUT THE LIGHTS...
THE SHADOW IS COMING!!
RUN...
THE SHADOW IS COMING!!
WHO'S COMING?
THE ENEMY?
HEY!!

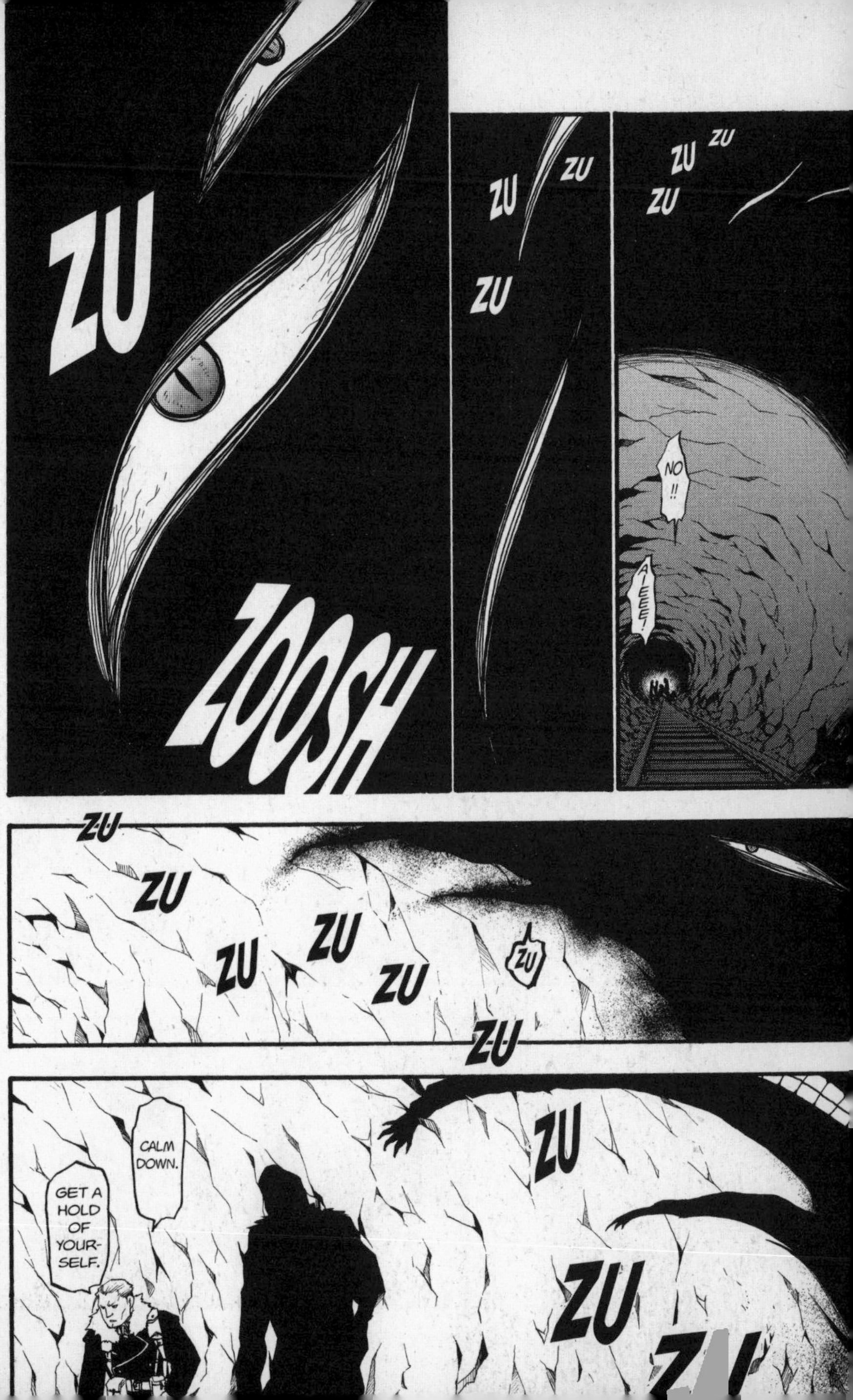
ZU
ZOOSH
ZU
ZU
ZU
ZU
ZU
ZU
NO!!
AIEEE!
Z-U
ZU
ZU
ZU
ZU
ZU
Z-U
ZU
CALM DOWN.
GET A HOLD OF YOUR-SELF.
ZU

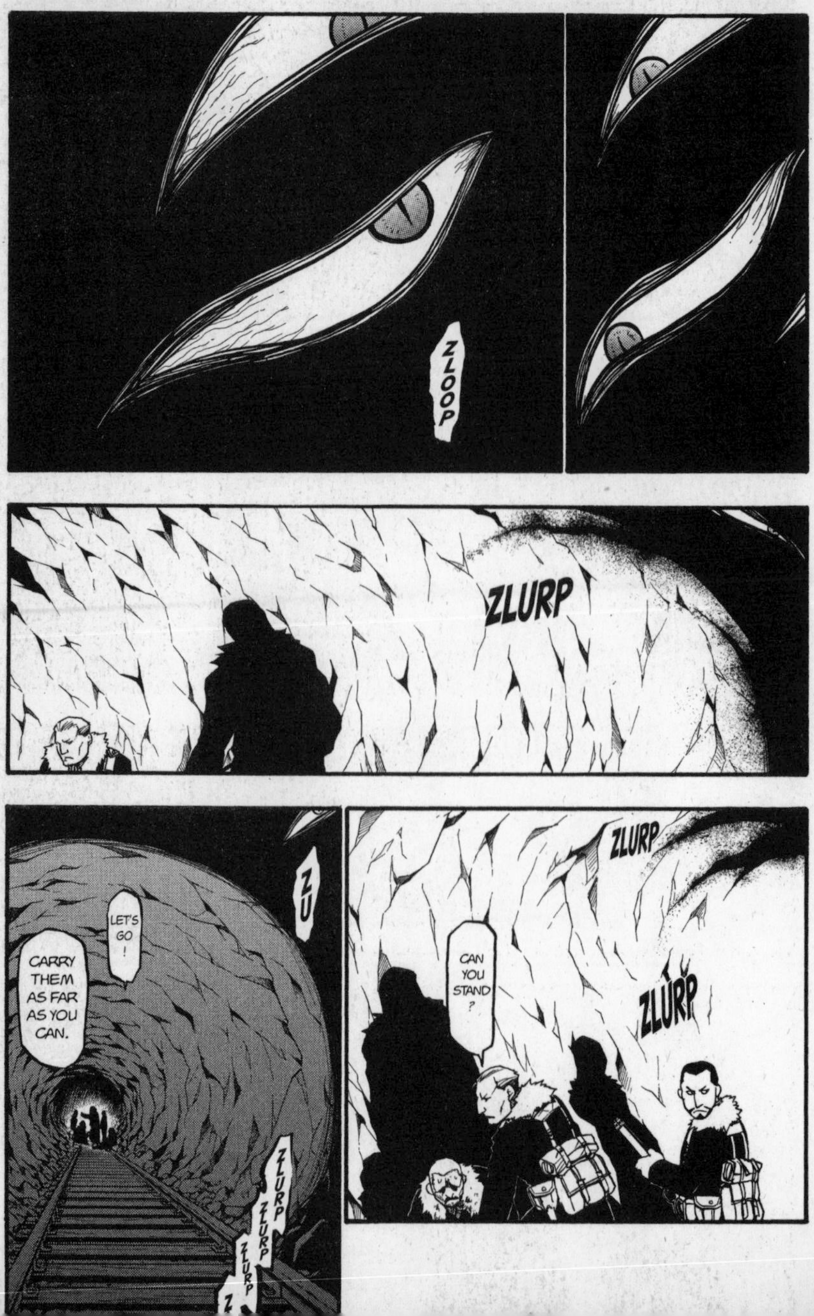
ZLOOP
ZLURP
ZLURP
CAN YOU STAND?
ZLURP
ZU
LET'S GO!
CARRY THEM AS FAR AS YOU CAN.
ZLURP
ZLURP
ZLURP

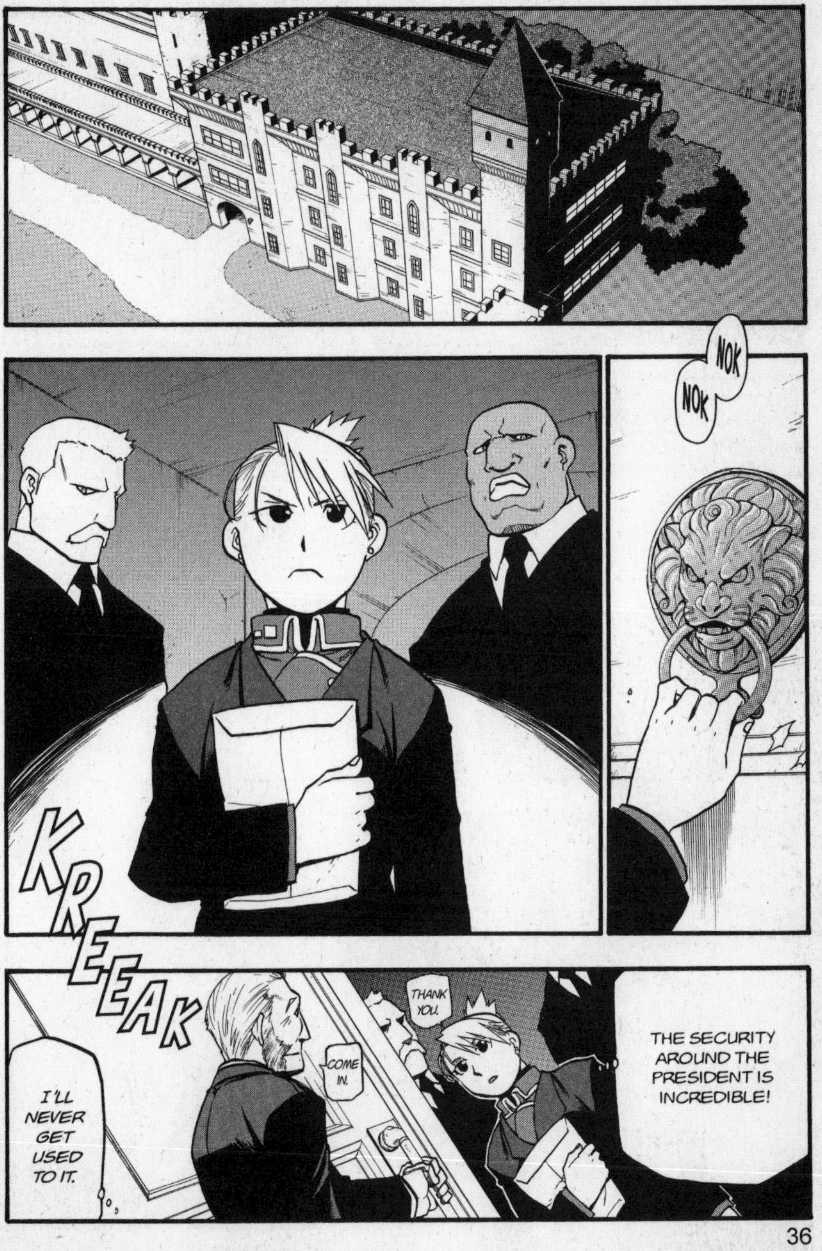
NOK
NOK
KREEAK
THE SECURITY AROUND THE PRESIDENT IS INCREDIBLE!
THANK YOU.
COME IN.
I'LL NEVER GET USED TO IT.

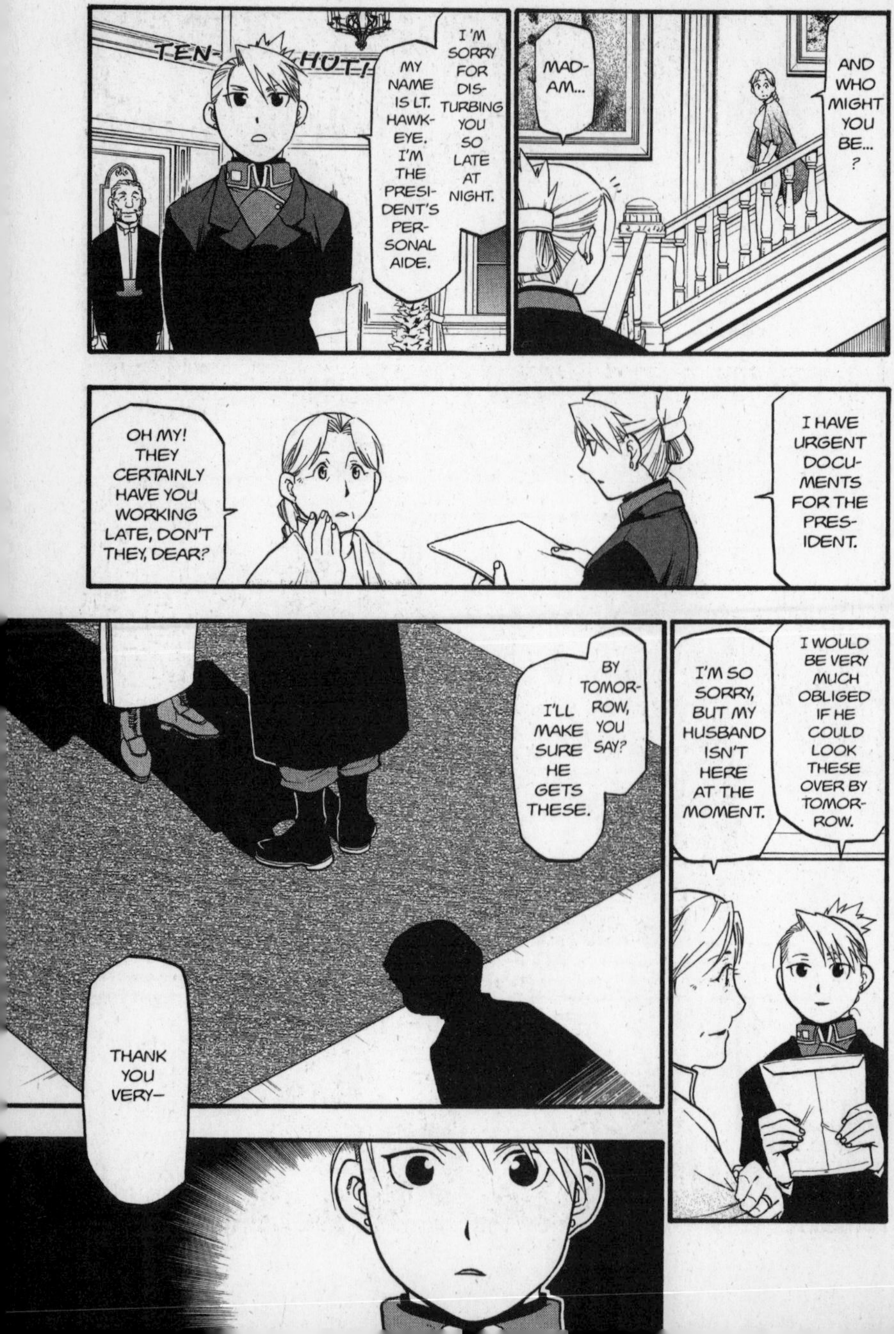
AND WHO MIGHT YOU BE...?
MADAM...
TEN-HUT!
I'M SORRY FOR DISTURBING YOU SO LATE AT NIGHT.
MY NAME IS LT. HAWKEYE. I'M THE PRESIDENT'S PERSONAL AIDE.
I HAVE URGENT DOCUMENTS FOR THE PRESIDENT.
OH MY! THEY CERTAINLY HAVE YOU WORKING LATE, DON'T THEY, DEAR?
I WOULD BE VERY MUCH OBLIGED IF HE COULD LOOK THESE OVER BY TOMORROW.
I'M SO SORRY, BUT MY HUSBAND ISN'T HERE AT THE MOMENT.
BY TOMORROW, YOU SAY?
I'LL MAKE SURE HE GETS THESE.
THANK YOU VERY—

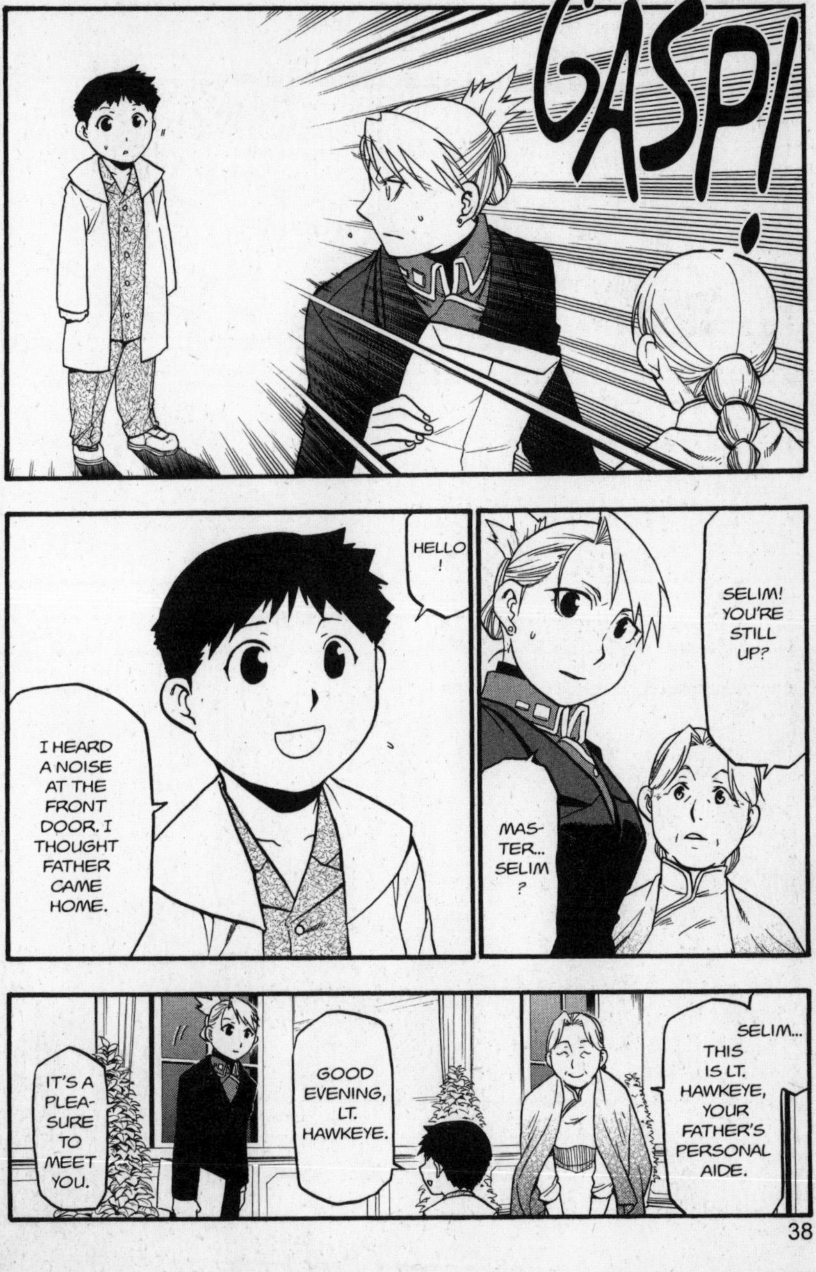
GASP!
SELIM! YOU'RE STILL UP?
MASTER... SELIM?
HELLO!
I HEARD A NOISE AT THE FRONT DOOR. I THOUGHT FATHER CAME HOME.
SELIM... THIS IS LT. HAWKEYE, YOUR FATHER'S PERSONAL AIDE.
GOOD EVENING, LT. HAWKEYE.
IT'S A PLEASURE TO MEET YOU.

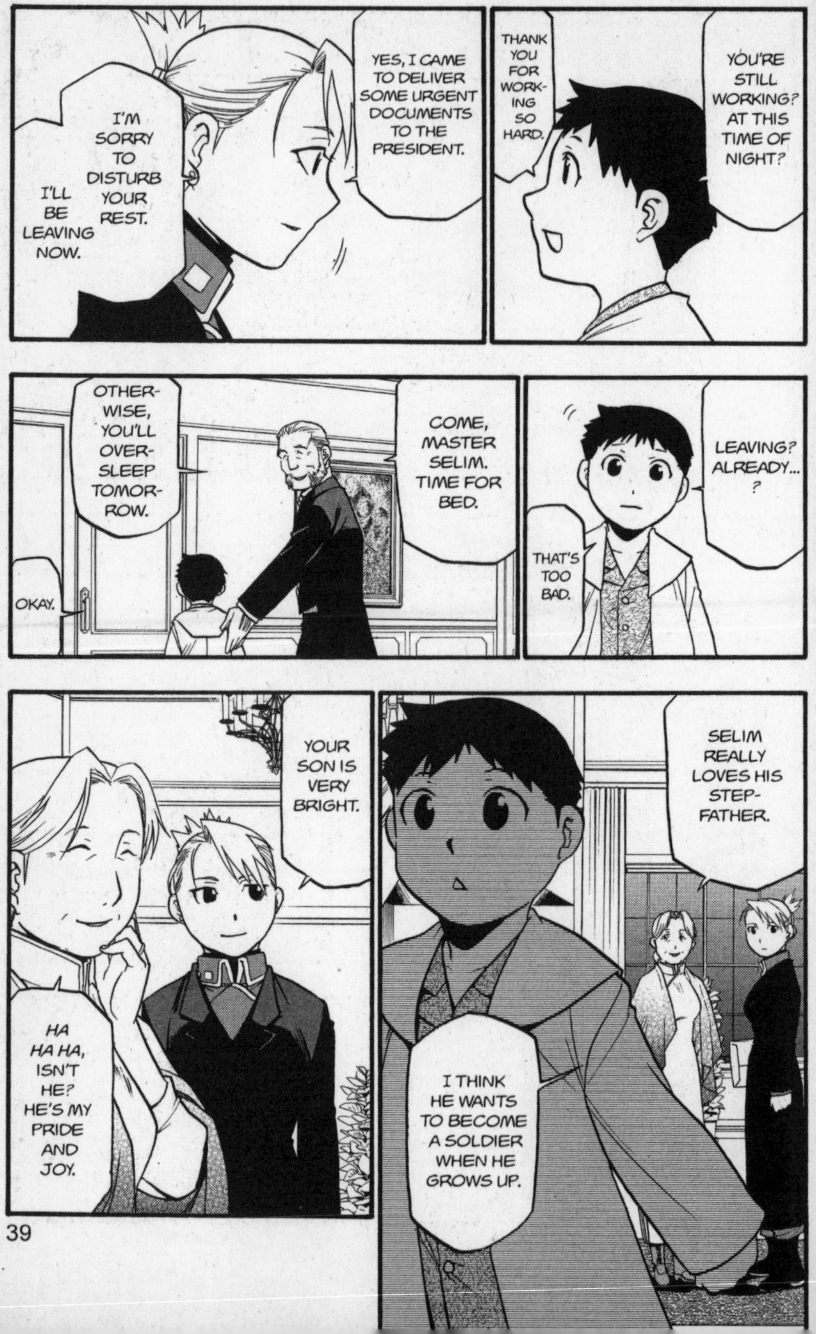
YOU'RE STILL WORKING? AT THIS TIME OF NIGHT?
THANK YOU FOR WORKING SO HARD.
YES, I CAME TO DELIVER SOME URGENT DOCUMENTS TO THE PRESIDENT.
I'M SORRY TO DISTURB YOUR REST.
I'LL BE LEAVING NOW.
LEAVING? ALREADY...?
THAT'S TOO BAD.
COME, MASTER SELIM. TIME FOR BED.
OTHERWISE, YOU'LL OVERSLEEP TOMORROW.
OKAY.
SELIM REALLY LOVES HIS STEPFATHER.
I THINK HE WANTS TO BECOME A SOLDIER WHEN HE GROWS UP.
YOUR SON IS VERY BRIGHT.
HA HA HA, ISN'T HE? HE'S MY PRIDE AND JOY.

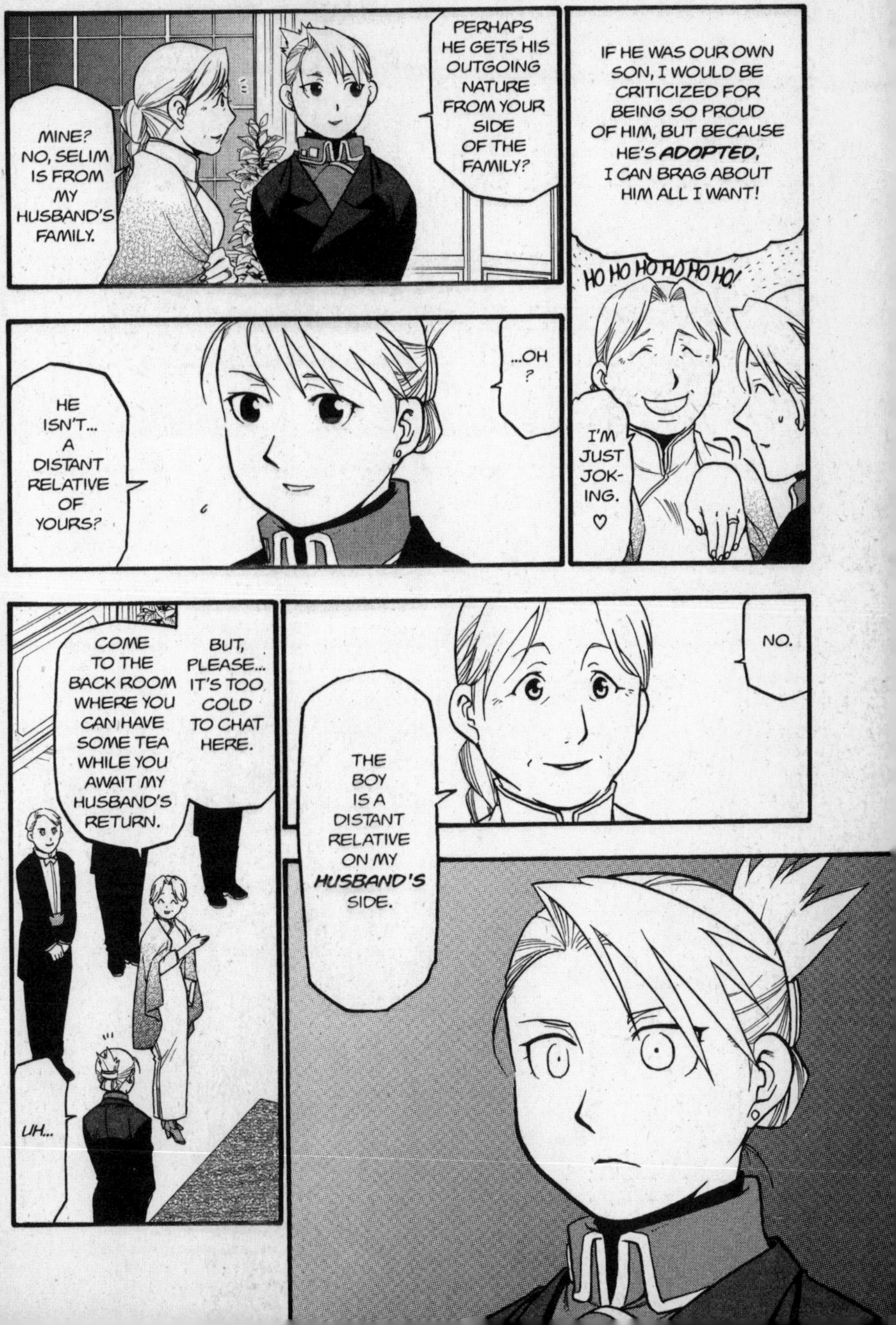
PERHAPS HE GETS HIS OUTGOING NATURE FROM YOUR SIDE OF THE FAMILY?
MINE? NO, SELIM IS FROM MY HUSBAND'S FAMILY.
IF HE WAS OUR OWN SON, I WOULD BE CRITICIZED FOR BEING SO PROUD OF HIM, BUT BECAUSE HE'S ***ADOPTED***, I CAN BRAG ABOUT HIM ALL I WANT!
HO HO HO HO HO HO!
I'M JUST JOK-ING. ♡
...OH?
HE ISN'T... A DISTANT RELATIVE OF YOURS?
NO.
THE BOY IS A DISTANT RELATIVE ON MY ***HUSBAND'S*** SIDE.
BUT, PLEASE... IT'S TOO COLD TO CHAT HERE.
COME TO THE BACK ROOM WHERE YOU CAN HAVE SOME TEA WHILE YOU AWAIT MY HUSBAND'S RETURN.
UH...

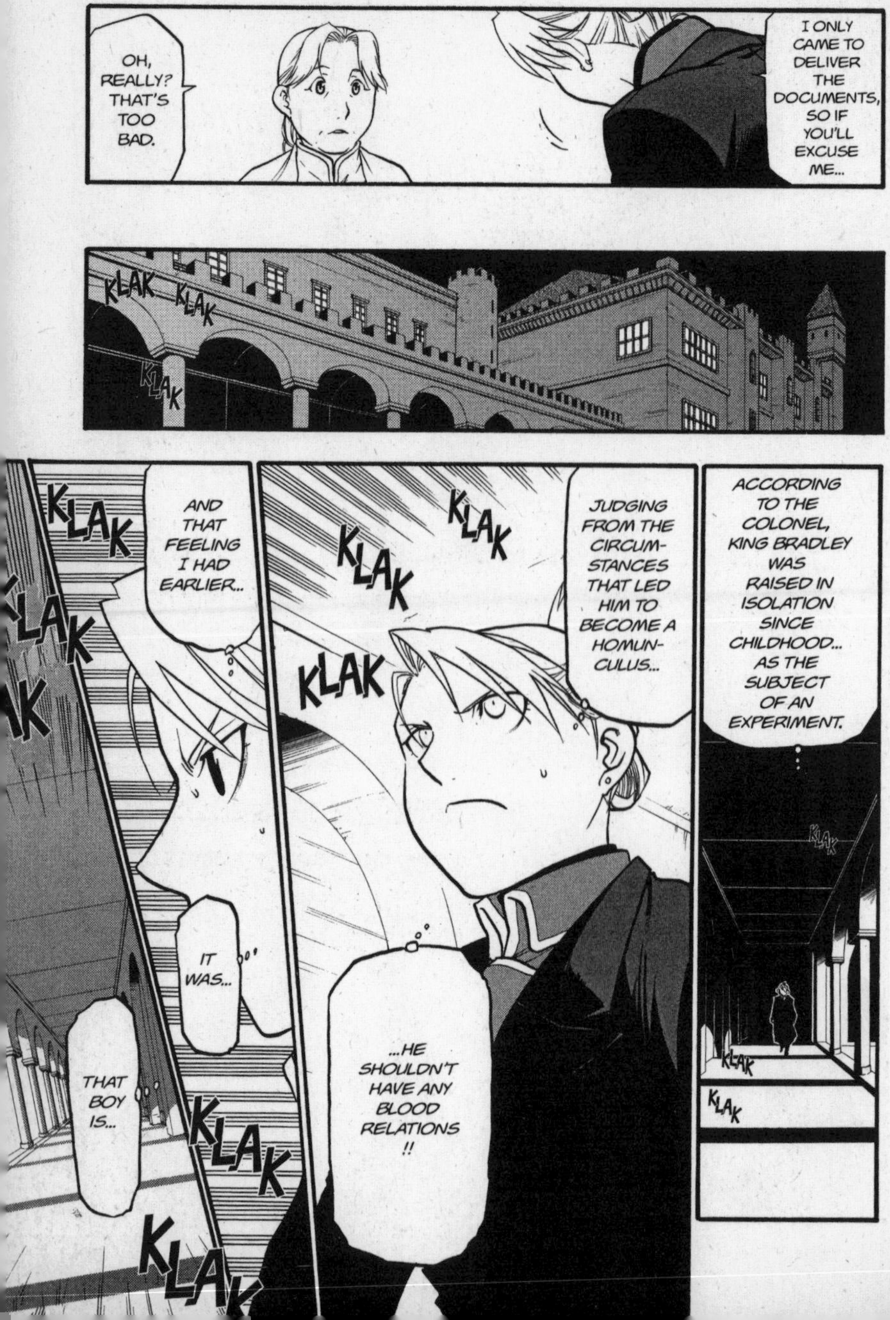
I ONLY CAME TO DELIVER THE DOCUMENTS, SO IF YOU'LL EXCUSE ME...
OH, REALLY? THAT'S TOO BAD.
KLAK KLAK
KLAK
ACCORDING TO THE COLONEL, KING BRADLEY WAS RAISED IN ISOLATION SINCE CHILDHOOD... AS THE SUBJECT OF AN EXPERIMENT.
KLAK
KLAK
KLAK
JUDGING FROM THE CIRCUM-STANCES THAT LED HIM TO BECOME A HOMUN-CULUS...
KLAK
KLAK
KLAK
...HE SHOULDN'T HAVE ANY BLOOD RELATIONS !!
AND THAT FEELING I HAD EARLIER...
KLAK
KLAK
IT WAS...
THAT BOY IS...
KLAK
KLAK

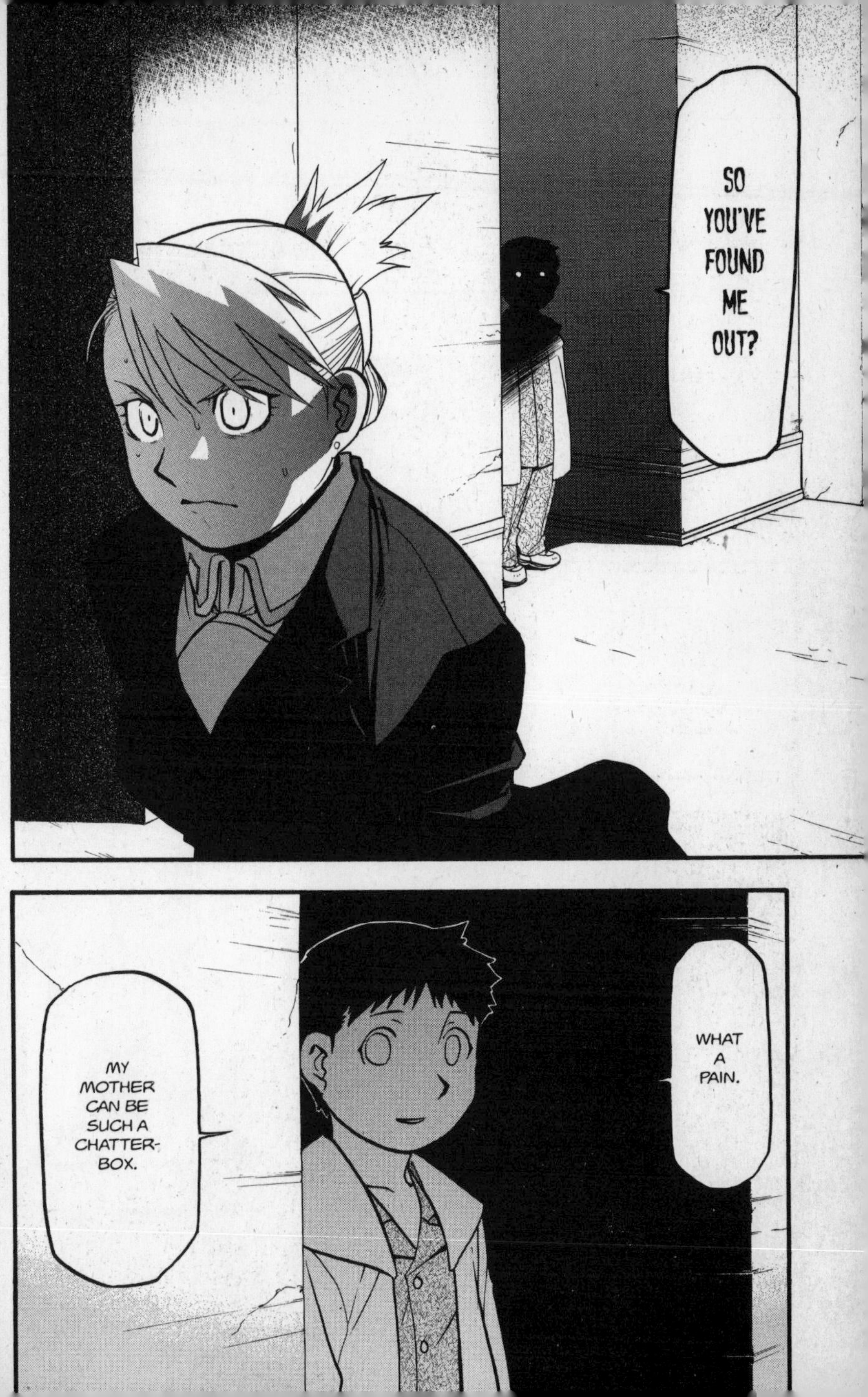
SO YOU'VE FOUND ME OUT?
WHAT A PAIN.
MY MOTHER CAN BE SUCH A CHATTER-BOX.

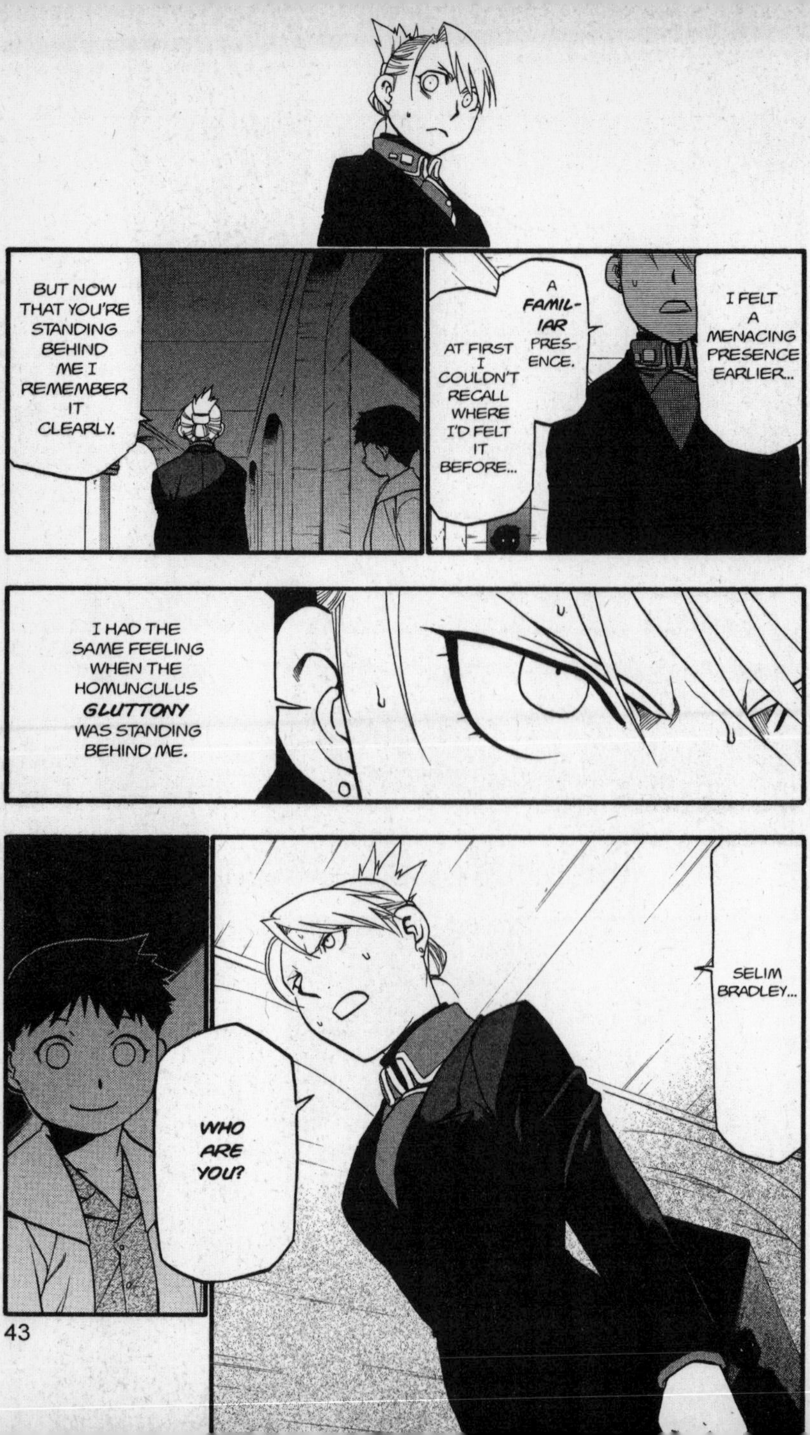
I FELT A MENACING PRESENCE EARLIER...
A FAMILIAR PRESENCE.
AT FIRST I COULDN'T RECALL WHERE I'D FELT IT BEFORE...
BUT NOW THAT YOU'RE STANDING BEHIND ME I REMEMBER IT CLEARLY.
I HAD THE SAME FEELING WHEN THE HOMUNCULUS GLUTTONY WAS STANDING BEHIND ME.
SELIM BRADLEY...
WHO ARE YOU?

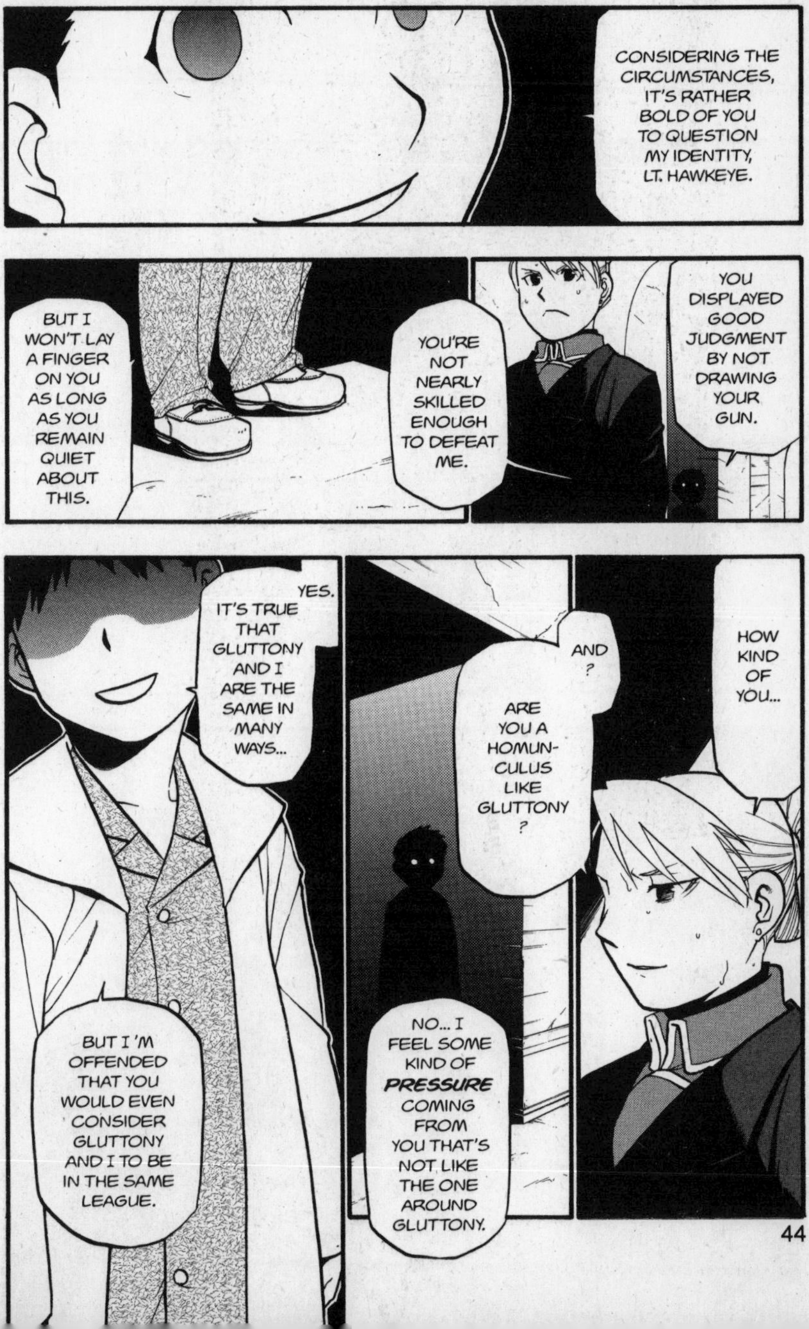
CONSIDERING THE CIRCUMSTANCES, IT'S RATHER BOLD OF YOU TO QUESTION MY IDENTITY, LT. HAWKEYE.
YOU DISPLAYED GOOD JUDGMENT BY NOT DRAWING YOUR GUN.
YOU'RE NOT NEARLY SKILLED ENOUGH TO DEFEAT ME.
BUT I WON'T LAY A FINGER ON YOU AS LONG AS YOU REMAIN QUIET ABOUT THIS.
HOW KIND OF YOU...
AND?
ARE YOU A HOMUNCULUS LIKE GLUTTONY?
NO... I FEEL SOME KIND OF *PRESSURE* COMING FROM YOU THAT'S NOT LIKE THE ONE AROUND GLUTTONY.
YES. IT'S TRUE THAT GLUTTONY AND I ARE THE SAME IN MANY WAYS...
BUT I'M OFFENDED THAT YOU WOULD EVEN CONSIDER GLUTTONY AND I TO BE IN THE SAME LEAGUE.

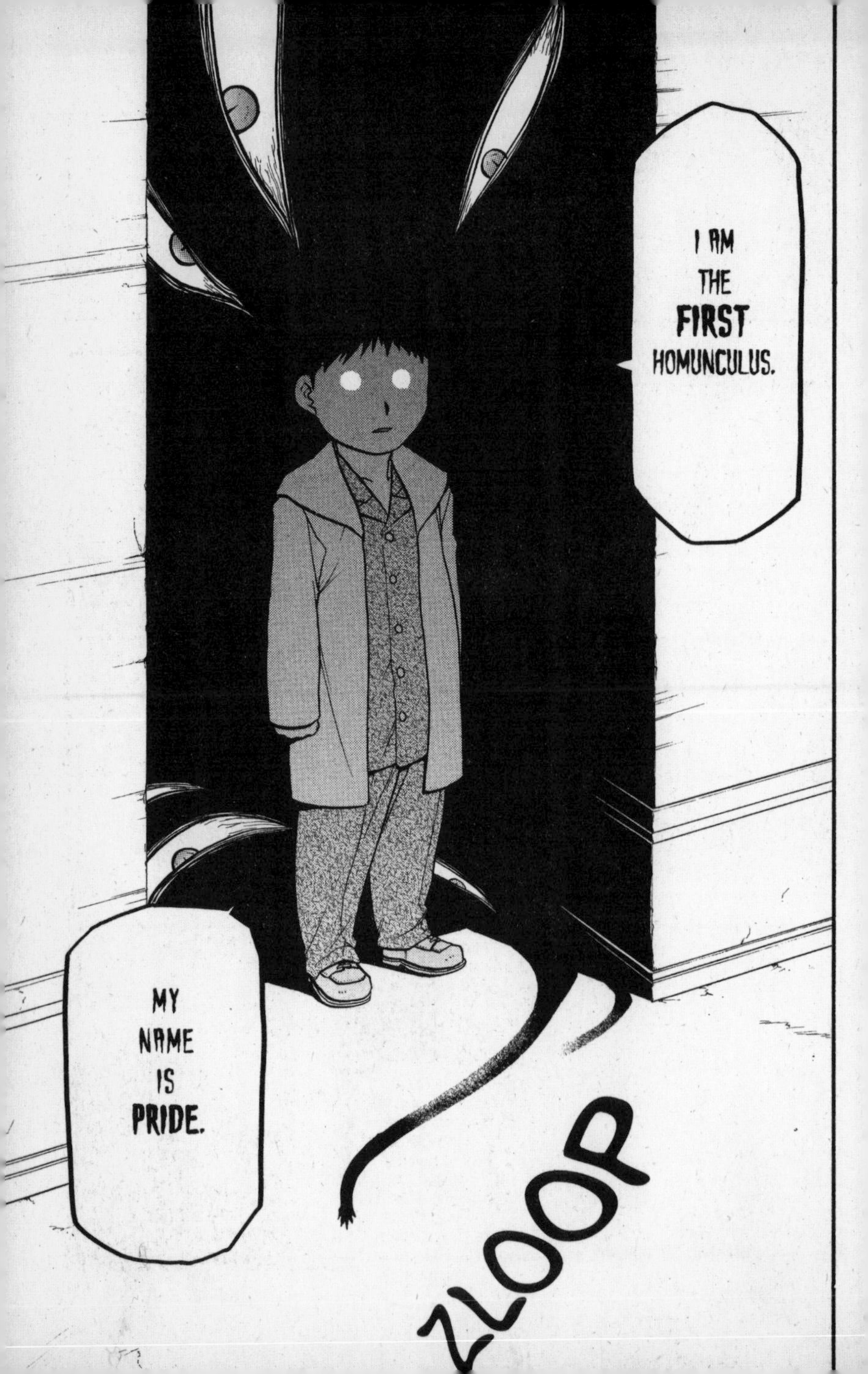
I AM THE FIRST HOMUNCULUS.
MY NAME IS PRIDE.
ZLOOP

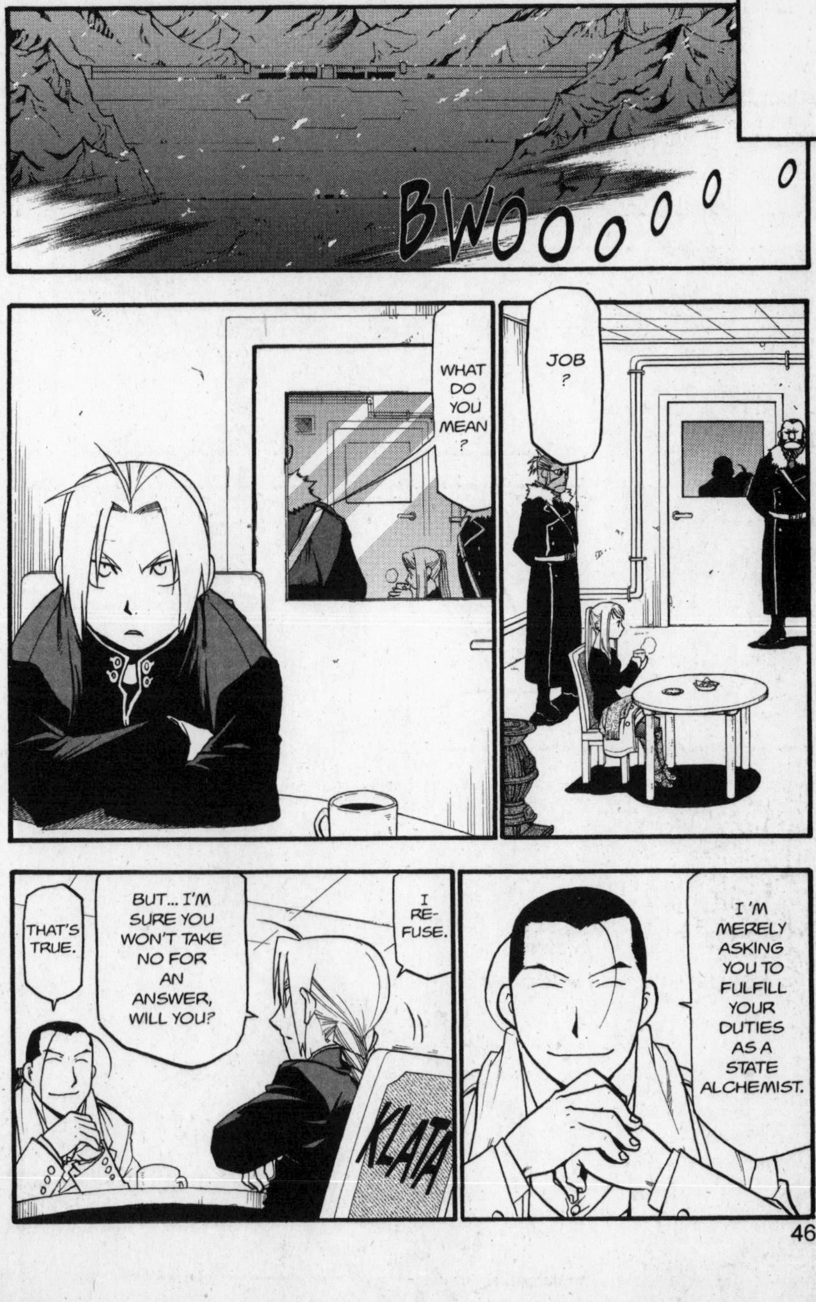
BWOOOOOOO
JOB?
WHAT DO YOU MEAN?
I'M MERELY ASKING YOU TO FULFILL YOUR DUTIES AS A STATE ALCHEMIST.
I RE-FUSE.
KLATA
BUT... I'M SURE YOU WON'T TAKE NO FOR AN ANSWER, WILL YOU?
THAT'S TRUE.

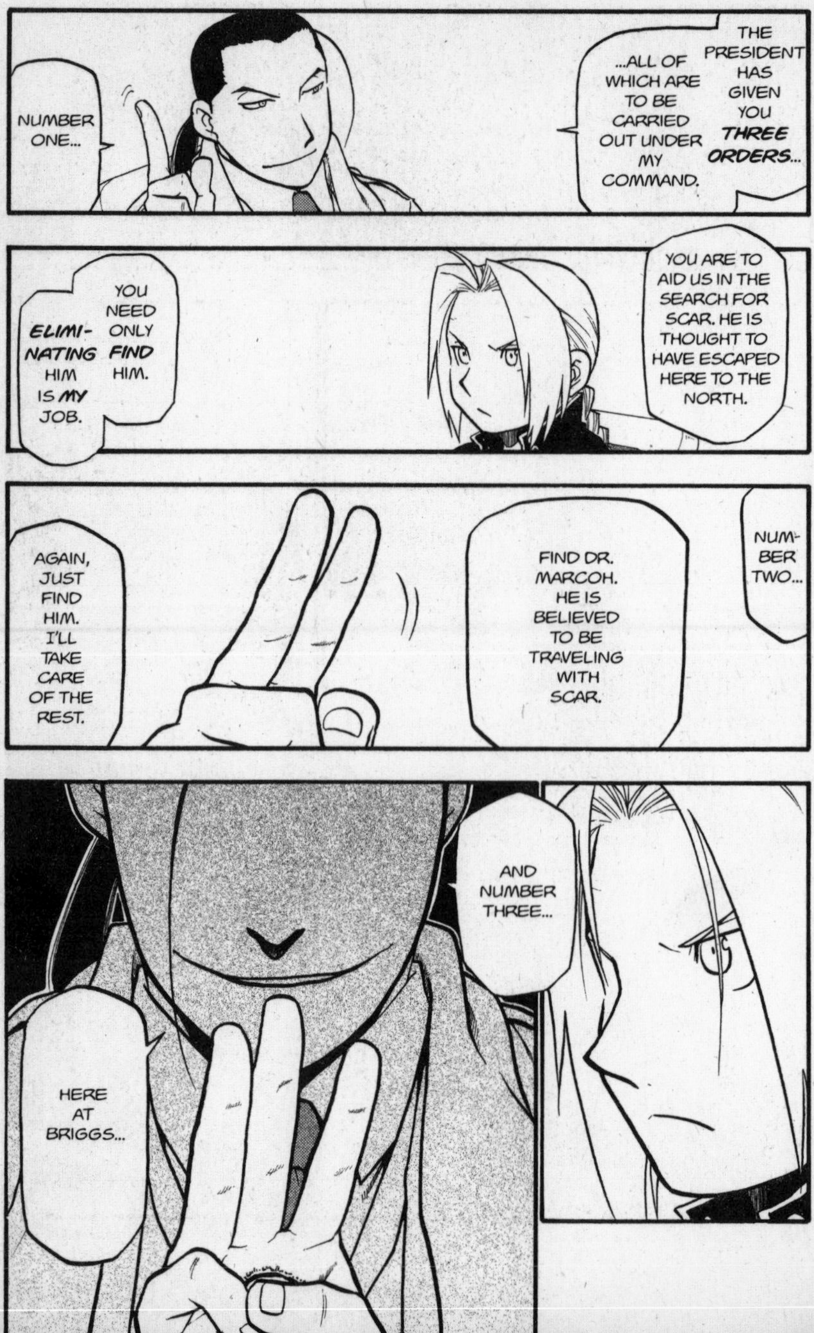
THE PRESIDENT HAS GIVEN YOU THREE ORDERS...
...ALL OF WHICH ARE TO BE CARRIED OUT UNDER MY COMMAND.
NUMBER ONE...
YOU ARE TO AID US IN THE SEARCH FOR SCAR. HE IS THOUGHT TO HAVE ESCAPED HERE TO THE NORTH.
YOU NEED ONLY FIND HIM.
ELIMI-NATING HIM IS MY JOB.
NUM-BER TWO...
FIND DR. MARCOH. HE IS BELIEVED TO BE TRAVELING WITH SCAR.
AGAIN, JUST FIND HIM. I'LL TAKE CARE OF THE REST.
AND NUMBER THREE...
HERE AT BRIGGS...

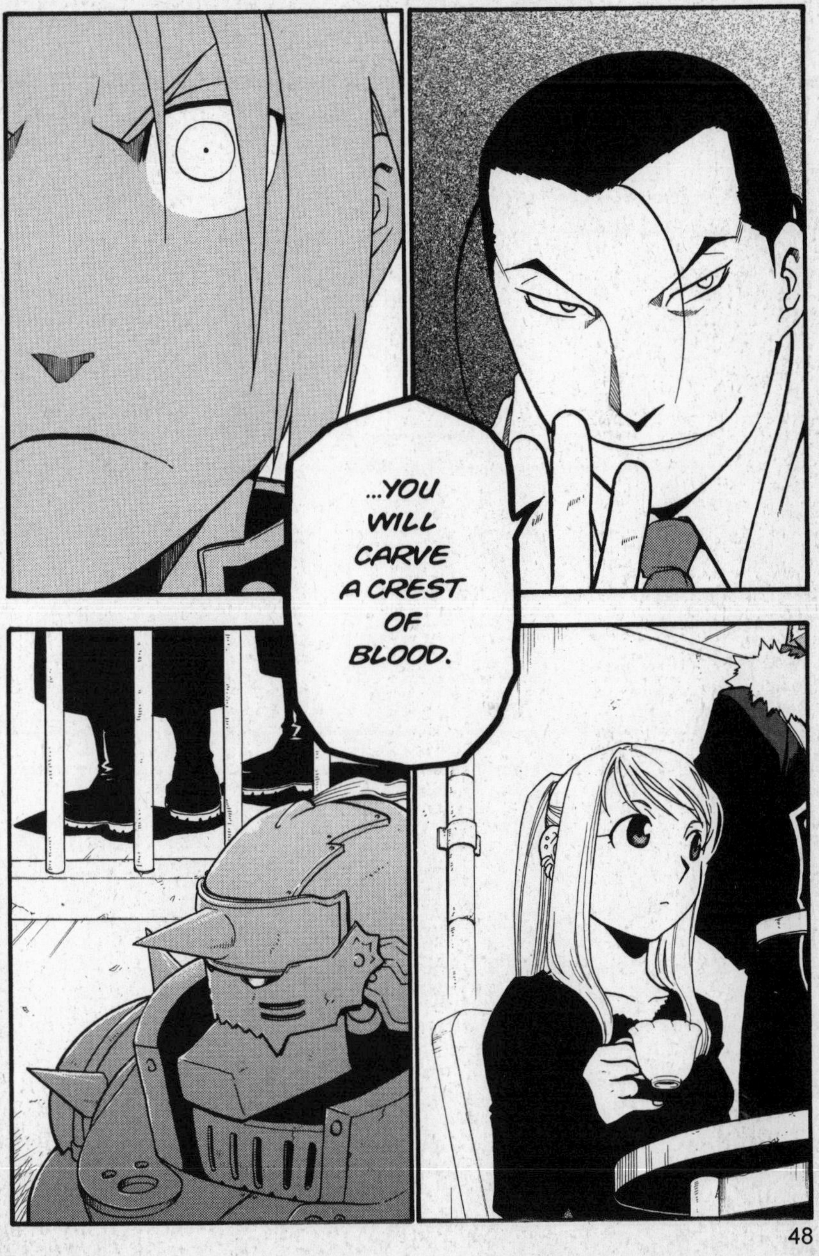
...YOU WILL CARVE A CREST OF BLOOD.

FULLMETAL

ALCHEMIST

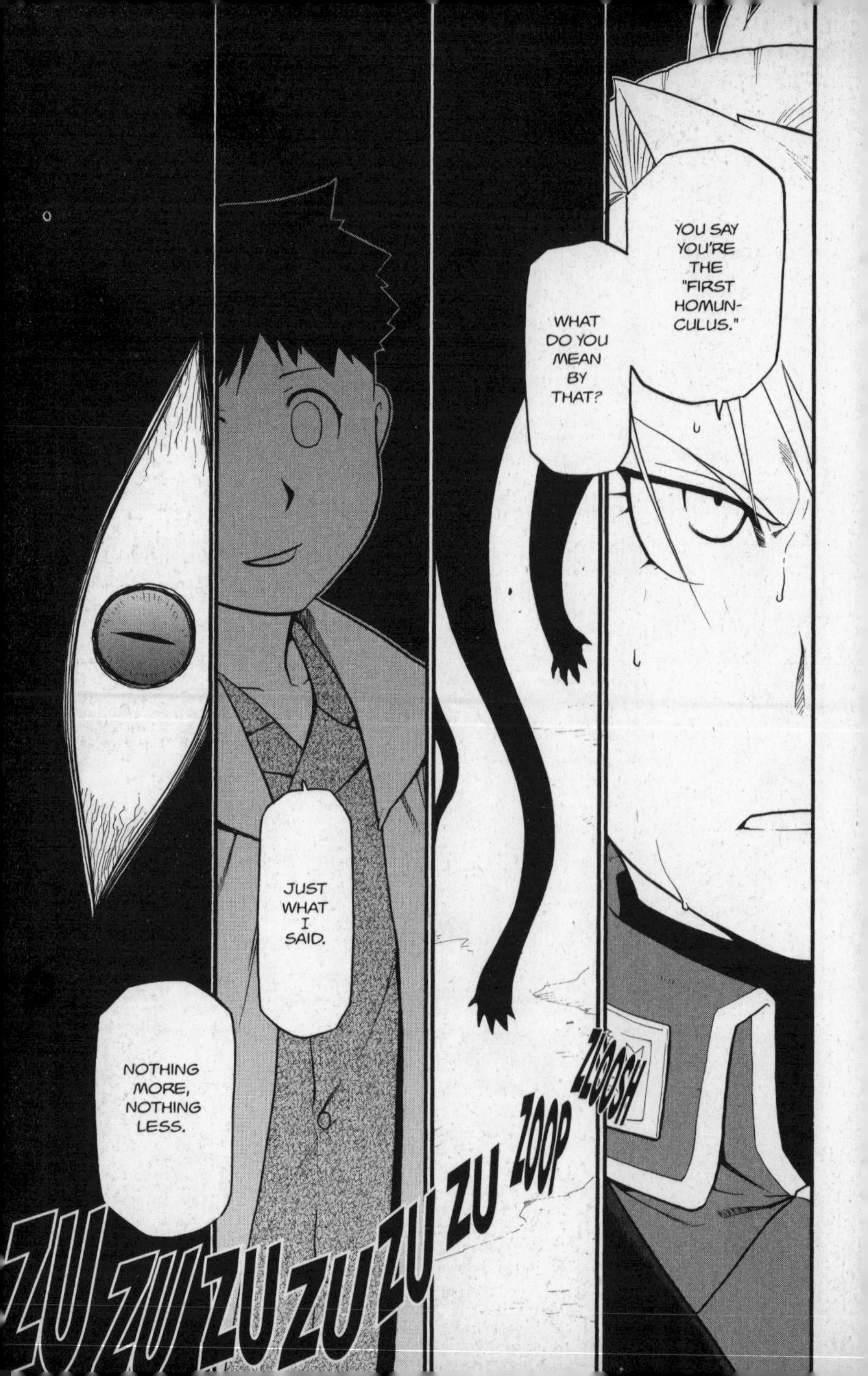
YOU SAY YOU'RE THE "FIRST HOMUN-CULUS."
WHAT DO YOU MEAN BY THAT?
JUST WHAT I SAID.
NOTHING MORE, NOTHING LESS.
ZU ZU ZU ZU ZU ZU ZU ZOOP ZLOOSH

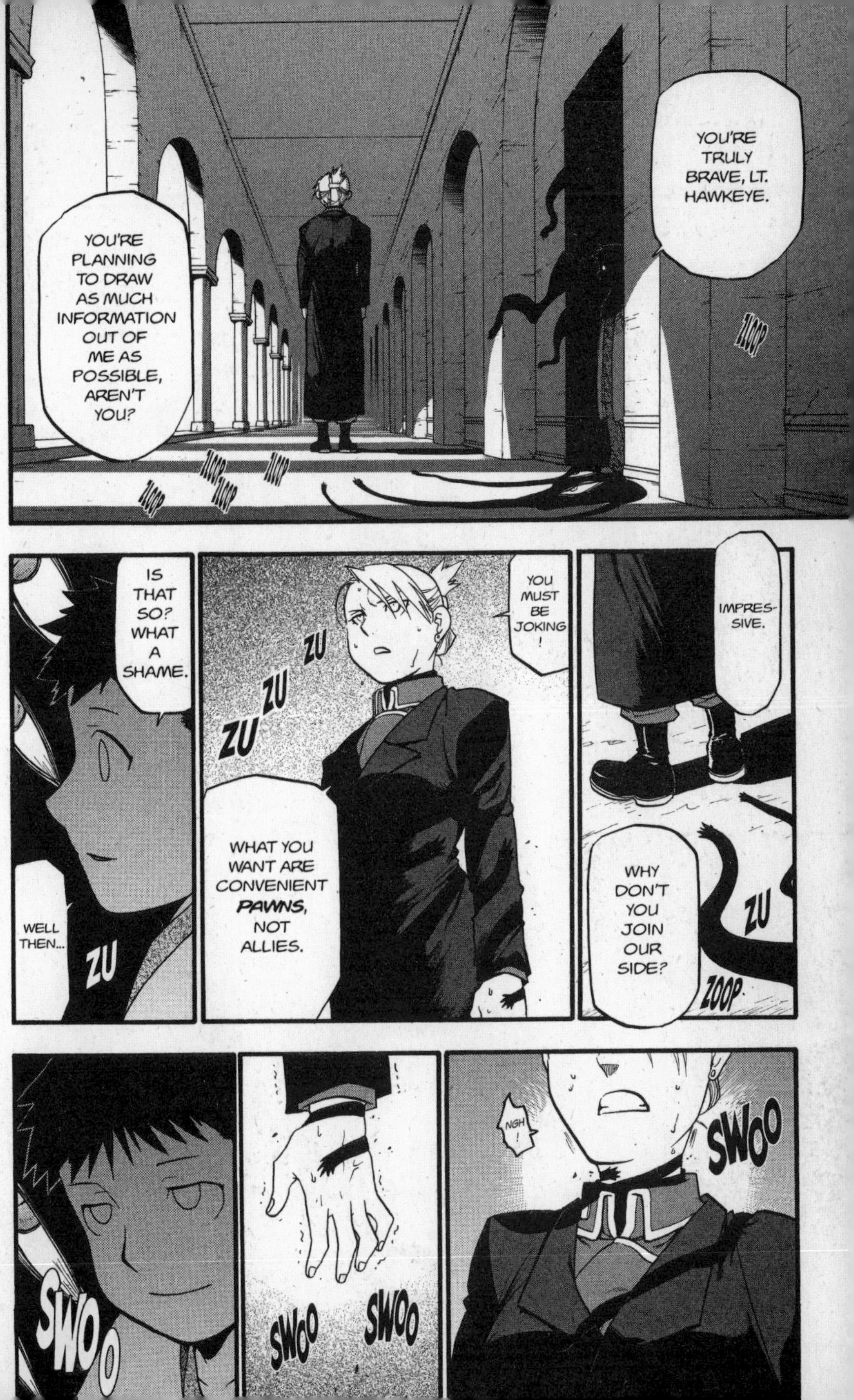
YOU'RE TRULY BRAVE, LT. HAWKEYE.
ZLOOP
YOU'RE PLANNING TO DRAW AS MUCH INFORMATION OUT OF ME AS POSSIBLE, AREN'T YOU?
ZLOOP ZLOOP ZLOOP ZLOOP
IMPRES-SIVE.
WHY DON'T YOU JOIN OUR SIDE?
ZU
ZOOP
YOU MUST BE JOKING!
ZU ZU ZU
WHAT YOU WANT ARE CONVENIENT *PAWNS*, NOT ALLIES.
IS THAT SO? WHAT A SHAME.
WELL THEN...
ZU
NGH!
SWOO
SWOO
SWOO
SWOO

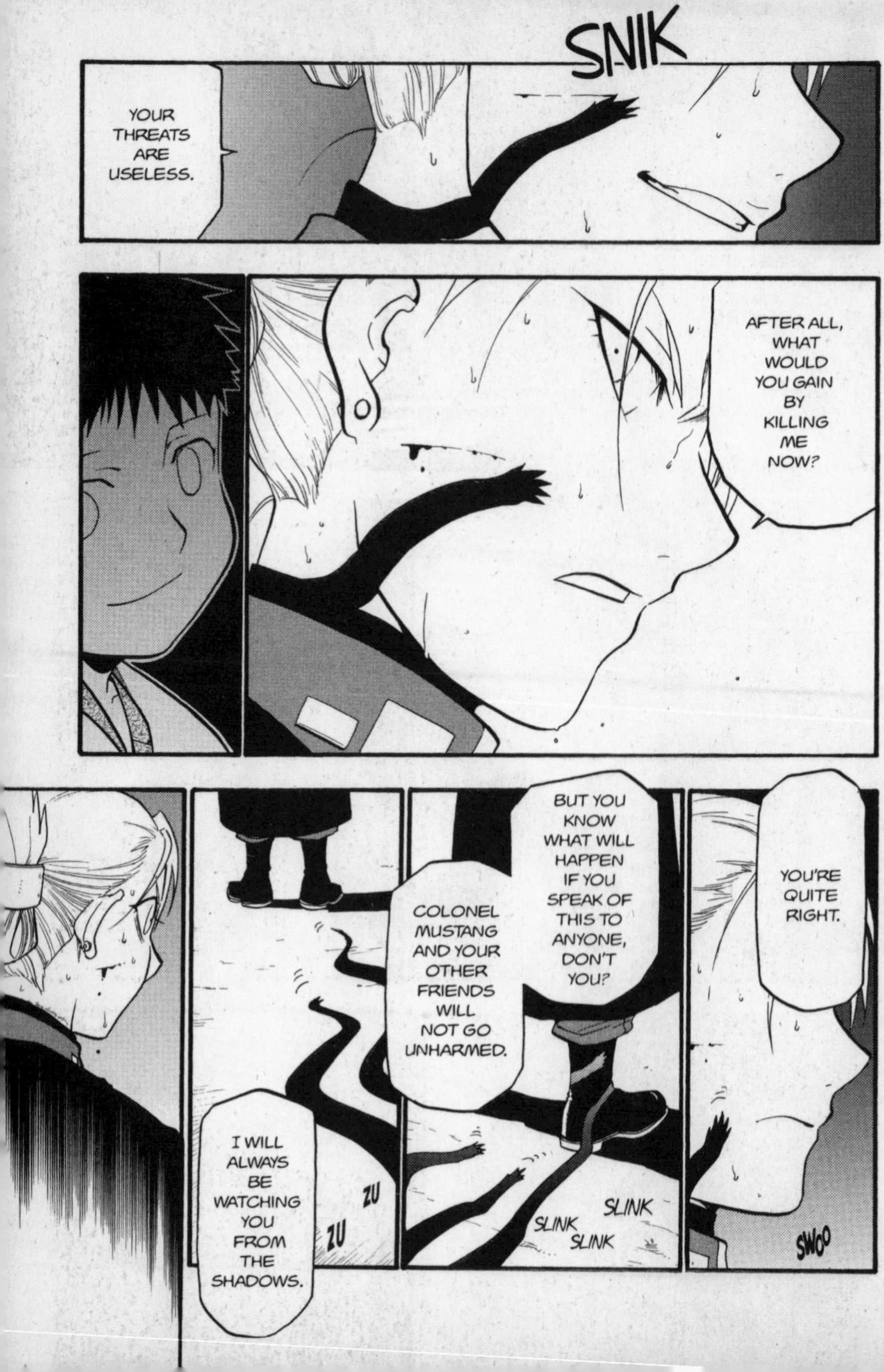
SNIK
YOUR THREATS ARE USELESS.
AFTER ALL, WHAT WOULD YOU GAIN BY KILLING ME NOW?
YOU'RE QUITE RIGHT.
SWOO
BUT YOU KNOW WHAT WILL HAPPEN IF YOU SPEAK OF THIS TO ANYONE, DON'T YOU?
COLONEL MUSTANG AND YOUR OTHER FRIENDS WILL NOT GO UNHARMED.
SLINK
SLINK
SLINK
ZU
ZU
I WILL ALWAYS BE WATCHING YOU FROM THE SHADOWS.

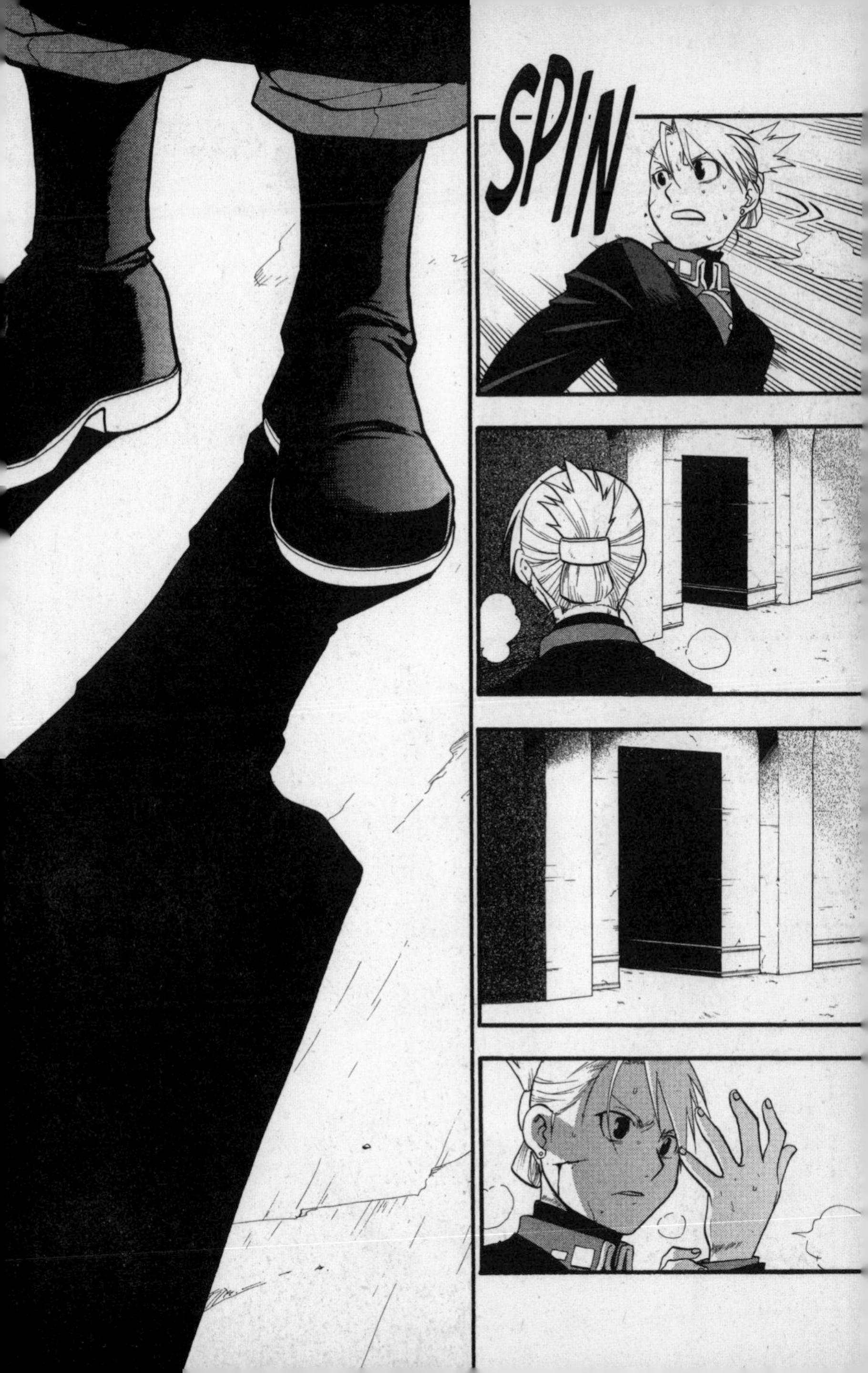
SPIN

Chapter 71
In the Grip of the Red Lotus

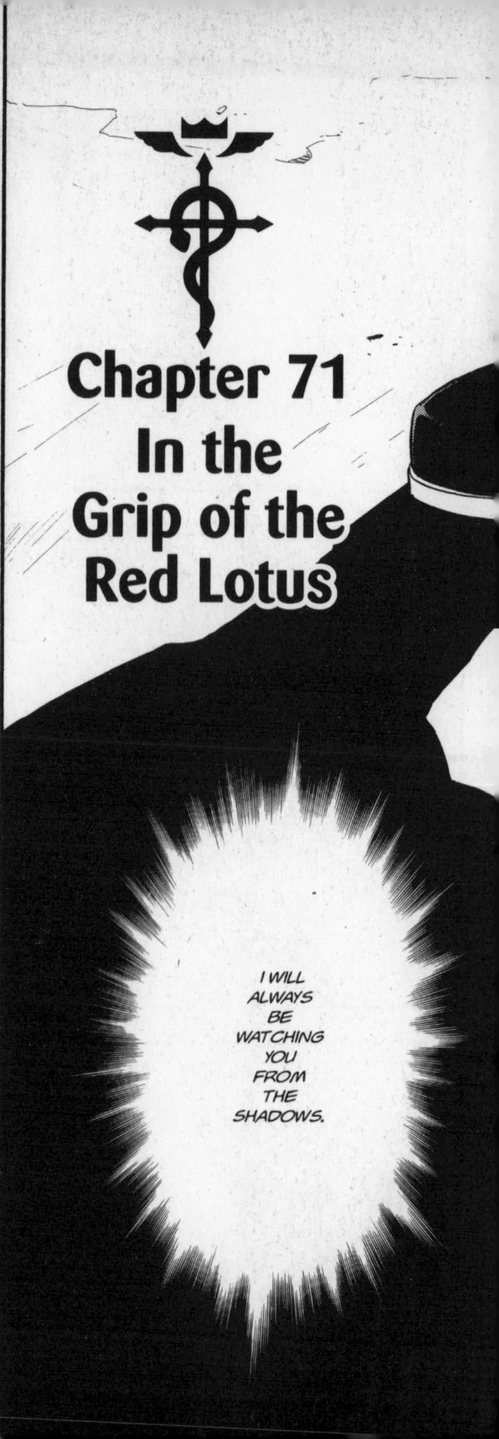
I WILL ALWAYS BE WATCHING YOU FROM THE SHADOWS.

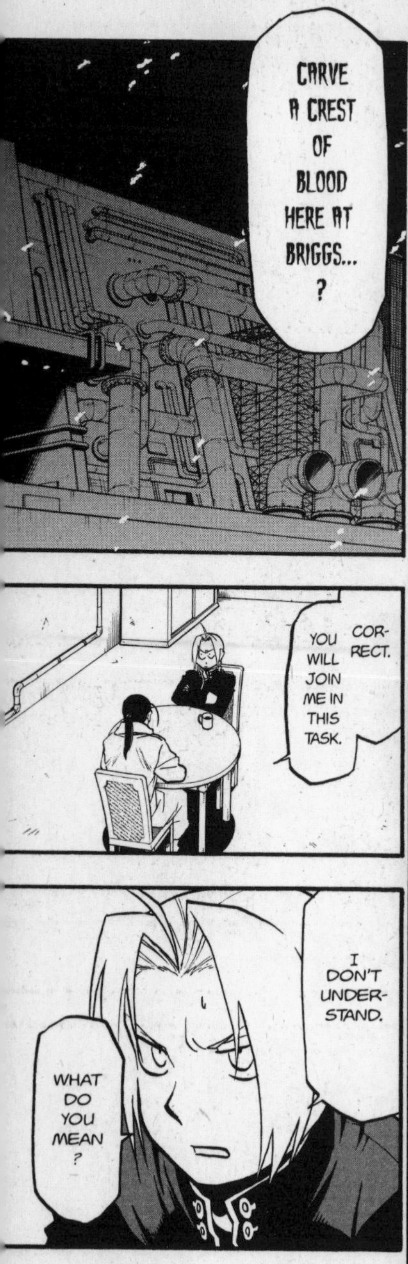
CARVE A CREST OF BLOOD HERE AT BRIGGS... ?
CORRECT.
YOU WILL JOIN ME IN THIS TASK.
I DON'T UNDERSTAND.
WHAT DO YOU MEAN ?

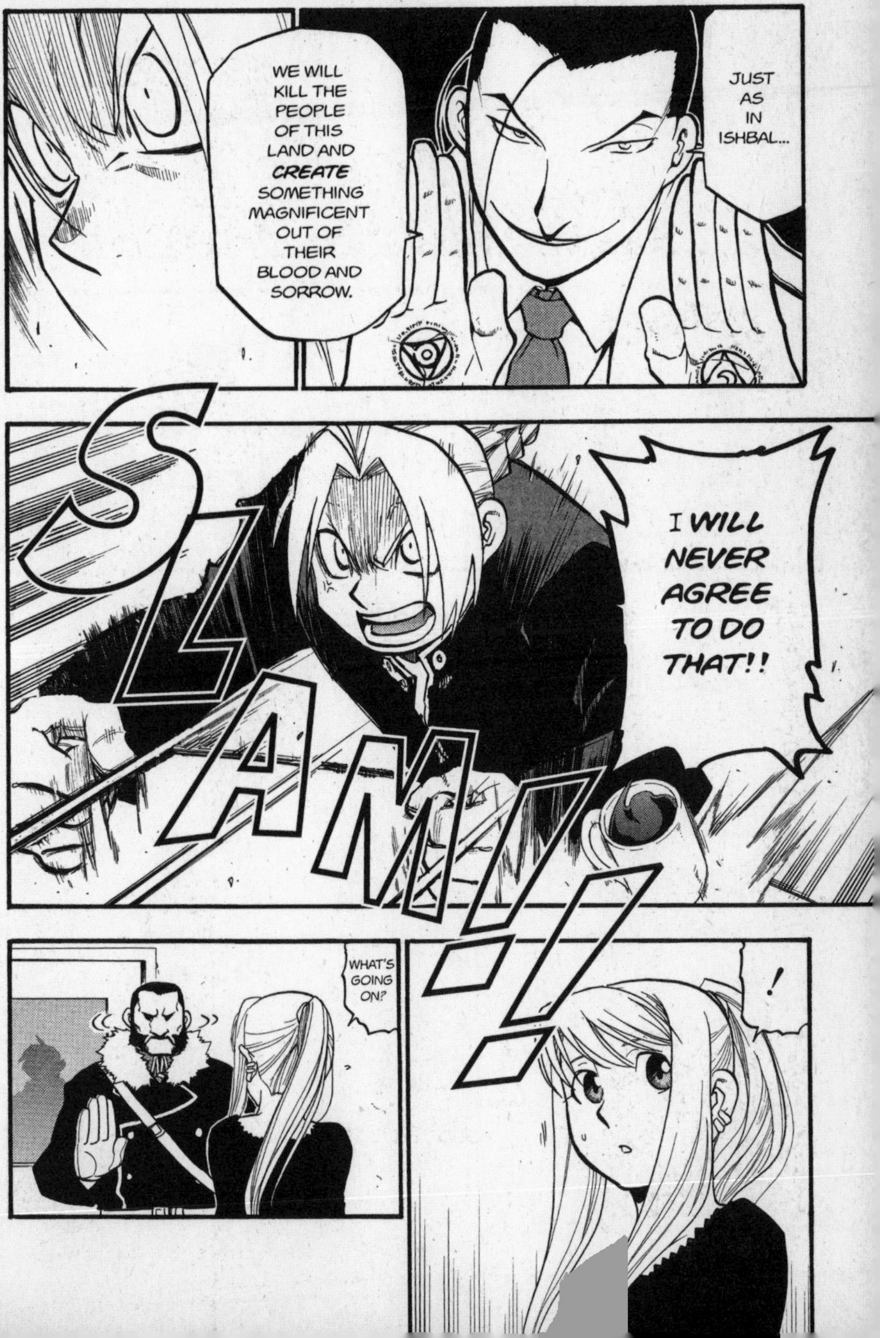
JUST AS IN ISHBAL...
WE WILL KILL THE PEOPLE OF THIS LAND AND CREATE SOMETHING MAGNIFICENT OUT OF THEIR BLOOD AND SORROW.
I WILL NEVER AGREE TO DO THAT!!
SLAM!!
!
WHAT'S GOING ON?

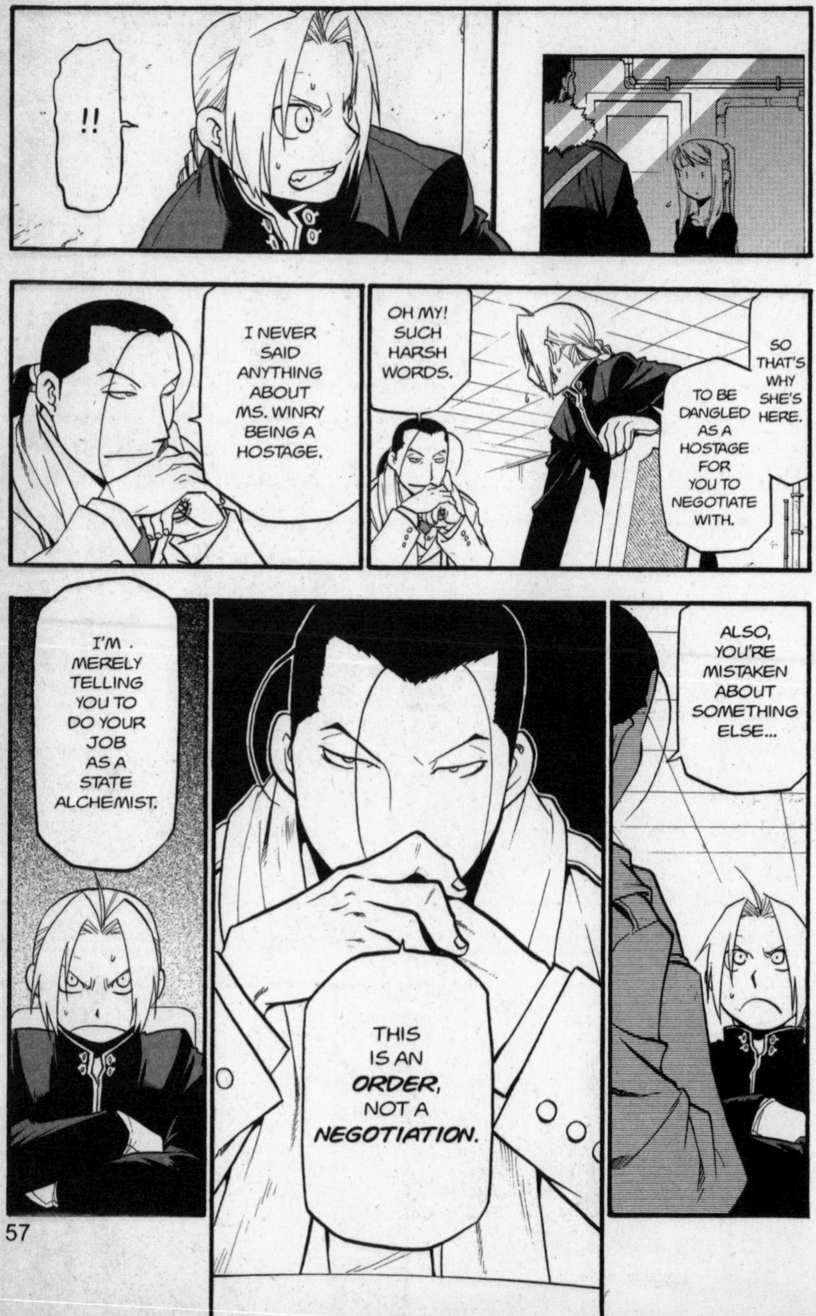
!!
SO THAT'S WHY SHE'S HERE.
TO BE DANGLED AS A HOSTAGE FOR YOU TO NEGOTIATE WITH.
OH MY! SUCH HARSH WORDS.
I NEVER SAID ANYTHING ABOUT MS. WINRY BEING A HOSTAGE.
ALSO, YOU'RE MISTAKEN ABOUT SOMETHING ELSE...
THIS IS AN *ORDER*, NOT A *NEGOTIATION*.
I'M MERELY TELLING YOU TO DO YOUR JOB AS A STATE ALCHEMIST.

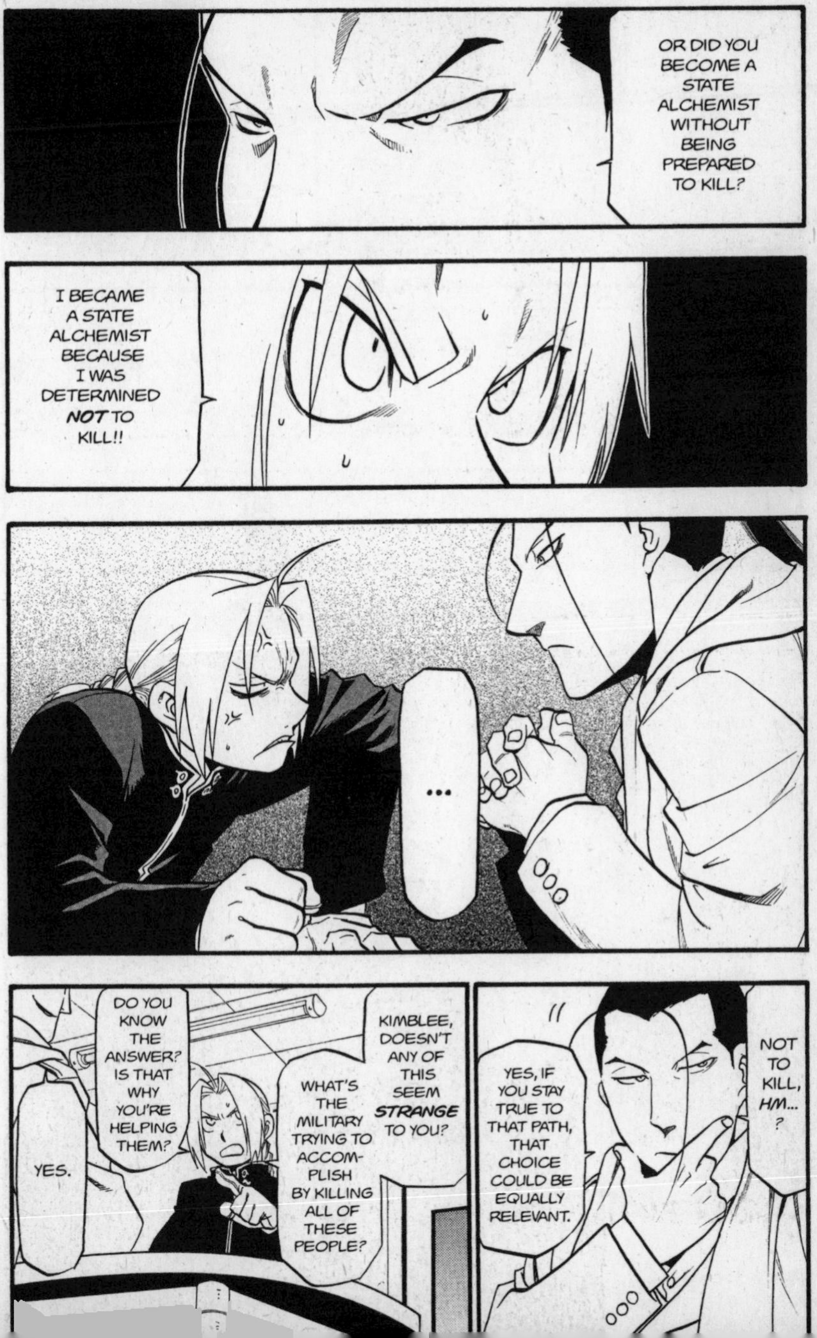
OR DID YOU BECOME A STATE ALCHEMIST WITHOUT BEING PREPARED TO KILL?
I BECAME A STATE ALCHEMIST BECAUSE I WAS DETERMINED ***NOT*** TO KILL!!
...
NOT TO KILL, ***HM...***?
YES, IF YOU STAY TRUE TO THAT PATH, THAT CHOICE COULD BE EQUALLY RELEVANT.
KIMBLEE, DOESN'T ANY OF THIS SEEM ***STRANGE*** TO YOU?
WHAT'S THE MILITARY TRYING TO ACCOMPLISH BY KILLING ALL OF THESE PEOPLE?
DO YOU KNOW THE ANSWER? IS THAT WHY YOU'RE HELPING THEM?
YES.

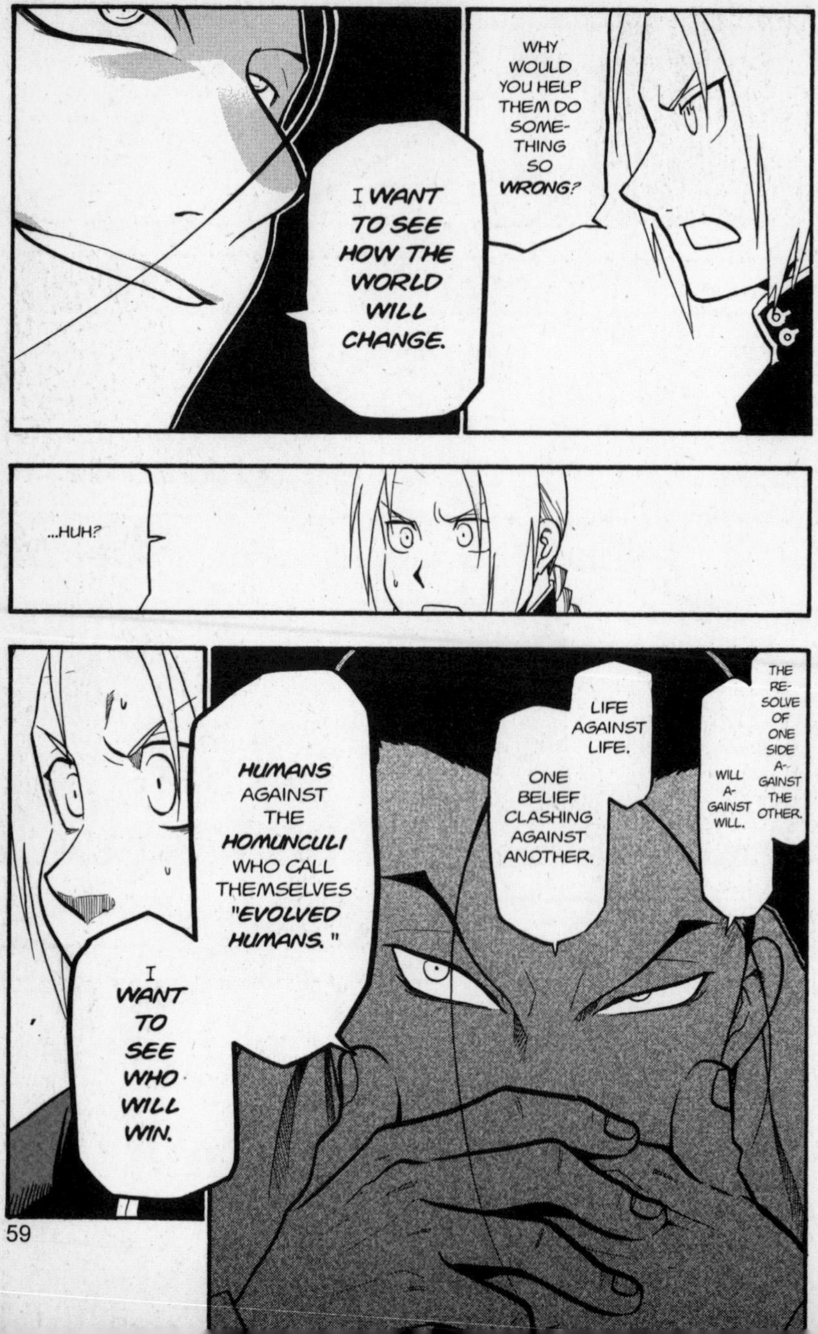
WHY WOULD YOU HELP THEM DO SOMETHING SO WRONG?
I WANT TO SEE HOW THE WORLD WILL CHANGE.
...HUH?
THE RESOLVE OF ONE SIDE AGAINST THE OTHER.
WILL AGAINST WILL.
LIFE AGAINST LIFE.
ONE BELIEF CLASHING AGAINST ANOTHER.
HUMANS AGAINST THE HOMUNCULI WHO CALL THEMSELVES "EVOLVED HUMANS."
I WANT TO SEE WHO WILL WIN.

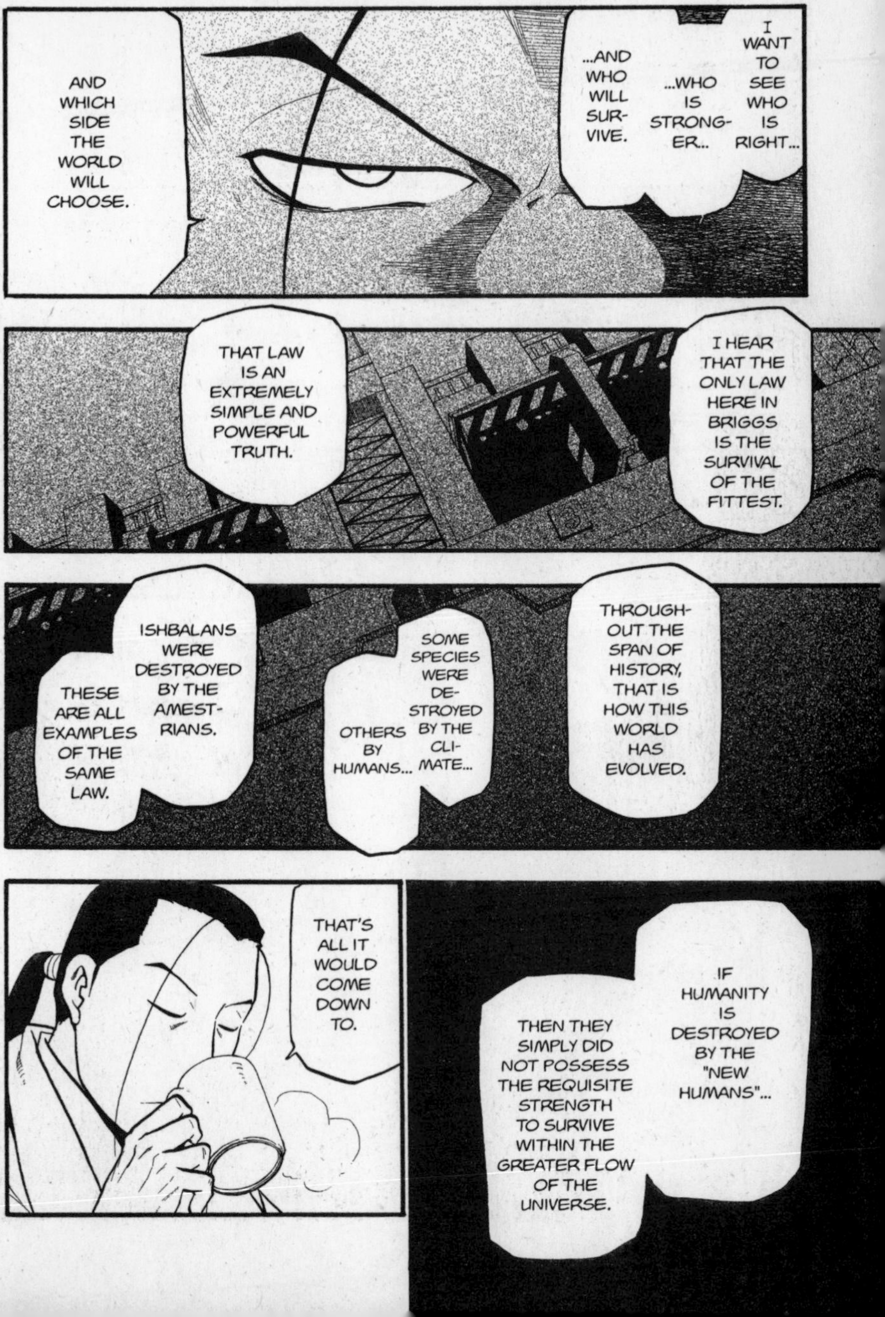
I WANT TO SEE WHO IS RIGHT...
...WHO IS STRONGER...
...AND WHO WILL SURVIVE.
AND WHICH SIDE THE WORLD WILL CHOOSE.
I HEAR THAT THE ONLY LAW HERE IN BRIGGS IS THE SURVIVAL OF THE FITTEST.
THAT LAW IS AN EXTREMELY SIMPLE AND POWERFUL TRUTH.
THROUGHOUT THE SPAN OF HISTORY, THAT IS HOW THIS WORLD HAS EVOLVED.
SOME SPECIES WERE DESTROYED BY THE CLIMATE...
OTHERS BY HUMANS...
ISHBALANS WERE DESTROYED BY THE AMESTRIANS.
THESE ARE ALL EXAMPLES OF THE SAME LAW.
IF HUMANITY IS DESTROYED BY THE "NEW HUMANS"...
THEN THEY SIMPLY DID NOT POSSESS THE REQUISITE STRENGTH TO SURVIVE WITHIN THE GREATER FLOW OF THE UNIVERSE.
THAT'S ALL IT WOULD COME DOWN TO.

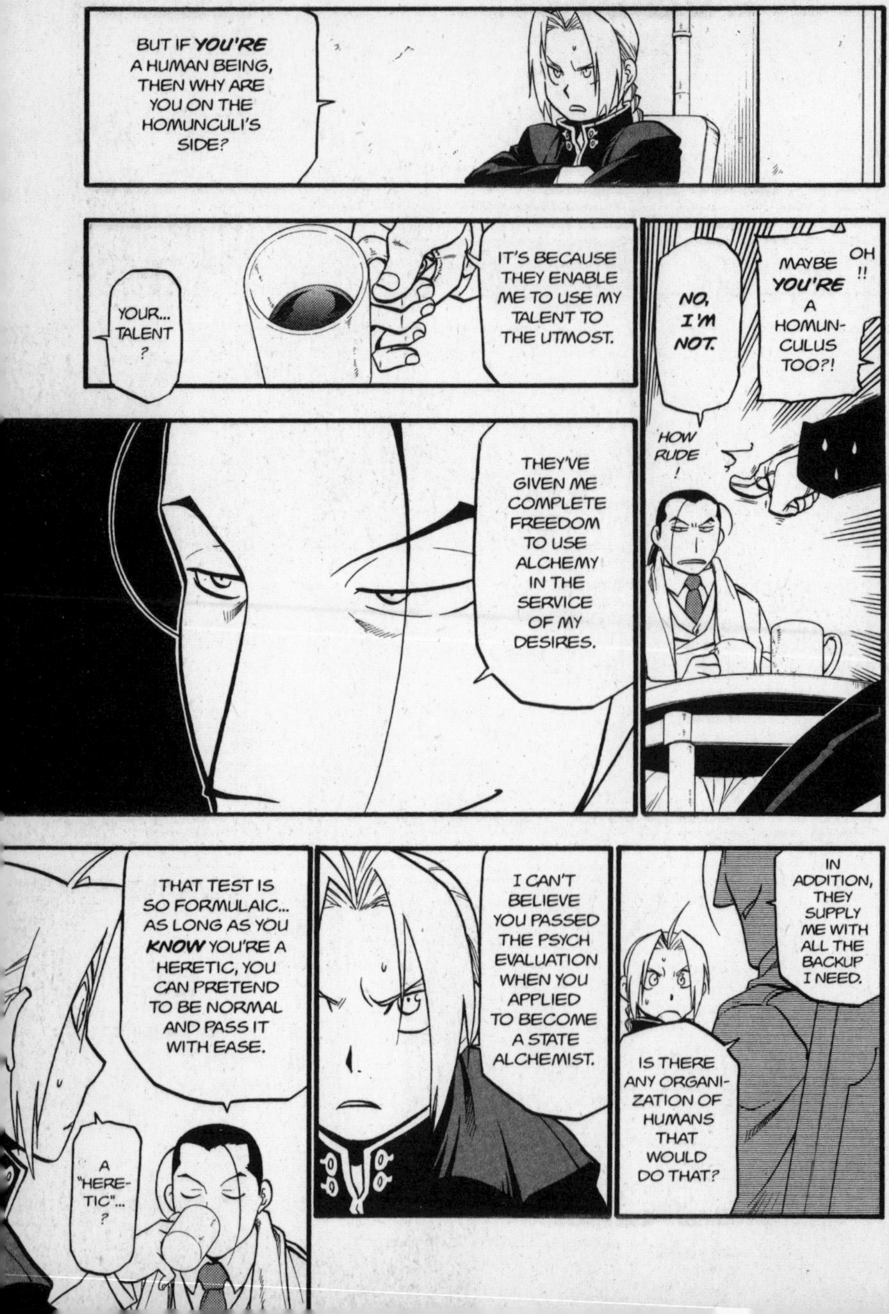
BUT IF YOU'RE A HUMAN BEING, THEN WHY ARE YOU ON THE HOMUNCULI'S SIDE?
MAYBE YOU'RE A HOMUNCULUS TOO?!
OH !!
NO, I'M NOT.
HOW RUDE !
IT'S BECAUSE THEY ENABLE ME TO USE MY TALENT TO THE UTMOST.
YOUR... TALENT ?
THEY'VE GIVEN ME COMPLETE FREEDOM TO USE ALCHEMY IN THE SERVICE OF MY DESIRES.
IN ADDITION, THEY SUPPLY ME WITH ALL THE BACKUP I NEED.
IS THERE ANY ORGANIZATION OF HUMANS THAT WOULD DO THAT?
I CAN'T BELIEVE YOU PASSED THE PSYCH EVALUATION WHEN YOU APPLIED TO BECOME A STATE ALCHEMIST.
THAT TEST IS SO FORMULAIC... AS LONG AS YOU KNOW YOU'RE A HERETIC, YOU CAN PRETEND TO BE NORMAL AND PASS IT WITH EASE.
A "HERETIC"... ?

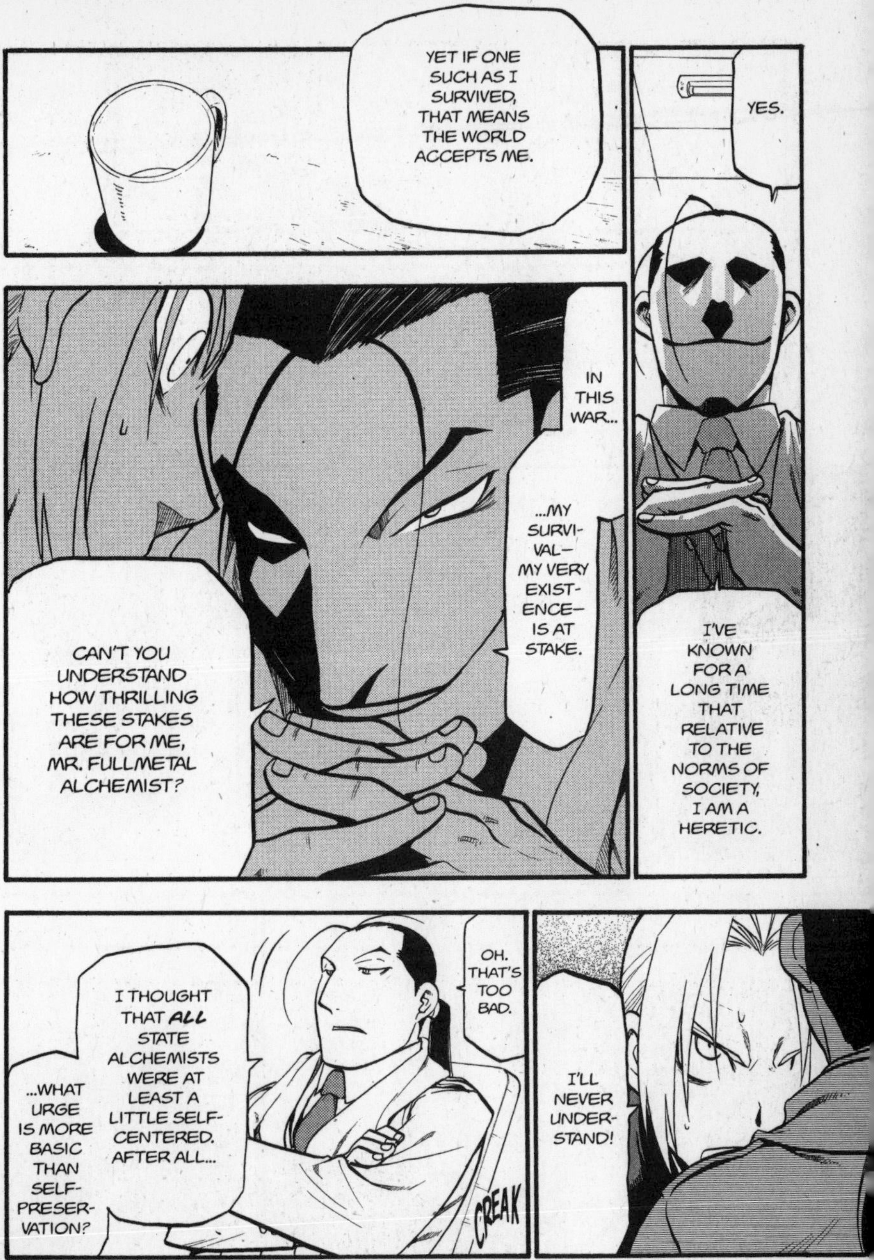
YES.
I'VE KNOWN FOR A LONG TIME THAT RELATIVE TO THE NORMS OF SOCIETY, I AM A HERETIC.
YET IF ONE SUCH AS I SURVIVED, THAT MEANS THE WORLD ACCEPTS ME.
IN THIS WAR...
...MY SURVIVAL— MY VERY EXISTENCE— IS AT STAKE.
CAN'T YOU UNDERSTAND HOW THRILLING THESE STAKES ARE FOR ME, MR. FULLMETAL ALCHEMIST?
I'LL NEVER UNDERSTAND!
OH. THAT'S TOO BAD.
I THOUGHT THAT ***ALL*** STATE ALCHEMISTS WERE AT LEAST A LITTLE SELF-CENTERED. AFTER ALL...
...WHAT URGE IS MORE BASIC THAN SELF-PRESERVATION?
CREAK

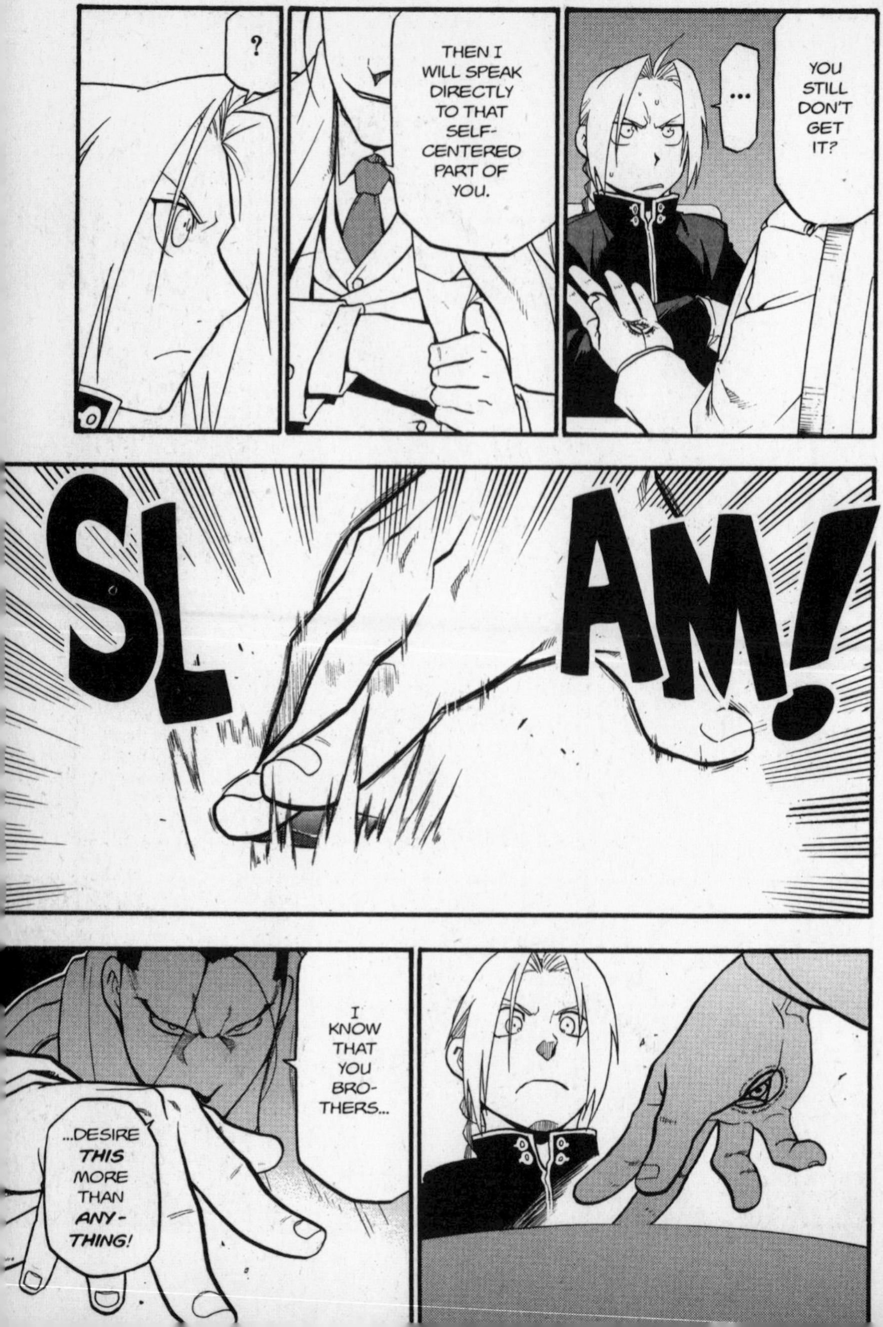
YOU STILL DON'T GET IT?
...
THEN I WILL SPEAK DIRECTLY TO THAT SELF-CENTERED PART OF YOU.
?
SLAM!
I KNOW THAT YOU BROTHERS...
...DESIRE THIS MORE THAN ANYTHING!

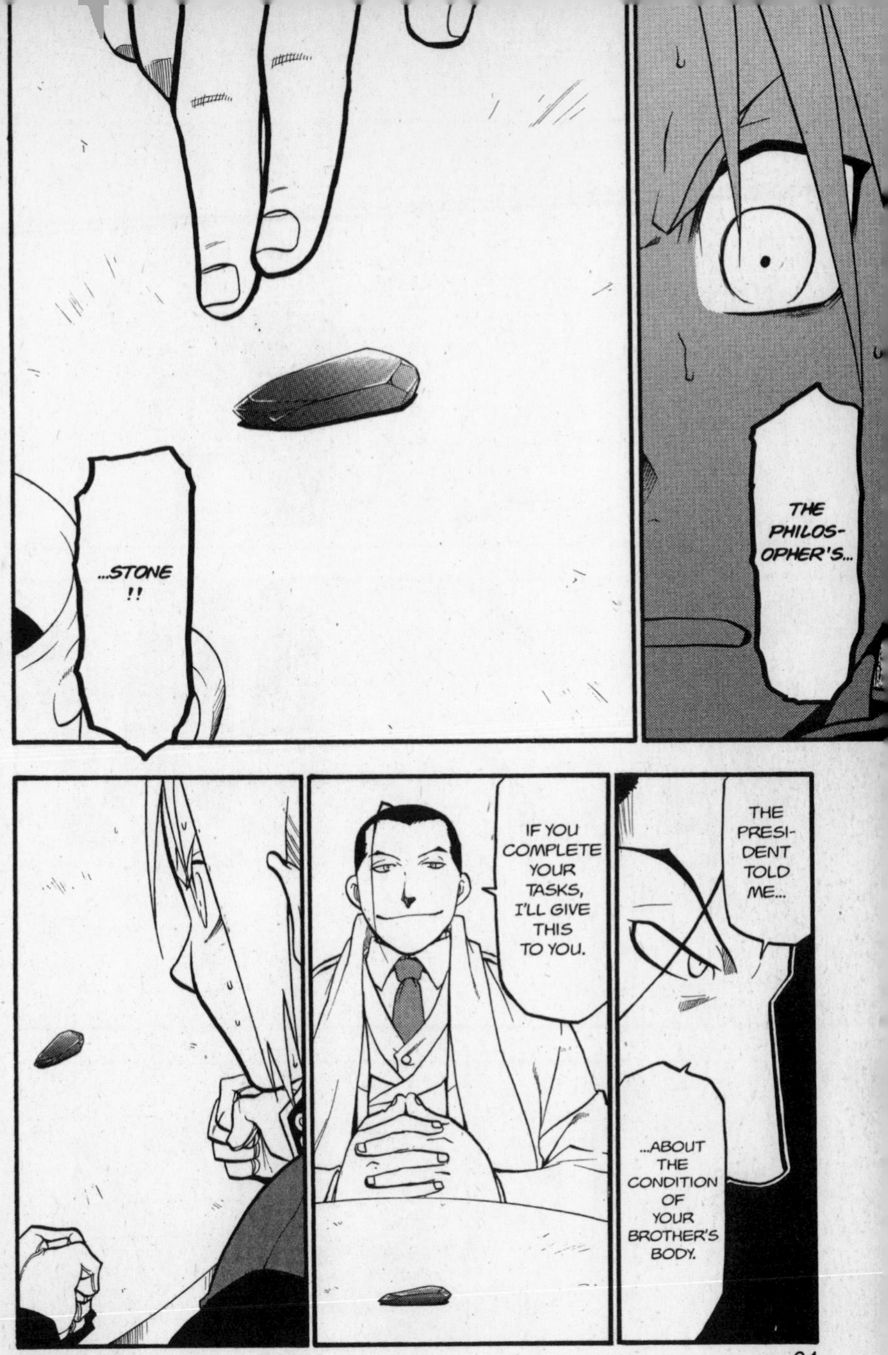
THE PHILOSOPHER'S...
...STONE !!
THE PRESIDENT TOLD ME...
...ABOUT THE CONDITION OF YOUR BROTHER'S BODY.
IF YOU COMPLETE YOUR TASKS, I'LL GIVE THIS TO YOU.

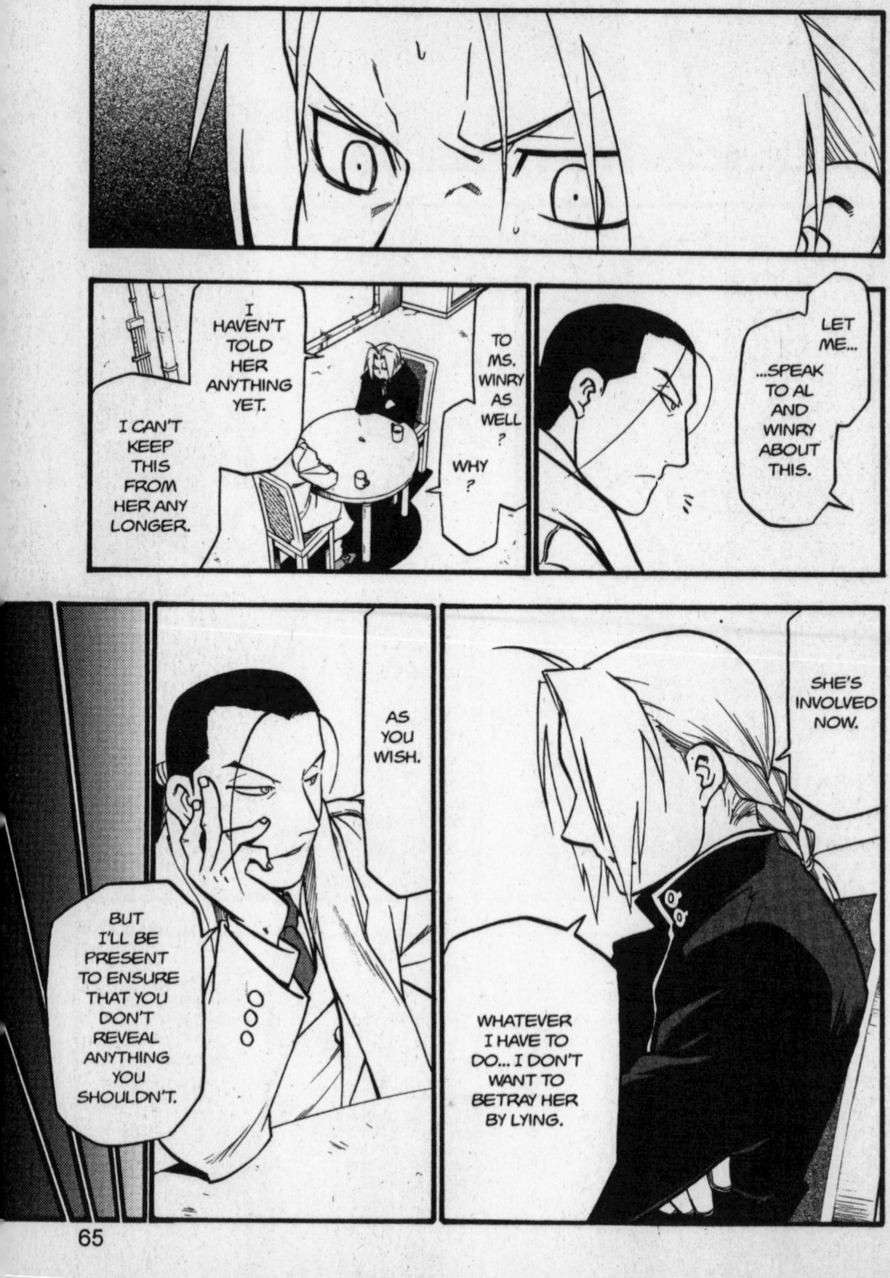
LET ME...
...SPEAK TO AL AND WINRY ABOUT THIS.
TO MS. WINRY AS WELL?
WHY?
I HAVEN'T TOLD HER ANYTHING YET.
I CAN'T KEEP THIS FROM HER ANY LONGER.
SHE'S INVOLVED NOW.
WHATEVER I HAVE TO DO... I DON'T WANT TO BETRAY HER BY LYING.
AS YOU WISH.
BUT I'LL BE PRESENT TO ENSURE THAT YOU DON'T REVEAL ANYTHING YOU SHOULDN'T.

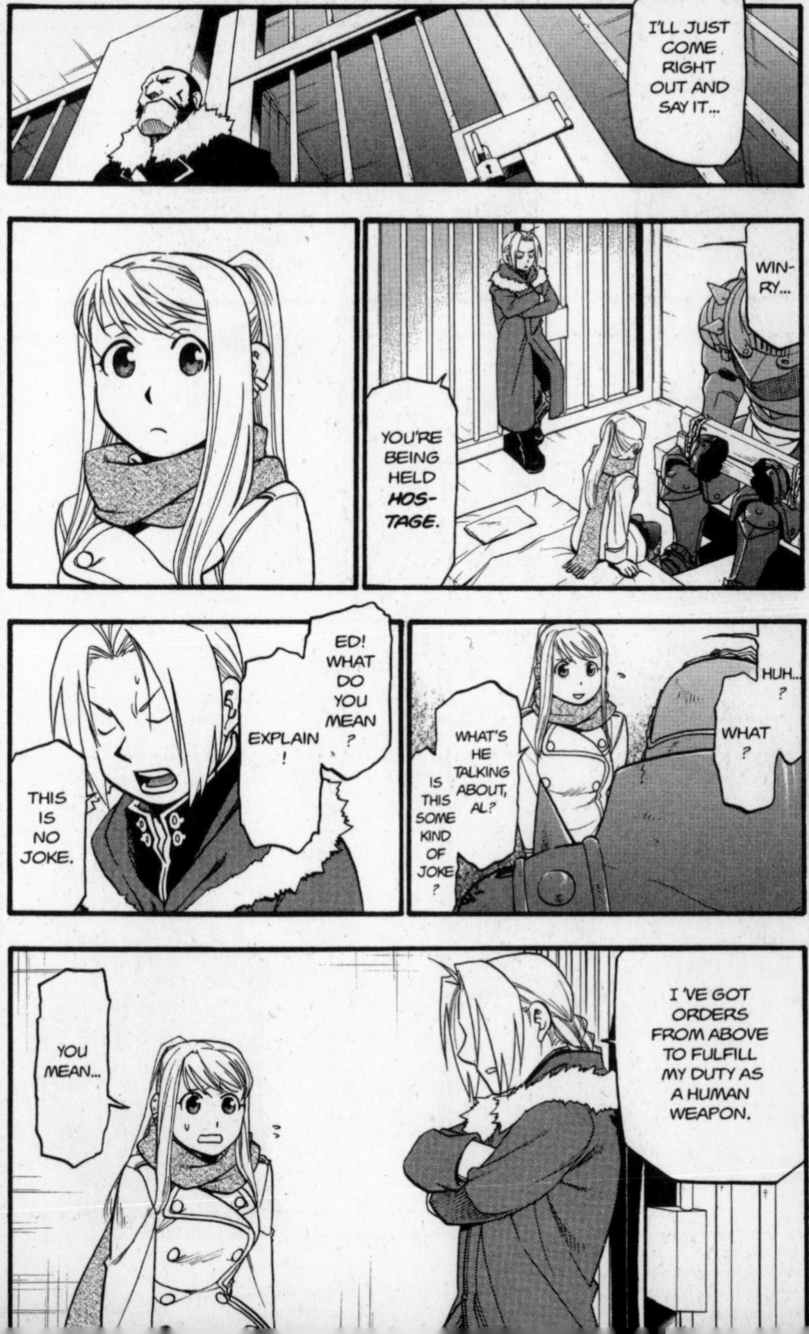
I'LL JUST COME RIGHT OUT AND SAY IT...
WIN-RY...
YOU'RE BEING HELD HOS-TAGE.
HUH...?
WHAT?
WHAT'S HE TALKING ABOUT, AL?
IS THIS SOME KIND OF JOKE?
ED! WHAT DO YOU MEAN?
EXPLAIN!
THIS IS NO JOKE.
I'VE GOT ORDERS FROM ABOVE TO FULFILL MY DUTY AS A HUMAN WEAPON.
YOU MEAN...

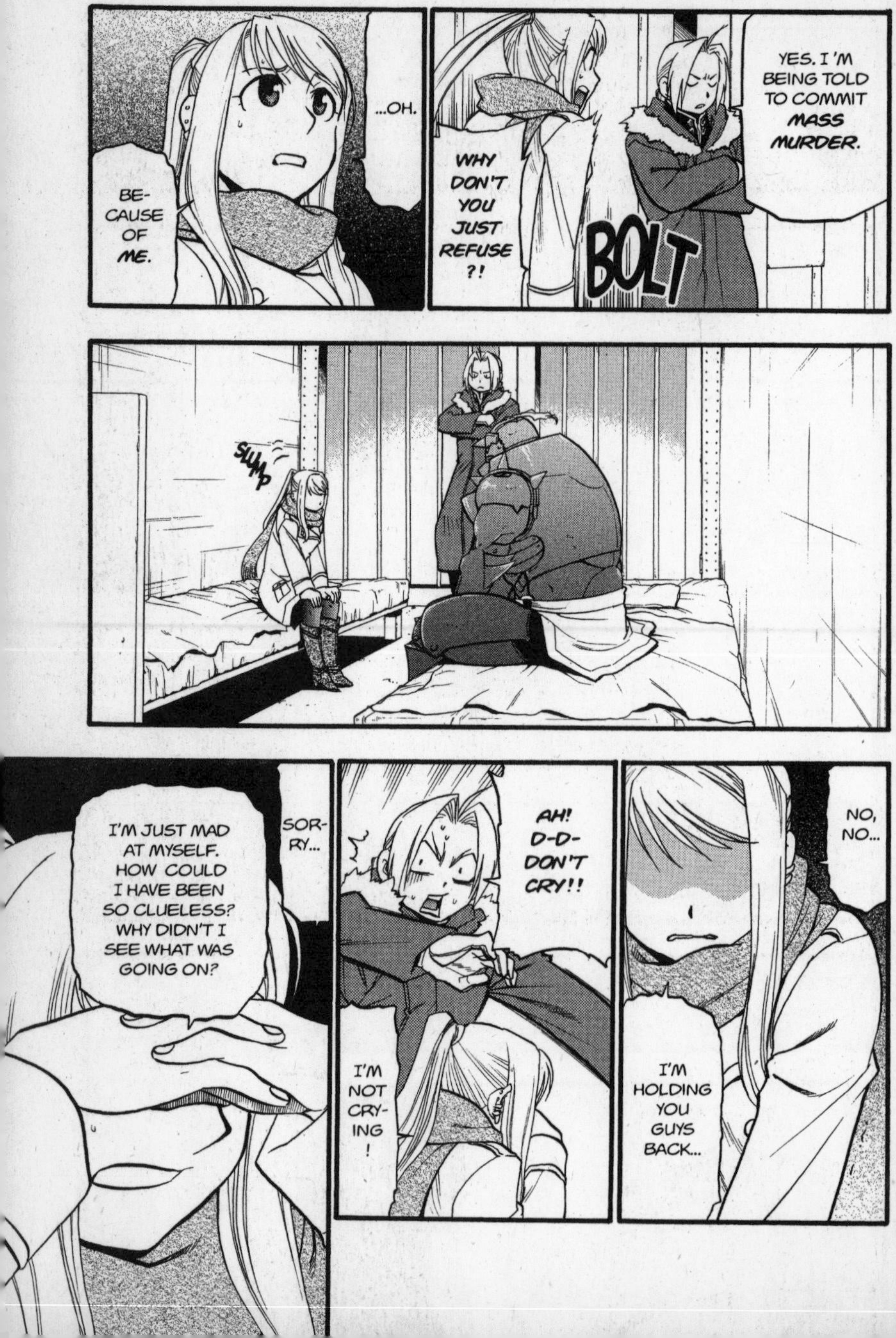
YES. I'M BEING TOLD TO COMMIT MASS MURDER.
BOLT
WHY DON'T YOU JUST REFUSE?!
...OH.
BE-CAUSE OF ME.
SLUMP
NO, NO...
I'M HOLDING YOU GUYS BACK...
AH! D-D-DON'T CRY!!
I'M NOT CRY-ING!
SOR-RY...
I'M JUST MAD AT MYSELF. HOW COULD I HAVE BEEN SO CLUELESS? WHY DIDN'T I SEE WHAT WAS GOING ON?

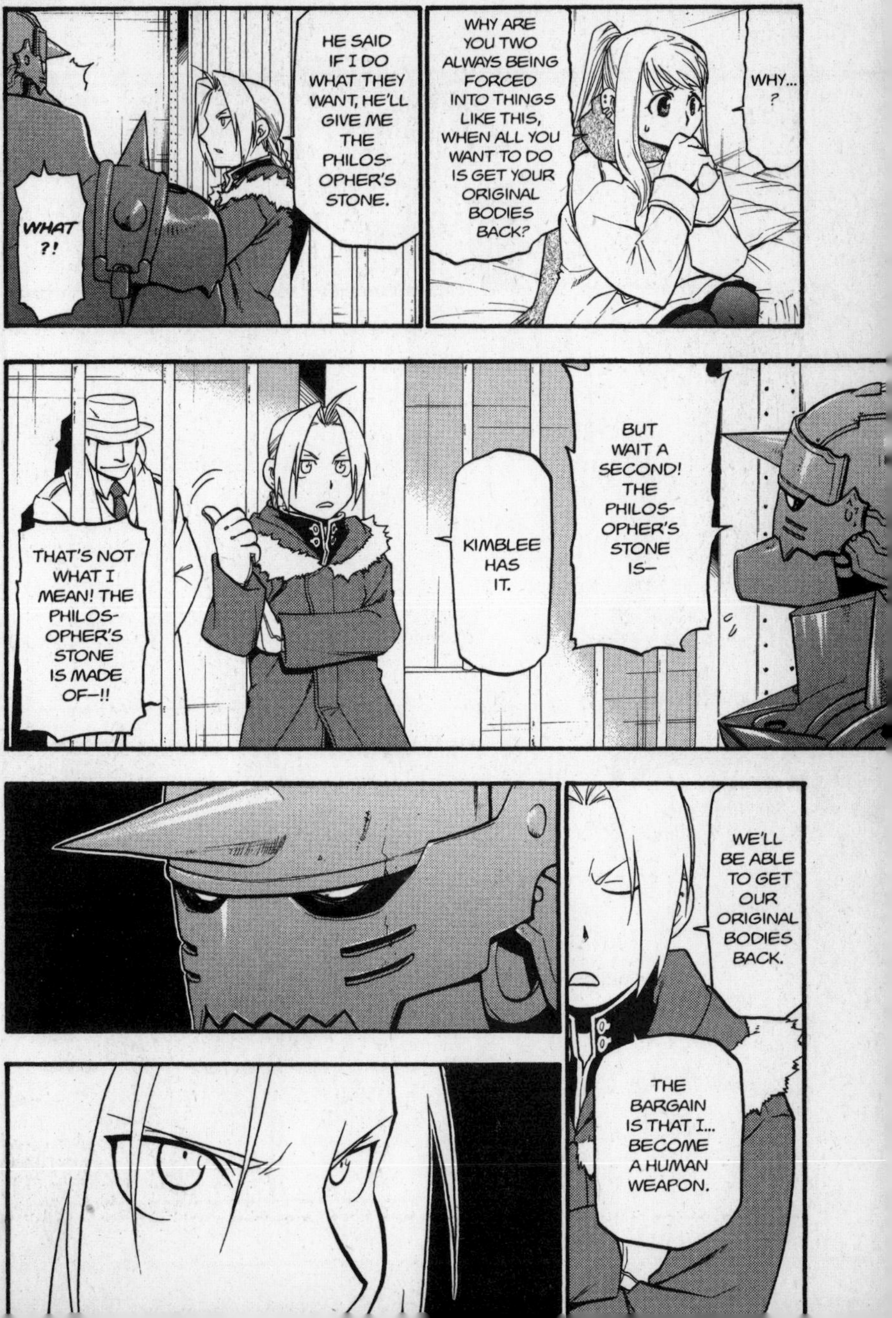
WHY... ?
WHY ARE YOU TWO ALWAYS BEING FORCED INTO THINGS LIKE THIS, WHEN ALL YOU WANT TO DO IS GET YOUR ORIGINAL BODIES BACK?
HE SAID IF I DO WHAT THEY WANT, HE'LL GIVE ME THE PHILOSOPHER'S STONE.
WHAT?!
BUT WAIT A SECOND! THE PHILOSOPHER'S STONE IS—
KIMBLEE HAS IT.
THAT'S NOT WHAT I MEAN! THE PHILOSOPHER'S STONE IS MADE OF—!!
WE'LL BE ABLE TO GET OUR ORIGINAL BODIES BACK.
THE BARGAIN IS THAT I... BECOME A HUMAN WEAPON.

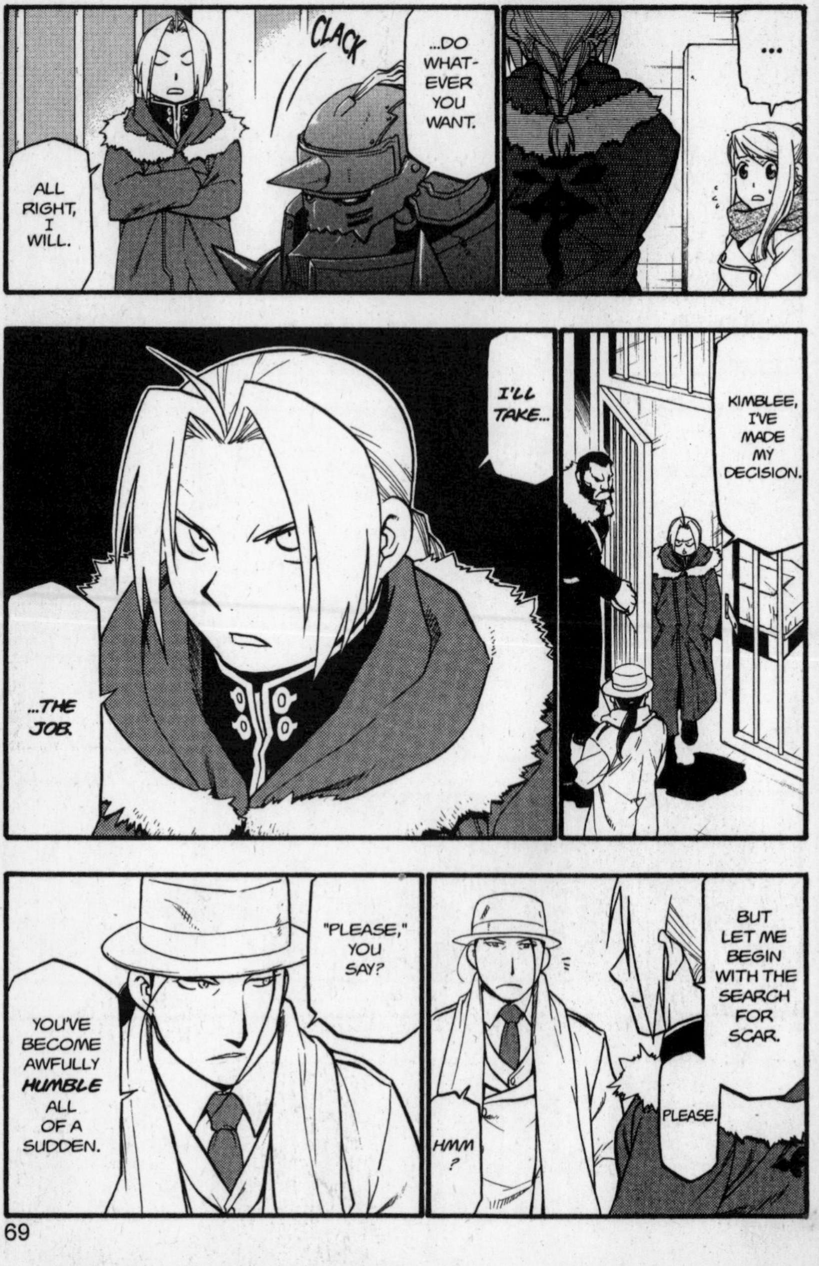
...
...DO WHATEVER YOU WANT.
CLACK
ALL RIGHT, I WILL.
KIMBLEE, I'VE MADE MY DECISION.
I'LL TAKE...
...THE JOB.
BUT LET ME BEGIN WITH THE SEARCH FOR SCAR.
PLEASE.
HMM?
"PLEASE," YOU SAY?
YOU'VE BECOME AWFULLY HUMBLE ALL OF A SUDDEN.

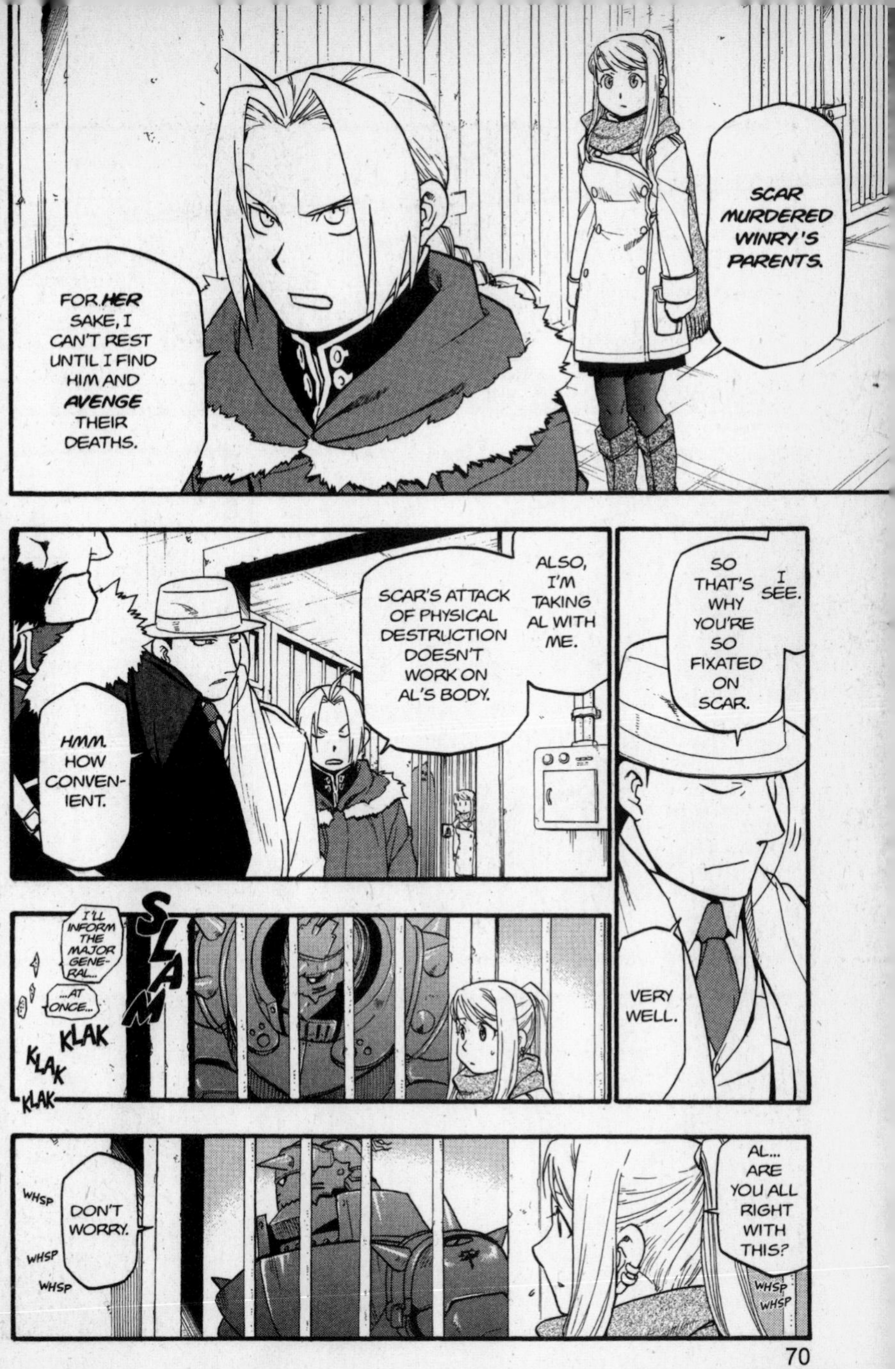
SCAR MURDERED WINRY'S PARENTS.
FOR HER SAKE, I CAN'T REST UNTIL I FIND HIM AND AVENGE THEIR DEATHS.
I SEE.
SO THAT'S WHY YOU'RE SO FIXATED ON SCAR.
VERY WELL.
ALSO, I'M TAKING AL WITH ME.
SCAR'S ATTACK OF PHYSICAL DESTRUCTION DOESN'T WORK ON AL'S BODY.
HMM. HOW CONVENIENT.
SLAM
I'LL INFORM THE MAJOR GENERAL...
...AT ONCE...
KLAK
KLAK
KLAK
AL... ARE YOU ALL RIGHT WITH THIS?
WHSP
WHSP
DON'T WORRY.
WHSP
WHSP
WHSP

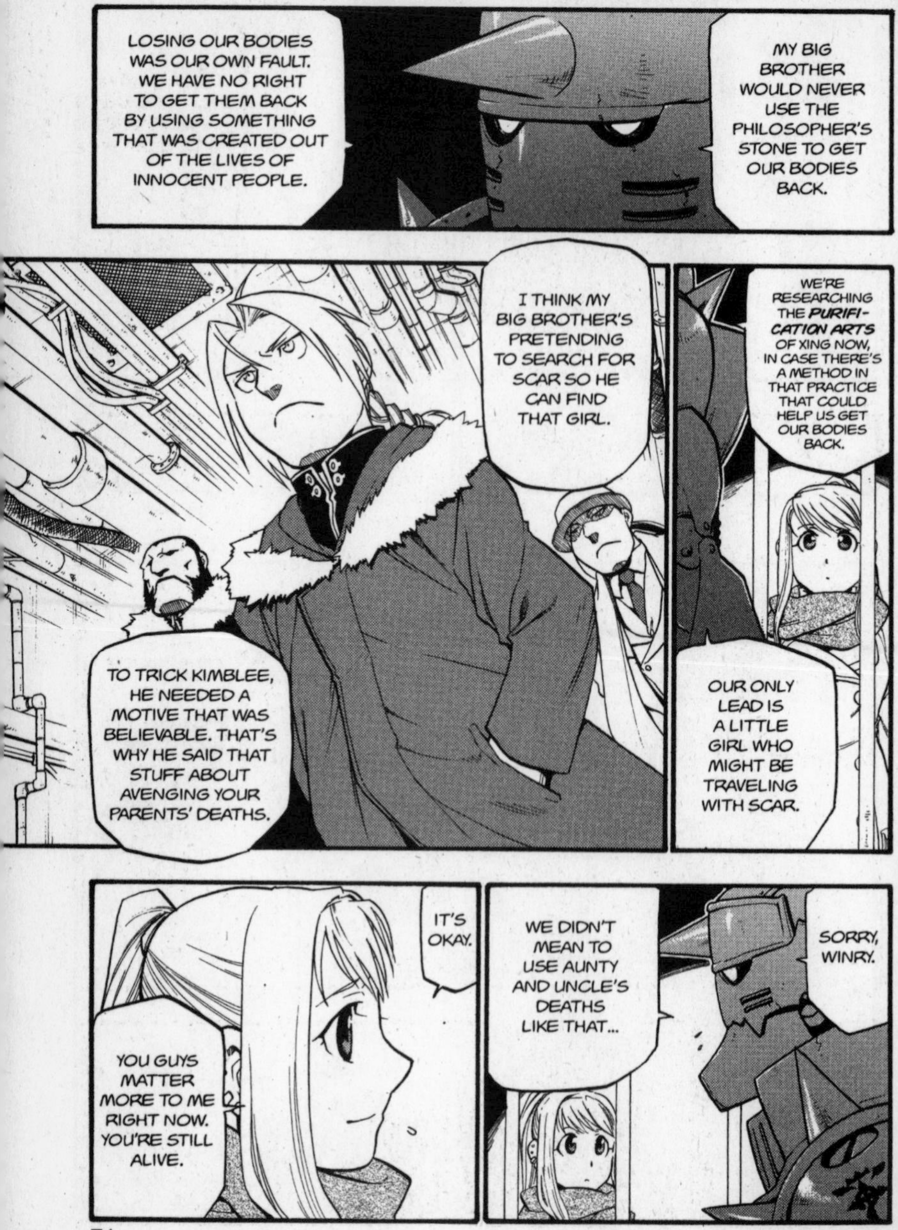
MY BIG BROTHER WOULD NEVER USE THE PHILOSOPHER'S STONE TO GET OUR BODIES BACK.
LOSING OUR BODIES WAS OUR OWN FAULT. WE HAVE NO RIGHT TO GET THEM BACK BY USING SOMETHING THAT WAS CREATED OUT OF THE LIVES OF INNOCENT PEOPLE.
WE'RE RESEARCHING THE *PURIFICATION ARTS* OF XING NOW, IN CASE THERE'S A METHOD IN THAT PRACTICE THAT COULD HELP US GET OUR BODIES BACK.
OUR ONLY LEAD IS A LITTLE GIRL WHO MIGHT BE TRAVELING WITH SCAR.
I THINK MY BIG BROTHER'S PRETENDING TO SEARCH FOR SCAR SO HE CAN FIND THAT GIRL.
TO TRICK KIMBLEE, HE NEEDED A MOTIVE THAT WAS BELIEVABLE. THAT'S WHY HE SAID THAT STUFF ABOUT AVENGING YOUR PARENTS' DEATHS.
SORRY, WINRY.
WE DIDN'T MEAN TO USE AUNTY AND UNCLE'S DEATHS LIKE THAT...
IT'S OKAY.
YOU GUYS MATTER MORE TO ME RIGHT NOW. YOU'RE STILL ALIVE.

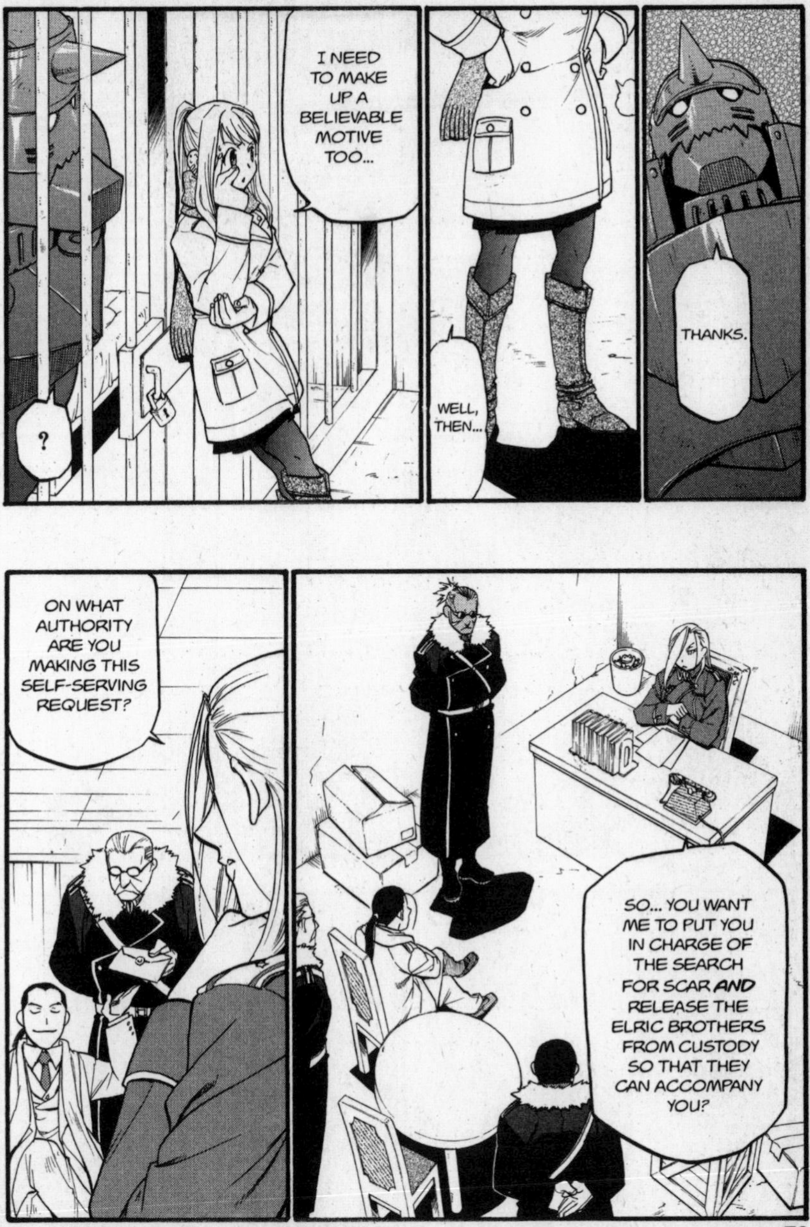
THANKS.
WELL, THEN...
I NEED TO MAKE UP A BELIEVABLE MOTIVE TOO...
?
SO... YOU WANT ME TO PUT YOU IN CHARGE OF THE SEARCH FOR SCAR AND RELEASE THE ELRIC BROTHERS FROM CUSTODY SO THAT THEY CAN ACCOMPANY YOU?
ON WHAT AUTHORITY ARE YOU MAKING THIS SELF-SERVING REQUEST?

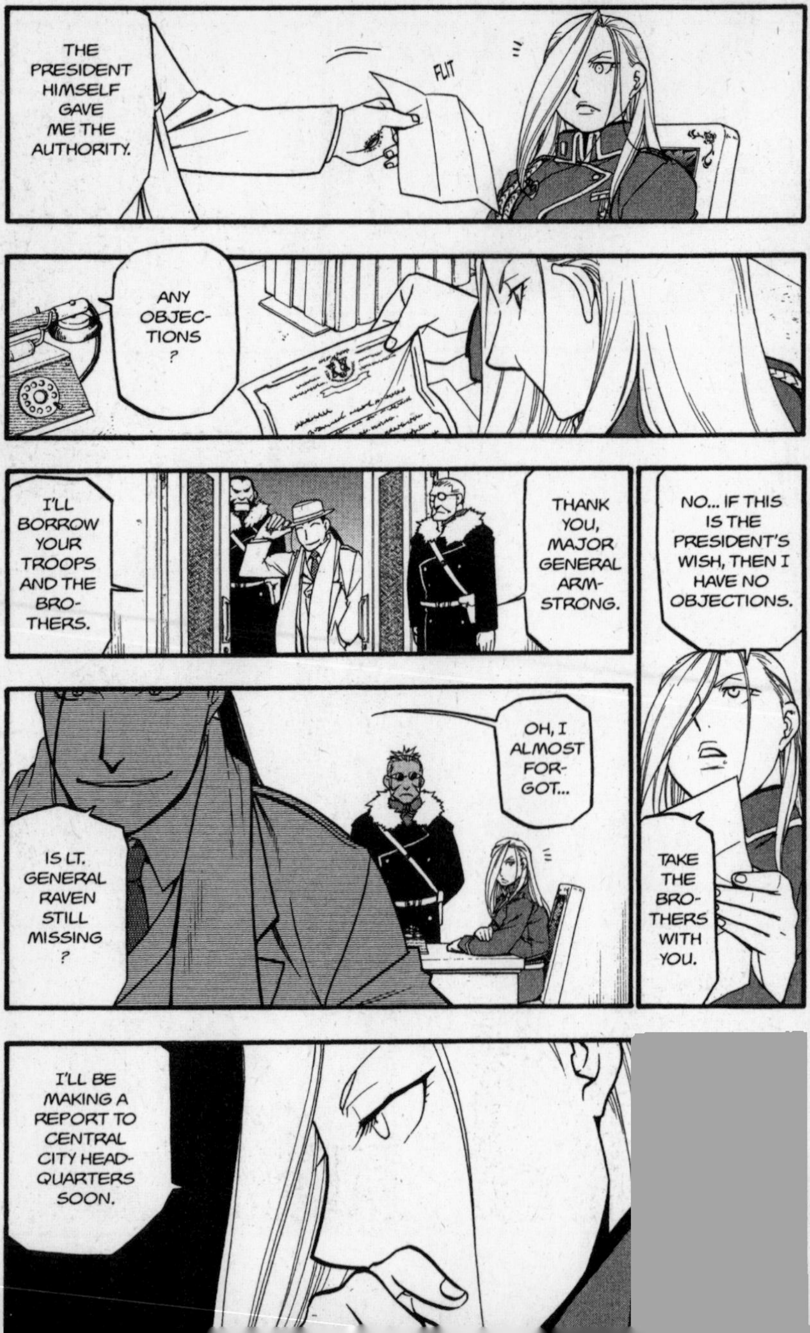
FLIT
THE PRESIDENT HIMSELF GAVE ME THE AUTHORITY.
ANY OBJECTIONS?
NO... IF THIS IS THE PRESIDENT'S WISH, THEN I HAVE NO OBJECTIONS.
TAKE THE BROTHERS WITH YOU.
THANK YOU, MAJOR GENERAL ARMSTRONG.
I'LL BORROW YOUR TROOPS AND THE BROTHERS.
OH, I ALMOST FORGOT...
IS LT. GENERAL RAVEN STILL MISSING?
I'LL BE MAKING A REPORT TO CENTRAL CITY HEADQUARTERS SOON.

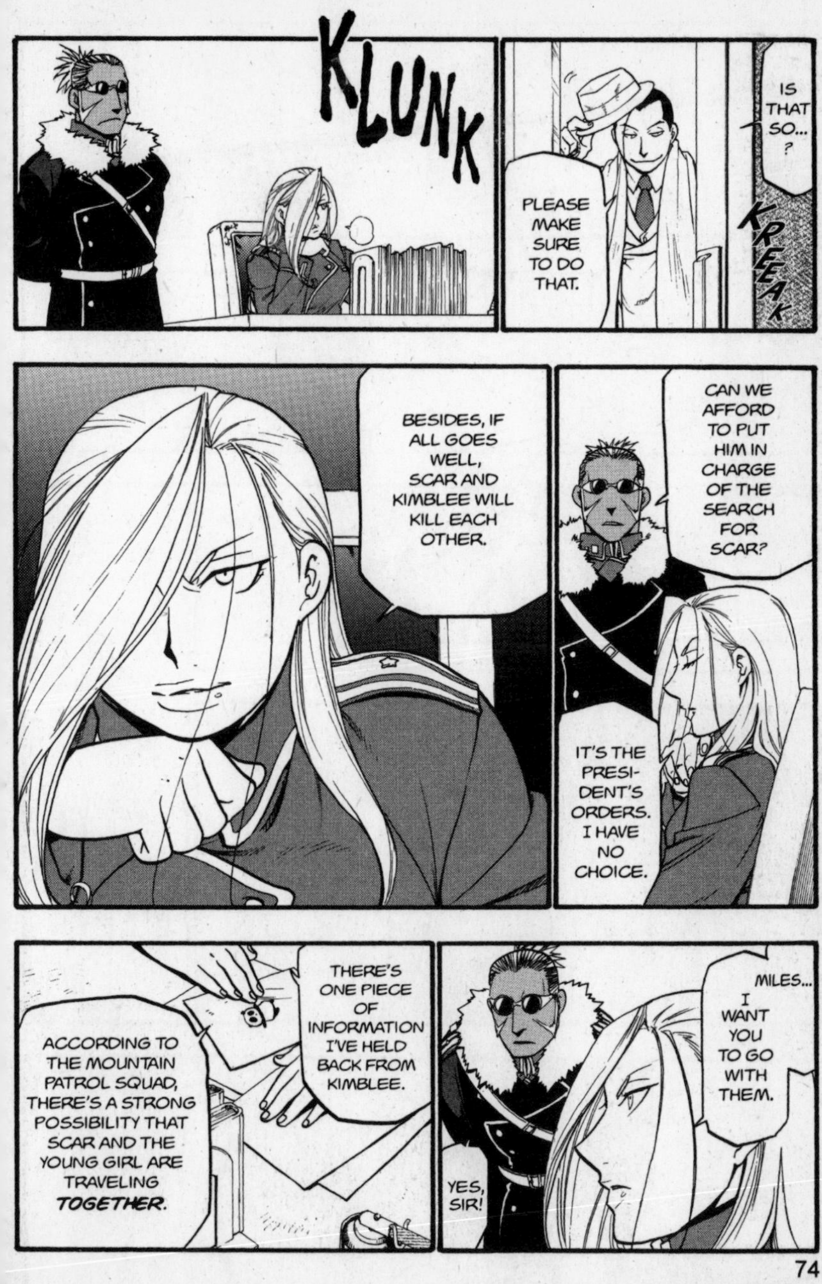
IS THAT SO...?
PLEASE MAKE SURE TO DO THAT.
KREEAK
KLUNK
CAN WE AFFORD TO PUT HIM IN CHARGE OF THE SEARCH FOR SCAR?
IT'S THE PRESIDENT'S ORDERS. I HAVE NO CHOICE.
BESIDES, IF ALL GOES WELL, SCAR AND KIMBLEE WILL KILL EACH OTHER.
MILES...
I WANT YOU TO GO WITH THEM.
YES, SIR!
THERE'S ONE PIECE OF INFORMATION I'VE HELD BACK FROM KIMBLEE.
ACCORDING TO THE MOUNTAIN PATROL SQUAD, THERE'S A STRONG POSSIBILITY THAT SCAR AND THE YOUNG GIRL ARE TRAVELING ***TOGETHER***.

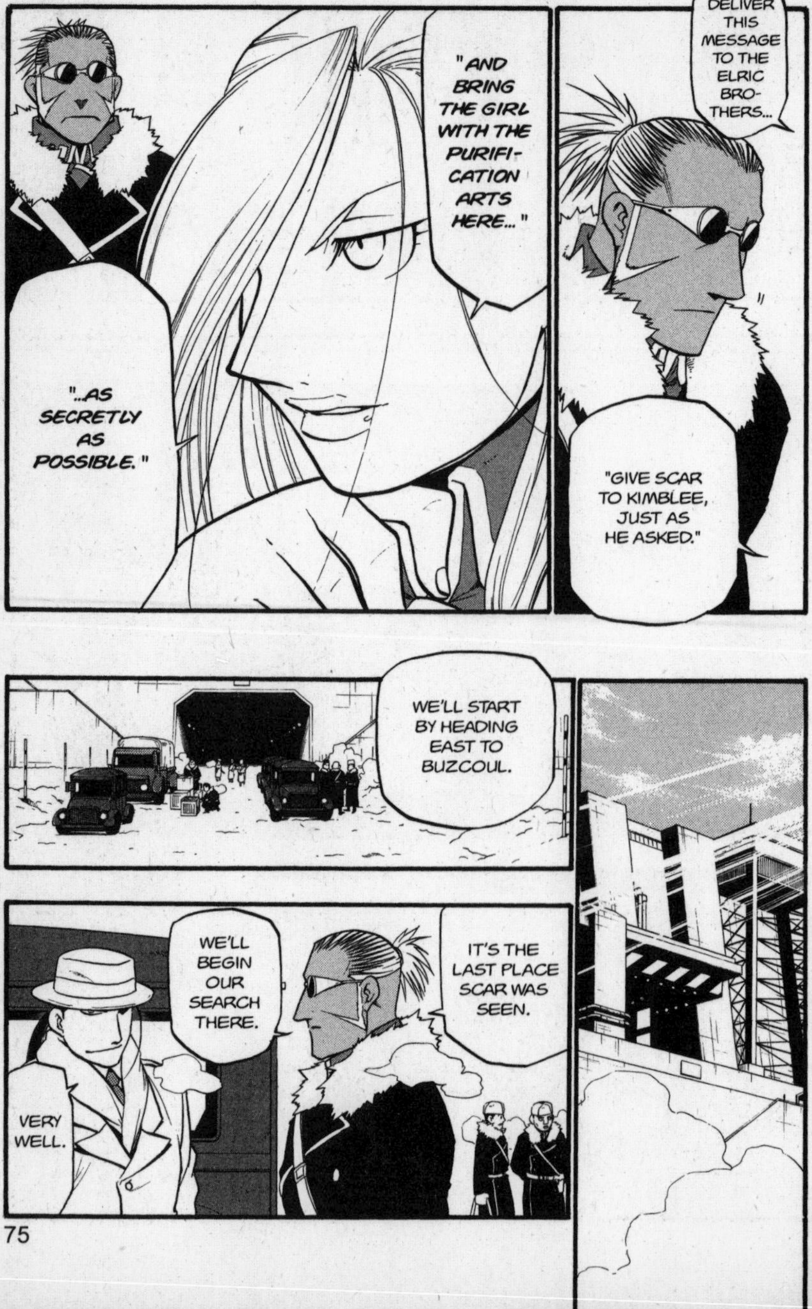
DELIVER THIS MESSAGE TO THE ELRIC BROTHERS...
"GIVE SCAR TO KIMBLEE, JUST AS HE ASKED."
"AND BRING THE GIRL WITH THE PURIFICATION ARTS HERE..."
"...AS SECRETLY AS POSSIBLE."
WE'LL START BY HEADING EAST TO BUZCOUL.
IT'S THE LAST PLACE SCAR WAS SEEN.
WE'LL BEGIN OUR SEARCH THERE.
VERY WELL.

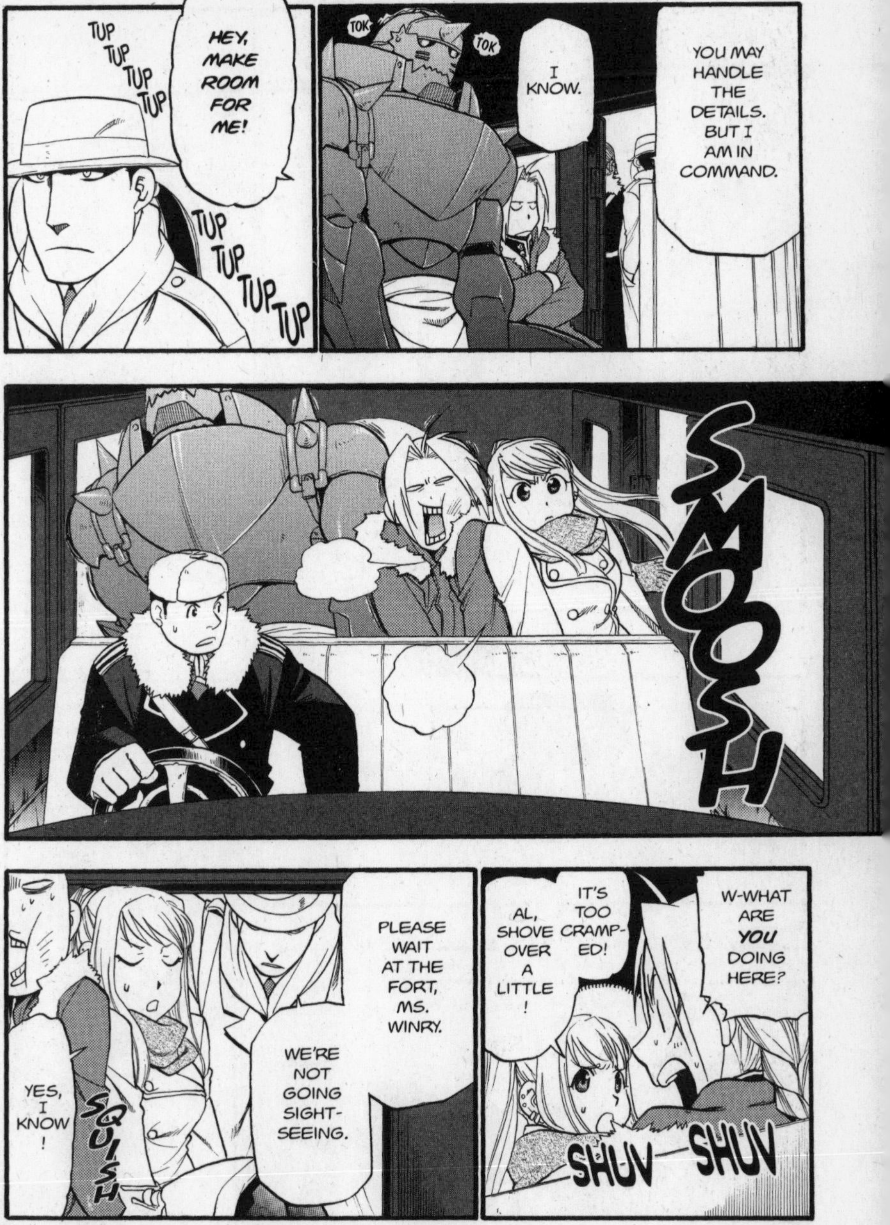
YOU MAY HANDLE THE DETAILS. BUT I AM IN COMMAND.
TOK
TOK
I KNOW.
HEY, MAKE ROOM FOR ME!
TUP TUP TUP TUP
TUP TUP TUP TUP
SMOOSH
W-WHAT ARE YOU DOING HERE?
IT'S TOO CRAMP-ED!
AL, SHOVE OVER A LITTLE!
SHUV SHUV
PLEASE WAIT AT THE FORT, MS. WINRY.
WE'RE NOT GOING SIGHT-SEEING.
YES, I KNOW!
SQUISH

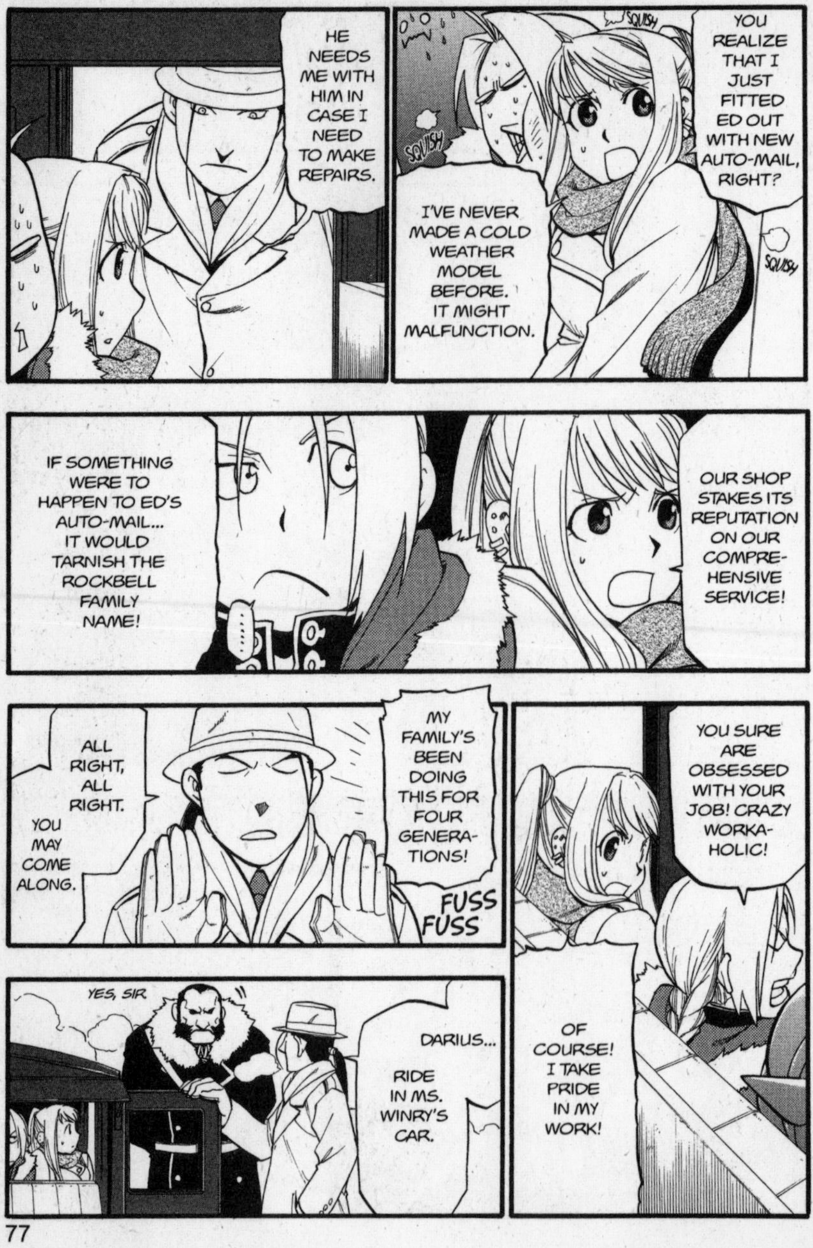
SQUISH
YOU REALIZE THAT I JUST FITTED ED OUT WITH NEW AUTO-MAIL, RIGHT?
SQUISH
SQUISH
I'VE NEVER MADE A COLD WEATHER MODEL BEFORE. IT MIGHT MALFUNCTION.
HE NEEDS ME WITH HIM IN CASE I NEED TO MAKE REPAIRS.
OUR SHOP STAKES ITS REPUTATION ON OUR COMPRE-HENSIVE SERVICE!
IF SOMETHING WERE TO HAPPEN TO ED'S AUTO-MAIL... IT WOULD TARNISH THE ROCKBELL FAMILY NAME!
MY FAMILY'S BEEN DOING THIS FOR FOUR GENERA-TIONS!
FUSS FUSS
ALL RIGHT, ALL RIGHT.
YOU MAY COME ALONG.
YOU SURE ARE OBSESSED WITH YOUR JOB! CRAZY WORKA-HOLIC!
OF COURSE! I TAKE PRIDE IN MY WORK!
DARIUS...
RIDE IN MS. WINRY'S CAR.
YES, SIR.

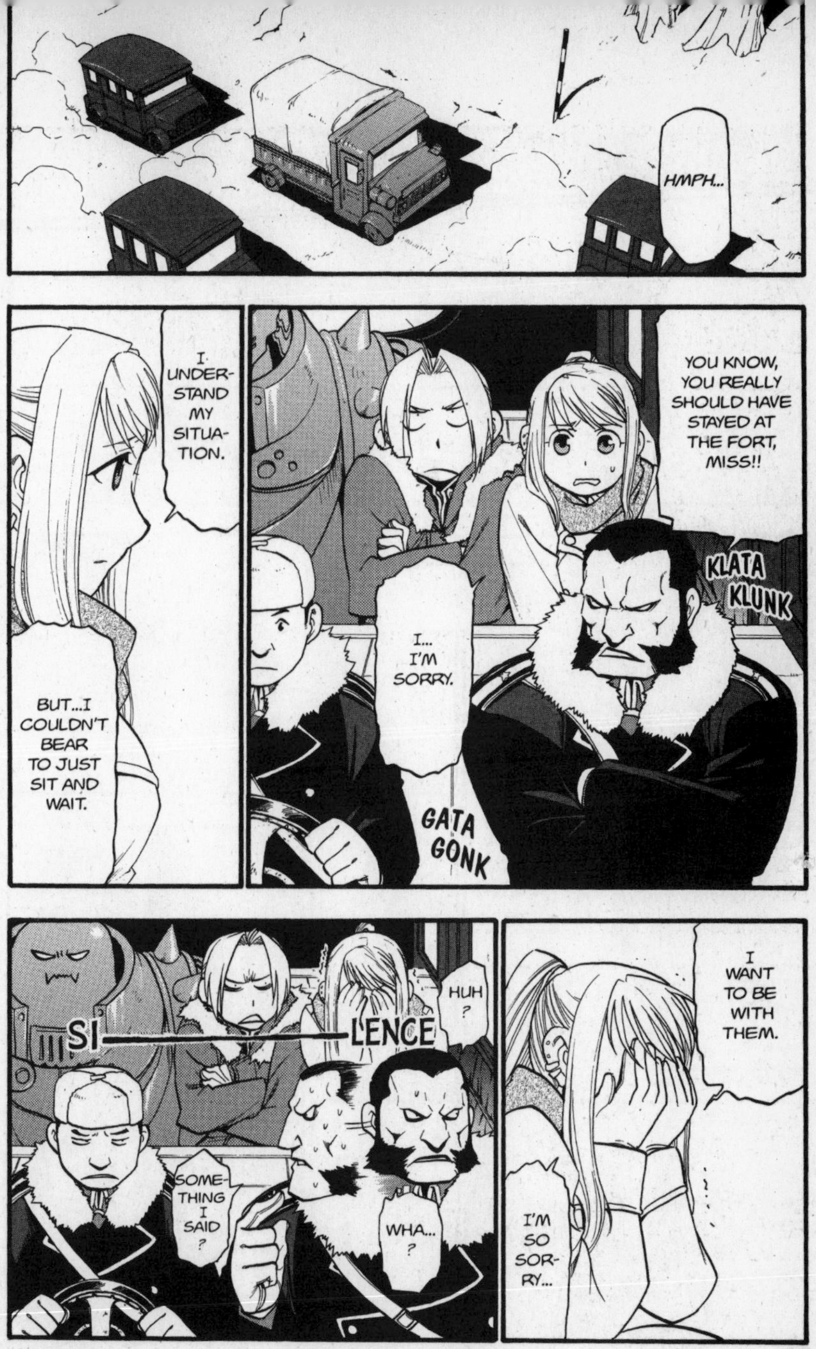
HMPH...
YOU KNOW, YOU REALLY SHOULD HAVE STAYED AT THE FORT, MISS!!
KLATA KLUNK
I... I'M SORRY.
GATA GONK
I UNDERSTAND MY SITUATION.
BUT...I COULDN'T BEAR TO JUST SIT AND WAIT.
I WANT TO BE WITH THEM.
...
I'M SO SORRY...
HUH?
SI—LENCE
SOMETHING I SAID?
WHA...?

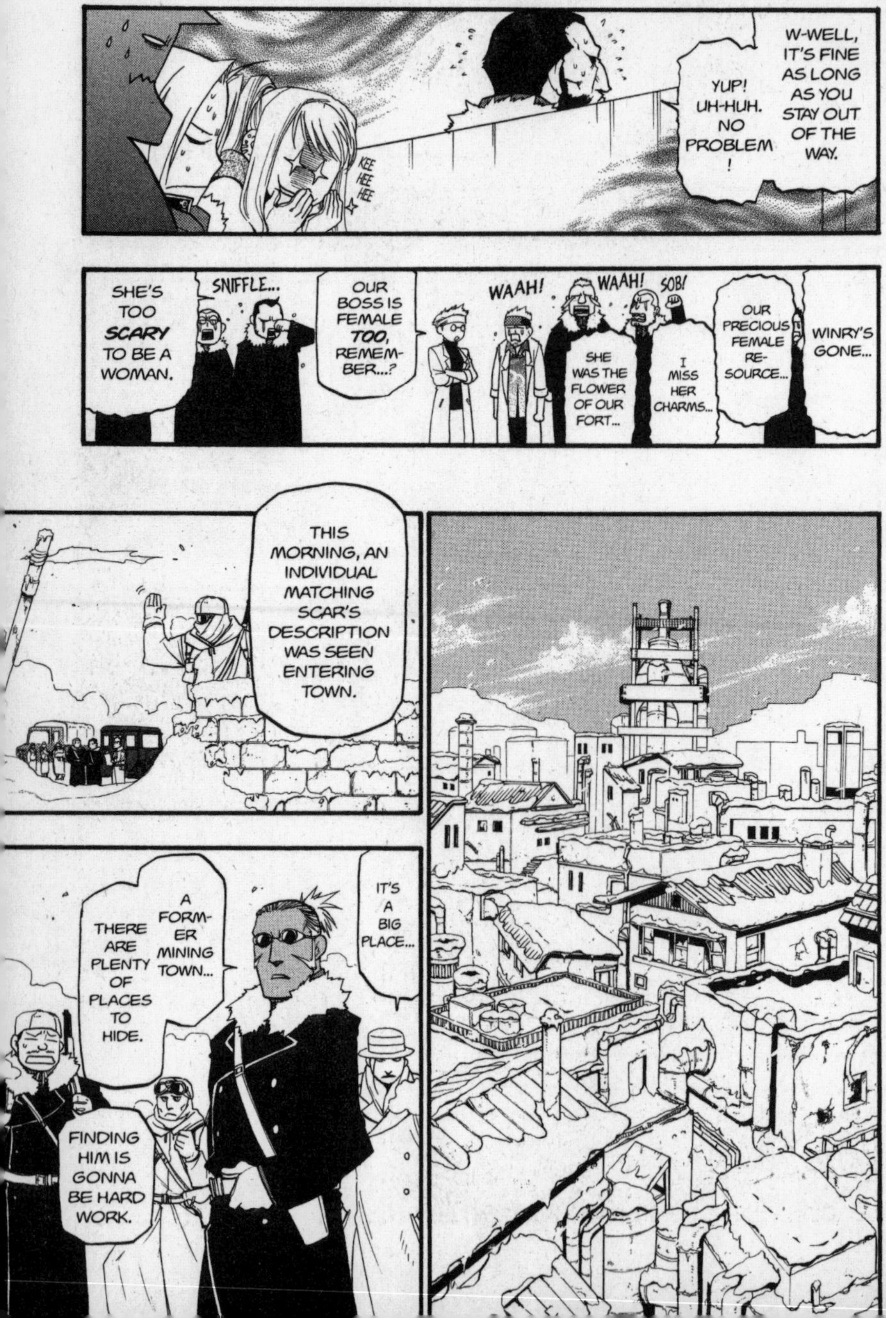
W-WELL, IT'S FINE AS LONG AS YOU STAY OUT OF THE WAY.
YUP! UH-HUH. NO PROBLEM!
KEE HEE HEE
WINRY'S GONE...
OUR PRECIOUS FEMALE RESOURCE...
I MISS HER CHARMS...
SOB!
WAAH!
SHE WAS THE FLOWER OF OUR FORT...
WAAH!
OUR BOSS IS FEMALE TOO, REMEMBER...?
SNIFFLE...
SHE'S TOO SCARY TO BE A WOMAN.
THIS MORNING, AN INDIVIDUAL MATCHING SCAR'S DESCRIPTION WAS SEEN ENTERING TOWN.
IT'S A BIG PLACE...
A FORMER MINING TOWN...
THERE ARE PLENTY OF PLACES TO HIDE.
FINDING HIM IS GONNA BE HARD WORK.

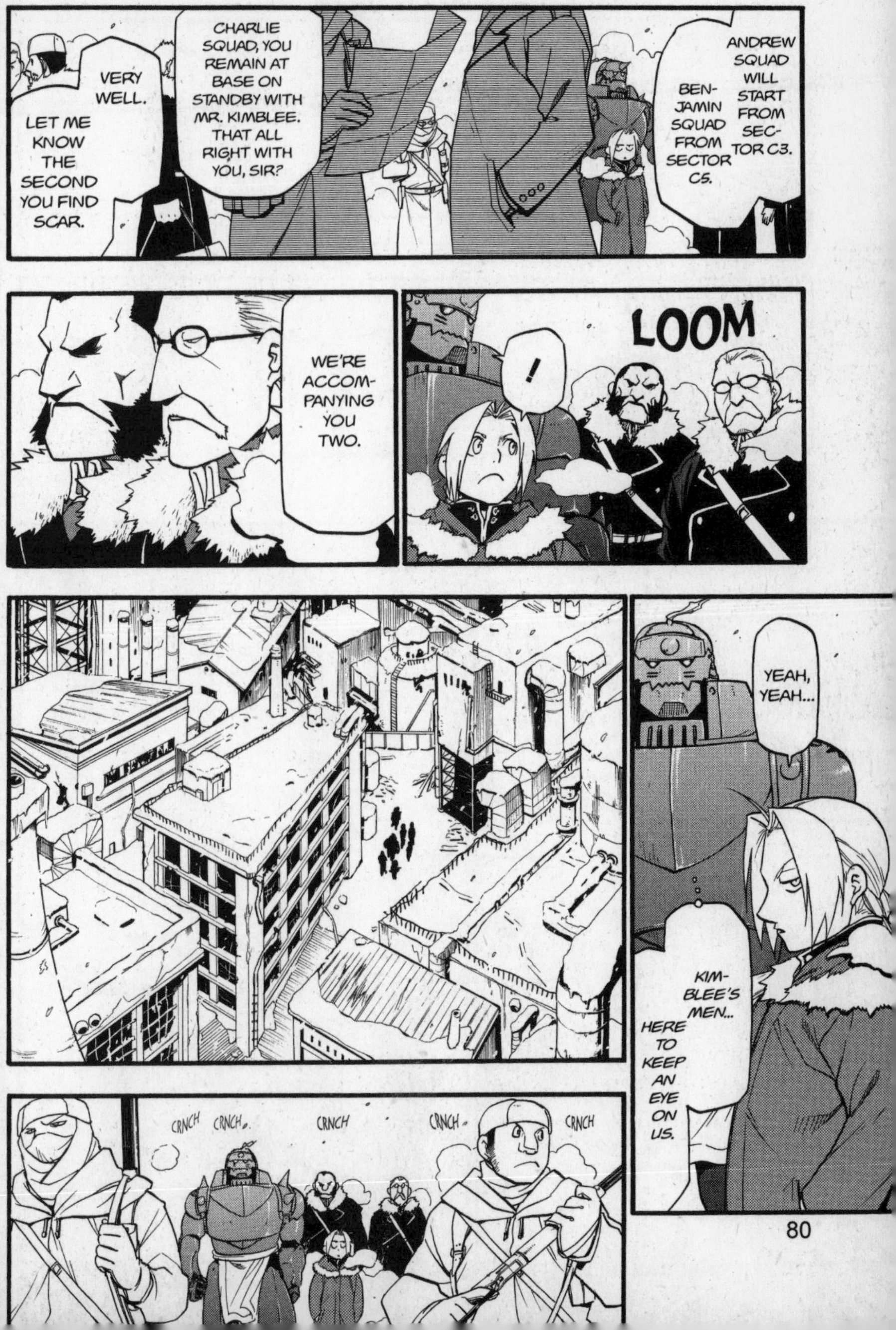
ANDREW SQUAD WILL START FROM SEC-TOR C3.
BEN-JAMIN SQUAD FROM SECTOR C5.
CHARLIE SQUAD, YOU REMAIN AT BASE ON STANDBY WITH MR. KIMBLEE. THAT ALL RIGHT WITH YOU, SIR?
VERY WELL.
LET ME KNOW THE SECOND YOU FIND SCAR.
LOOM
!
WE'RE ACCOM-PANYING YOU TWO.
YEAH, YEAH...
KIM-BLEE'S MEN...
HERE TO KEEP AN EYE ON US.
CRNCH
CRNCH
CRNCH
CRNCH
CRNCH

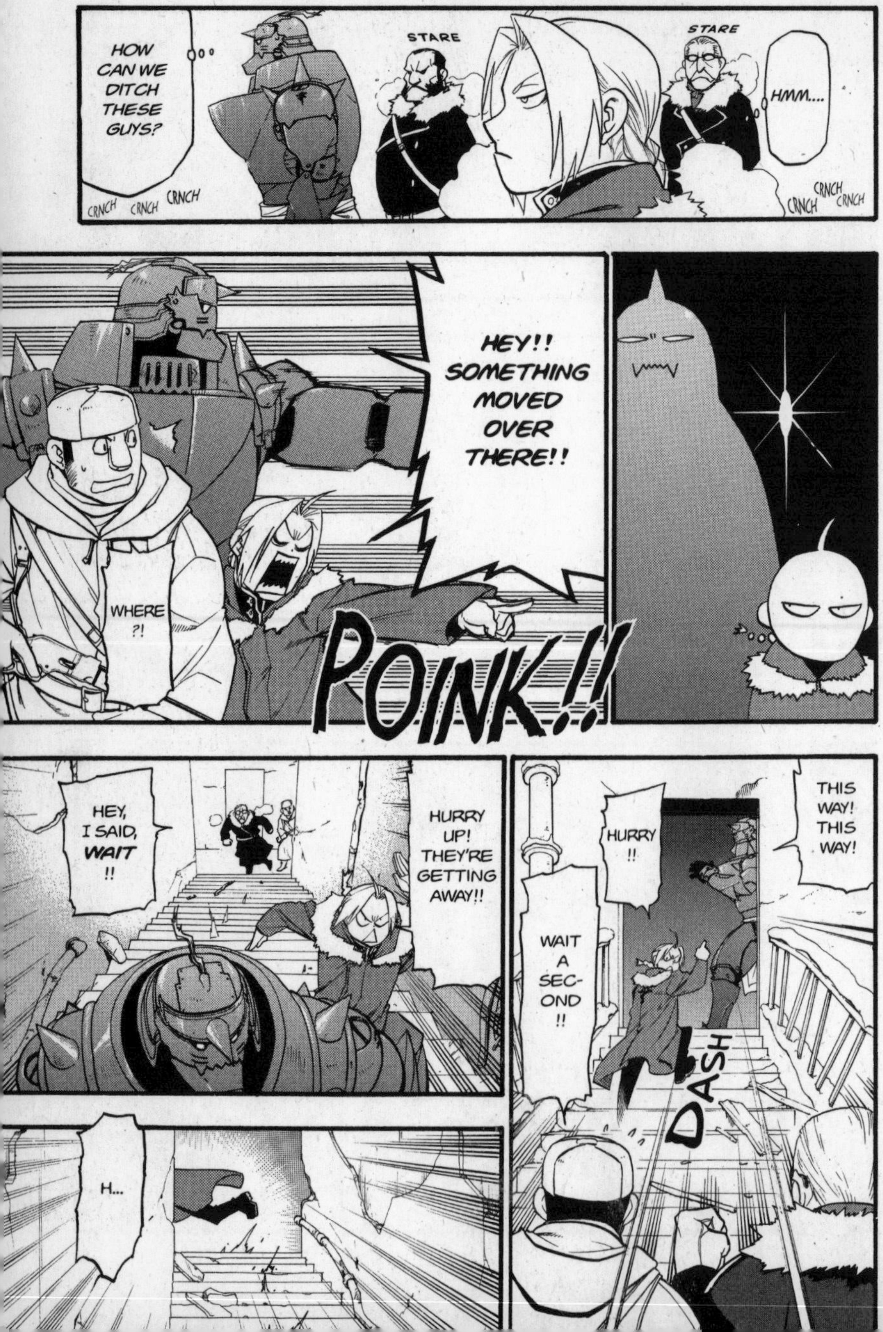
HMM....
STARE
STARE
HOW CAN WE DITCH THESE GUYS?
CRNCH CRNCH CRNCH
CRNCH CRNCH CRNCH
HEY!! SOMETHING MOVED OVER THERE!!
POINK!!
WHERE ?!
THIS WAY! THIS WAY!
HURRY !!
WAIT A SEC-OND !!
DASH
HURRY UP! THEY'RE GETTING AWAY!!
HEY, I SAID, WAIT !!
H...

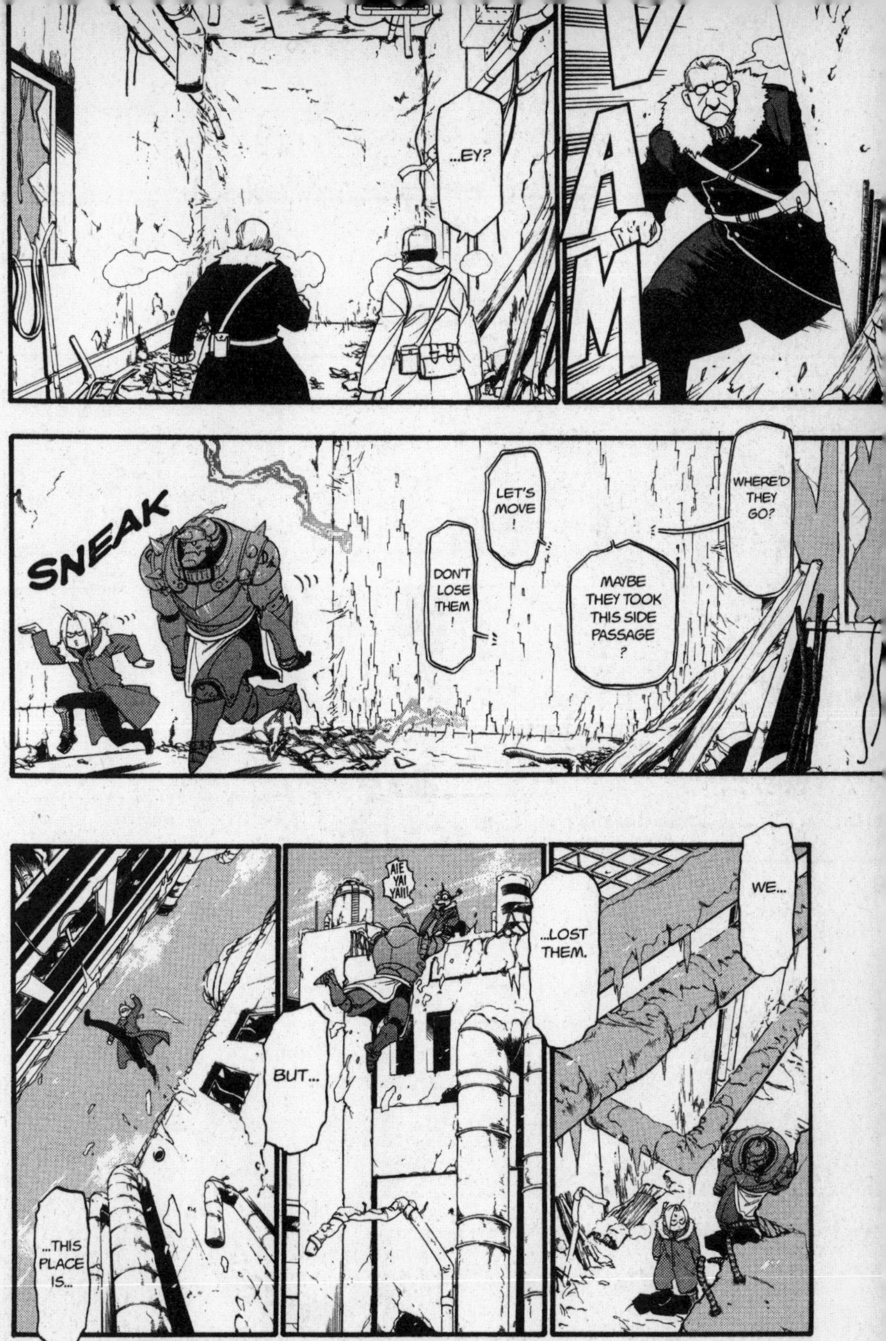
VAM
...EY?
WHERE'D THEY GO?
MAYBE THEY TOOK THIS SIDE PASSAGE?
LET'S MOVE!
DON'T LOSE THEM!
SNEAK
WE...
...LOST THEM.
AIE YAI YAI!!
BUT...
...THIS PLACE IS...

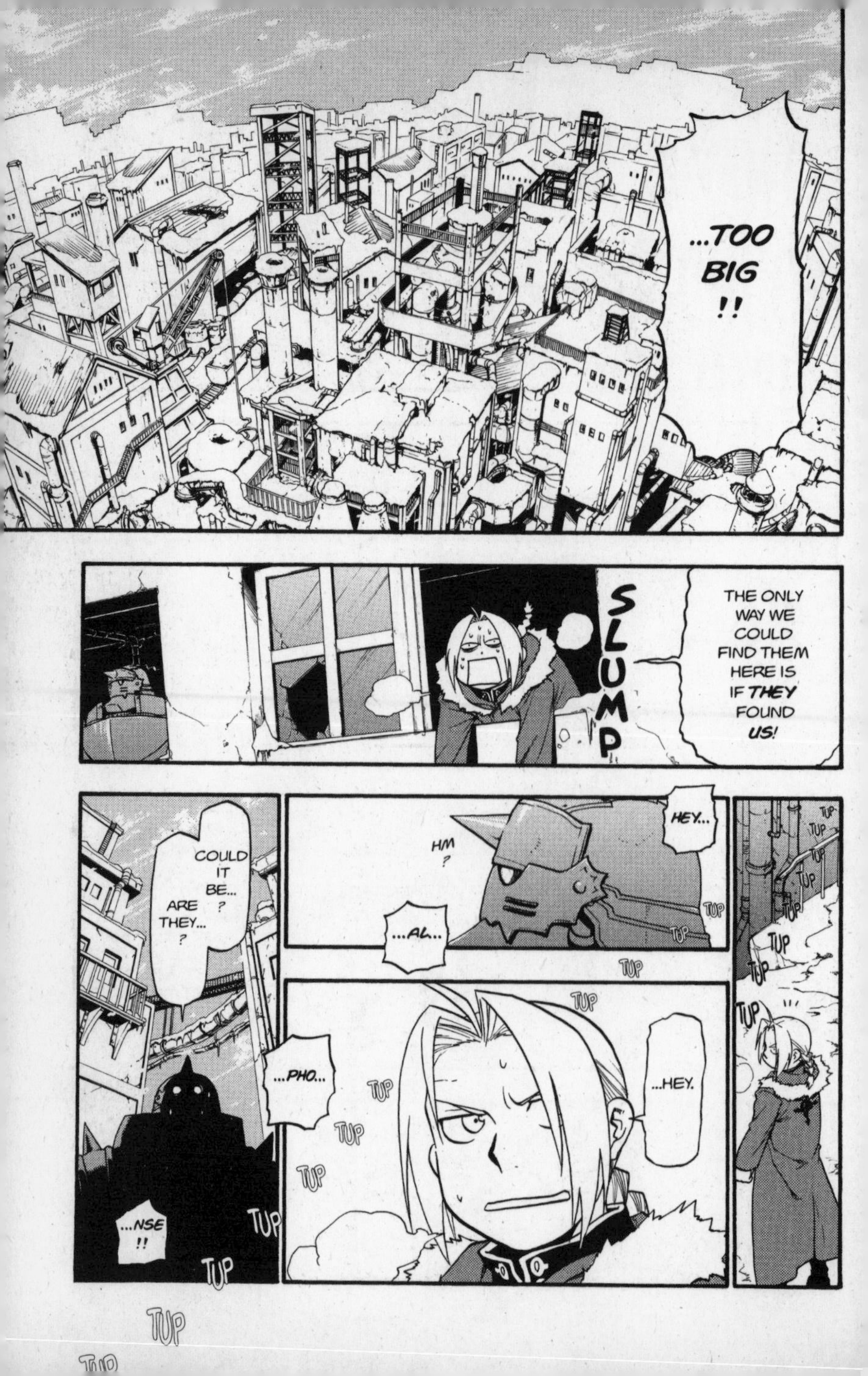
...TOO BIG !!
THE ONLY WAY WE COULD FIND THEM HERE IS IF THEY FOUND US!
SLUMP
TUP TUP TUP TUP TUP TUP TUP TUP
HEY...
HM ?
...AL...
TUP TUP
TUP
...HEY.
TUP TUP TUP TUP
COULD IT BE... ?
ARE THEY... ?
...PHO...
...NSE !!
TUP TUP
TUP

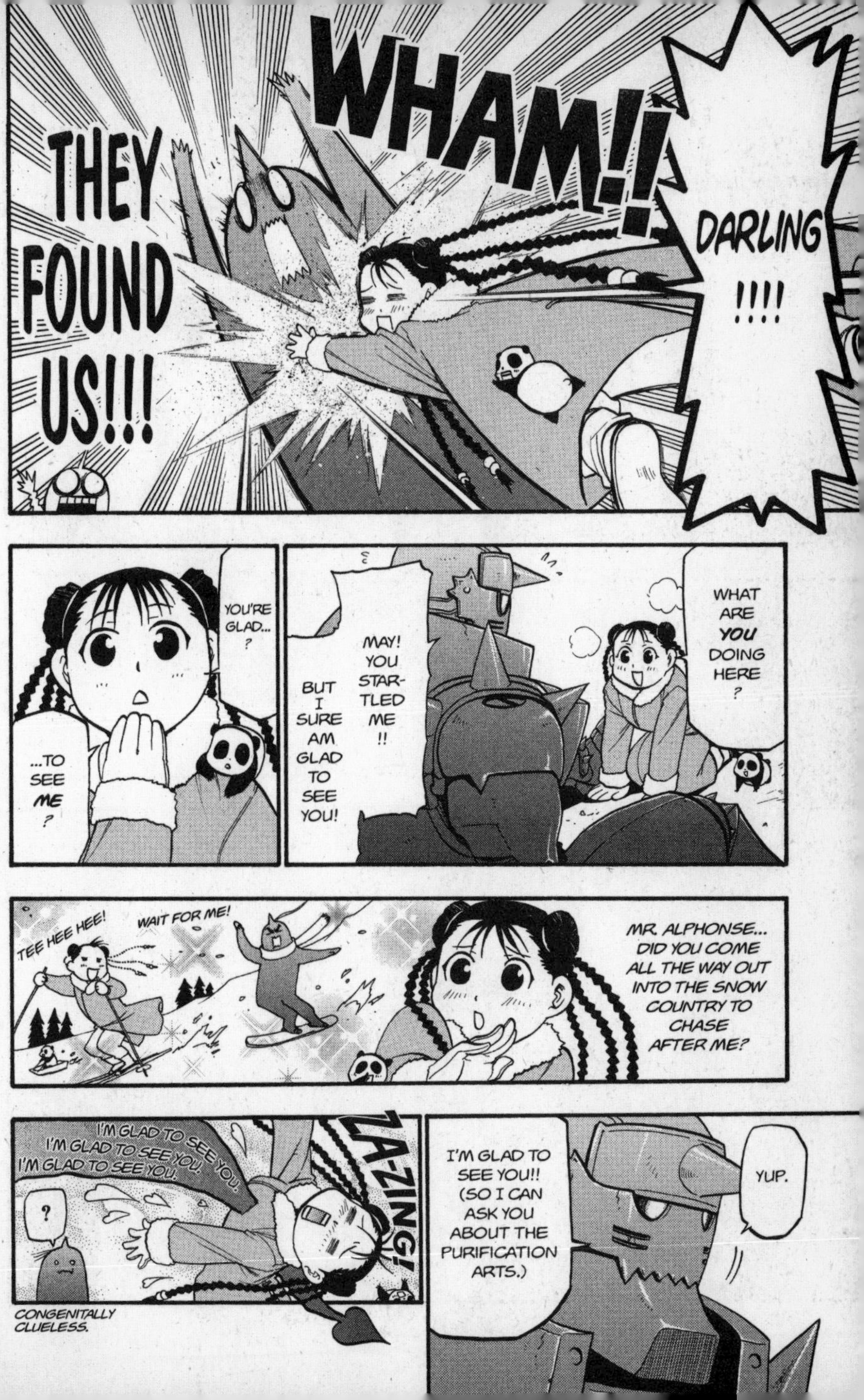
DARLING !!!!
WHAM!!
THEY FOUND US!!!
WHAT ARE YOU DOING HERE?
MAY! YOU STARTLED ME!!
BUT I SURE AM GLAD TO SEE YOU!
YOU'RE GLAD...?
...TO SEE ME?
MR. ALPHONSE... DID YOU COME ALL THE WAY OUT INTO THE SNOW COUNTRY TO CHASE AFTER ME?
WAIT FOR ME!
TEE HEE HEE!
YUP.
I'M GLAD TO SEE YOU!! (SO I CAN ASK YOU ABOUT THE PURIFICATION ARTS.)
ZA-ZING!
I'M GLAD TO SEE YOU.
I'M GLAD TO SEE YOU.
I'M GLAD TO SEE YOU.
?
CONGENITALLY CLUELESS.

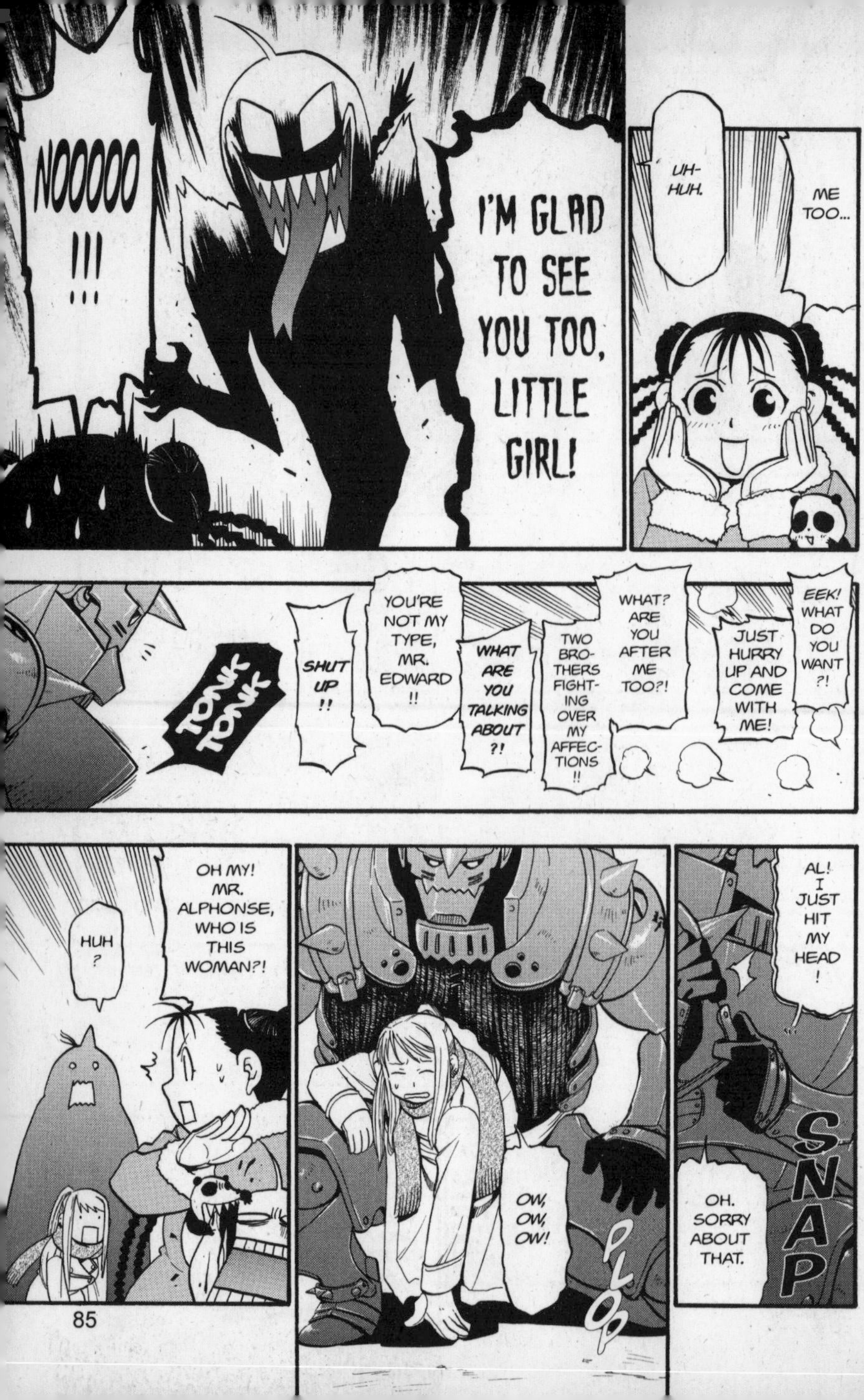
ME TOO...
UH-HUH.
I'M GLAD TO SEE YOU TOO, LITTLE GIRL!
NOOOOO!!!!!!
EEK! WHAT DO YOU WANT?!
JUST HURRY UP AND COME WITH ME!
WHAT? ARE YOU AFTER ME TOO?!
TWO BROTHERS FIGHTING OVER MY AFFECTIONS!!
WHAT ARE YOU TALKING ABOUT?!
YOU'RE NOT MY TYPE, MR. EDWARD!!
SHUT UP!!
TONK TONK
AL! I JUST HIT MY HEAD!
SNAP
OH. SORRY ABOUT THAT.
OW, OW, OW!
PLOP
OH MY! MR. ALPHONSE, WHO IS THIS WOMAN?!
HUH?

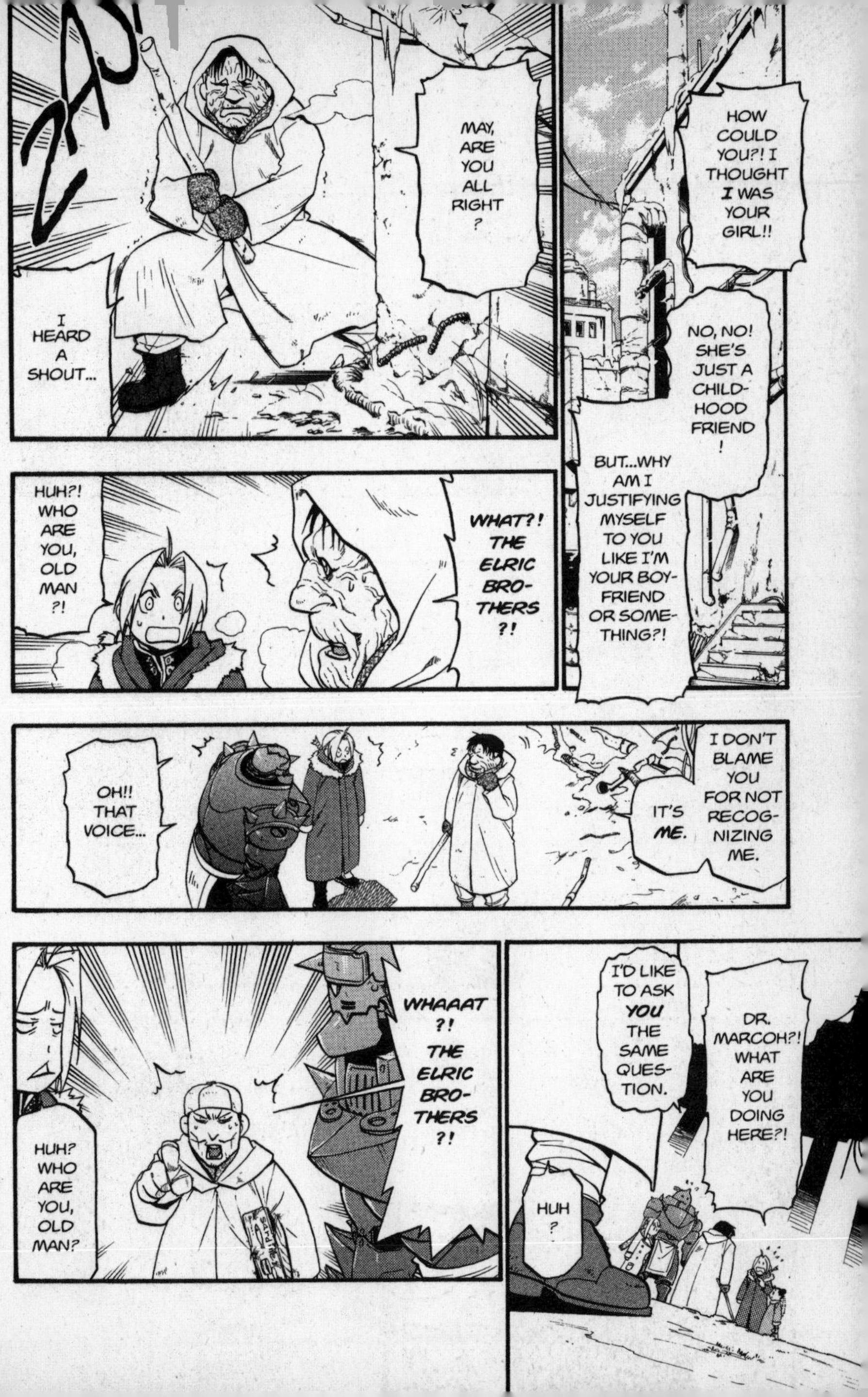
HOW COULD YOU?! I THOUGHT I WAS YOUR GIRL!!
NO, NO! SHE'S JUST A CHILDHOOD FRIEND!
BUT...WHY AM I JUSTIFYING MYSELF TO YOU LIKE I'M YOUR BOYFRIEND OR SOMETHING?!
MAY, ARE YOU ALL RIGHT?
I HEARD A SHOUT...
WHAT?! THE ELRIC BROTHERS?!
HUH?! WHO ARE YOU, OLD MAN?!
I DON'T BLAME YOU FOR NOT RECOGNIZING ME.
IT'S ME.
OH!! THAT VOICE...
DR. MARCOH?! WHAT ARE YOU DOING HERE?!
I'D LIKE TO ASK YOU THE SAME QUESTION.
HUH?
WHAAAT?! THE ELRIC BROTHERS?!
HUH? WHO ARE YOU, OLD MAN?

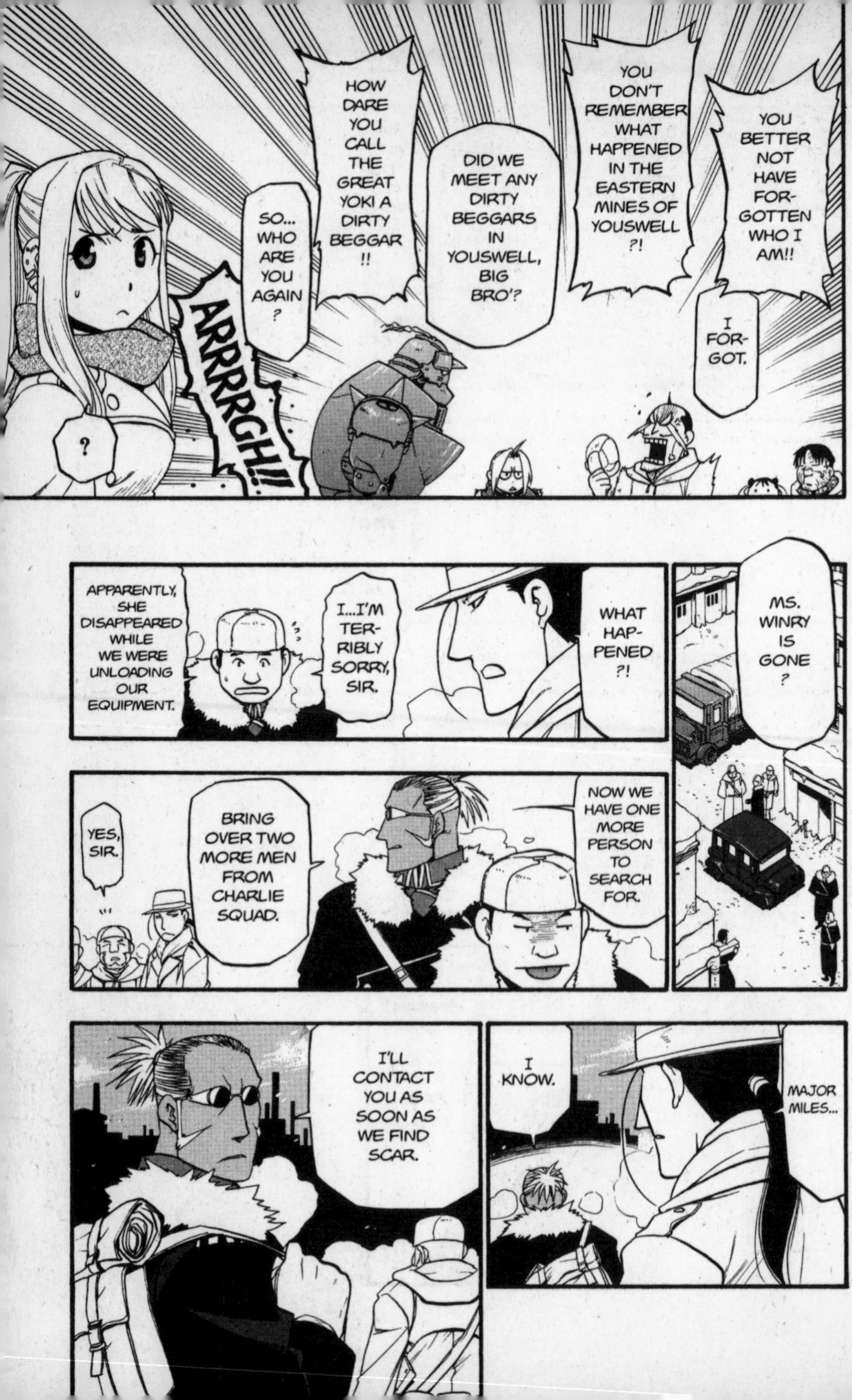
YOU BETTER NOT HAVE FOR-GOTTEN WHO I AM!!
I FOR-GOT.
YOU DON'T REMEMBER WHAT HAPPENED IN THE EASTERN MINES OF YOUSWELL ?!
DID WE MEET ANY DIRTY BEGGARS IN YOUSWELL, BIG BRO'?
HOW DARE YOU CALL THE GREAT YOKI A DIRTY BEGGAR !!
SO... WHO ARE YOU AGAIN ?
ARRRRGH!!!
?
MS. WINRY IS GONE ?
WHAT HAP-PENED ?!
I...I'M TER-RIBLY SORRY, SIR.
APPARENTLY, SHE DISAPPEARED WHILE WE WERE UNLOADING OUR EQUIPMENT.
NOW WE HAVE ONE MORE PERSON TO SEARCH FOR.
BRING OVER TWO MORE MEN FROM CHARLIE SQUAD.
YES, SIR.
MAJOR MILES...
I KNOW.
I'LL CONTACT YOU AS SOON AS WE FIND SCAR.

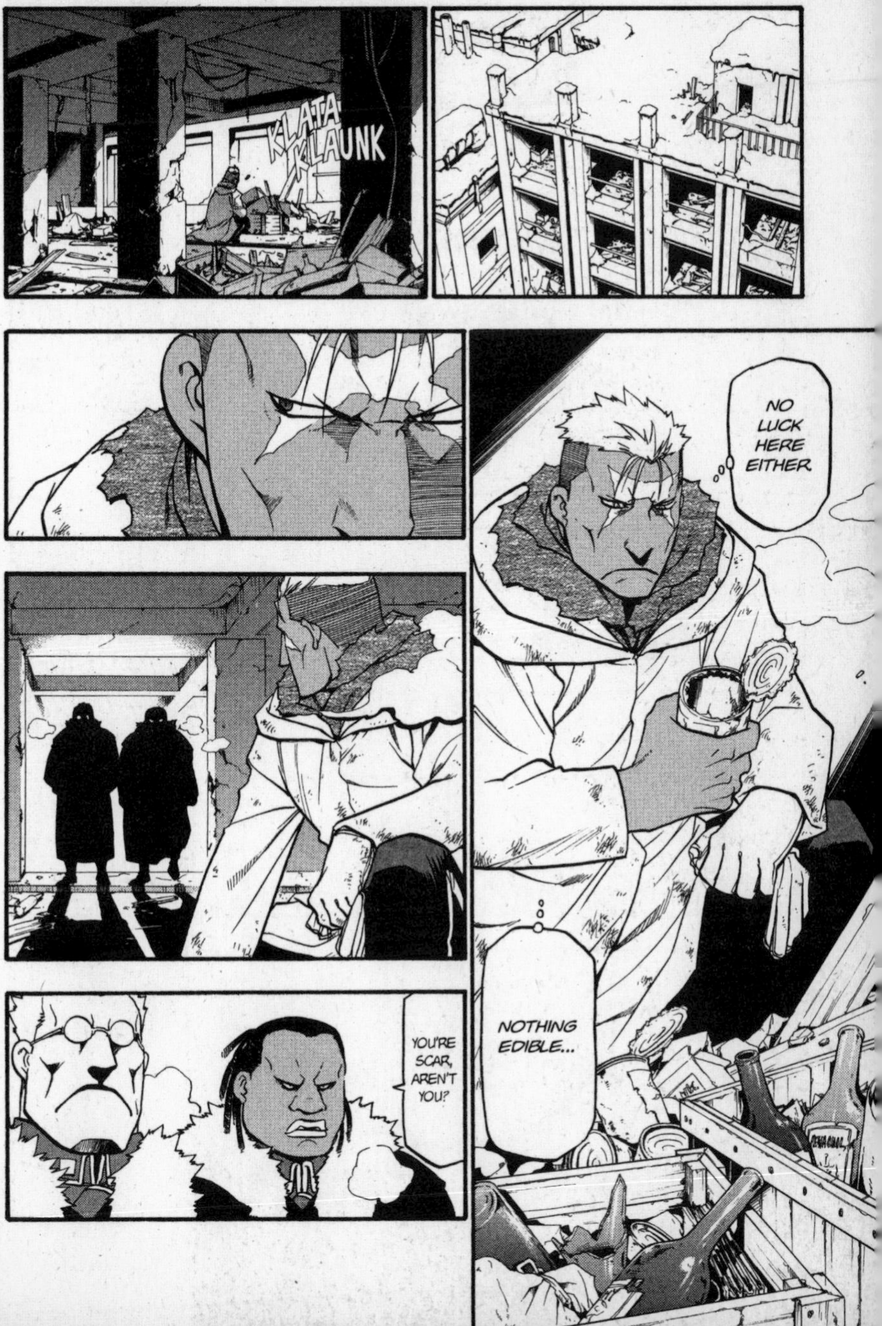
KLATA KLAUNK
NO LUCK HERE EITHER
NOTHING EDIBLE...
YOU'RE SCAR, AREN'T YOU?

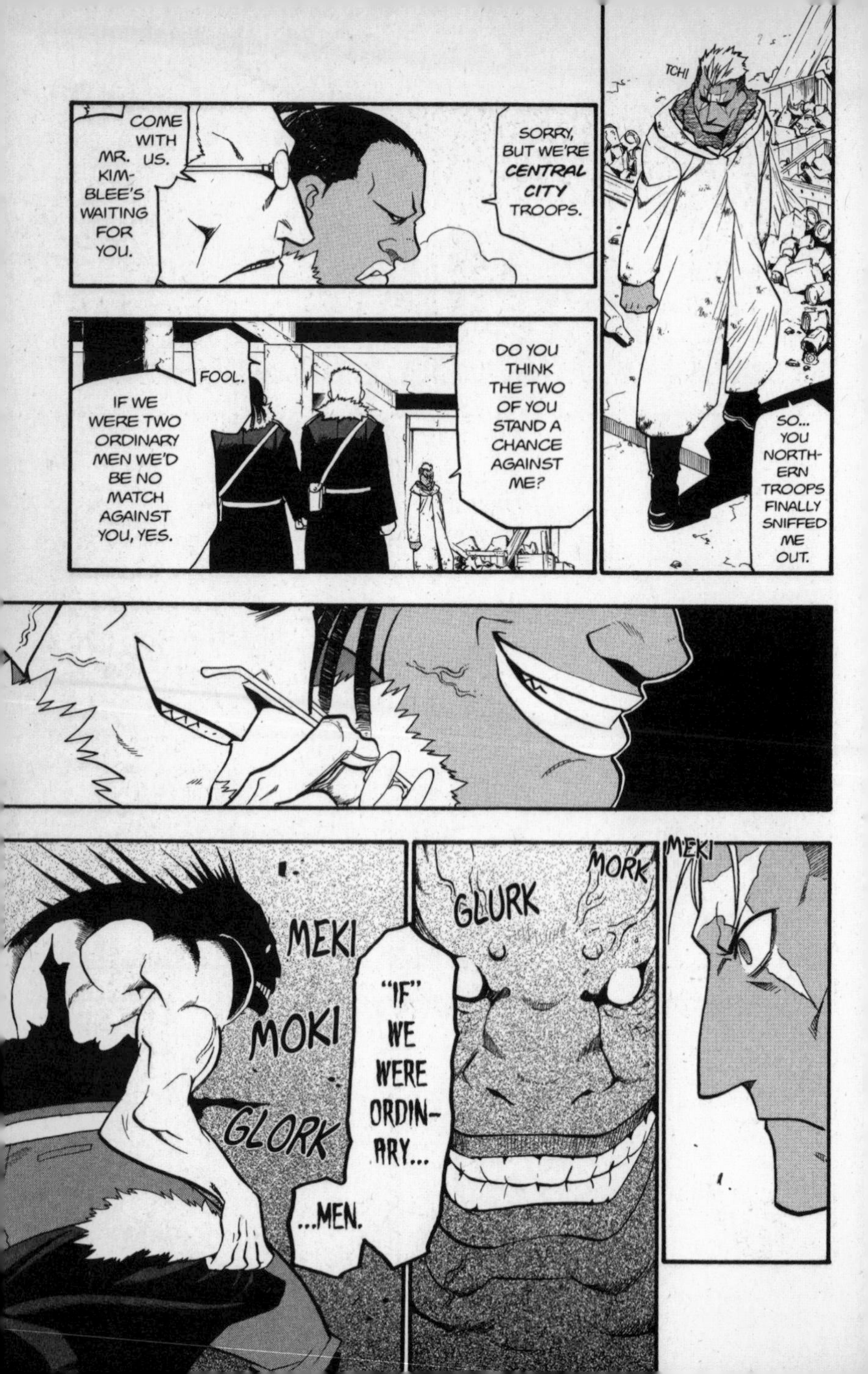
TCHI
SO... YOU NORTHERN TROOPS FINALLY SNIFFED ME OUT.
SORRY, BUT WE'RE CENTRAL CITY TROOPS.
COME WITH US.
MR. KIMBLEE'S WAITING FOR YOU.
DO YOU THINK THE TWO OF YOU STAND A CHANCE AGAINST ME?
FOOL.
IF WE WERE TWO ORDINARY MEN WE'D BE NO MATCH AGAINST YOU, YES.
MEKI
MORK
GLURK
"IF" WE WERE ORDINARY...
...MEN.
MEKI
MOKI
GLORK

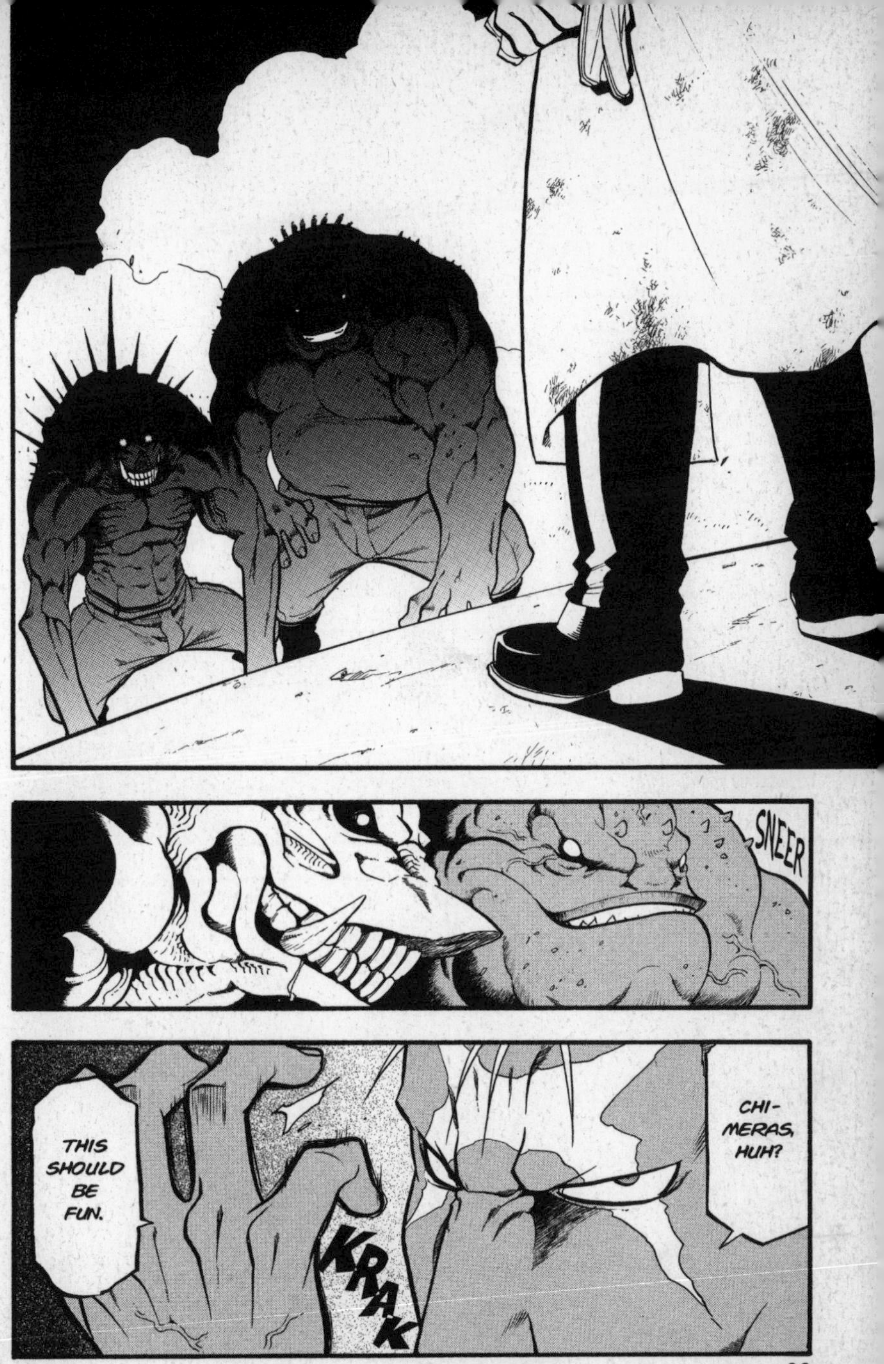
SNEER
CHI-MERAS, HUH?
THIS SHOULD BE FUN.
KRAK

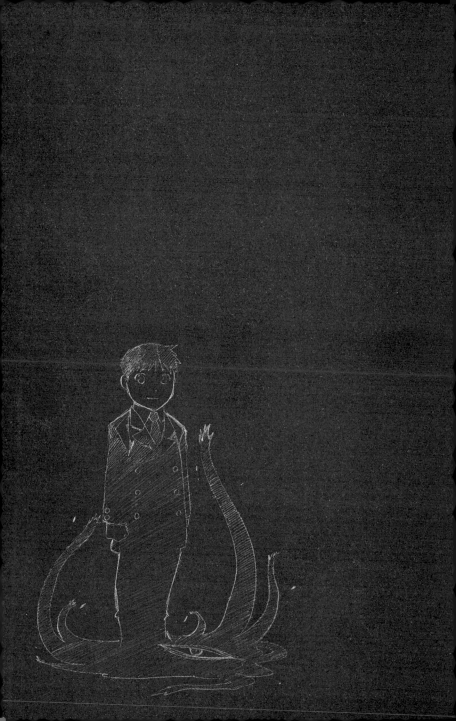

FULLMETAL
ALCHEMIST

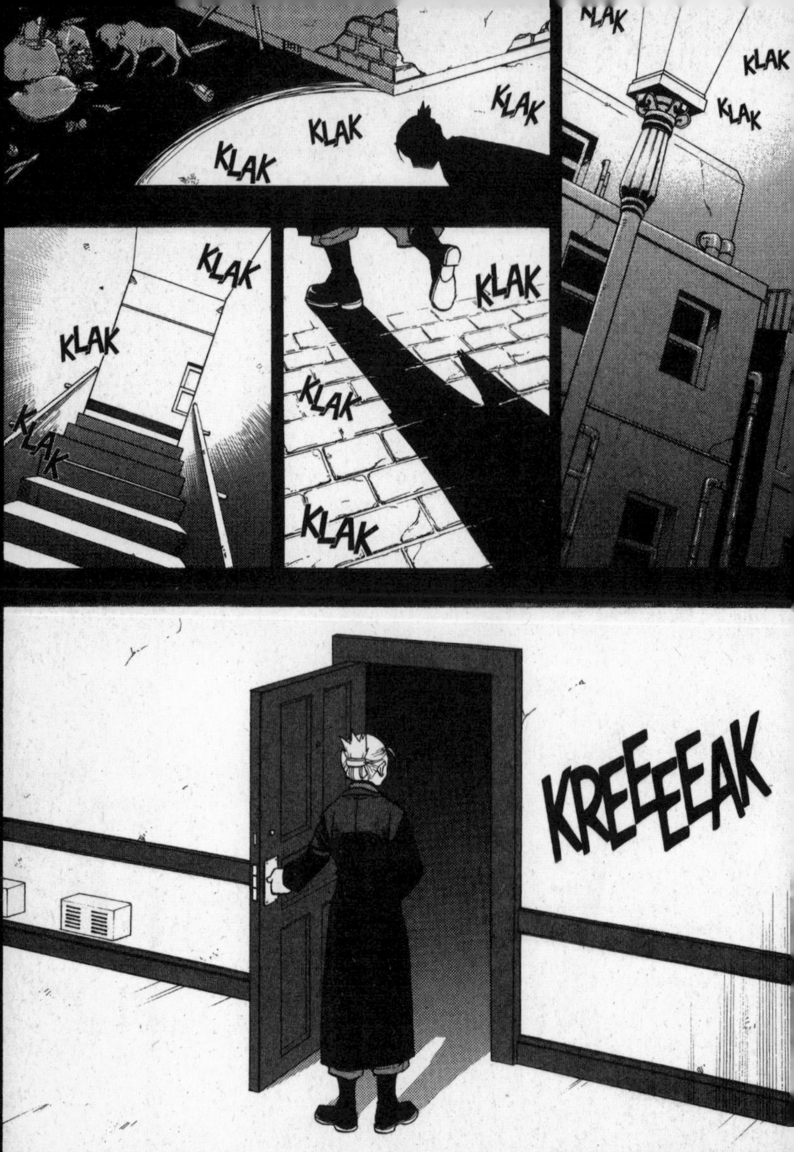
KLAK
KLAK
KLAK
KLAK
KLAK
KLAK
KLAK
KLAK
KLAK
KLAK
KLAK
KLAK
KREEEEAK

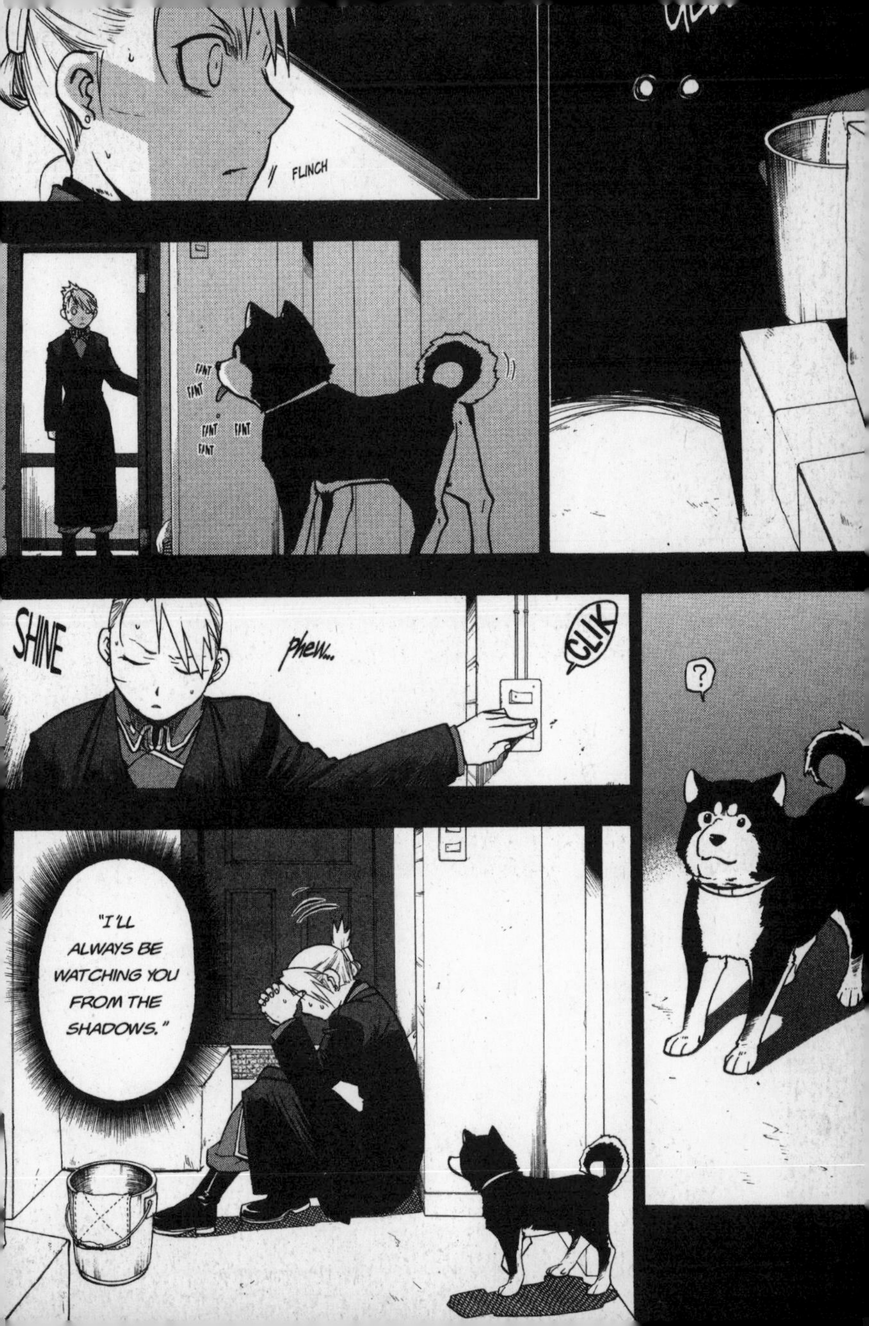
FLINCH
PANT
PANT
PANT
PANT
PANT
?
CLIK
phew...
SHINE
"I'LL ALWAYS BE WATCHING YOU FROM THE SHADOWS."

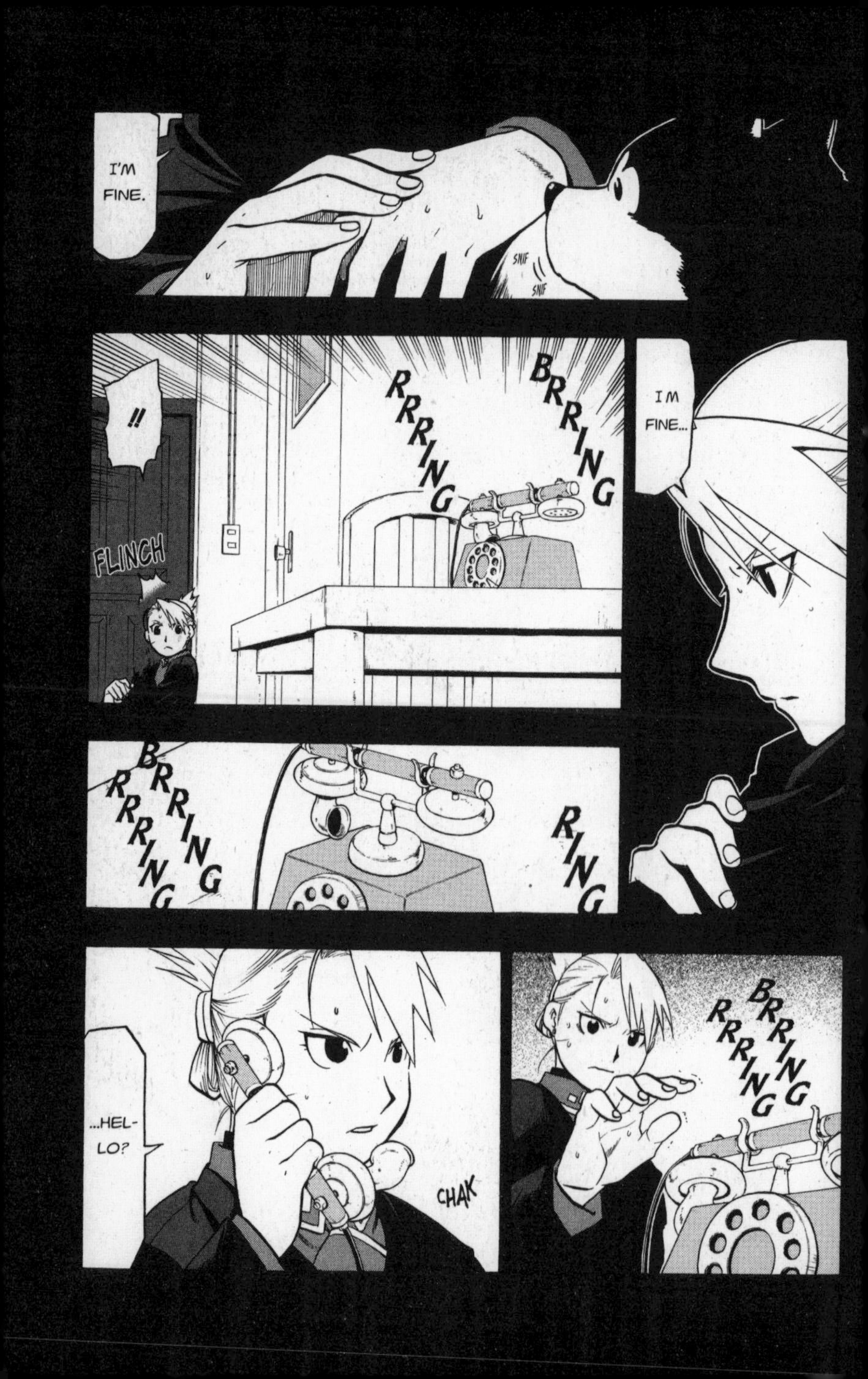
I'M FINE.
SNIF
SNIF
I'M FINE...
BRRRING
RRRING
!!
FLINCH
BRRRING
RRRING
RING
BRRRING
RRRING
...HEL-
LO?
CHAK

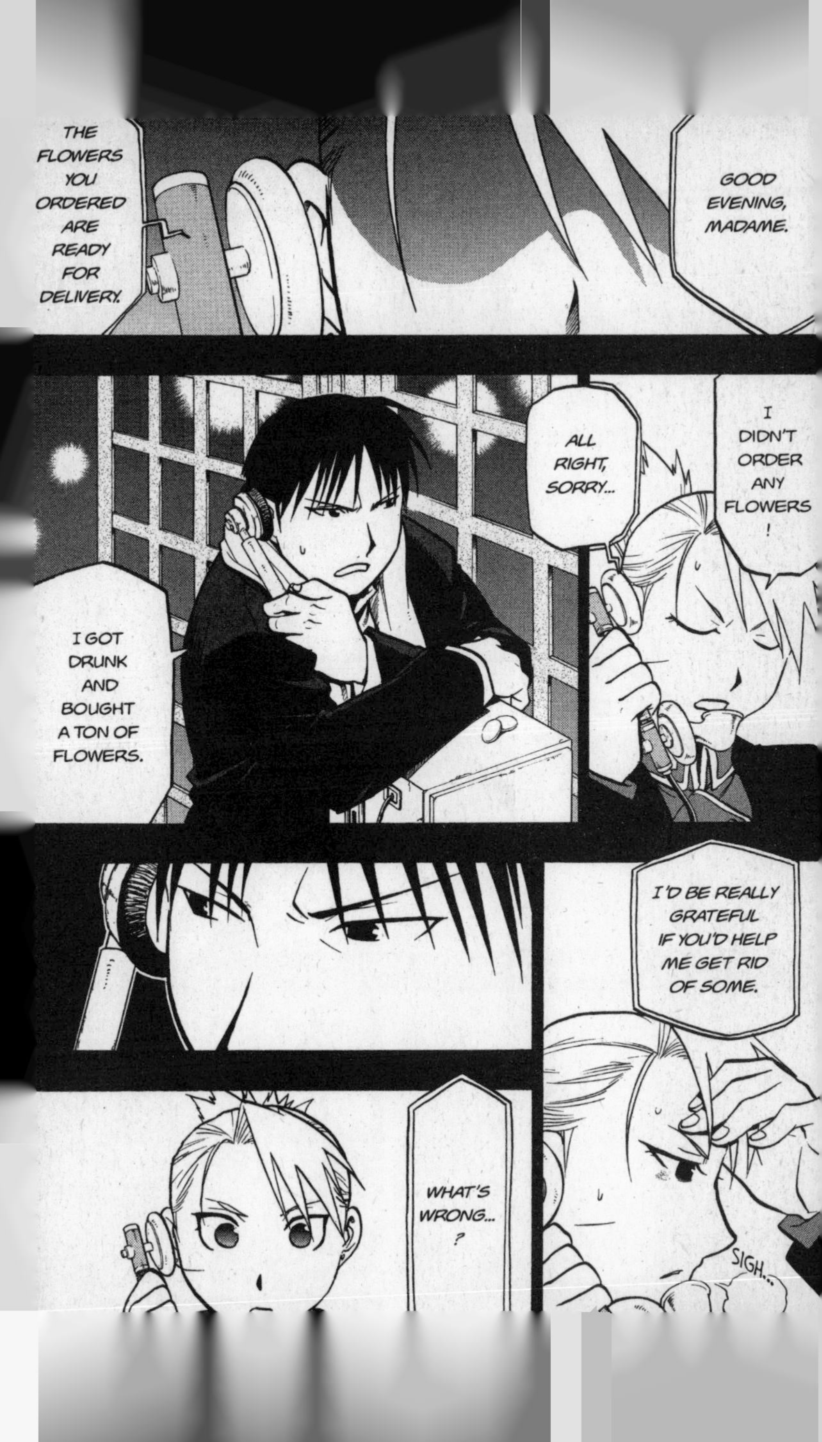
GOOD EVENING, MADAME.
THE FLOWERS YOU ORDERED ARE READY FOR DELIVERY.
I DIDN'T ORDER ANY FLOWERS!
ALL RIGHT, SORRY...
I GOT DRUNK AND BOUGHT A TON OF FLOWERS.
I'D BE REALLY GRATEFUL IF YOU'D HELP ME GET RID OF SOME.
SIGH...
WHAT'S WRONG...?

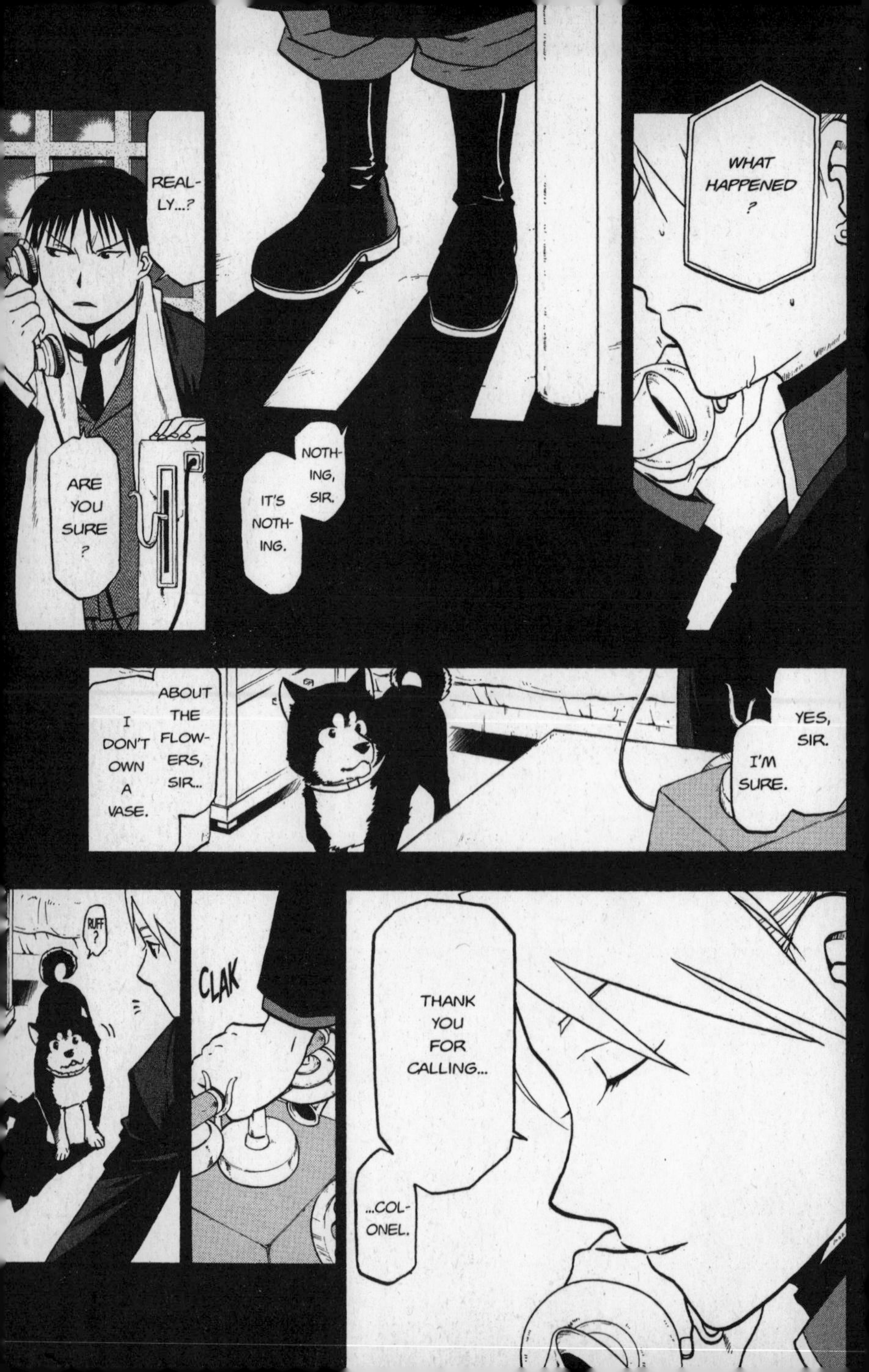
WHAT HAPPENED ?
NOTHING, SIR.
IT'S NOTHING.
REALLY...?
ARE YOU SURE ?
YES, SIR.
I'M SURE.
ABOUT THE FLOWERS, SIR...
I DON'T OWN A VASE.
THANK YOU FOR CALLING...
...COLONEL.
CLAK
RUFF ?

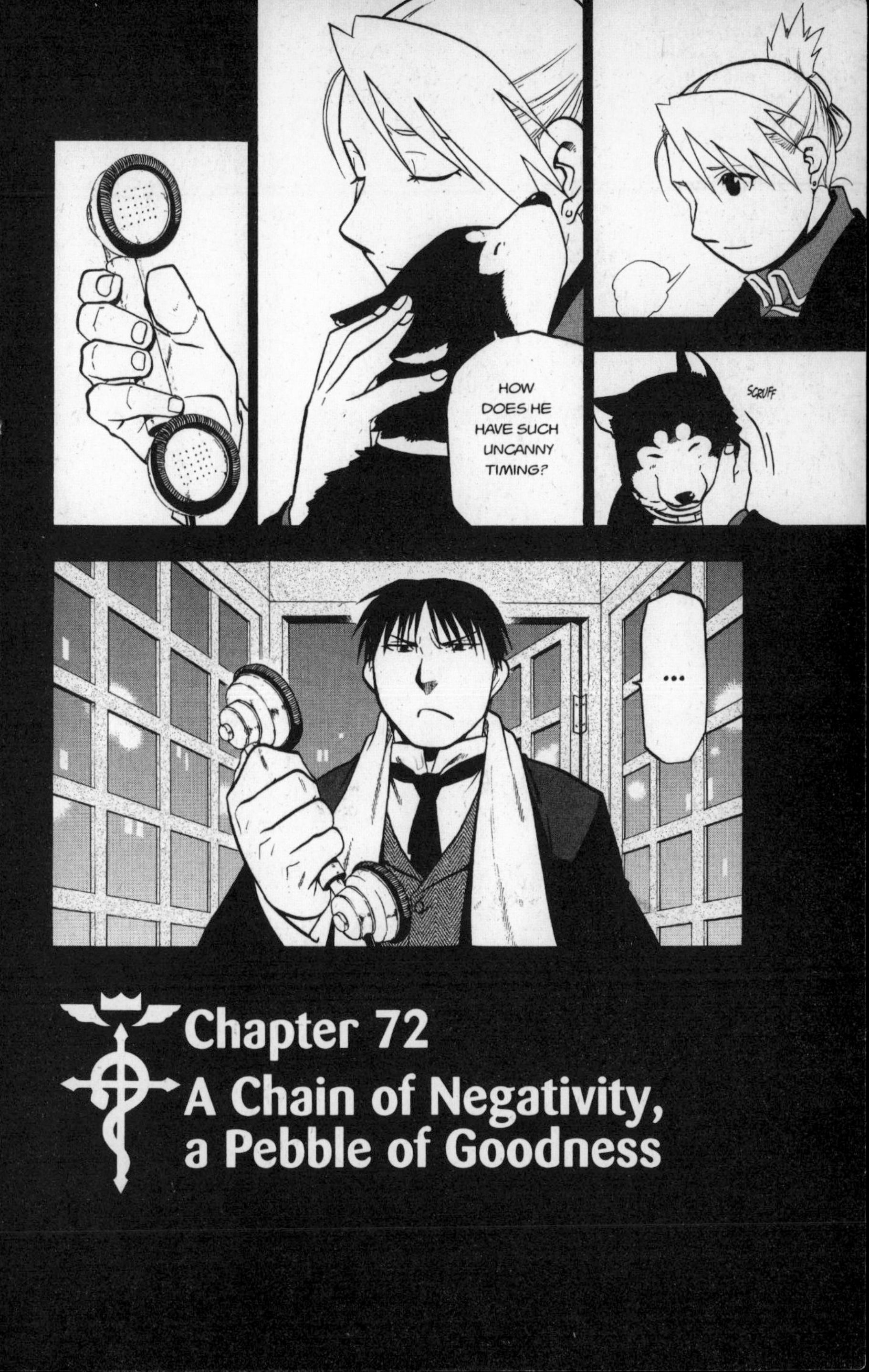
SCRUFF
HOW DOES HE HAVE SUCH UNCANNY TIMING?
...

Chapter 72
A Chain of Negativity, a Pebble of Goodness

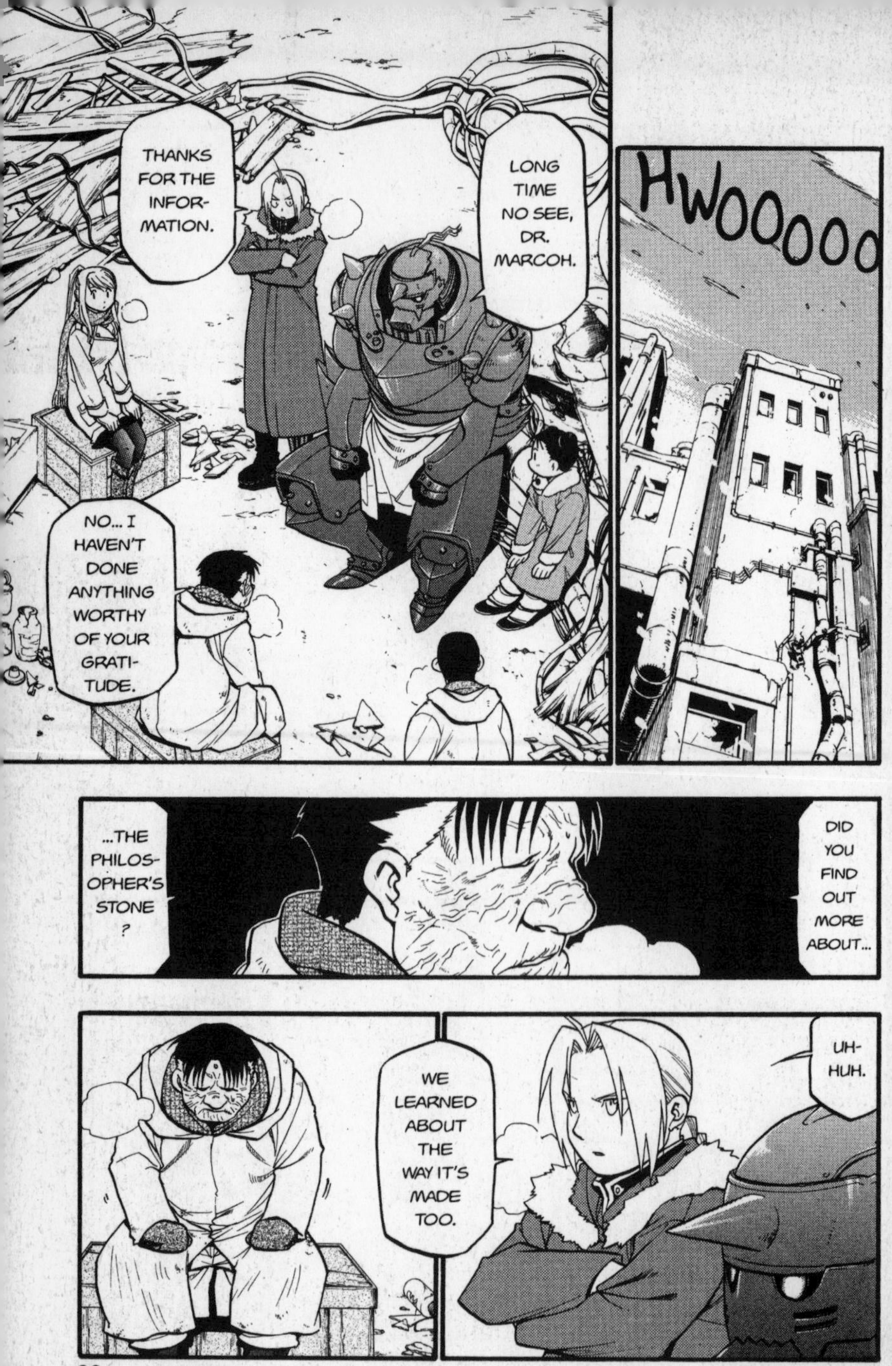
HWOOOOO
LONG TIME NO SEE, DR. MARCOH.
THANKS FOR THE INFOR-MATION.
NO... I HAVEN'T DONE ANYTHING WORTHY OF YOUR GRATI-TUDE.
DID YOU FIND OUT MORE ABOUT...
...THE PHILOS-OPHER'S STONE ?
UH-HUH.
WE LEARNED ABOUT THE WAY IT'S MADE TOO.

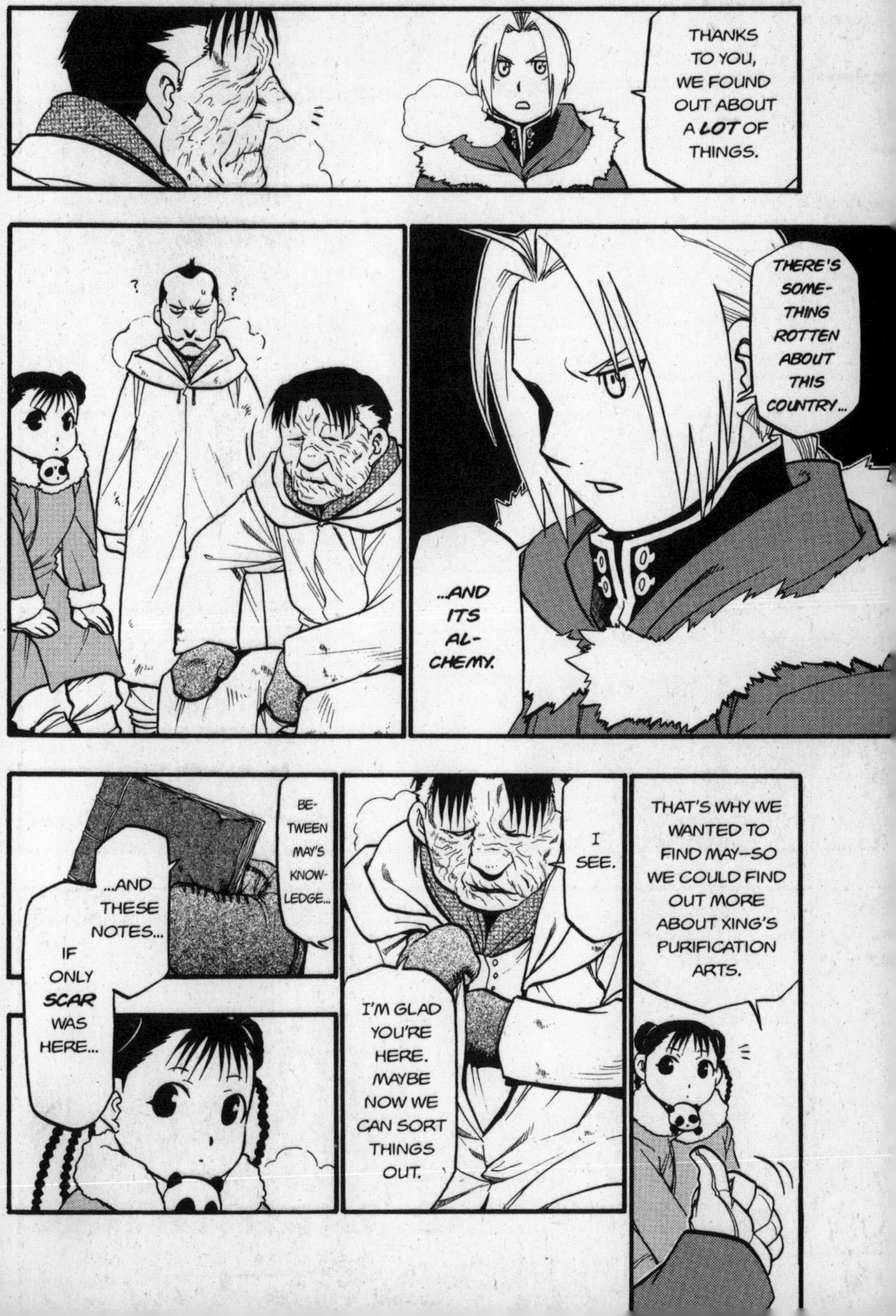
THANKS TO YOU, WE FOUND OUT ABOUT A **LOT** OF THINGS.
THERE'S SOMETHING ROTTEN ABOUT THIS COUNTRY...
...AND ITS ALCHEMY.
THAT'S WHY WE WANTED TO FIND MAY—SO WE COULD FIND OUT MORE ABOUT XING'S PURIFICATION ARTS.
I SEE.
I'M GLAD YOU'RE HERE. MAYBE NOW WE CAN SORT THINGS OUT.
BETWEEN MAY'S KNOWLEDGE...
...AND THESE NOTES...
IF ONLY ***SCAR*** WAS HERE...

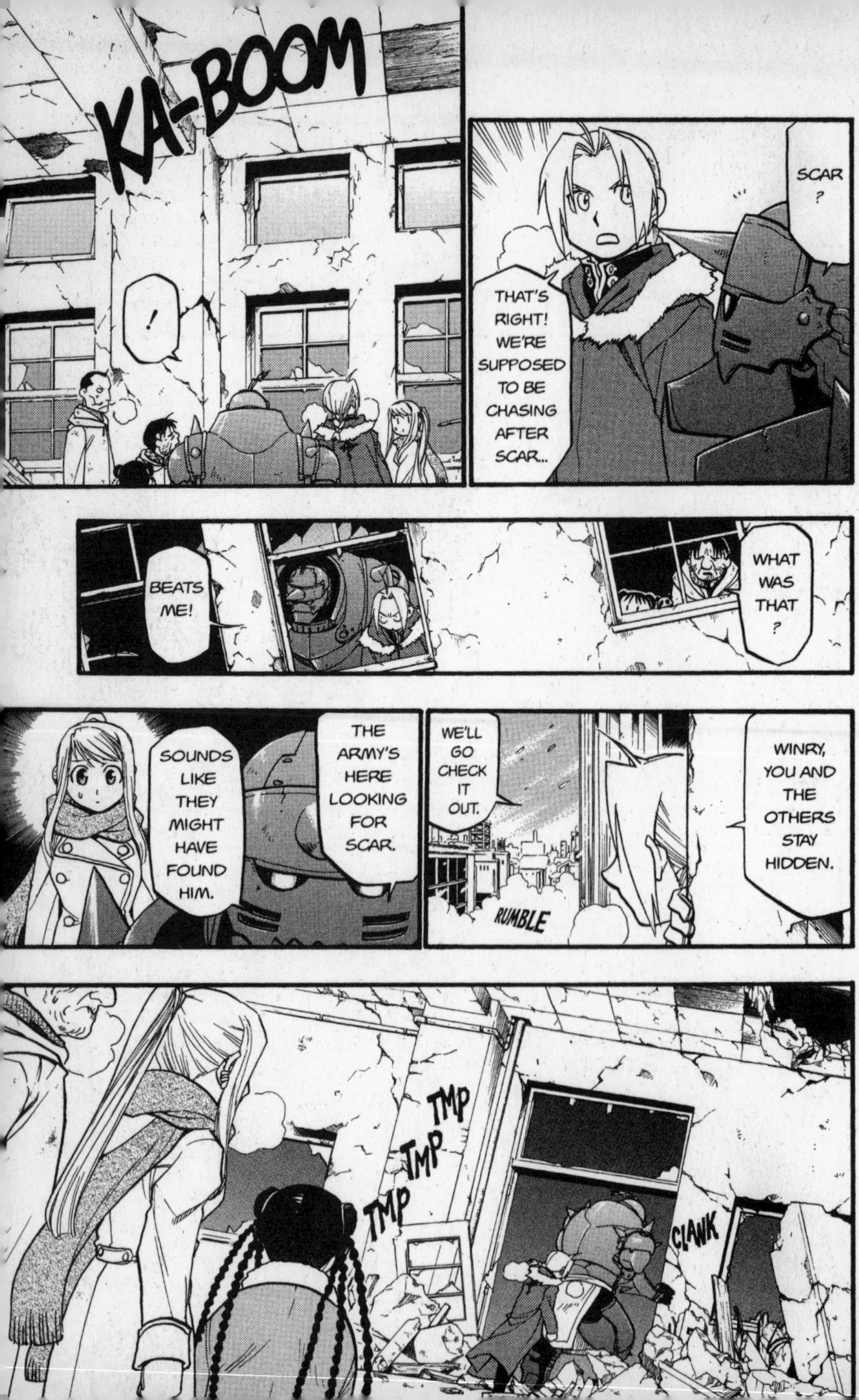
SCAR ?
THAT'S RIGHT! WE'RE SUPPOSED TO BE CHASING AFTER SCAR...
KA-BOOM
!
WHAT WAS THAT ?
BEATS ME!
WINRY, YOU AND THE OTHERS STAY HIDDEN.
WE'LL GO CHECK IT OUT.
RUMBLE
THE ARMY'S HERE LOOKING FOR SCAR.
SOUNDS LIKE THEY MIGHT HAVE FOUND HIM.
CLANK
TMP
TMP
TMP
TMP

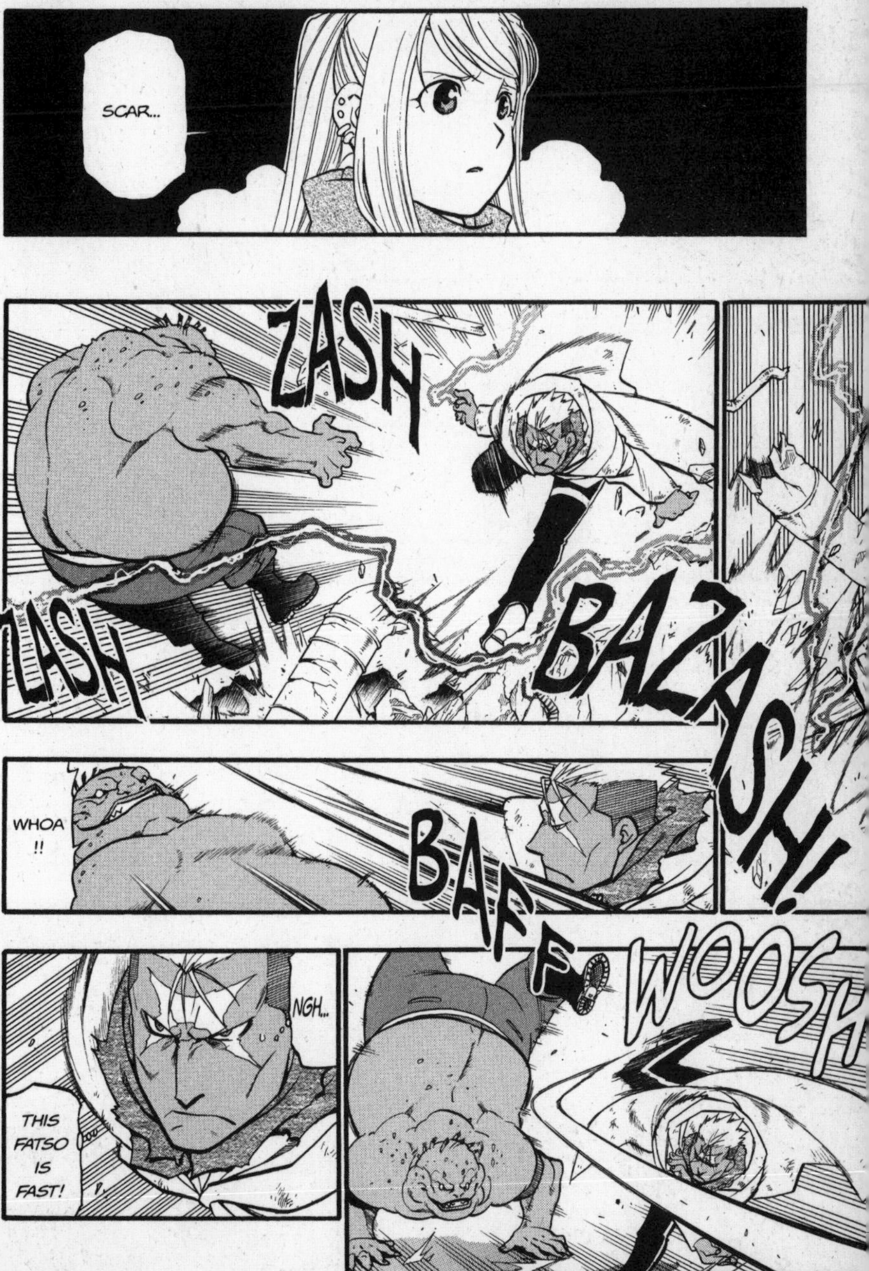

SCAR...
BAZASH!
ZASH
ZASH
WHOA !!
BAFF
WOOSH
NGH...
THIS FATSO IS FAST!

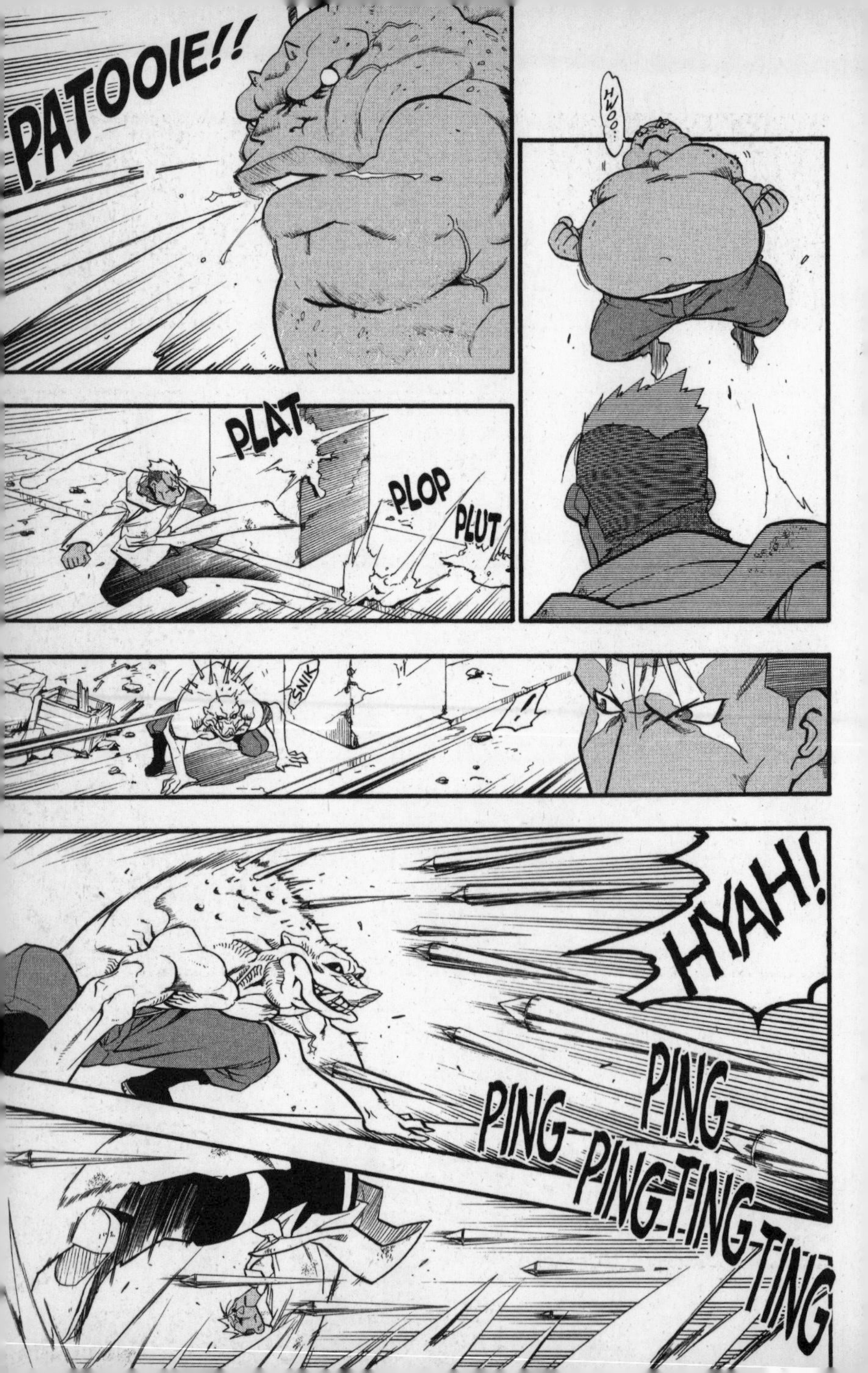
HWOO...
PATOOIE!!
PLAT
PLOP
PLUT
SNIK
HYAH!
PING
PING
PING-TING-TING-TING

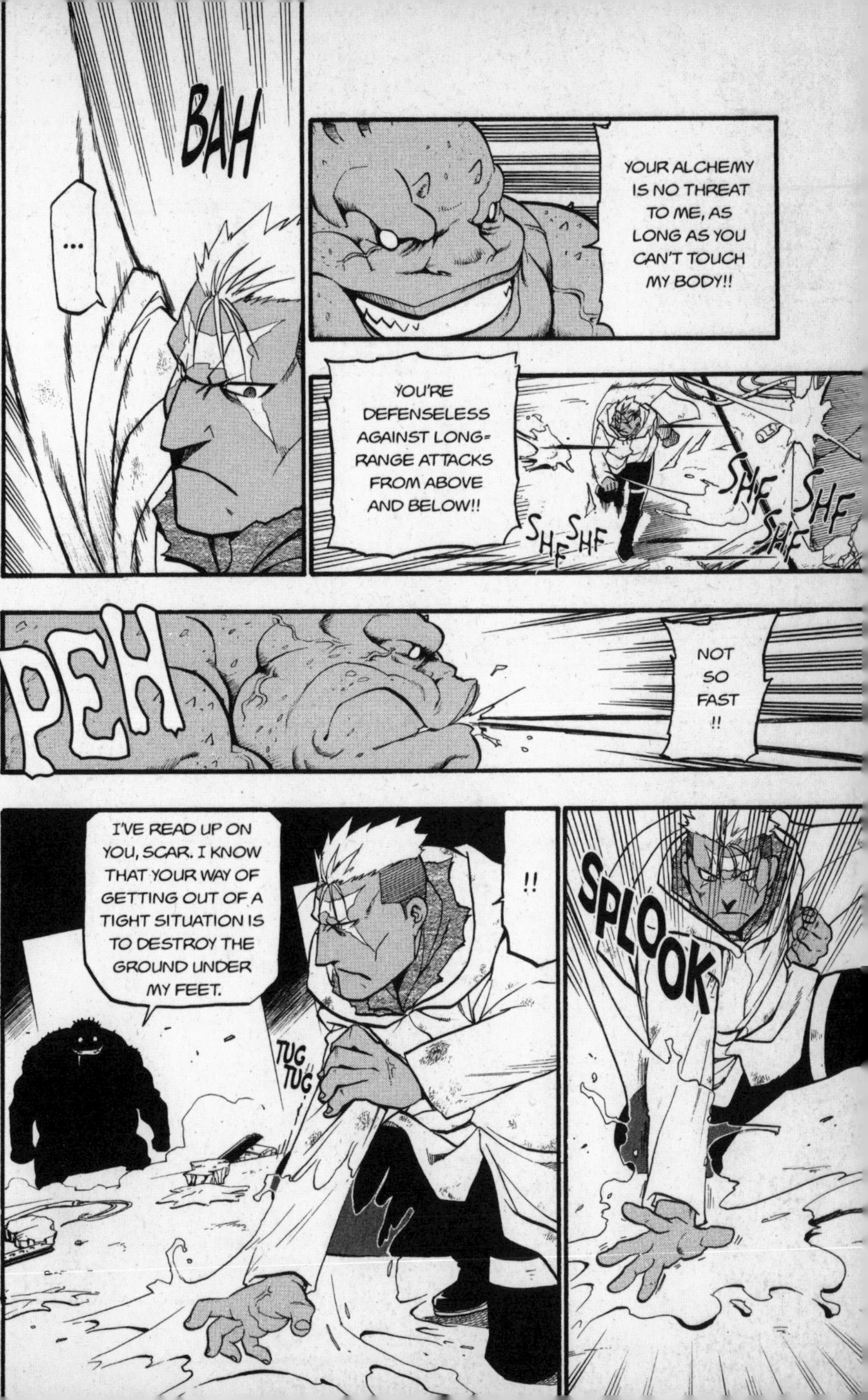
YOUR ALCHEMY IS NO THREAT TO ME, AS LONG AS YOU CAN'T TOUCH MY BODY!!
YOU'RE DEFENSELESS AGAINST LONG=RANGE ATTACKS FROM ABOVE AND BELOW!!
SHF SHF
SHF SHF
SHF
SHF
BAH
...
NOT SO FAST !!
PEH
SPLOOK
!!
I'VE READ UP ON YOU, SCAR. I KNOW THAT YOUR WAY OF GETTING OUT OF A TIGHT SITUATION IS TO DESTROY THE GROUND UNDER MY FEET.
TUG TUG

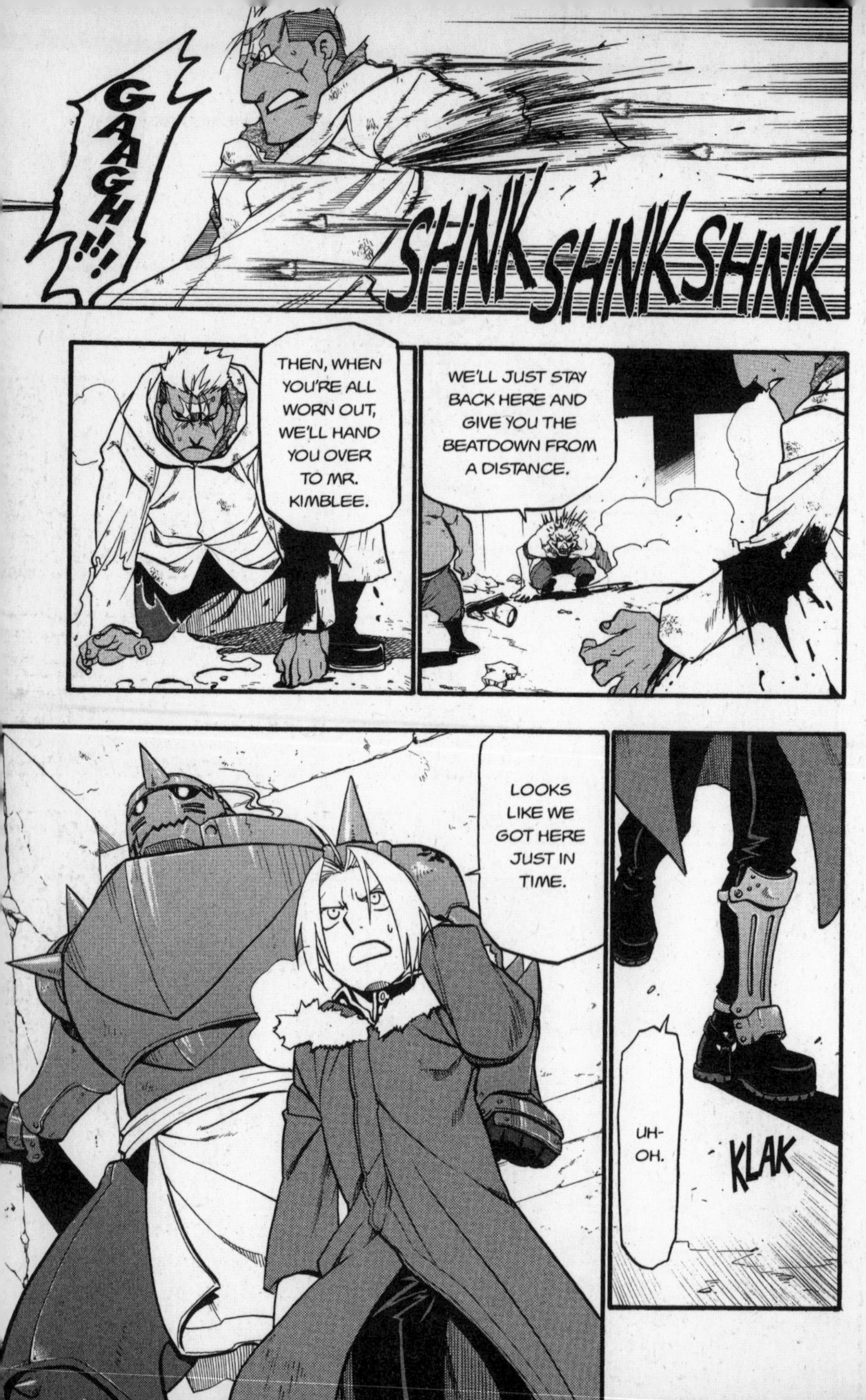
SHNK SHNK SHNK
GAAGH!!!
WE'LL JUST STAY BACK HERE AND GIVE YOU THE BEATDOWN FROM A DISTANCE.
THEN, WHEN YOU'RE ALL WORN OUT, WE'LL HAND YOU OVER TO MR. KIMBLEE.
UH-OH.
KLAK
LOOKS LIKE WE GOT HERE JUST IN TIME.

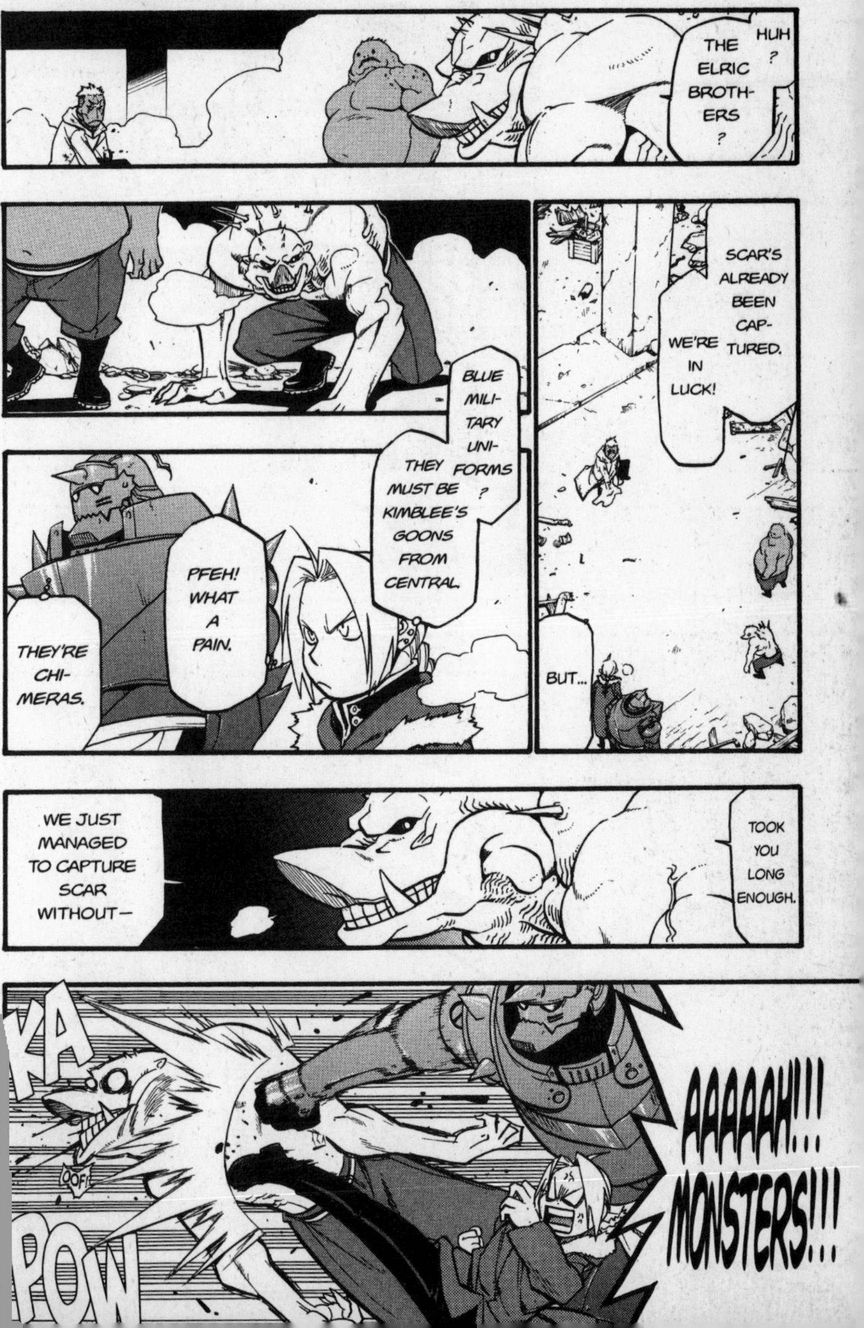
HUH?
THE ELRIC BROTHERS?
SCAR'S ALREADY BEEN CAPTURED.
WE'RE IN LUCK!
BUT...
BLUE MILITARY UNIFORMS?
THEY MUST BE KIMBLEE'S GOONS FROM CENTRAL.
PFEH! WHAT A PAIN.
THEY'RE CHIMERAS.
TOOK YOU LONG ENOUGH.
WE JUST MANAGED TO CAPTURE SCAR WITHOUT—
AAAAAH!!! MONSTERS!!!
OOF!
KA
POW

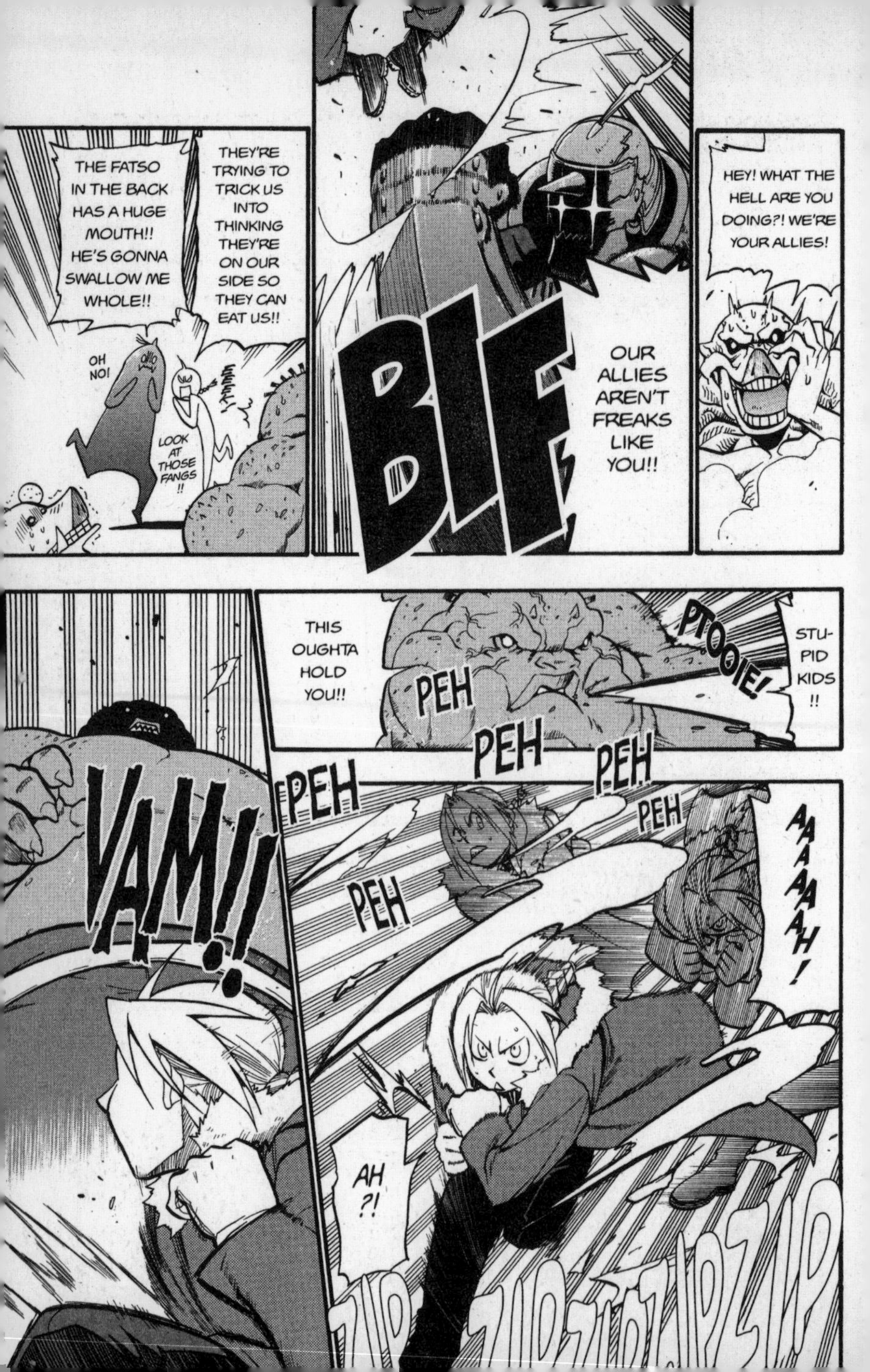

HEY! WHAT THE HELL ARE YOU DOING?! WE'RE YOUR ALLIES!
BIF
OUR ALLIES AREN'T FREAKS LIKE YOU!!
THEY'RE TRYING TO TRICK US INTO THINKING THEY'RE ON OUR SIDE SO THEY CAN EAT US!!
THE FATSO IN THE BACK HAS A HUGE MOUTH!! HE'S GONNA SWALLOW ME WHOLE!!
OH NO!
LOOK AT THOSE FANGS!!
STU-PID KIDS!!
PTOOIE!
THIS OUGHTA HOLD YOU!!
PEH
PEH
PEH
PEH
PEH
PEH
AAAAAAH!
AH?!
ZIP ZIP ZIP ZIP ZIP
YAM!!

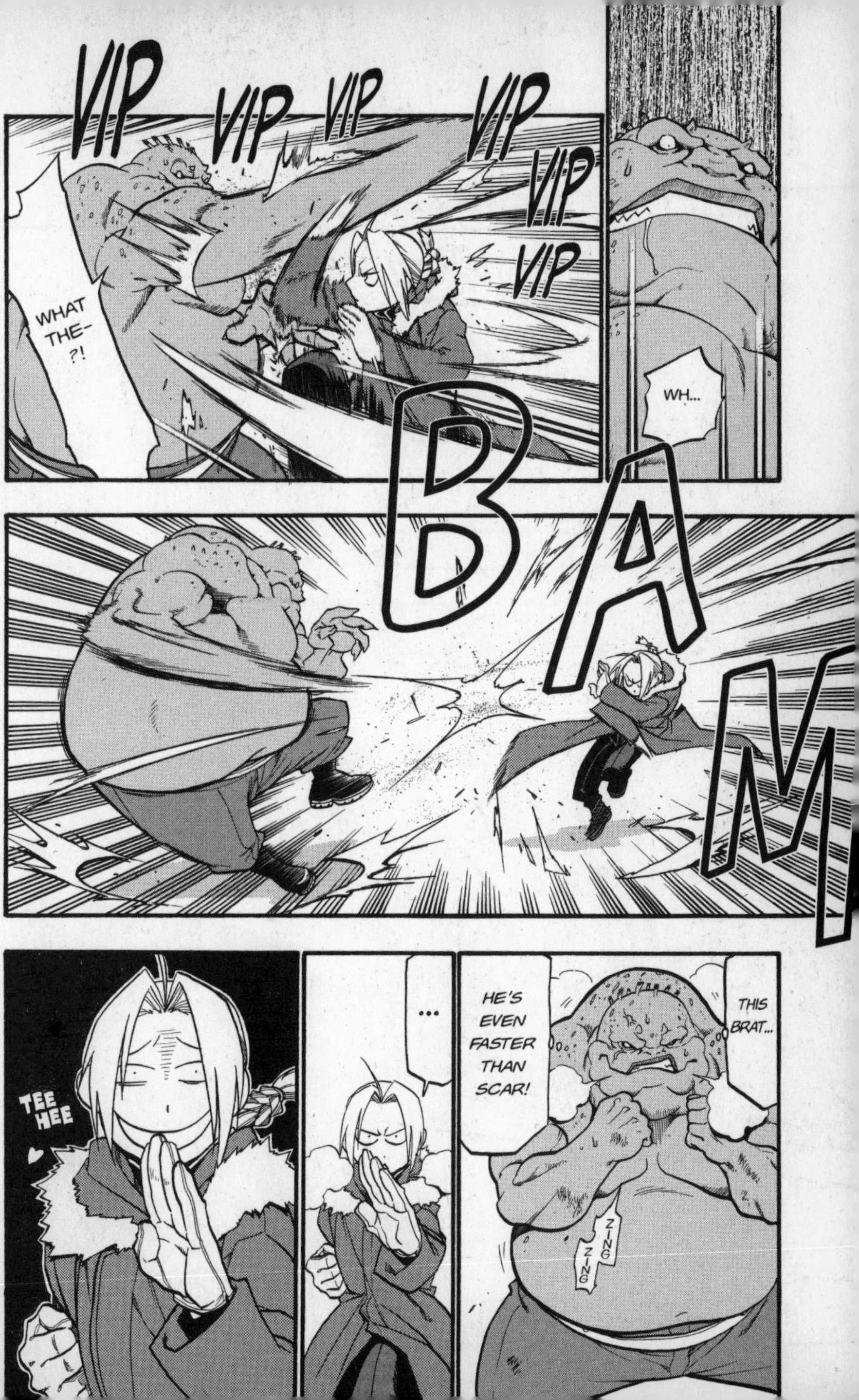
WH...
VIP VIP VIP VIP VIP VIP
WHAT THE- ?!
BAM
THIS BRAT...
HE'S EVEN FASTER THAN SCAR!
ZING ZING
...
TEE HEE

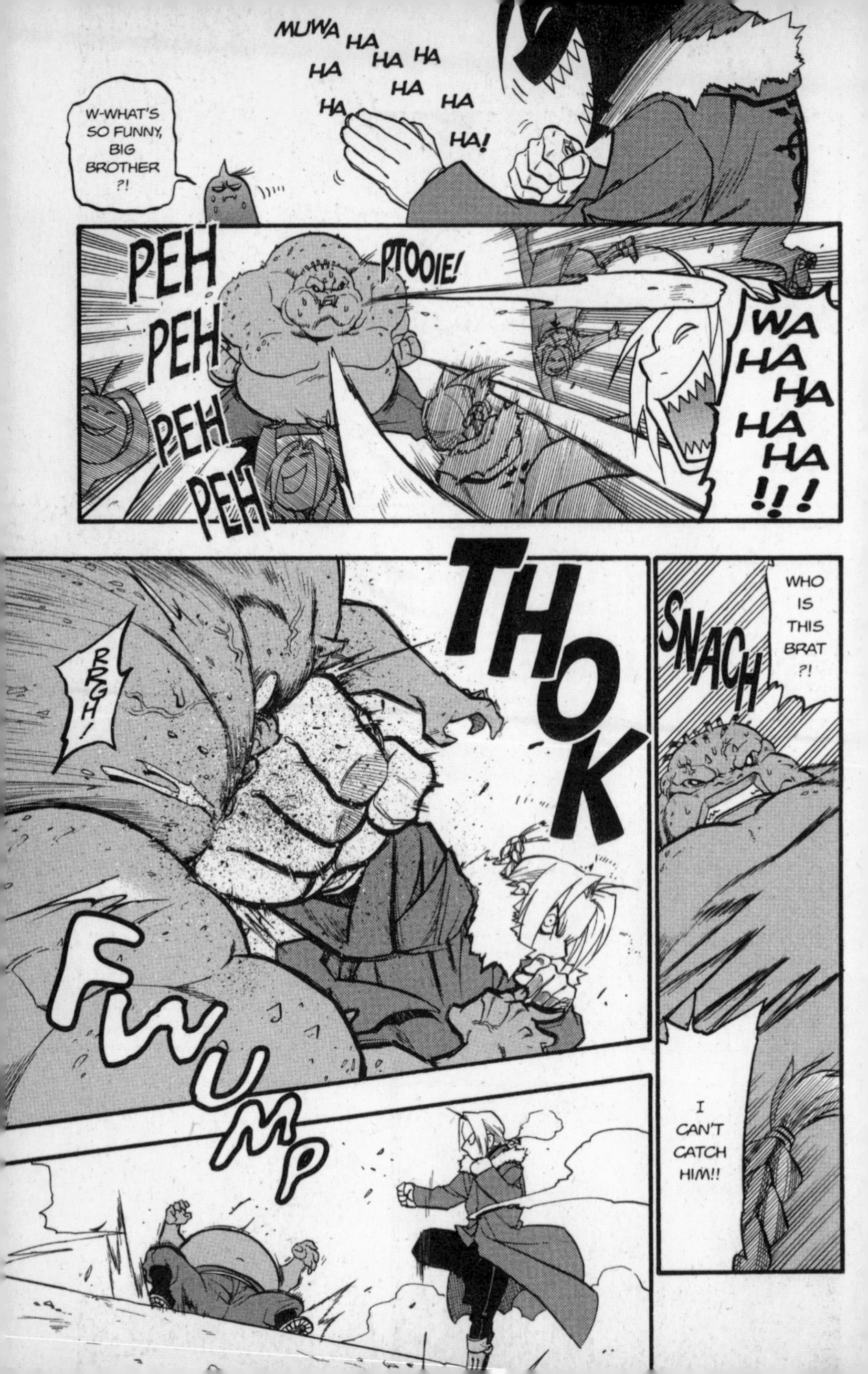
MUWA HA HA HA HA HA HA HA HA!
W-WHAT'S SO FUNNY, BIG BROTHER ?!
WA HA HA HA HA !!!
PTOOIE!
PEH PEH PEH PEH
SNACH
WHO IS THIS BRAT ?!
I CAN'T CATCH HIM!!
THOK
RRGH!
FWUMP

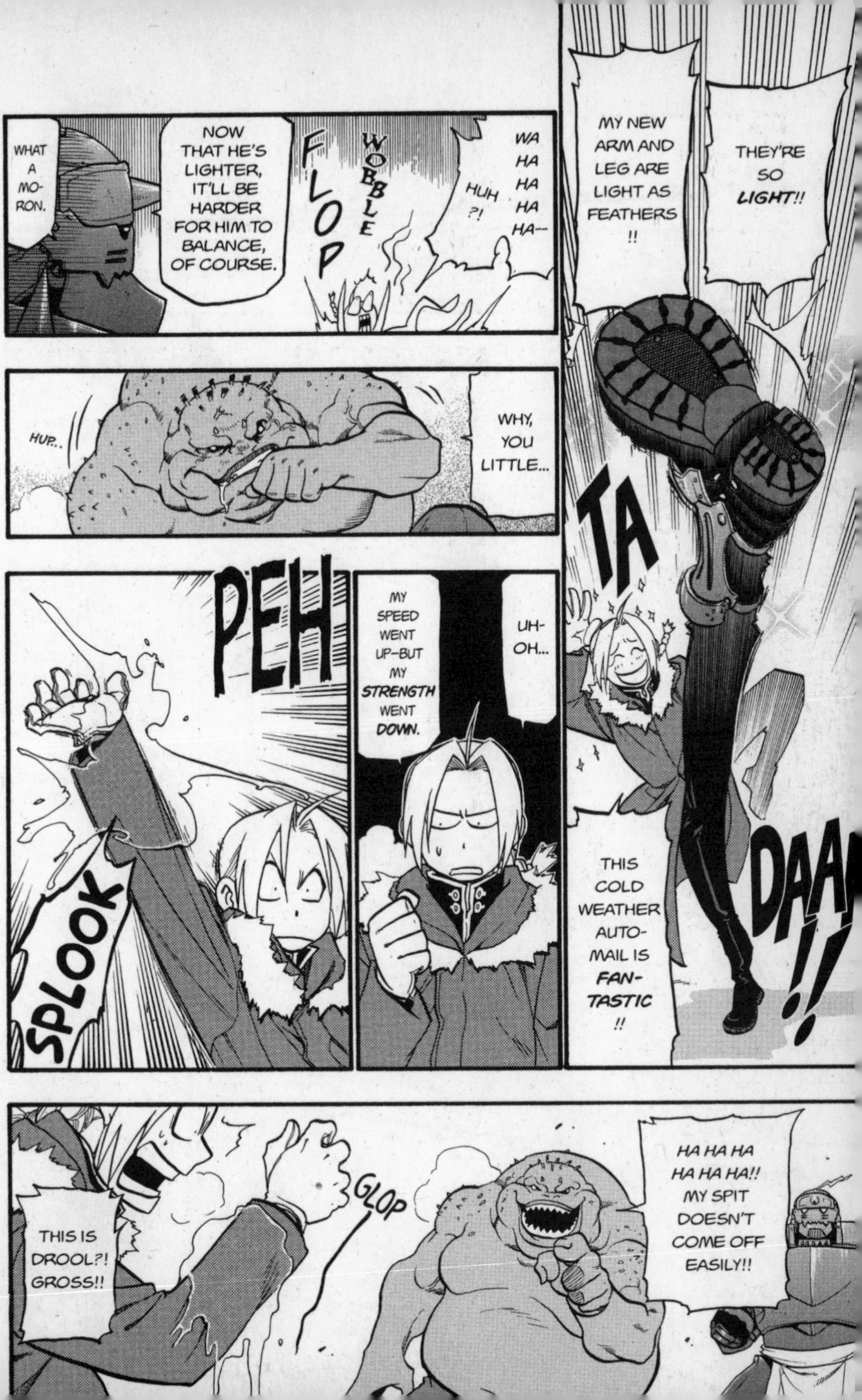
THEY'RE SO LIGHT!!
MY NEW ARM AND LEG ARE LIGHT AS FEATHERS!!
TA
DAA!!
THIS COLD WEATHER AUTO-MAIL IS FANTASTIC!!
WA HA HA HA HA--
HUH?!
WOBBLE
FLOP
NOW THAT HE'S LIGHTER, IT'LL BE HARDER FOR HIM TO BALANCE, OF COURSE.
WHAT A MO-RON.
WHY, YOU LITTLE...
HUP...
UH-OH...
MY SPEED WENT UP—BUT MY STRENGTH WENT DOWN.
PEH
SPLOOK
HA HA HA HA HA HA!! MY SPIT DOESN'T COME OFF EASILY!!
GLOP
THIS IS DROOL?! GROSS!!

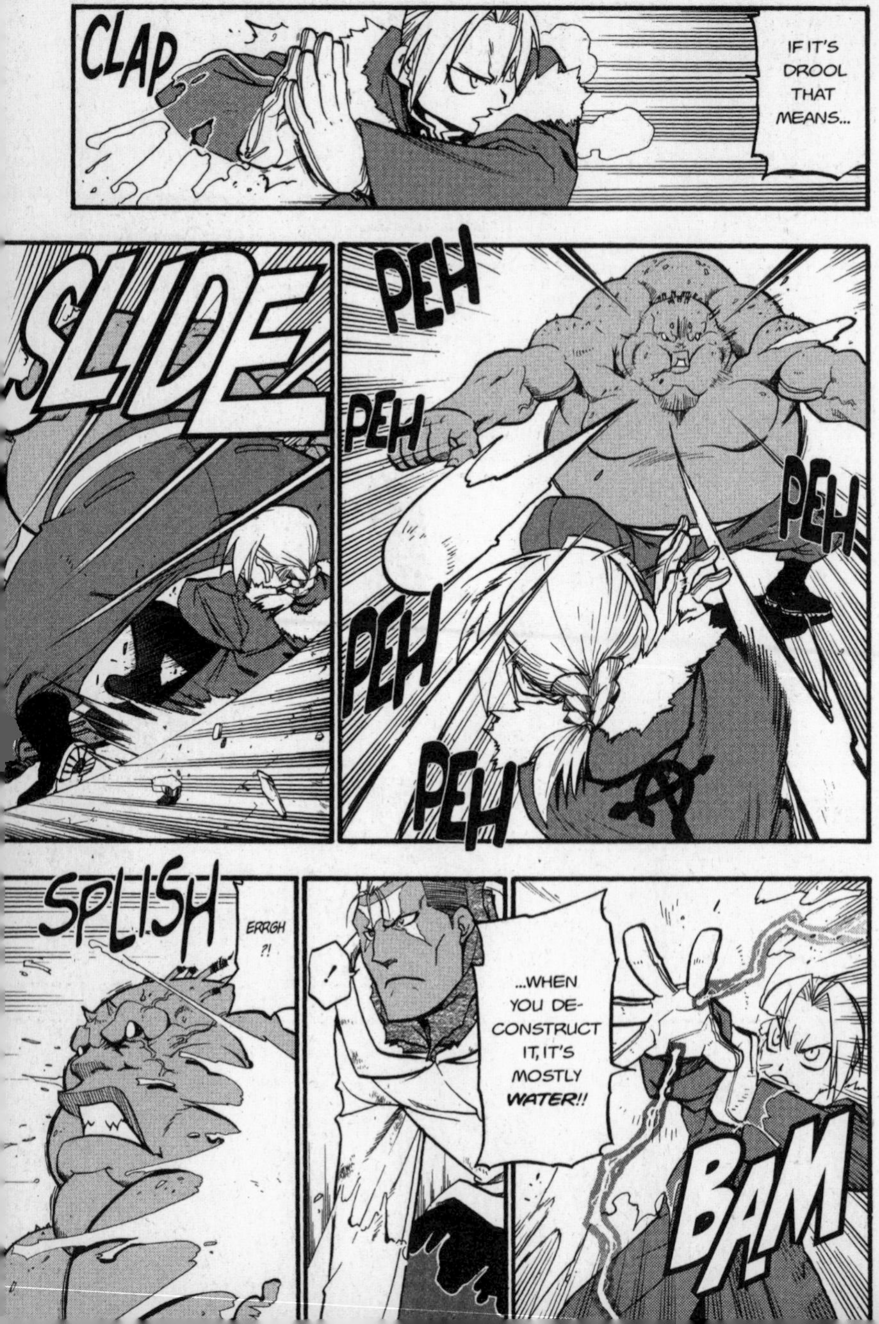
IF IT'S DROOL THAT MEANS...
CLAP
PEH
PEH
PEH
PEH
PEH
SLIDE
BAM
!
...WHEN YOU DE-CONSTRUCT IT, IT'S MOSTLY WATER!!
SPLISH
ERRGH ?!

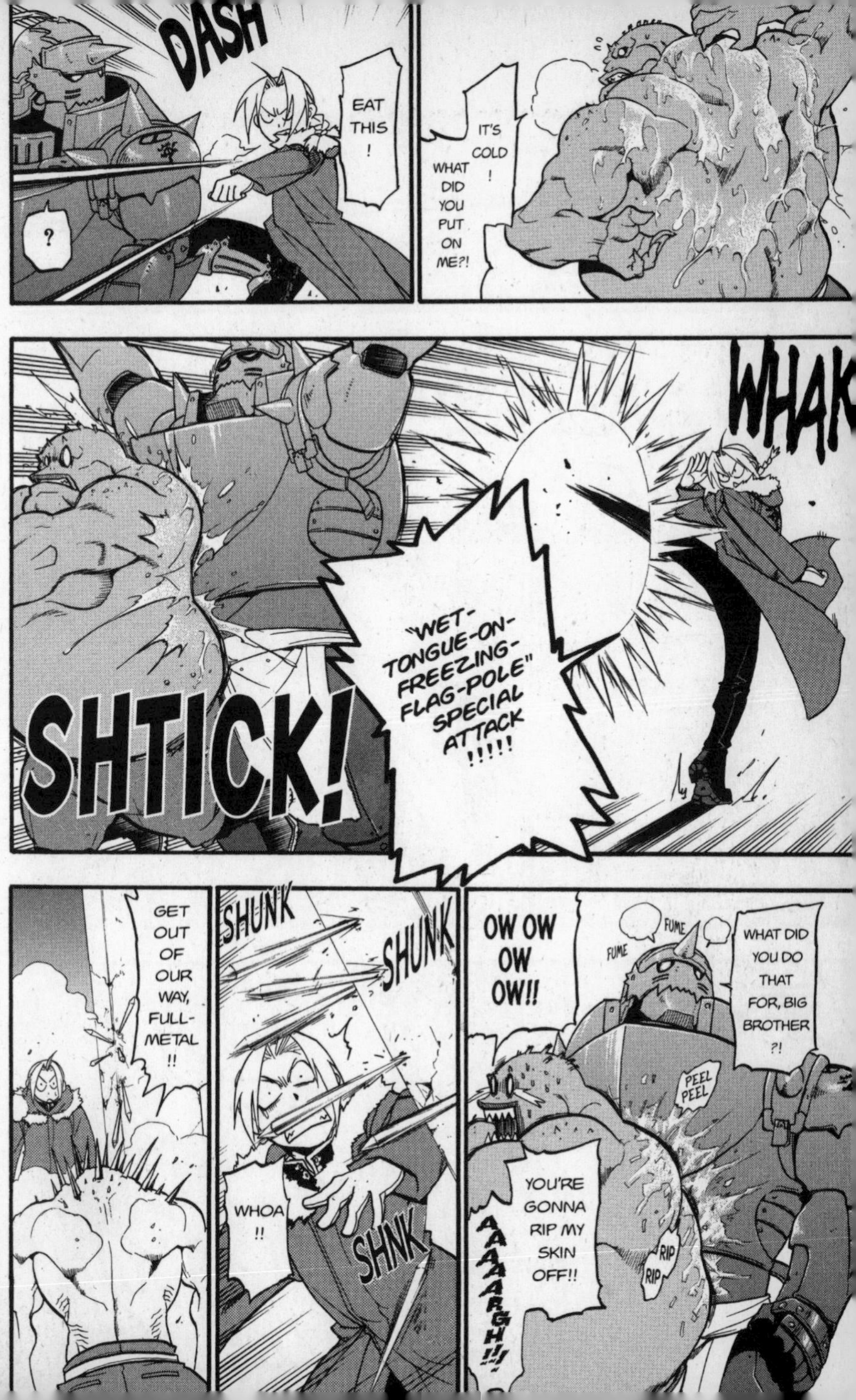
IT'S COLD!
WHAT DID YOU PUT ON ME?!
DASH
EAT THIS!
?
WHAK
"WET-TONGUE-ON-FREEZING-FLAG-POLE" SPECIAL ATTACK!!!!!
SHTICK!
FUME
FUME
WHAT DID YOU DO THAT FOR, BIG BROTHER?!
OW OW OW OW!!
PEEL PEEL
YOU'RE GONNA RIP MY SKIN OFF!!
RIP
RIP
AAAAARGH!!!
SHUNK
SHUNK
WHOA!!
SHNK
GET OUT OF OUR WAY, FULL-METAL!!

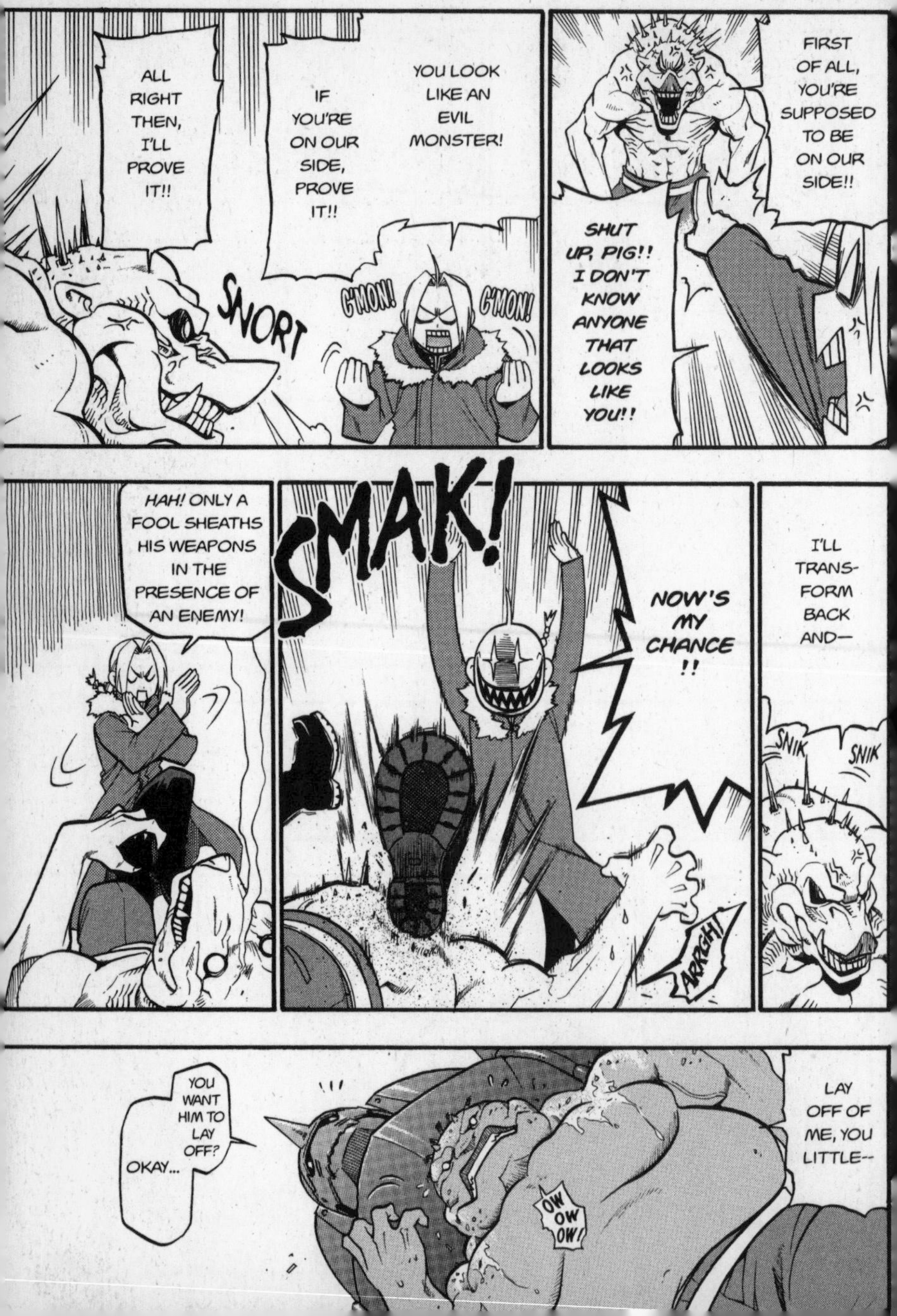
FIRST OF ALL, YOU'RE SUPPOSED TO BE ON OUR SIDE!!
SHUT UP, PIG!! I DON'T KNOW ANYONE THAT LOOKS LIKE YOU!!
YOU LOOK LIKE AN EVIL MONSTER!
IF YOU'RE ON OUR SIDE, PROVE IT!!
ALL RIGHT THEN, I'LL PROVE IT!!
C'MON!
C'MON!
SNORT
I'LL TRANS-FORM BACK AND—
SNIK
SNIK
SMAK!
NOW'S MY CHANCE!!
ARRGH!
HAH! ONLY A FOOL SHEATHS HIS WEAPONS IN THE PRESENCE OF AN ENEMY!
LAY OFF OF ME, YOU LITTLE--
OW OW OW!
YOU WANT HIM TO LAY OFF? OKAY...

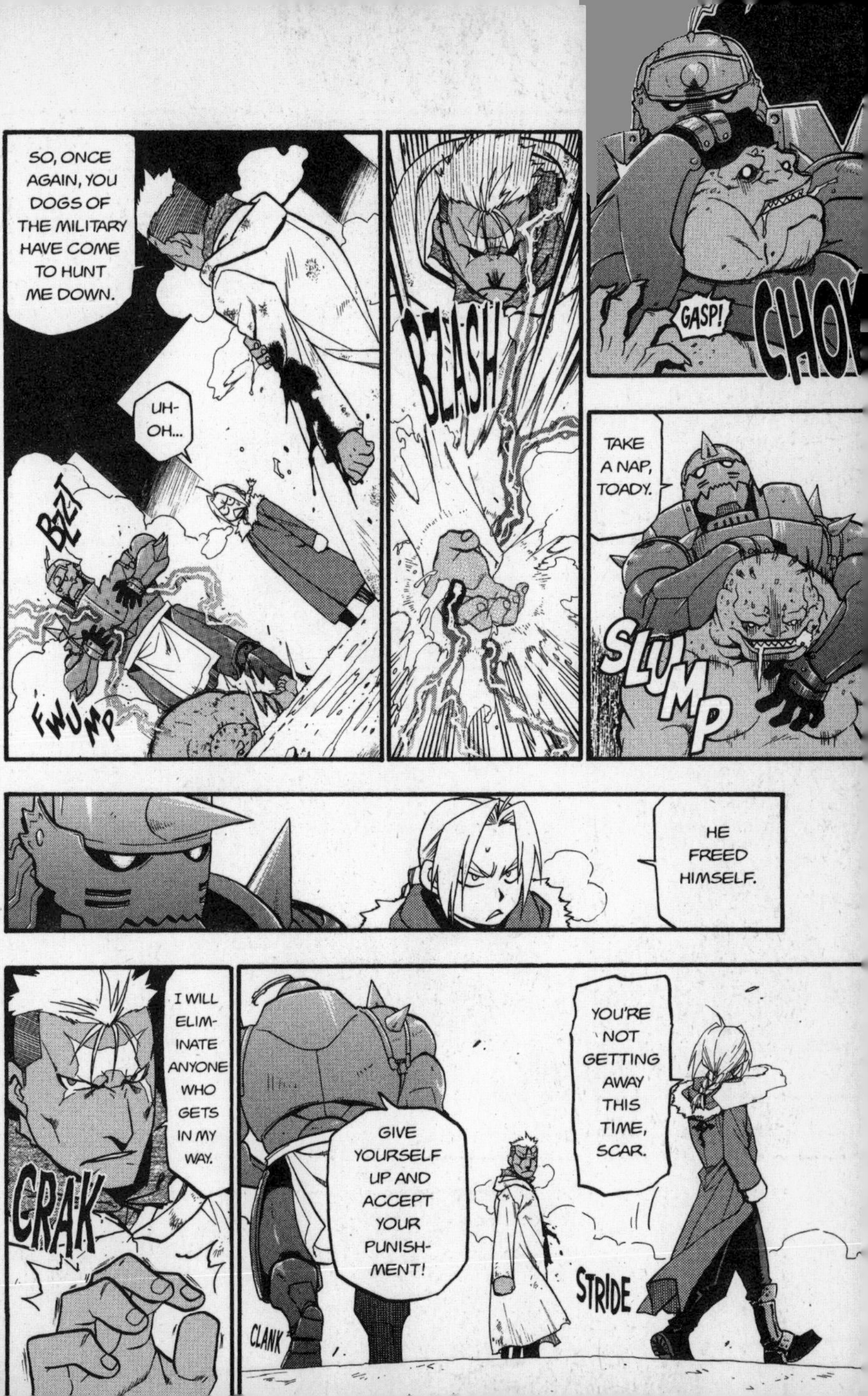
GASP!
CHOK
TAKE A NAP, TOADY.
SLUMP
BZASH
SO, ONCE AGAIN, YOU DOGS OF THE MILITARY HAVE COME TO HUNT ME DOWN.
UH-OH...
BZZT
FWUMP
HE FREED HIMSELF.
YOU'RE NOT GETTING AWAY THIS TIME, SCAR.
GIVE YOURSELF UP AND ACCEPT YOUR PUNISHMENT!
STRIDE
CLANK
I WILL ELIMINATE ANYONE WHO GETS IN MY WAY.
CRAK

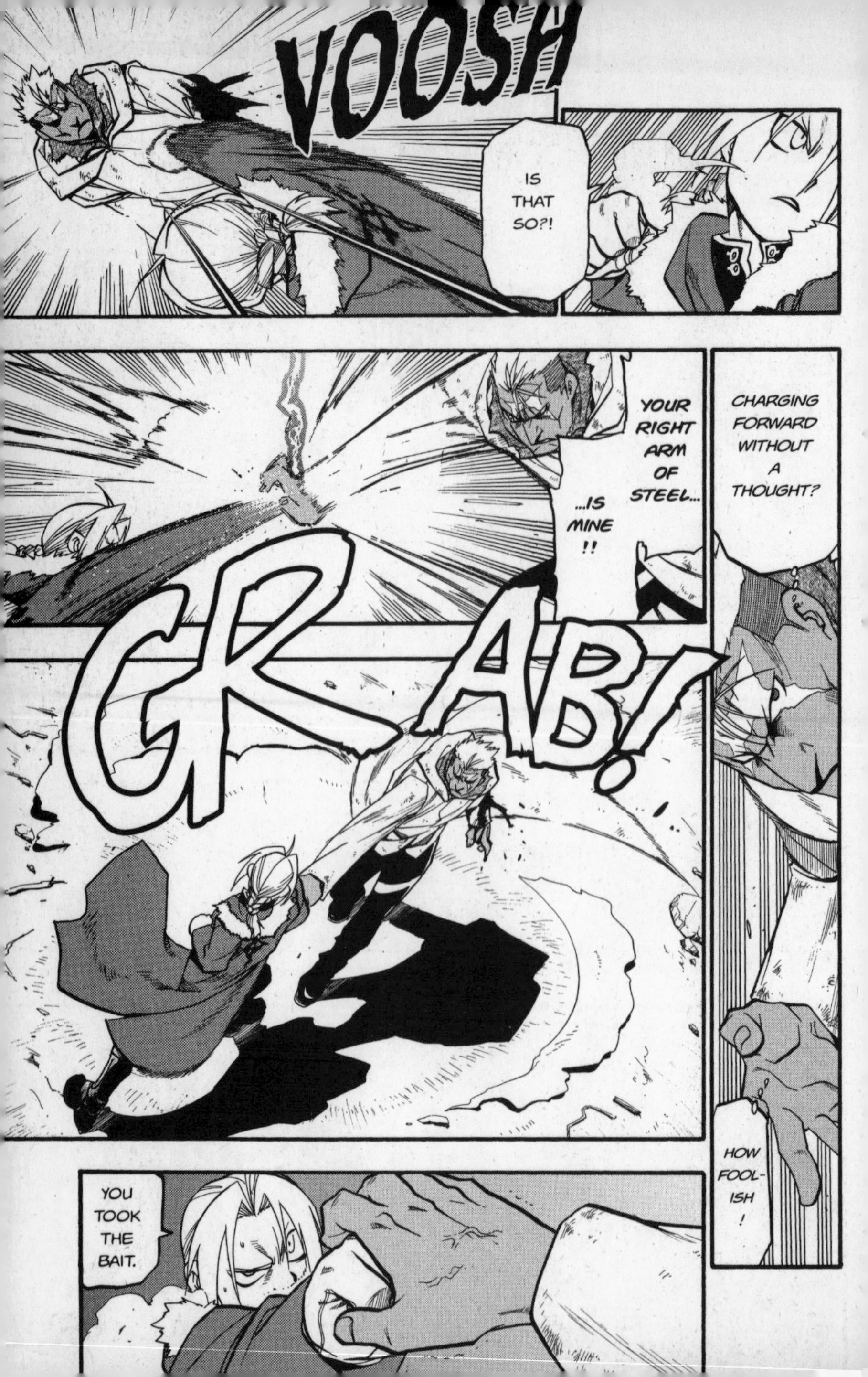
IS THAT SO?!
VOOSH
CHARGING FORWARD WITHOUT A THOUGHT?
HOW FOOL-ISH!
YOUR RIGHT ARM OF STEEL...
...IS MINE!!
GRAB!
YOU TOOK THE BAIT.

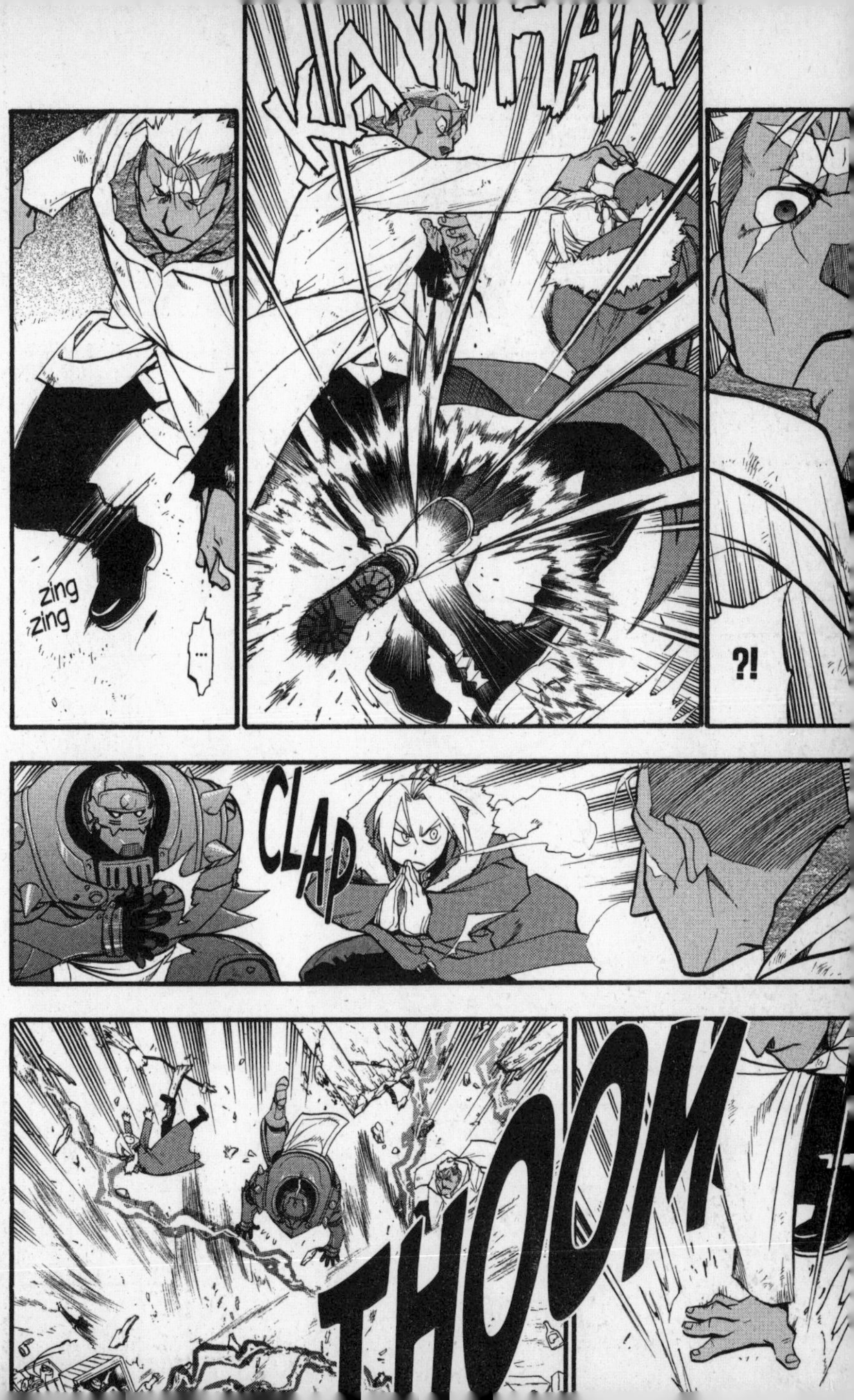
?!
KAWHAM
zing
zing
...
CLAP
THOOM

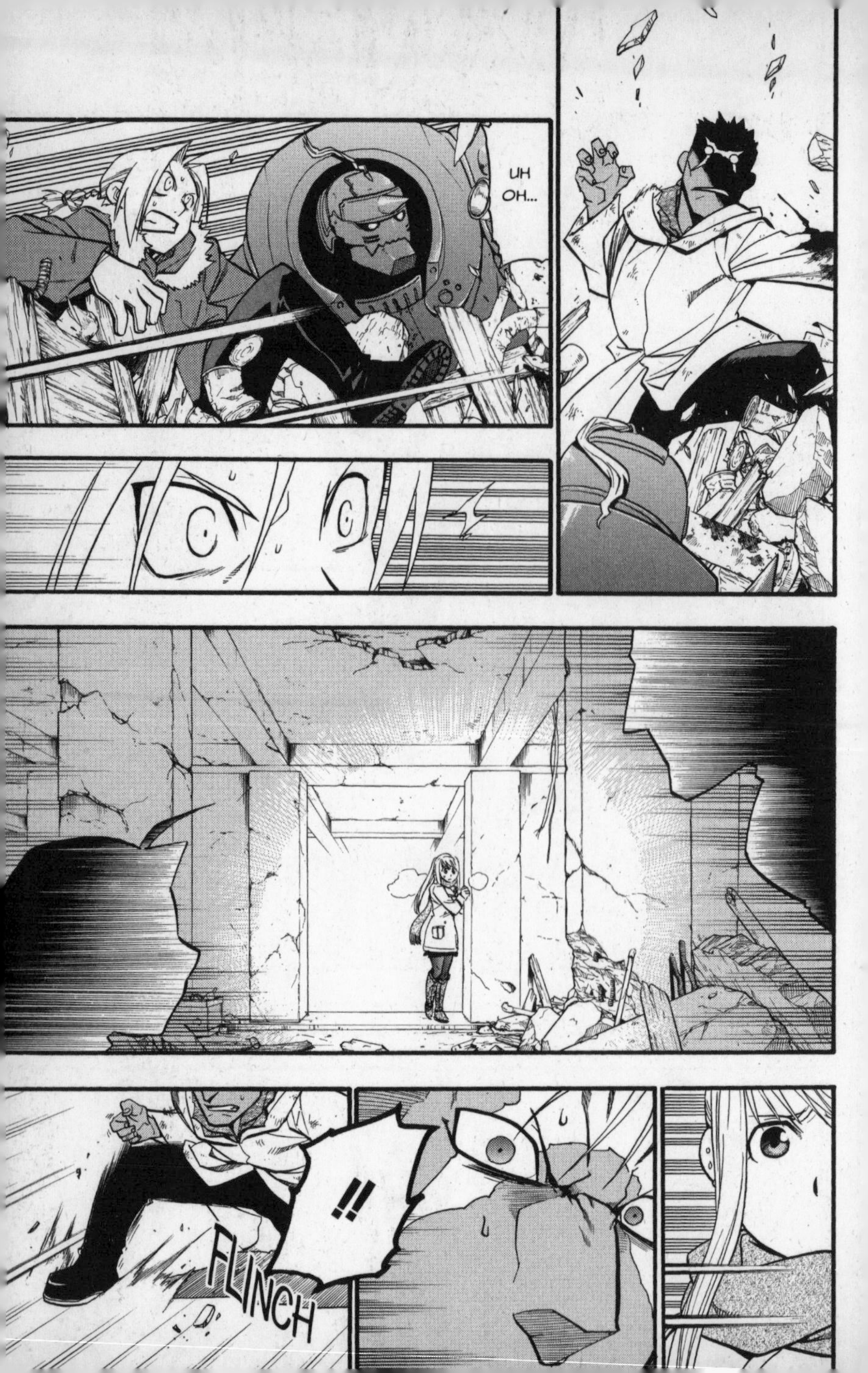
UH OH...
!!
FLINCH

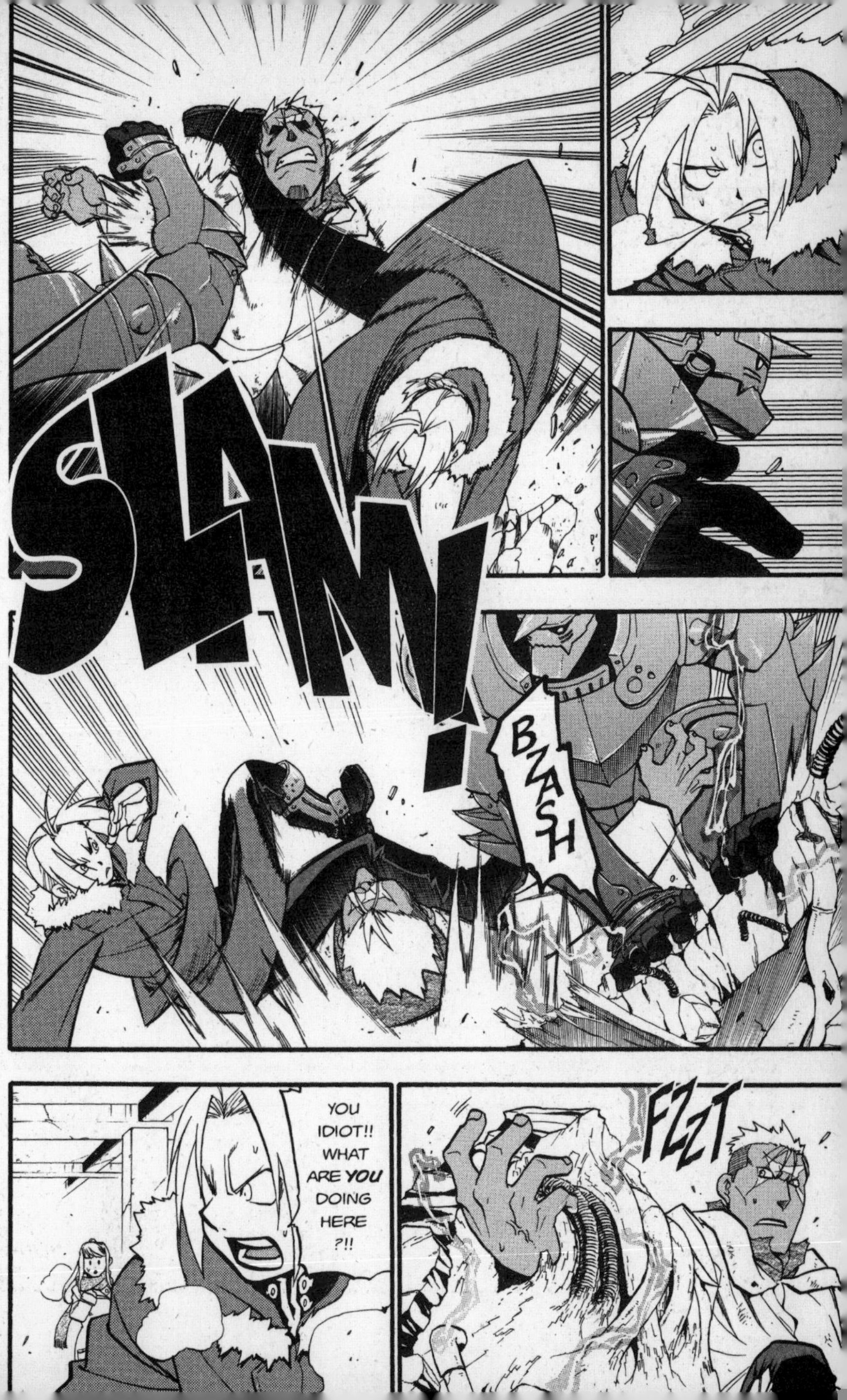
SLAM!
BZASH
FZZT
YOU IDIOT!! WHAT ARE *YOU* DOING HERE ?!!

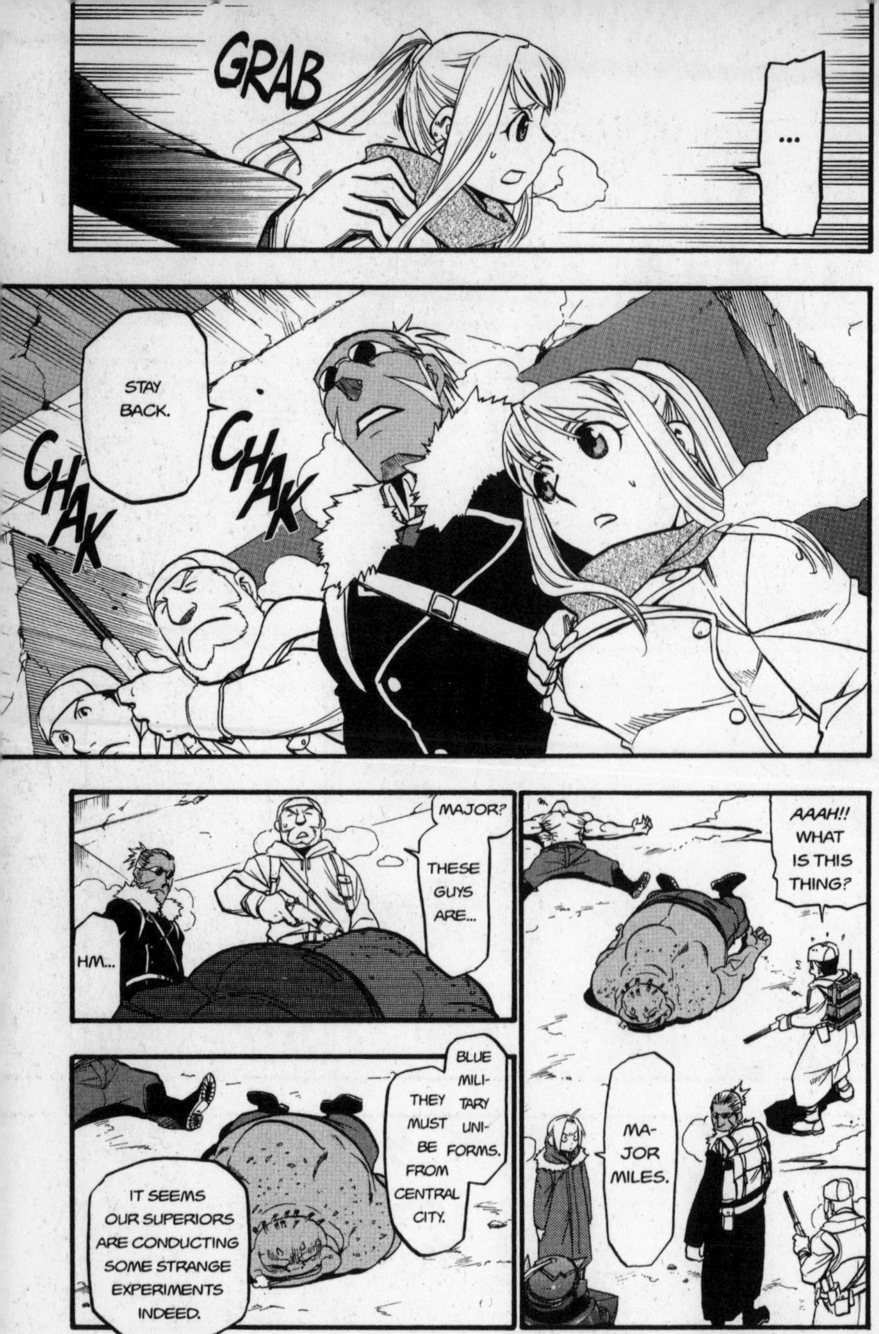
...
GRAB
STAY BACK.
CHAK
CHAK
AAAH!! WHAT IS THIS THING?
MAJOR MILES.
MAJOR?
THESE GUYS ARE...
HM...
BLUE MILITARY UNIFORMS.
THEY MUST BE FROM CENTRAL CITY.
IT SEEMS OUR SUPERIORS ARE CONDUCTING SOME STRANGE EXPERIMENTS INDEED.

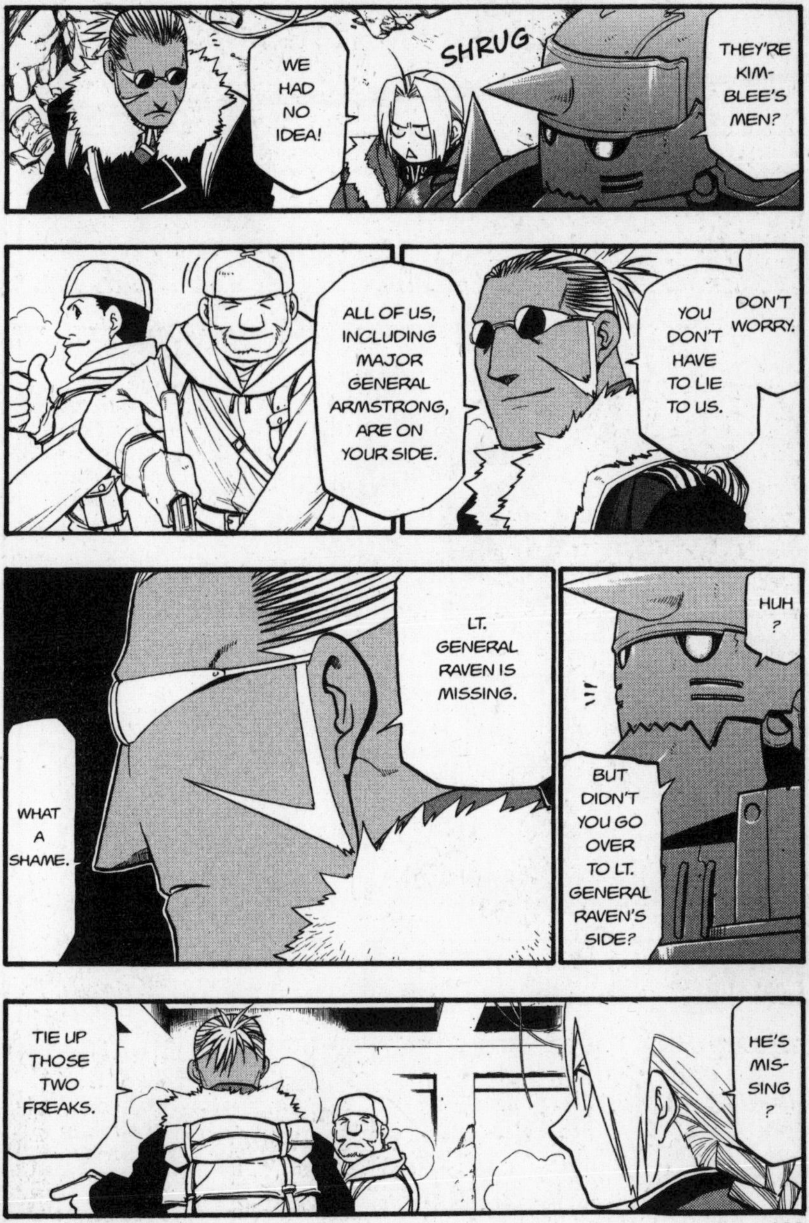
THEY'RE KIM-BLEE'S MEN?
SHRUG
WE HAD NO IDEA!
DON'T WORRY.
YOU DON'T HAVE TO LIE TO US.
ALL OF US, INCLUDING MAJOR GENERAL ARMSTRONG, ARE ON YOUR SIDE.
HUH?
BUT DIDN'T YOU GO OVER TO LT. GENERAL RAVEN'S SIDE?
LT. GENERAL RAVEN IS MISSING.
WHAT A SHAME.
HE'S MIS-SING?
TIE UP THOSE TWO FREAKS.

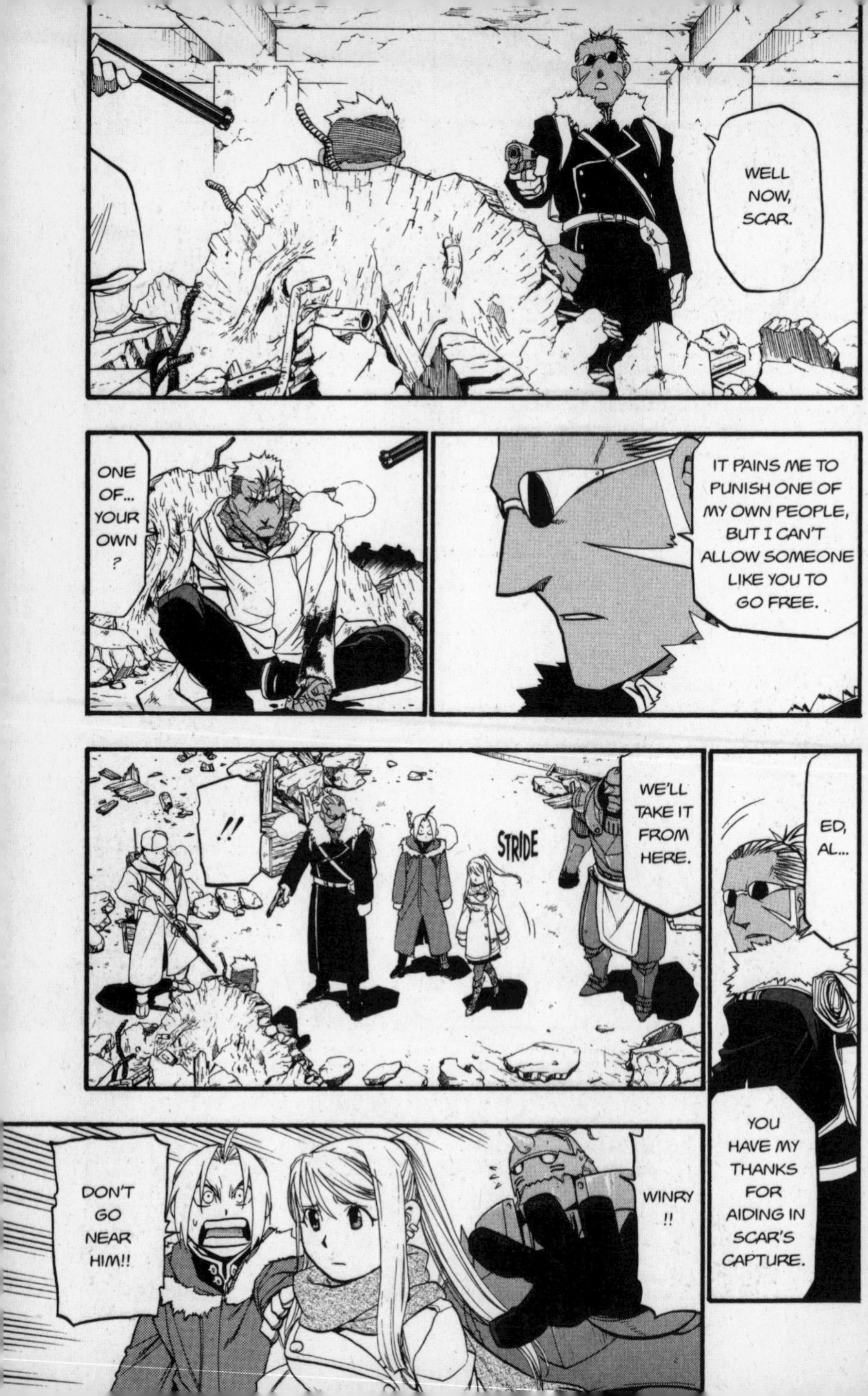
WELL NOW, SCAR.
IT PAINS ME TO PUNISH ONE OF MY OWN PEOPLE, BUT I CAN'T ALLOW SOMEONE LIKE YOU TO GO FREE.
ONE OF... YOUR OWN ?
ED, AL...
YOU HAVE MY THANKS FOR AIDING IN SCAR'S CAPTURE.
WE'LL TAKE IT FROM HERE.
STRIDE
!!
WINRY !!
DON'T GO NEAR HIM!!

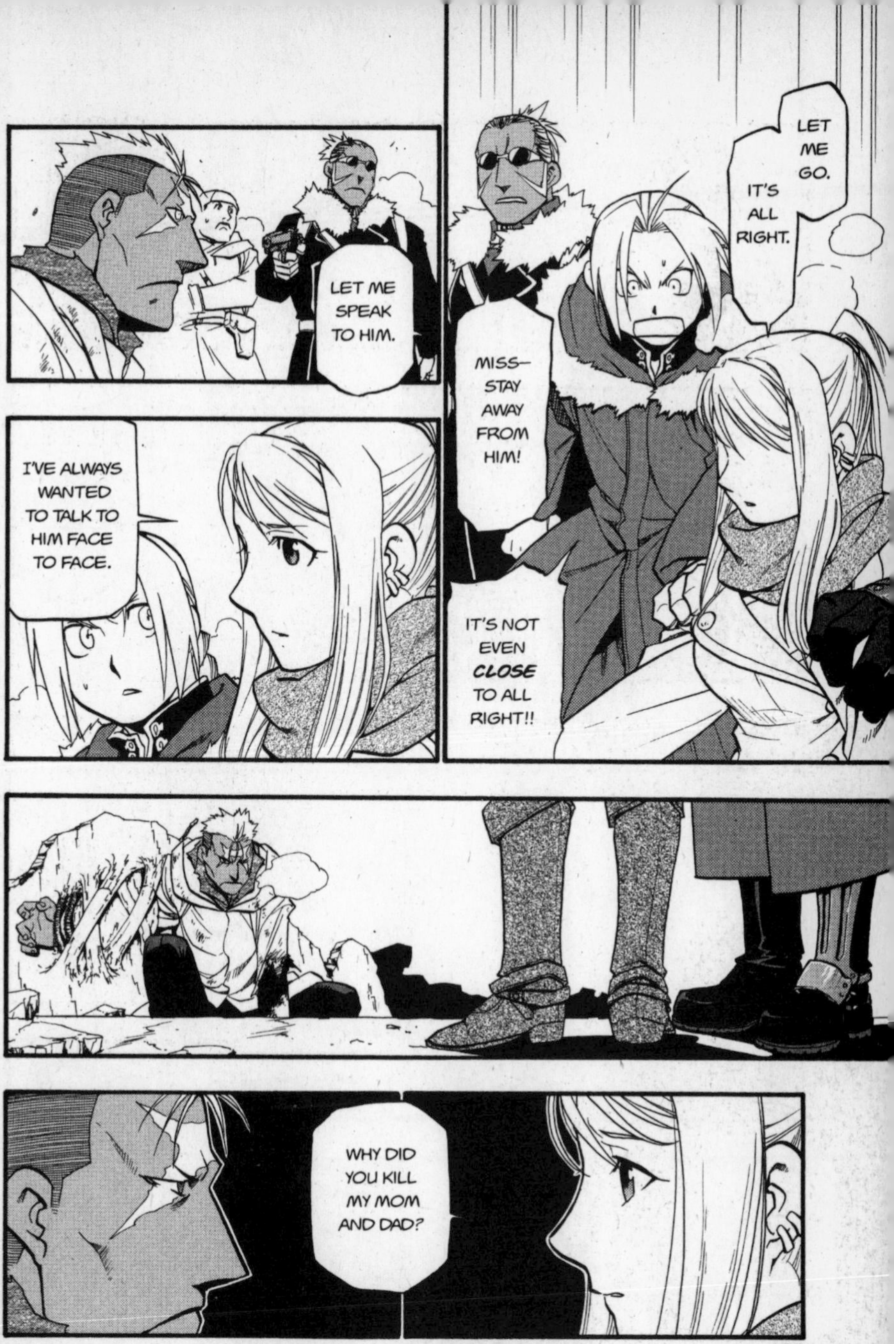
LET ME GO.
IT'S ALL RIGHT.
MISS—STAY AWAY FROM HIM!
IT'S NOT EVEN **CLOSE** TO ALL RIGHT!!
LET ME SPEAK TO HIM.
I'VE ALWAYS WANTED TO TALK TO HIM FACE TO FACE.
WHY DID YOU KILL MY MOM AND DAD?

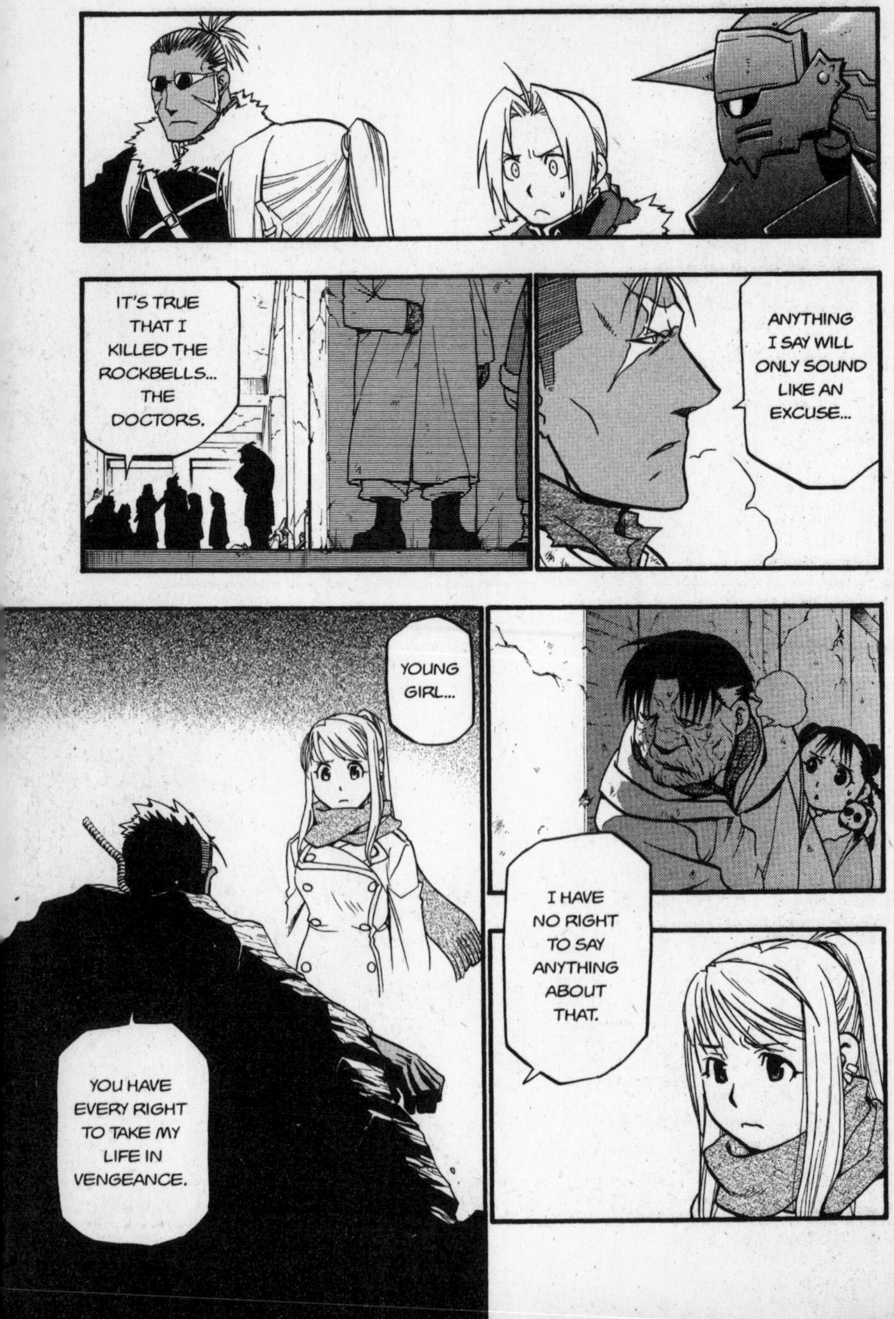
ANYTHING I SAY WILL ONLY SOUND LIKE AN EXCUSE...
IT'S TRUE THAT I KILLED THE ROCKBELLS... THE DOCTORS.
YOUNG GIRL...
YOU HAVE EVERY RIGHT TO TAKE MY LIFE IN VENGEANCE.
I HAVE NO RIGHT TO SAY ANYTHING ABOUT THAT.

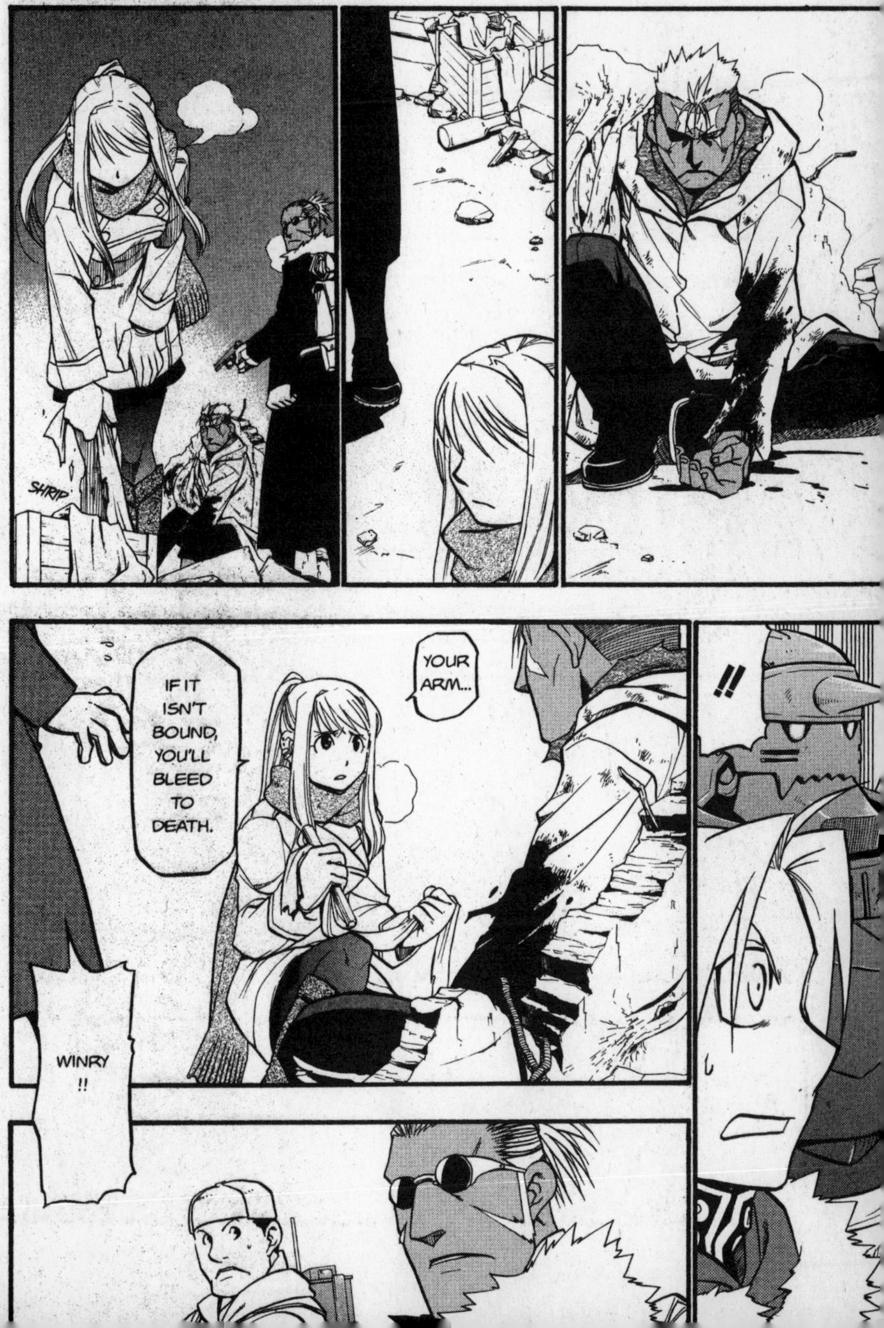
SHRIP
!!
YOUR ARM...
IF IT ISN'T BOUND, YOU'LL BLEED TO DEATH.
WINRY !!

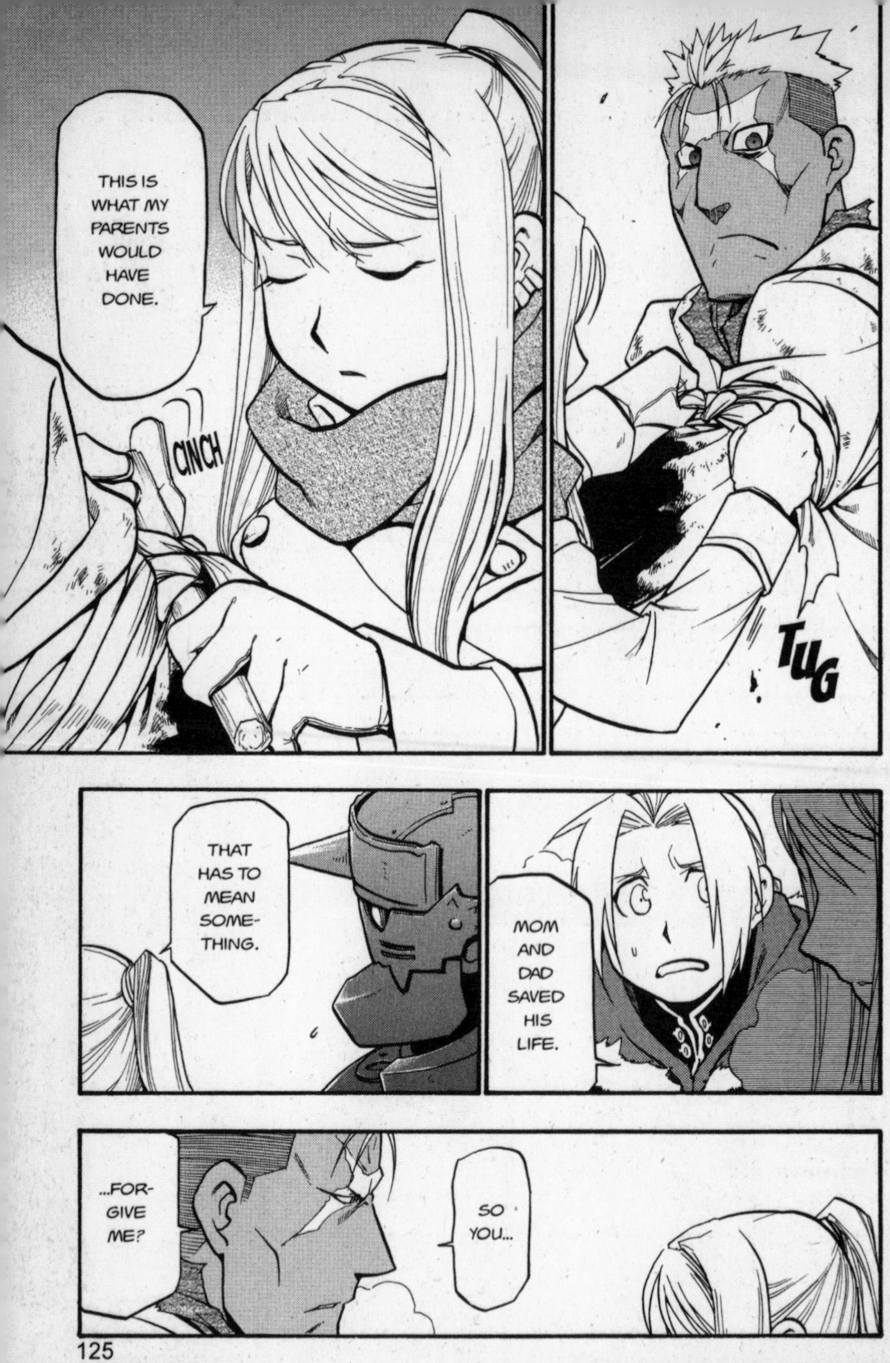
TUG
THIS IS WHAT MY PARENTS WOULD HAVE DONE.
CINCH
MOM AND DAD SAVED HIS LIFE.
THAT HAS TO MEAN SOME-THING.
SO YOU...
...FOR-GIVE ME?

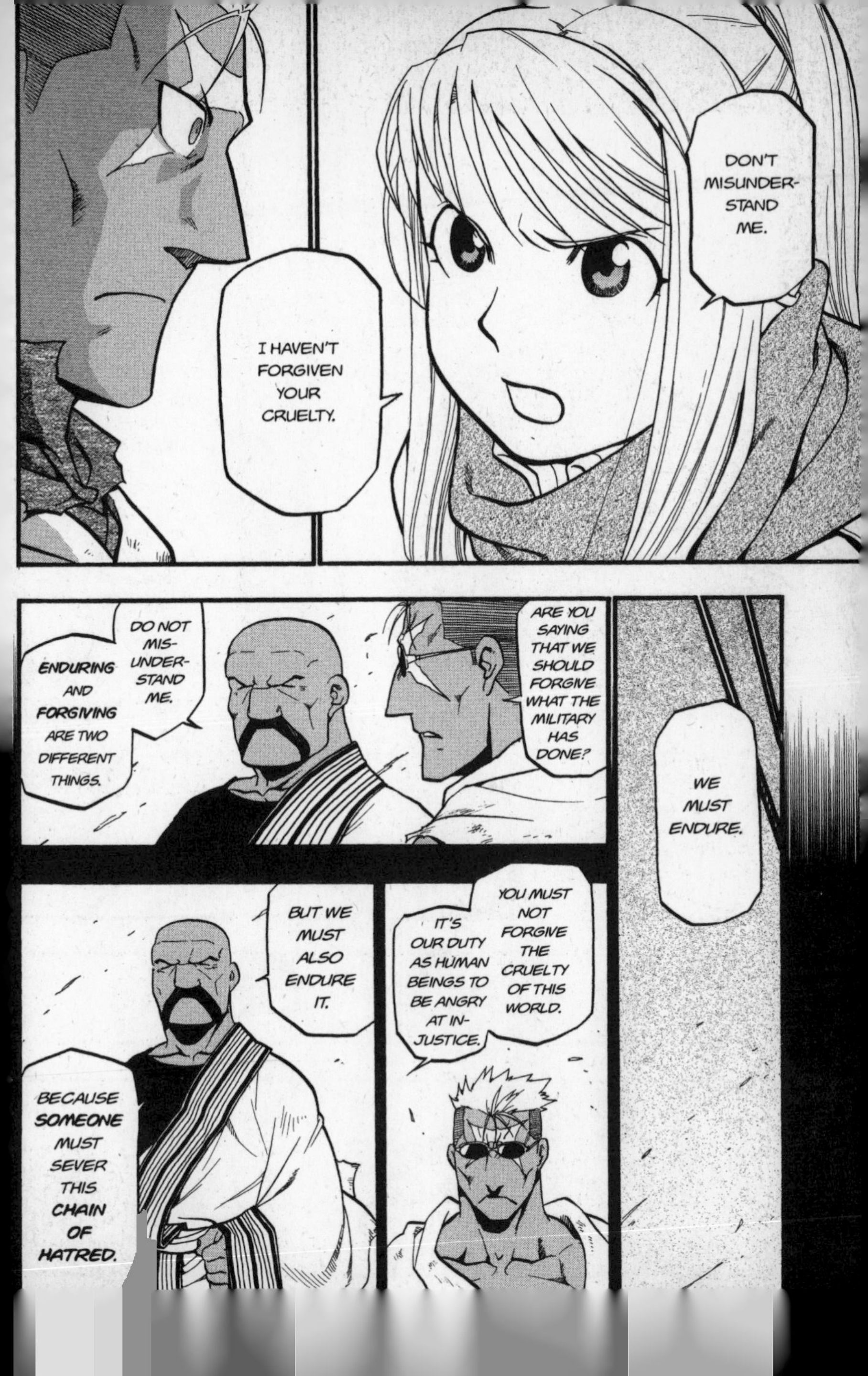
DON'T MISUNDERSTAND ME.
I HAVEN'T FORGIVEN YOUR CRUELTY.
WE MUST ENDURE.
ARE YOU SAYING THAT WE SHOULD FORGIVE WHAT THE MILITARY HAS DONE?
DO NOT MISUNDERSTAND ME.
ENDURING AND FORGIVING ARE TWO DIFFERENT THINGS.
YOU MUST NOT FORGIVE THE CRUELTY OF THIS WORLD.
IT'S OUR DUTY AS HUMAN BEINGS TO BE ANGRY AT INJUSTICE.
BUT WE MUST ALSO ENDURE IT.
BECAUSE SOMEONE MUST SEVER THIS CHAIN OF HATRED.

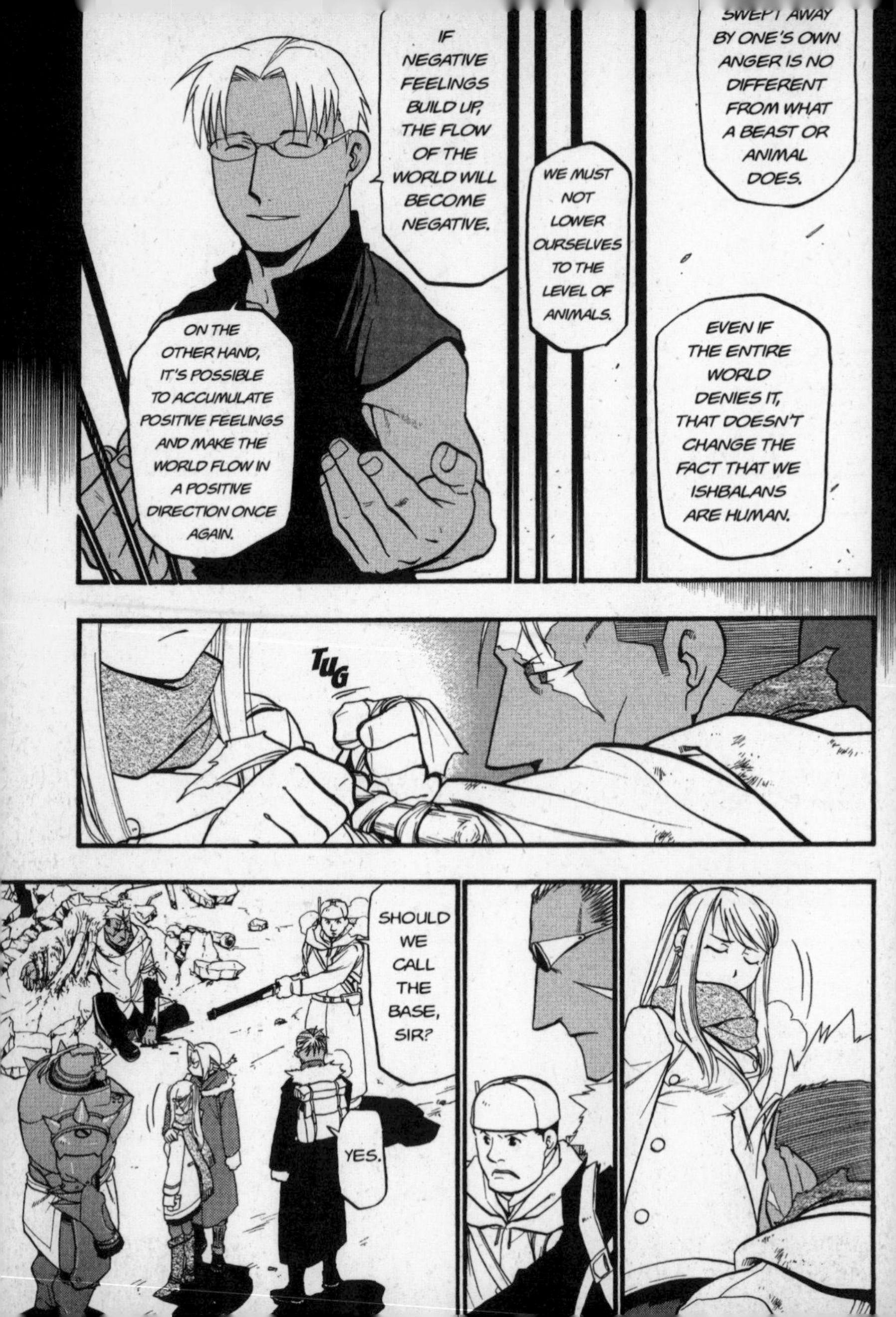
SWEPT AWAY BY ONE'S OWN ANGER IS NO DIFFERENT FROM WHAT A BEAST OR ANIMAL DOES.
EVEN IF THE ENTIRE WORLD DENIES IT, THAT DOESN'T CHANGE THE FACT THAT WE ISHBALANS ARE HUMAN.
WE MUST NOT LOWER OURSELVES TO THE LEVEL OF ANIMALS.
IF NEGATIVE FEELINGS BUILD UP, THE FLOW OF THE WORLD WILL BECOME NEGATIVE.
ON THE OTHER HAND, IT'S POSSIBLE TO ACCUMULATE POSITIVE FEELINGS AND MAKE THE WORLD FLOW IN A POSITIVE DIRECTION ONCE AGAIN.
TUG
SHOULD WE CALL THE BASE, SIR?
YES.

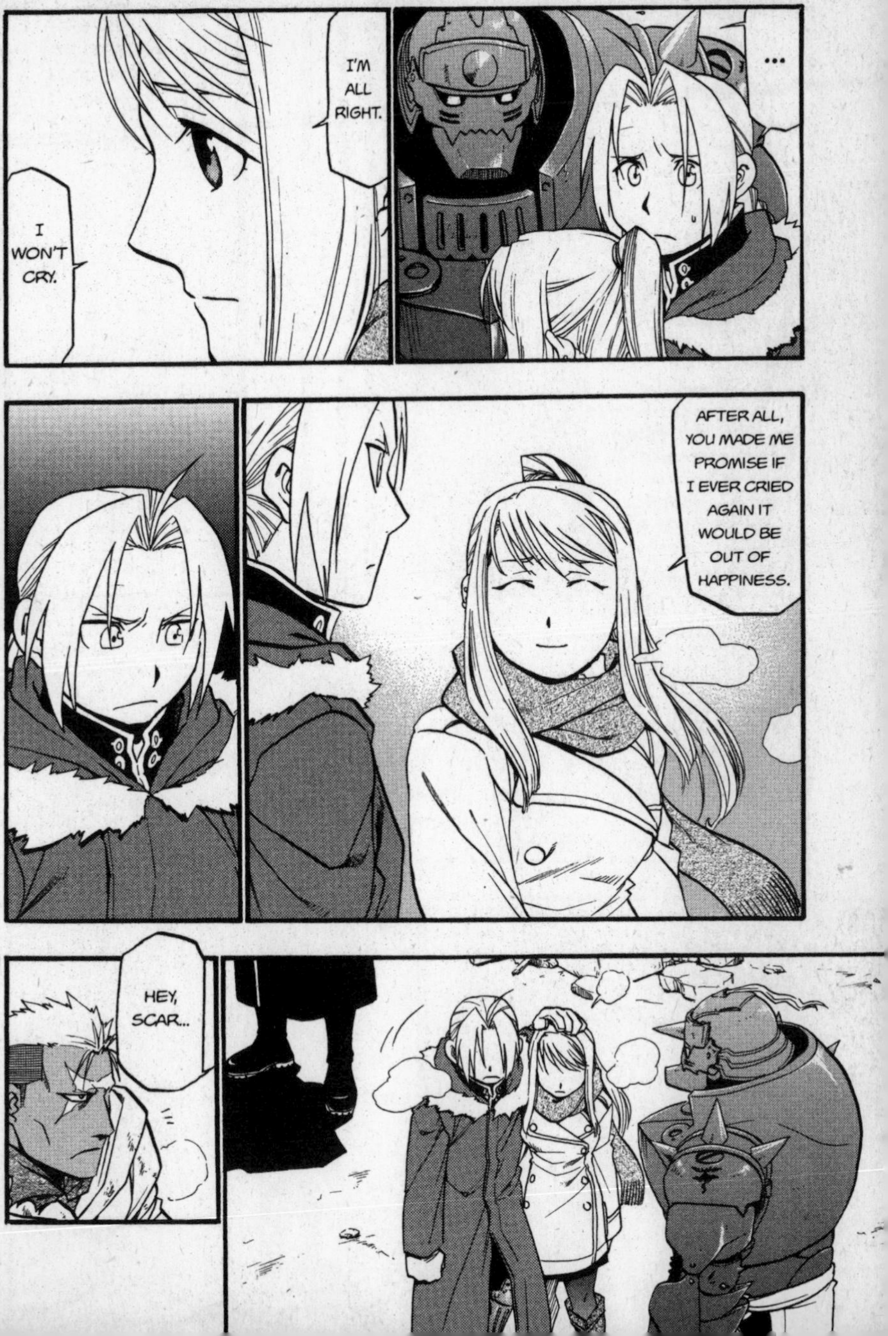
...
I'M ALL RIGHT.
I WON'T CRY.
AFTER ALL, YOU MADE ME PROMISE IF I EVER CRIED AGAIN IT WOULD BE OUT OF HAPPINESS.
HEY, SCAR...

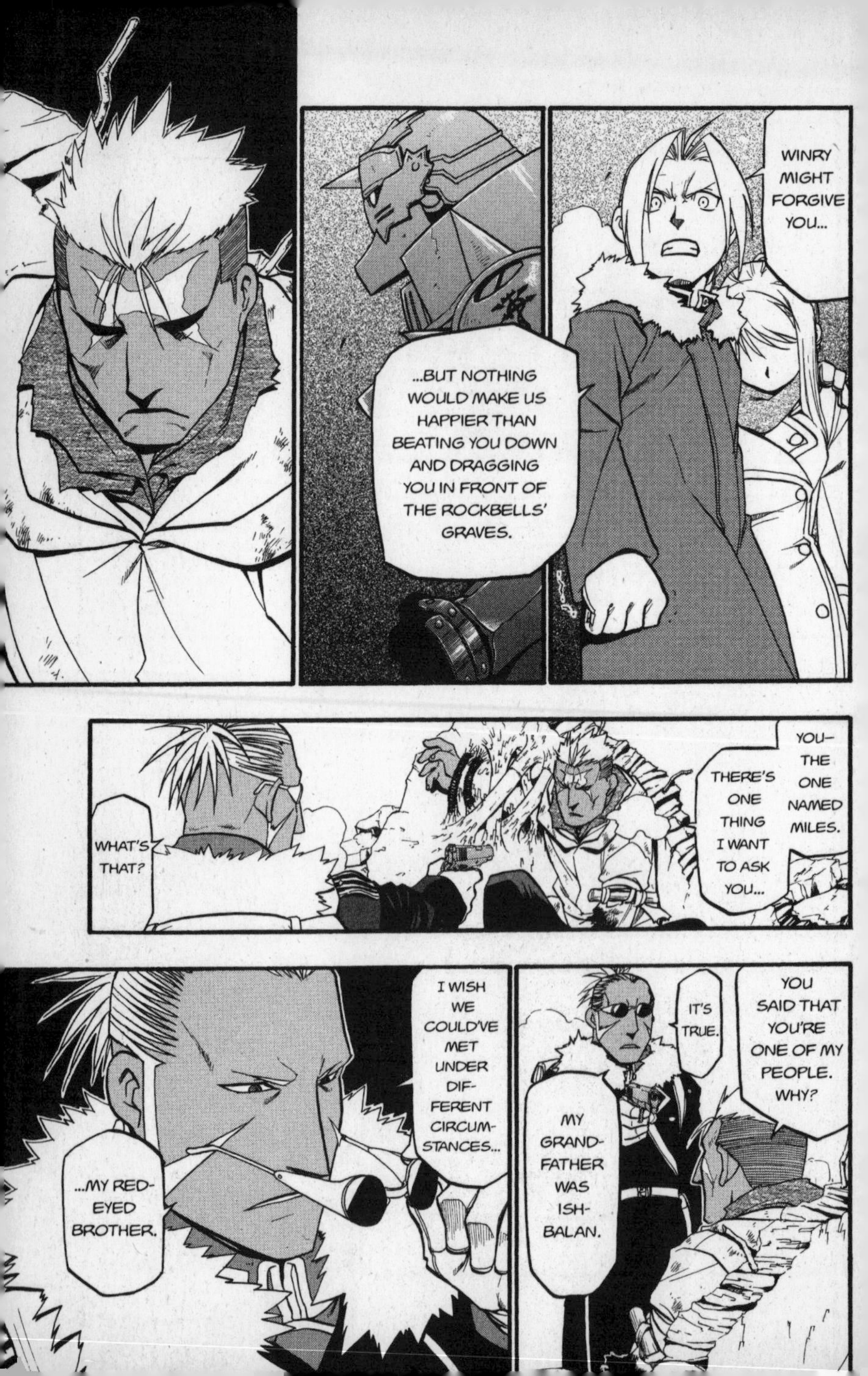
WINRY MIGHT FORGIVE YOU...
...BUT NOTHING WOULD MAKE US HAPPIER THAN BEATING YOU DOWN AND DRAGGING YOU IN FRONT OF THE ROCKBELLS' GRAVES.
YOU— THE ONE NAMED MILES.
THERE'S ONE THING I WANT TO ASK YOU...
WHAT'S THAT?
YOU SAID THAT YOU'RE ONE OF MY PEOPLE. WHY?
IT'S TRUE.
MY GRANDFATHER WAS ISHBALAN.
I WISH WE COULD'VE MET UNDER DIFFERENT CIRCUMSTANCES...
...MY RED-EYED BROTHER.

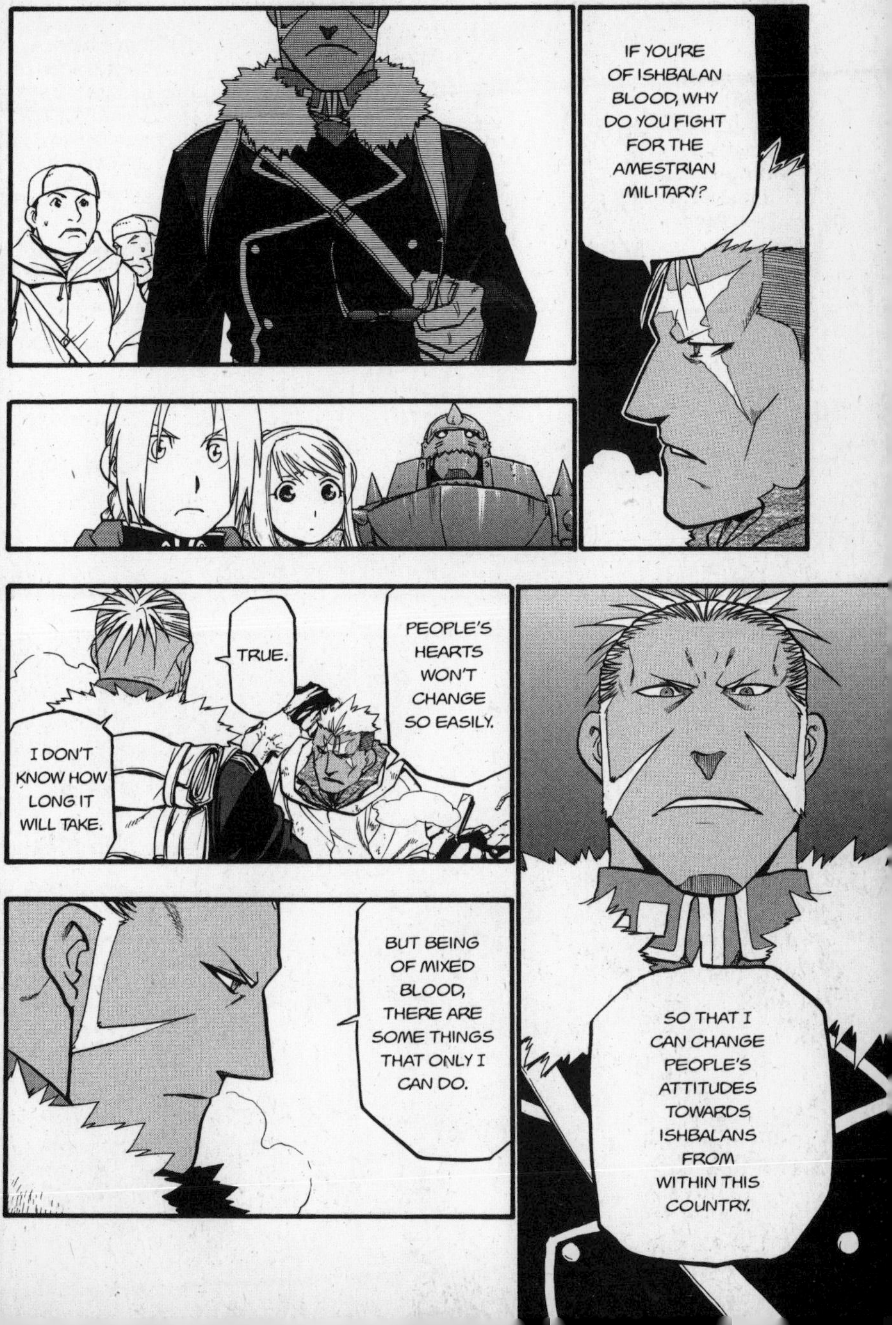
IF YOU'RE OF ISHBALAN BLOOD, WHY DO YOU FIGHT FOR THE AMESTRIAN MILITARY?
SO THAT I CAN CHANGE PEOPLE'S ATTITUDES TOWARDS ISHBALANS FROM WITHIN THIS COUNTRY.
PEOPLE'S HEARTS WON'T CHANGE SO EASILY.
TRUE.
I DON'T KNOW HOW LONG IT WILL TAKE.
BUT BEING OF MIXED BLOOD, THERE ARE SOME THINGS THAT ONLY I CAN DO.

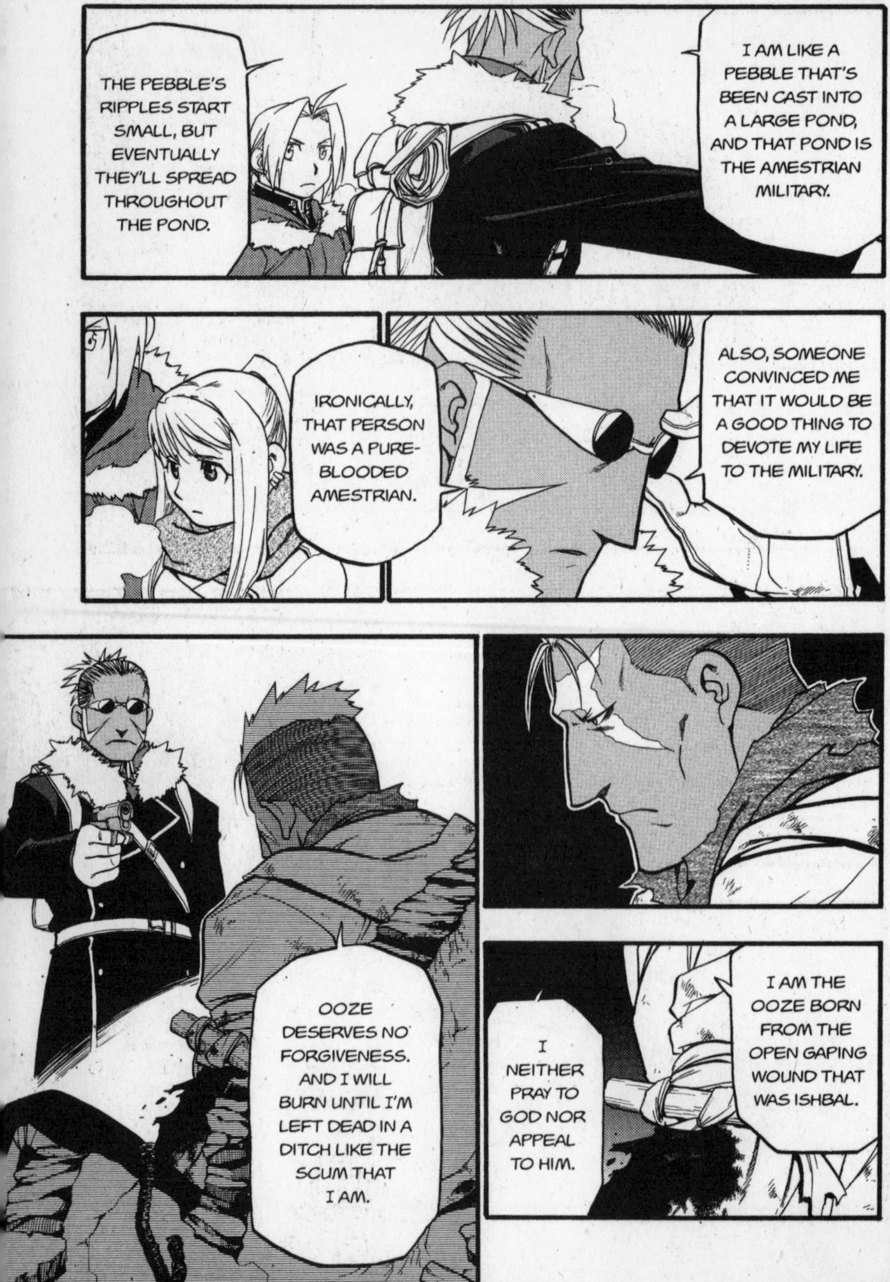
I AM LIKE A PEBBLE THAT'S BEEN CAST INTO A LARGE POND, AND THAT POND IS THE AMESTRIAN MILITARY.
THE PEBBLE'S RIPPLES START SMALL, BUT EVENTUALLY THEY'LL SPREAD THROUGHOUT THE POND.
ALSO, SOMEONE CONVINCED ME THAT IT WOULD BE A GOOD THING TO DEVOTE MY LIFE TO THE MILITARY.
IRONICALLY, THAT PERSON WAS A PURE-BLOODED AMESTRIAN.
I AM THE OOZE BORN FROM THE OPEN GAPING WOUND THAT WAS ISHBAL.
I NEITHER PRAY TO GOD NOR APPEAL TO HIM.
OOZE DESERVES NO FORGIVENESS. AND I WILL BURN UNTIL I'M LEFT DEAD IN A DITCH LIKE THE SCUM THAT I AM.

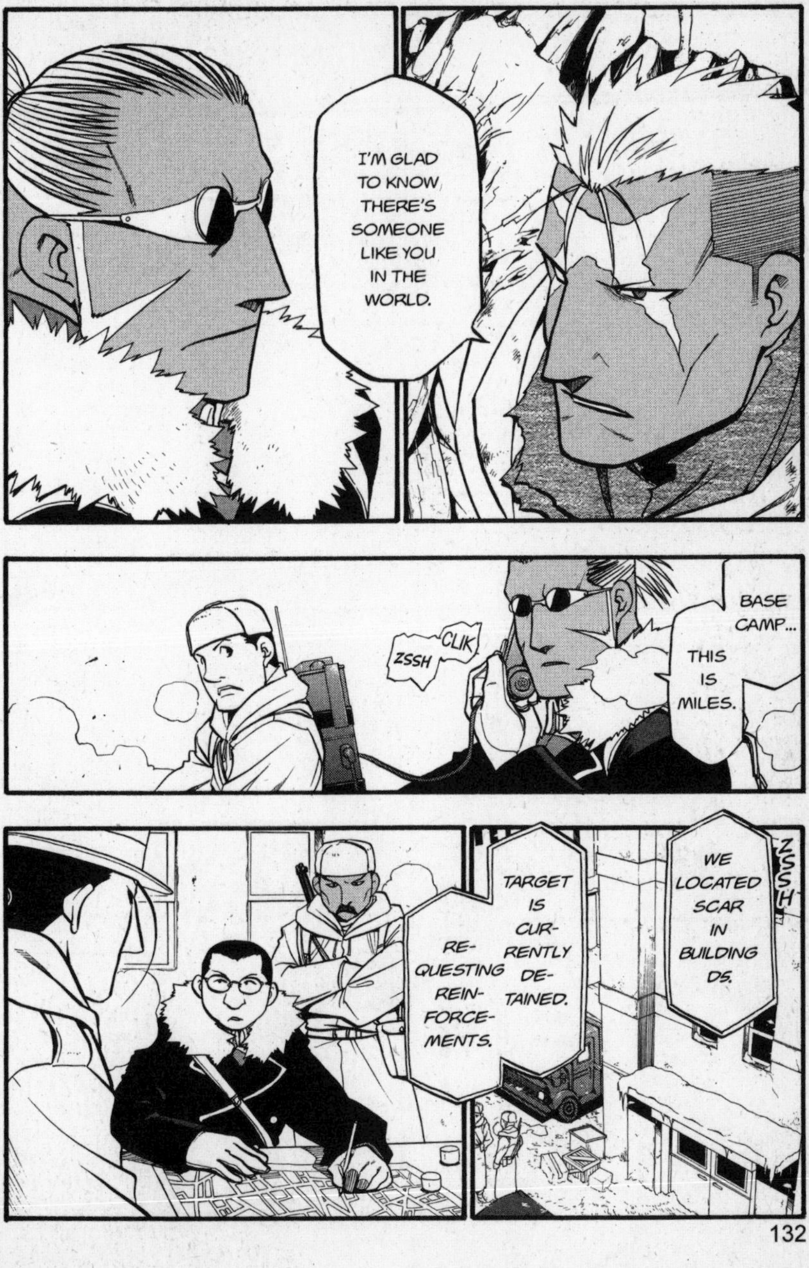
I'M GLAD TO KNOW THERE'S SOMEONE LIKE YOU IN THE WORLD.
BASE CAMP... THIS IS MILES.
CLIK
ZSSH
ZSSH
WE LOCATED SCAR IN BUILDING D5.
TARGET IS CURRENTLY DETAINED.
REQUESTING REINFORCEMENTS.

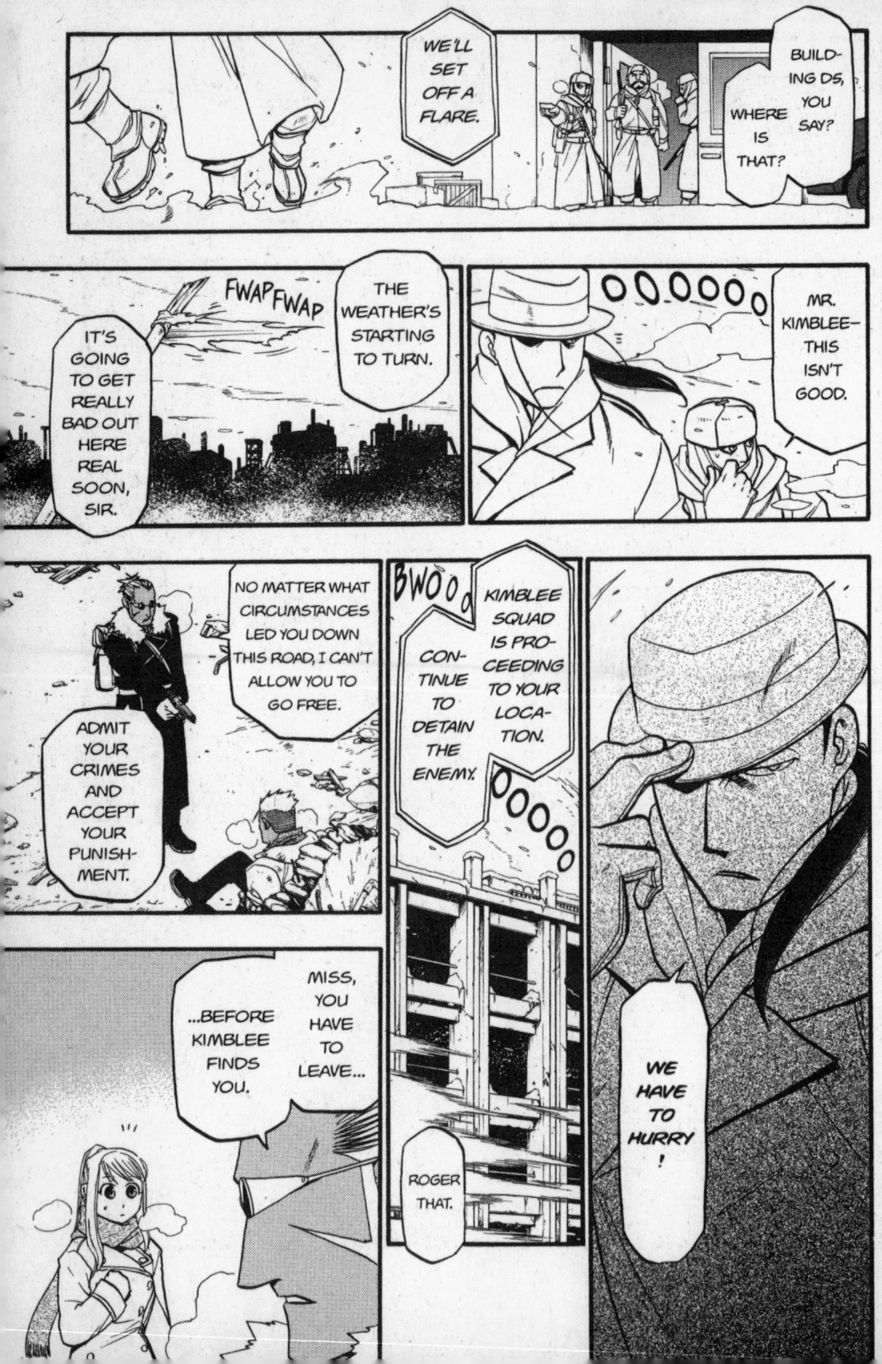
BUILDING DS, YOU SAY?
WHERE IS THAT?
WE'LL SET OFF A FLARE.
OOOOOO
MR. KIMBLEE— THIS ISN'T GOOD.
THE WEATHER'S STARTING TO TURN.
FWAP FWAP
IT'S GOING TO GET REALLY BAD OUT HERE REAL SOON, SIR.
WE HAVE TO HURRY!
BWOOO
KIMBLEE SQUAD IS PROCEEDING TO YOUR LOCATION.
CONTINUE TO DETAIN THE ENEMY.
OOOOO
ROGER THAT.
NO MATTER WHAT CIRCUMSTANCES LED YOU DOWN THIS ROAD, I CAN'T ALLOW YOU TO GO FREE.
ADMIT YOUR CRIMES AND ACCEPT YOUR PUNISHMENT.
MISS, YOU HAVE TO LEAVE...
...BEFORE KIMBLEE FINDS YOU.

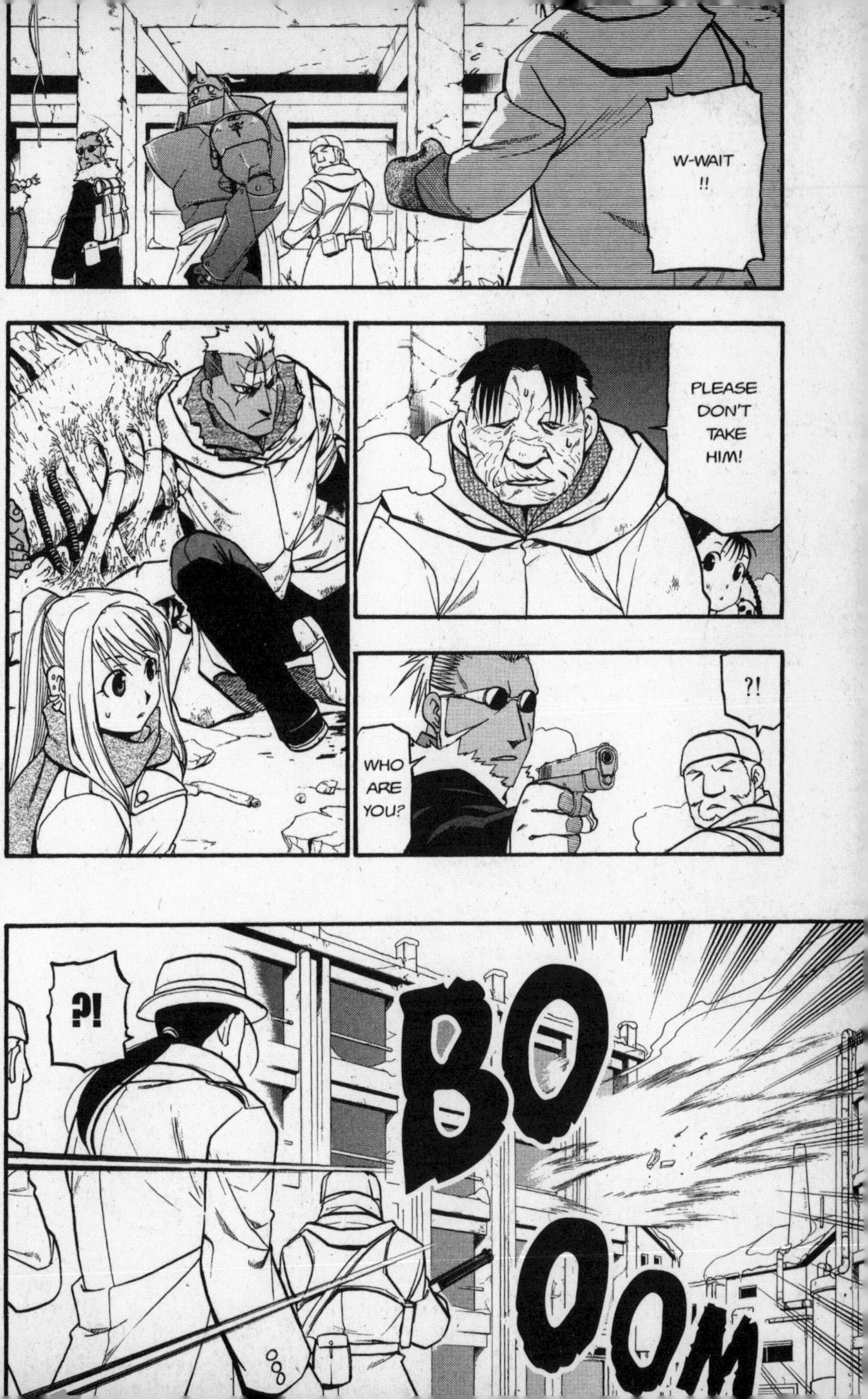
W-WAIT !!
PLEASE DON'T TAKE HIM!
?!
WHO ARE YOU?
?!
BOOOOM

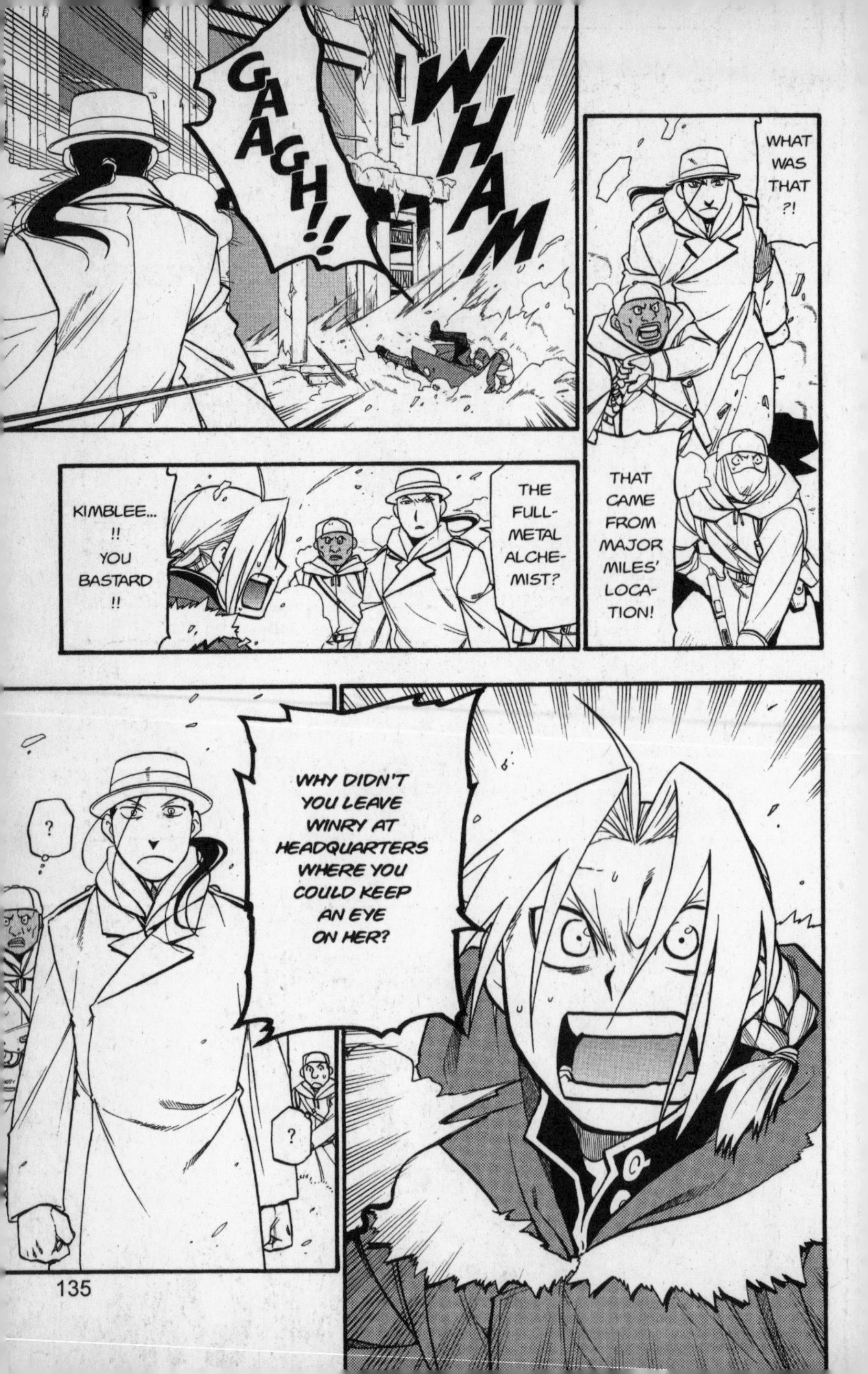
WHAM
GAGH!!
WHAT WAS THAT ?!
THAT CAME FROM MAJOR MILES' LOCATION!
THE FULL-METAL ALCHE-MIST?
KIMBLEE... !! YOU BASTARD !!
WHY DIDN'T YOU LEAVE WINRY AT HEADQUARTERS WHERE YOU COULD KEEP AN EYE ON HER?
?
?

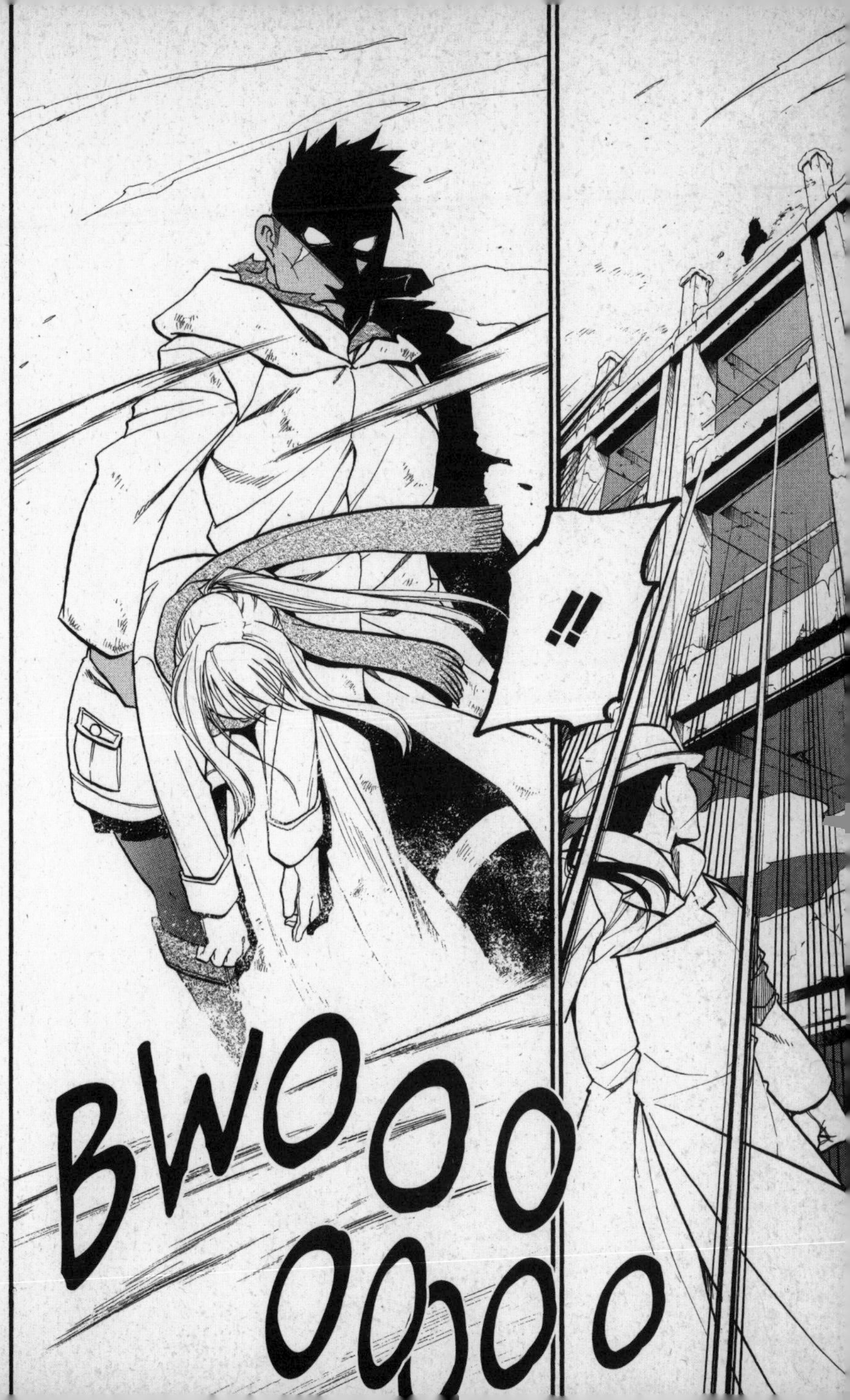
!!
BWOOOOOOOO

FULLMETAL
ALCHEMIST

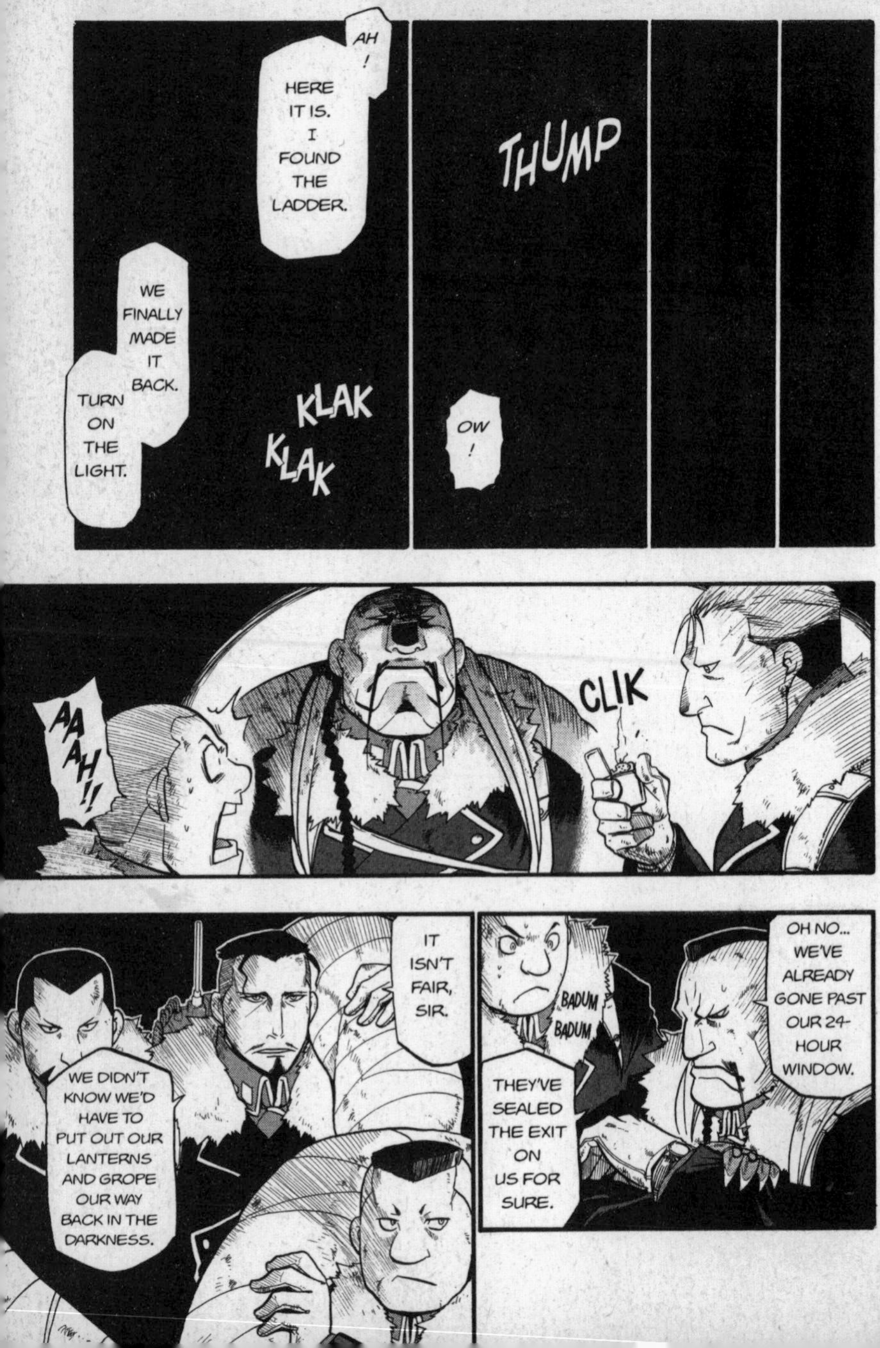
THUMP
OW!
AH!
HERE IT IS. I FOUND THE LADDER.
WE FINALLY MADE IT BACK.
KLAK KLAK
TURN ON THE LIGHT.
CLIK
AAAH!!
OH NO... WE'VE ALREADY GONE PAST OUR 24-HOUR WINDOW.
BADUM BADUM
THEY'VE SEALED THE EXIT ON US FOR SURE.
IT ISN'T FAIR, SIR.
WE DIDN'T KNOW WE'D HAVE TO PUT OUT OUR LANTERNS AND GROPE OUR WAY BACK IN THE DARKNESS.

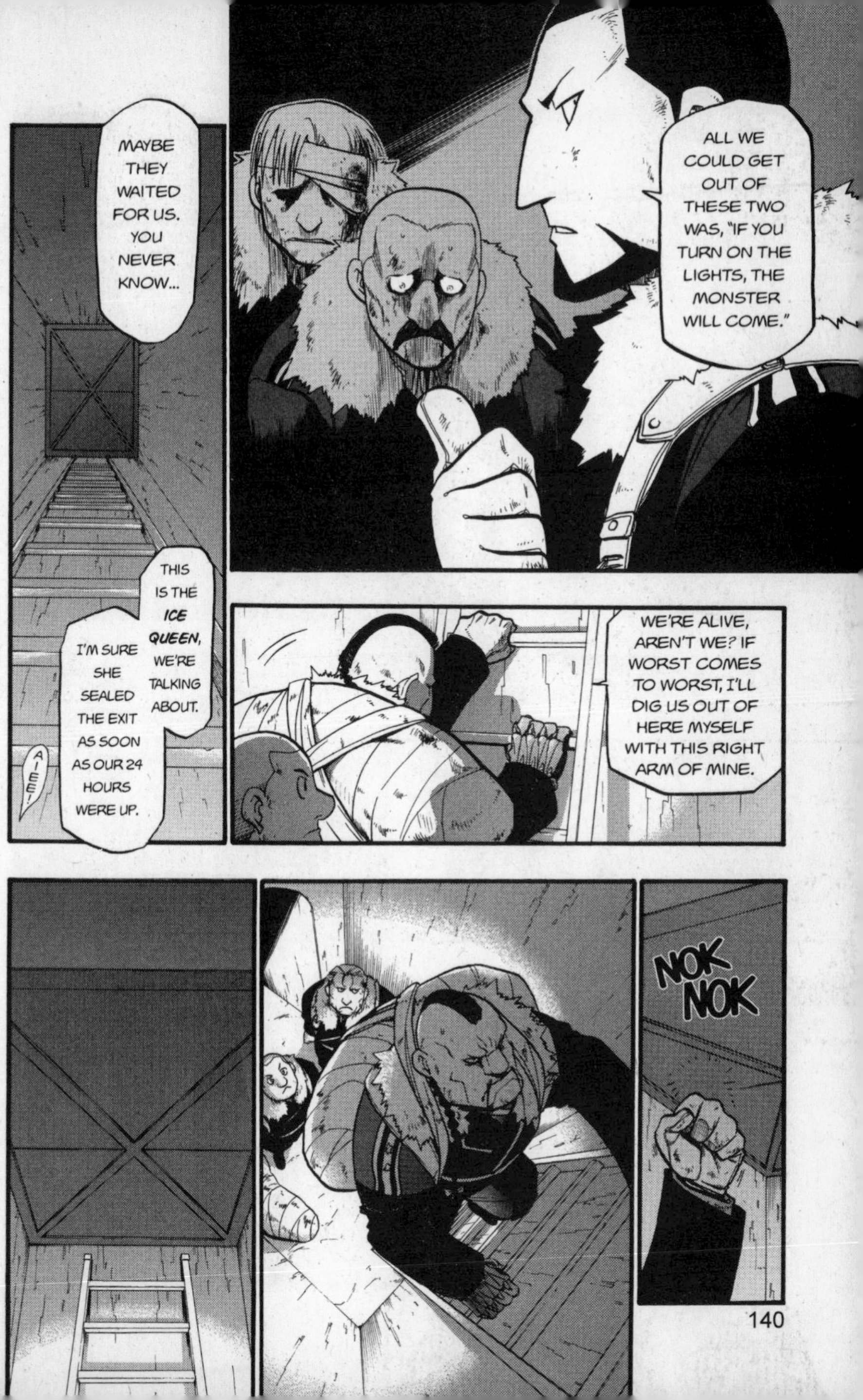
ALL WE COULD GET OUT OF THESE TWO WAS, "IF YOU TURN ON THE LIGHTS, THE MONSTER WILL COME."
WE'RE ALIVE, AREN'T WE? IF WORST COMES TO WORST, I'LL DIG US OUT OF HERE MYSELF WITH THIS RIGHT ARM OF MINE.
MAYBE THEY WAITED FOR US. YOU NEVER KNOW...
THIS IS THE ICE QUEEN, WE'RE TALKING ABOUT.
I'M SURE SHE SEALED THE EXIT AS SOON AS OUR 24 HOURS WERE UP.
AIEE!
NOK NOK

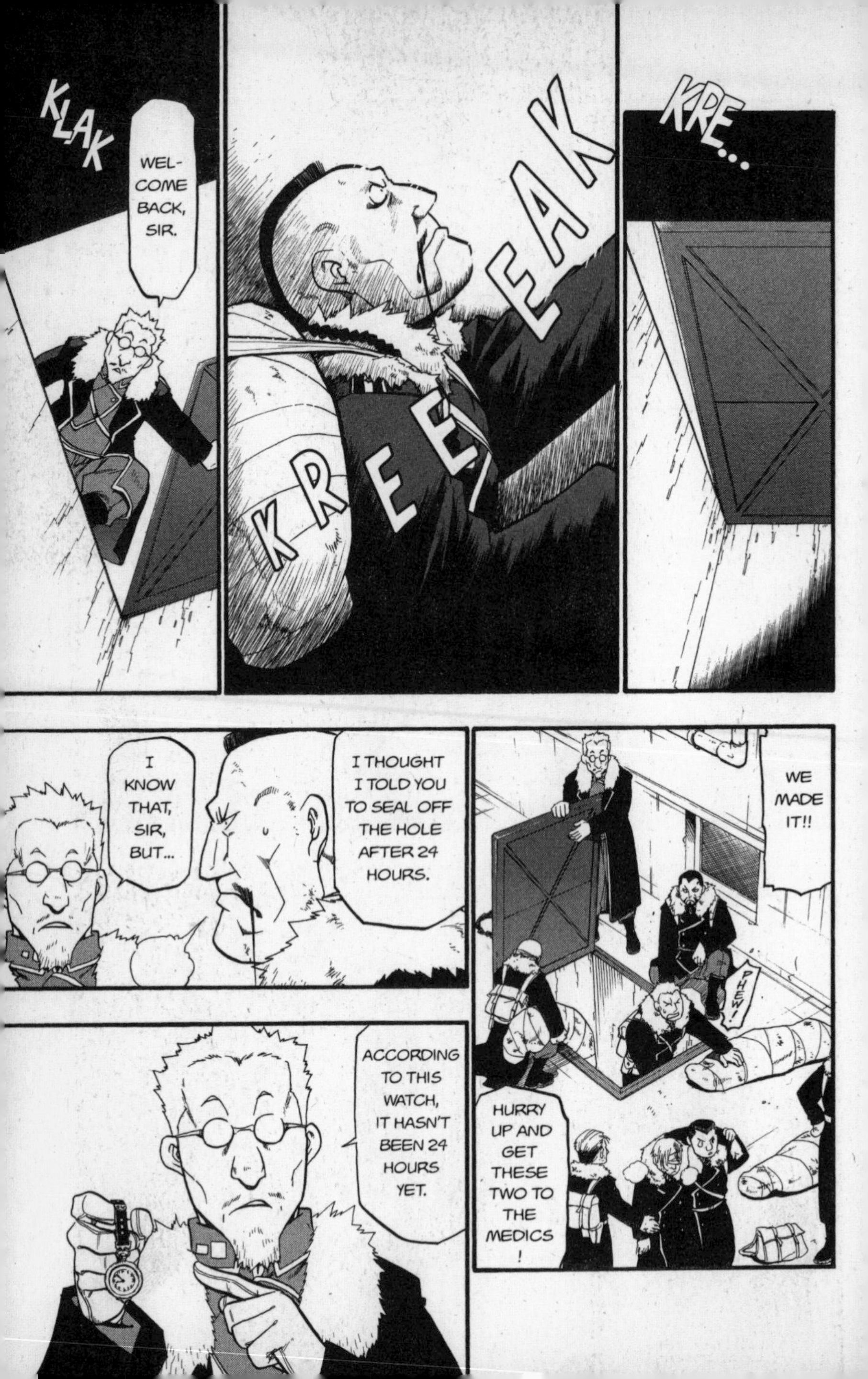
KRE...
KREEEAK
KLAK
WEL-COME BACK, SIR.
WE MADE IT!!
PHEW!
HURRY UP AND GET THESE TWO TO THE MEDICS!
I THOUGHT I TOLD YOU TO SEAL OFF THE HOLE AFTER 24 HOURS.
I KNOW THAT, SIR, BUT...
ACCORDING TO THIS WATCH, IT HASN'T BEEN 24 HOURS YET.

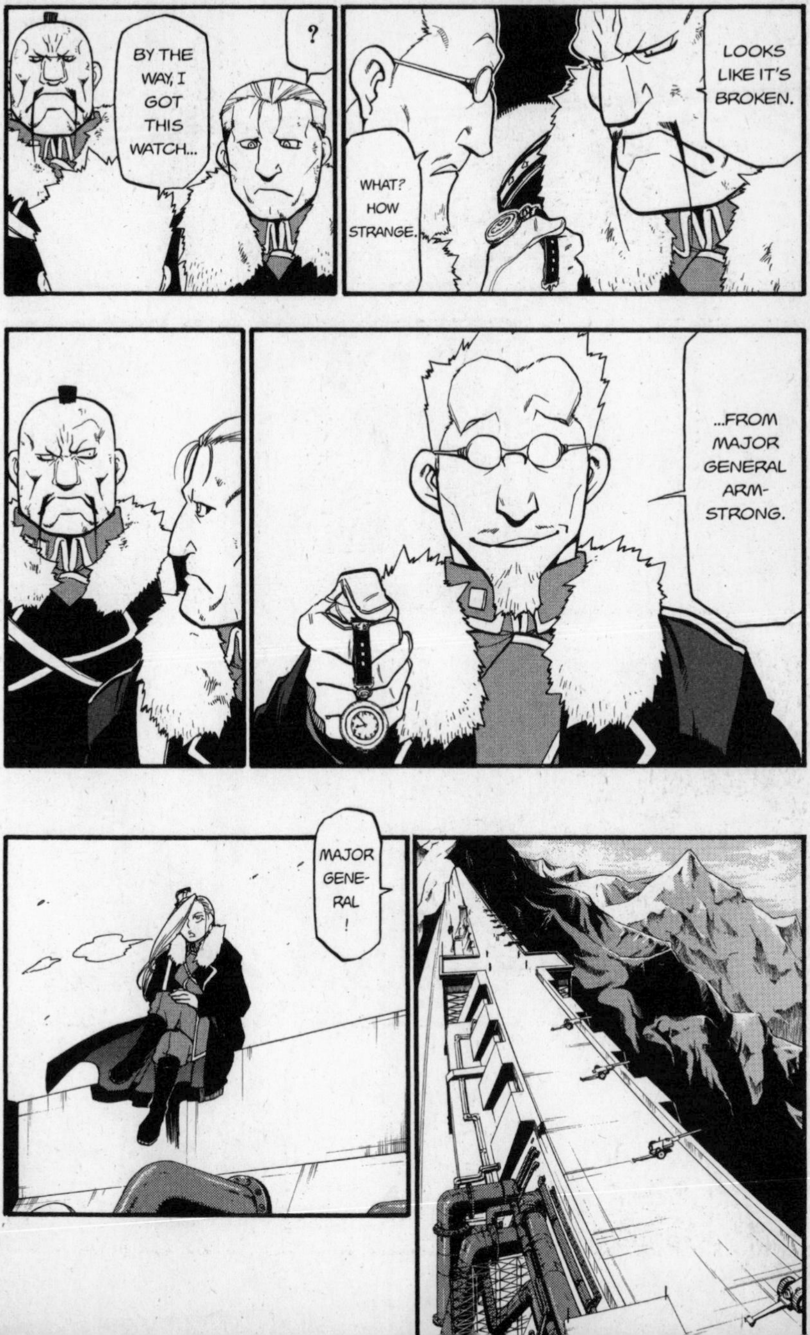
LOOKS LIKE IT'S BROKEN.
WHAT? HOW STRANGE.
?
BY THE WAY, I GOT THIS WATCH...
...FROM MAJOR GENERAL ARM-STRONG.
MAJOR GENE-RAL!

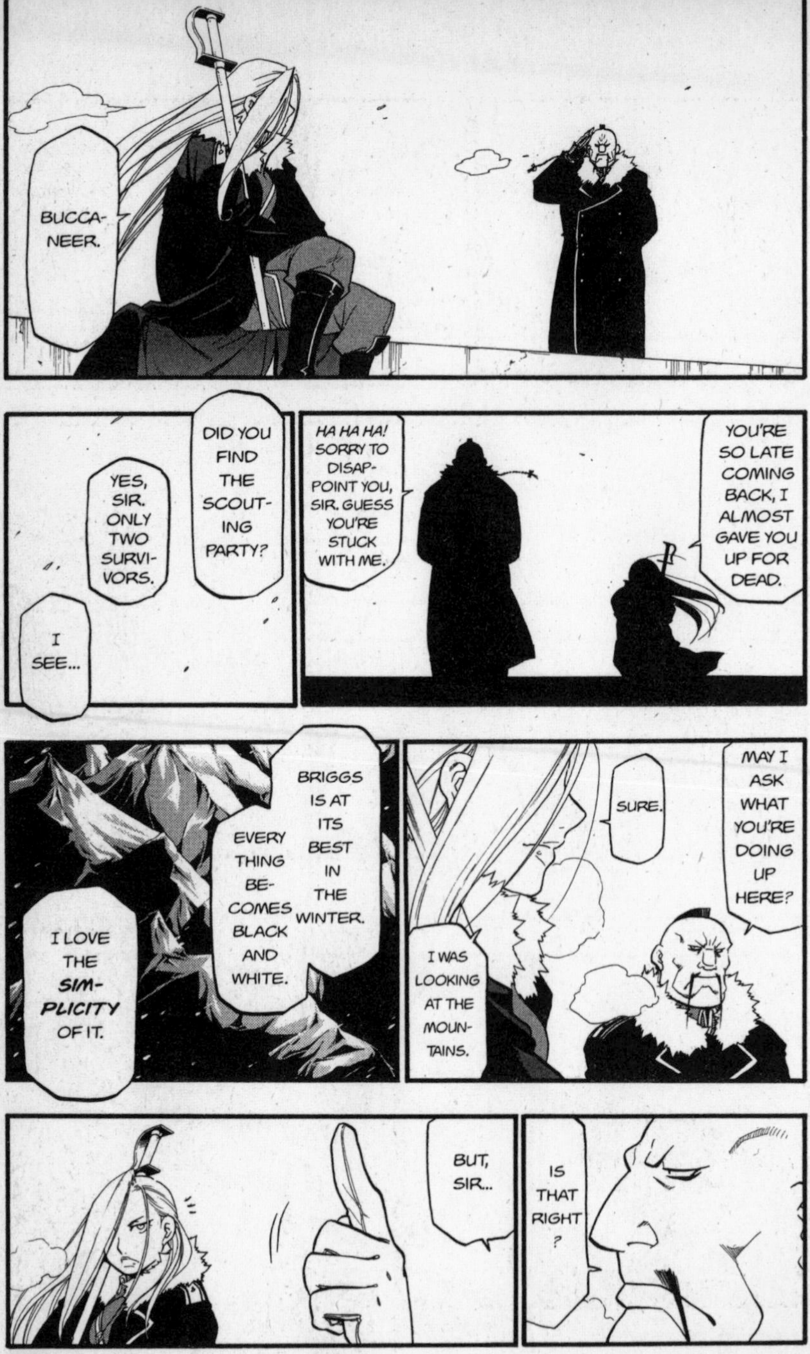
BUCCANEER.
YOU'RE SO LATE COMING BACK, I ALMOST GAVE YOU UP FOR DEAD.
HA HA HA! SORRY TO DISAPPOINT YOU, SIR. GUESS YOU'RE STUCK WITH ME.
DID YOU FIND THE SCOUTING PARTY?
YES, SIR. ONLY TWO SURVIVORS.
I SEE...
MAY I ASK WHAT YOU'RE DOING UP HERE?
SURE.
I WAS LOOKING AT THE MOUNTAINS.
BRIGGS IS AT ITS BEST IN THE WINTER.
EVERY THING BECOMES BLACK AND WHITE.
I LOVE THE ***SIMPLICITY*** OF IT.
IS THAT RIGHT?
BUT, SIR...

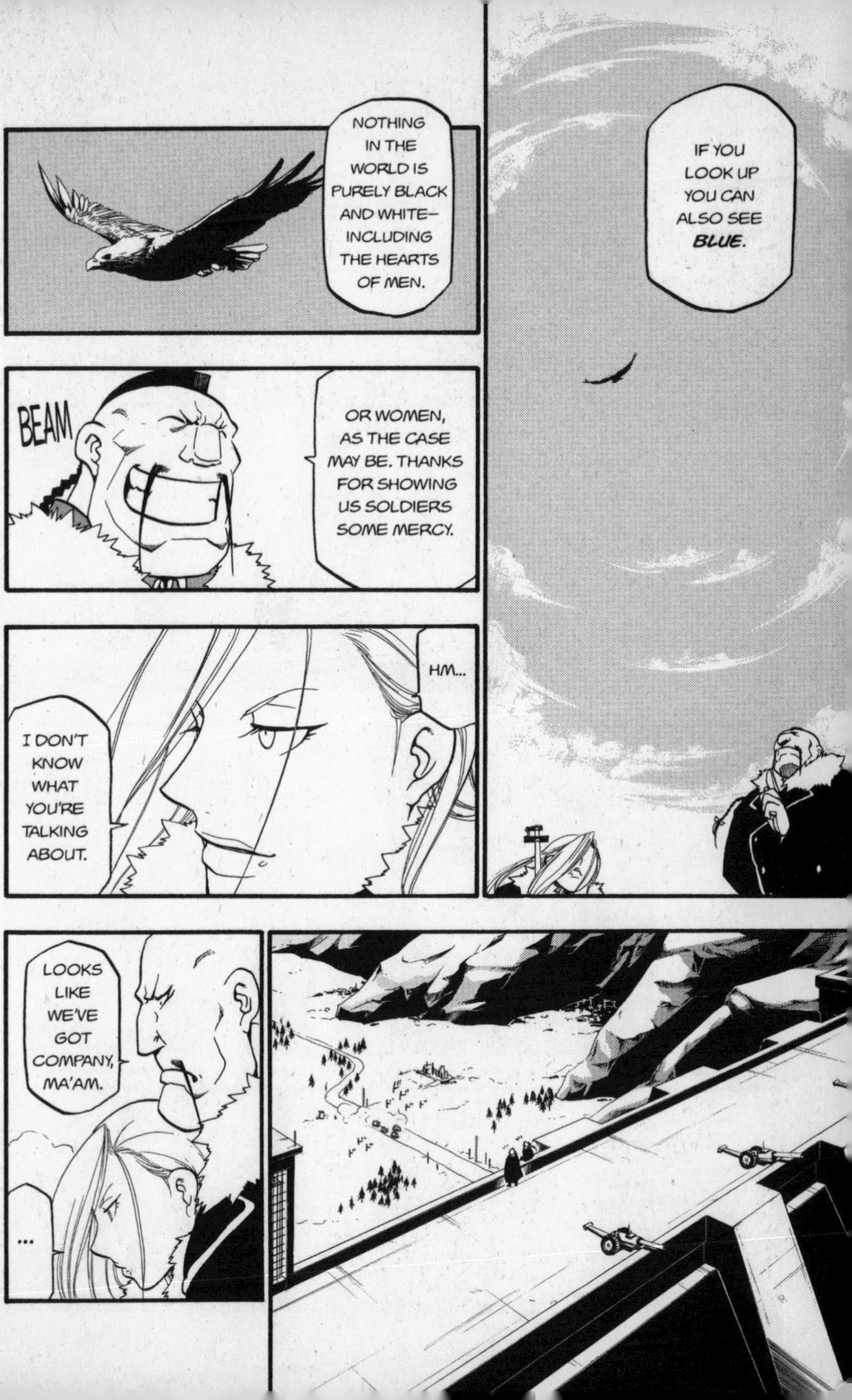
IF YOU LOOK UP YOU CAN ALSO SEE ***BLUE***.
NOTHING IN THE WORLD IS PURELY BLACK AND WHITE— INCLUDING THE HEARTS OF MEN.
OR WOMEN, AS THE CASE MAY BE. THANKS FOR SHOWING US SOLDIERS SOME MERCY.
BEAM
HM...
I DON'T KNOW WHAT YOU'RE TALKING ABOUT.
LOOKS LIKE WE'VE GOT COMPANY, MA'AM.
...

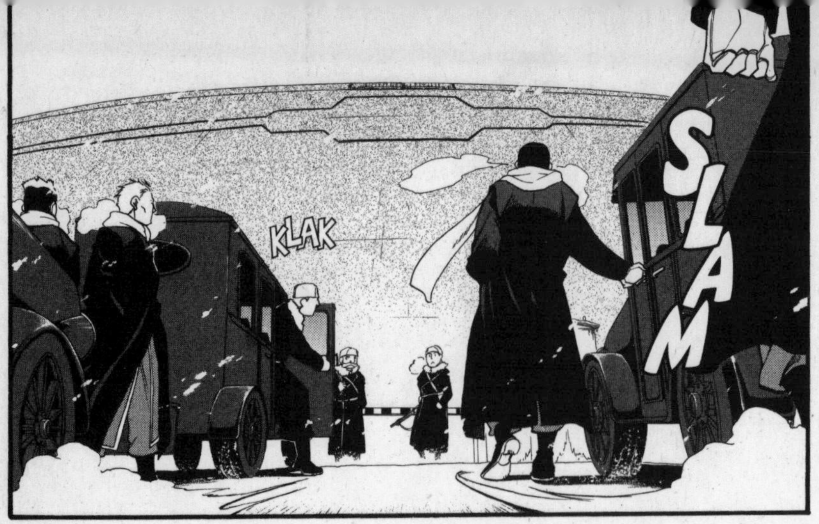
SLAM
KLAK

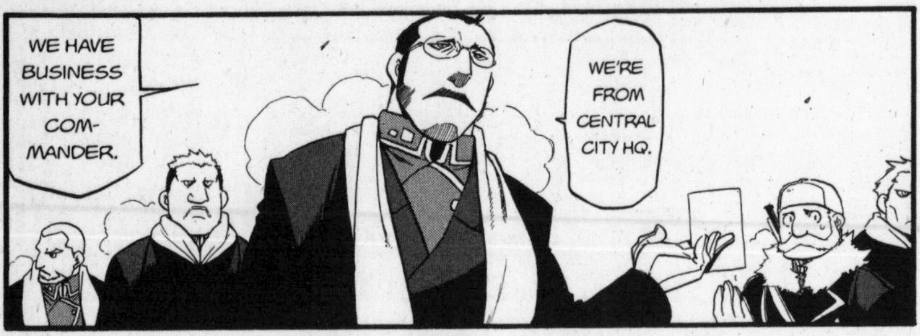
WE'RE FROM CENTRAL CITY HQ.
WE HAVE BUSINESS WITH YOUR COM-MANDER.

Chapter 73 A Daydream

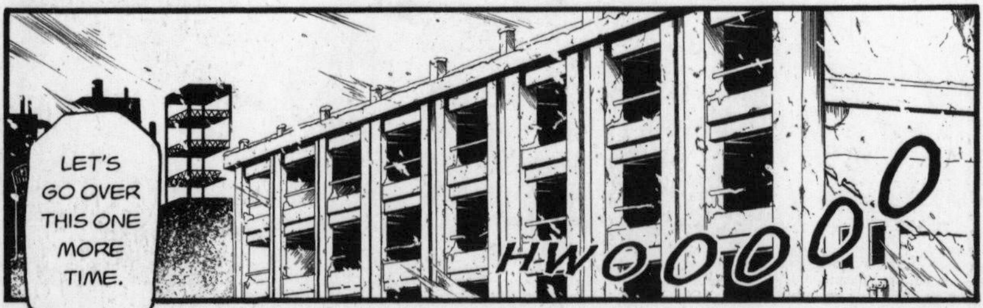
HWOOOOO
LET'S GO OVER THIS ONE MORE TIME.

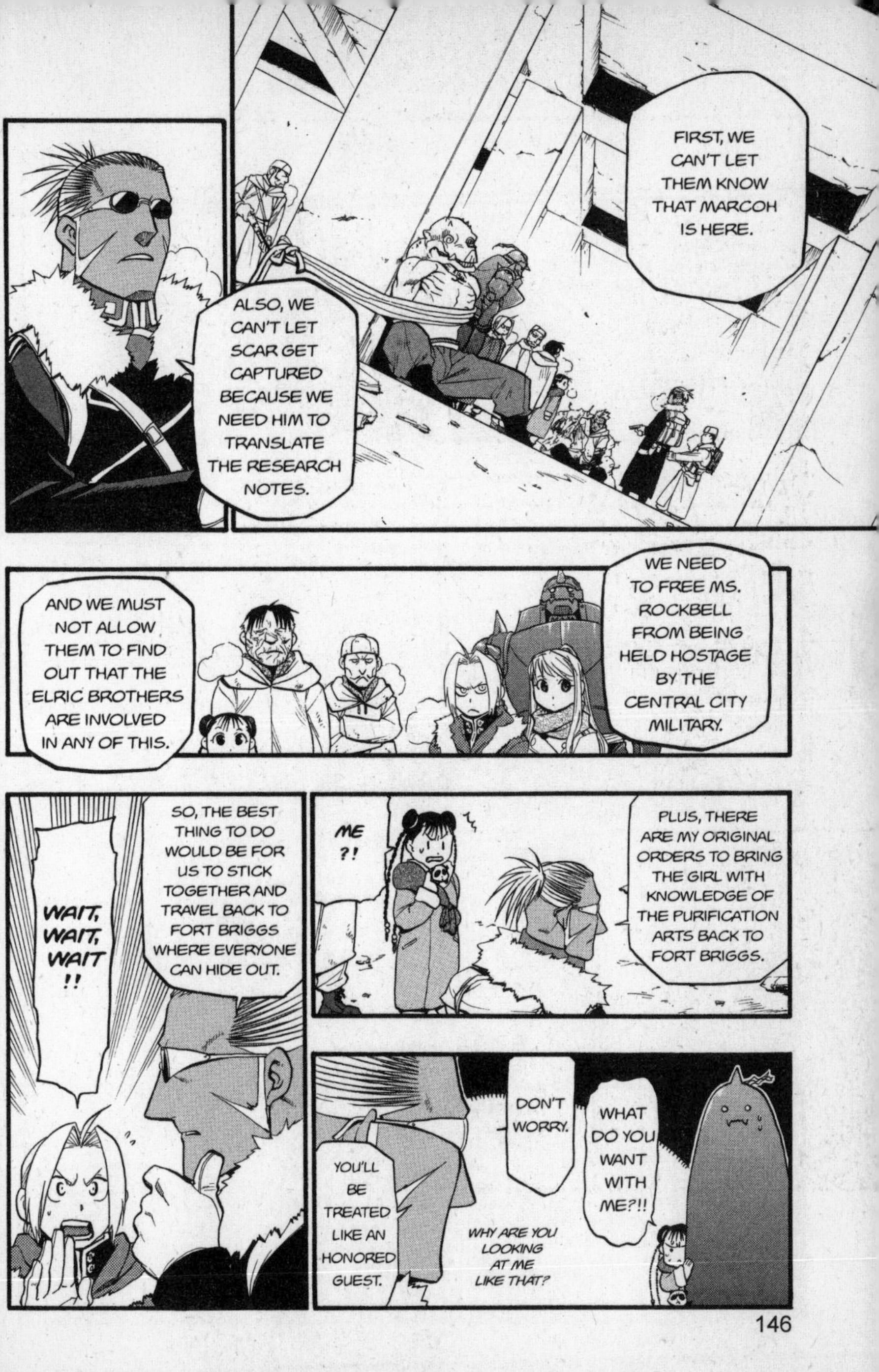
FIRST, WE CAN'T LET THEM KNOW THAT MARCOH IS HERE.
ALSO, WE CAN'T LET SCAR GET CAPTURED BECAUSE WE NEED HIM TO TRANSLATE THE RESEARCH NOTES.
WE NEED TO FREE MS. ROCKBELL FROM BEING HELD HOSTAGE BY THE CENTRAL CITY MILITARY.
AND WE MUST NOT ALLOW THEM TO FIND OUT THAT THE ELRIC BROTHERS ARE INVOLVED IN ANY OF THIS.
PLUS, THERE ARE MY ORIGINAL ORDERS TO BRING THE GIRL WITH KNOWLEDGE OF THE PURIFICATION ARTS BACK TO FORT BRIGGS.
ME?!
WHAT DO YOU WANT WITH ME?!!
DON'T WORRY.
YOU'LL BE TREATED LIKE AN HONORED GUEST.
WHY ARE YOU LOOKING AT ME LIKE THAT?
SO, THE BEST THING TO DO WOULD BE FOR US TO STICK TOGETHER AND TRAVEL BACK TO FORT BRIGGS WHERE EVERYONE CAN HIDE OUT.
WAIT, WAIT, WAIT!!

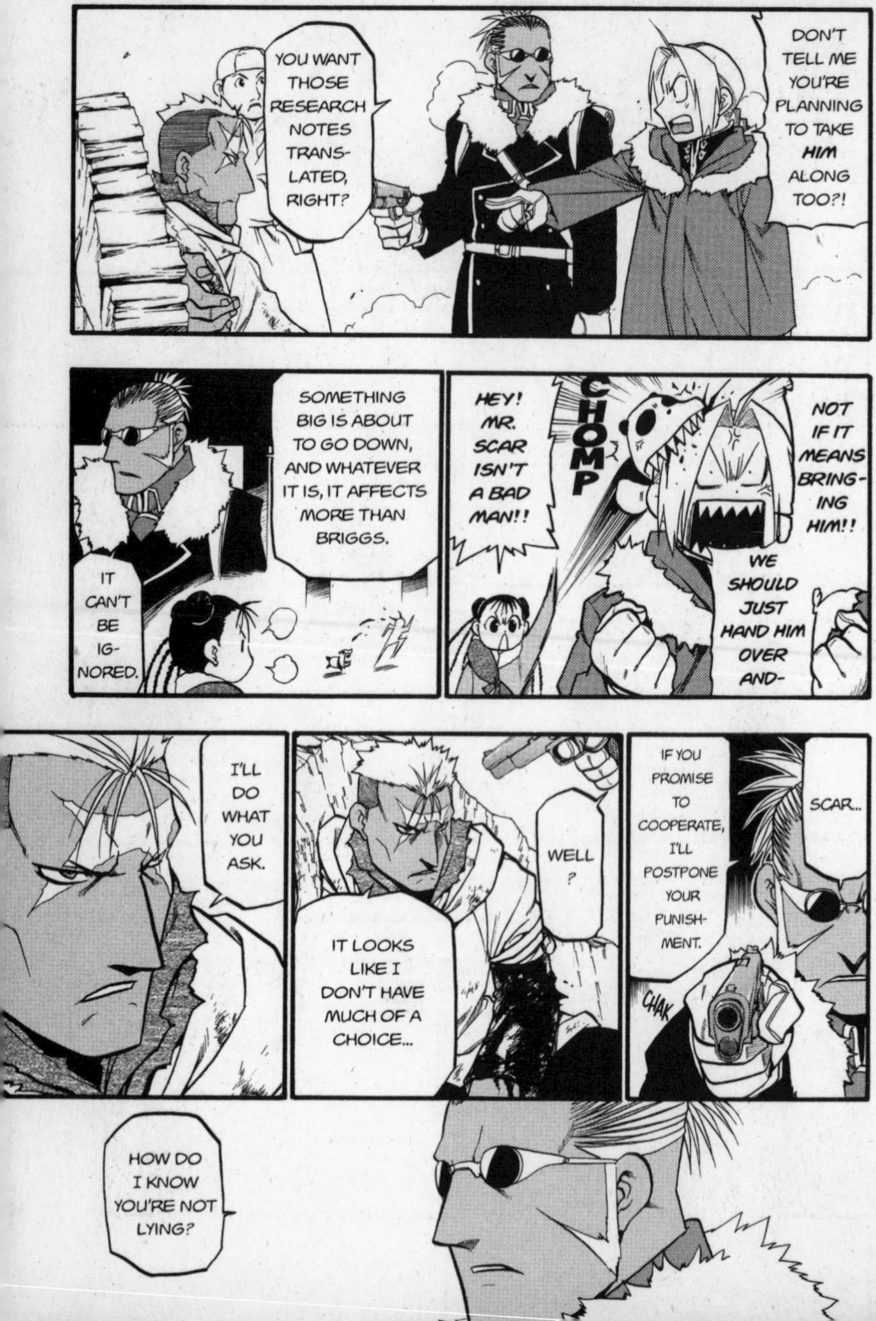
DON'T TELL ME YOU'RE PLANNING TO TAKE HIM ALONG TOO?!
YOU WANT THOSE RESEARCH NOTES TRANSLATED, RIGHT?
NOT IF IT MEANS BRINGING HIM!!
WE SHOULD JUST HAND HIM OVER AND-
CHOMP
HEY! MR. SCAR ISN'T A BAD MAN!!
SOMETHING BIG IS ABOUT TO GO DOWN, AND WHATEVER IT IS, IT AFFECTS MORE THAN BRIGGS.
IT CAN'T BE IGNORED.
SCAR...
IF YOU PROMISE TO COOPERATE, I'LL POSTPONE YOUR PUNISHMENT.
CHAK
WELL?
IT LOOKS LIKE I DON'T HAVE MUCH OF A CHOICE...
I'LL DO WHAT YOU ASK.
HOW DO I KNOW YOU'RE NOT LYING?

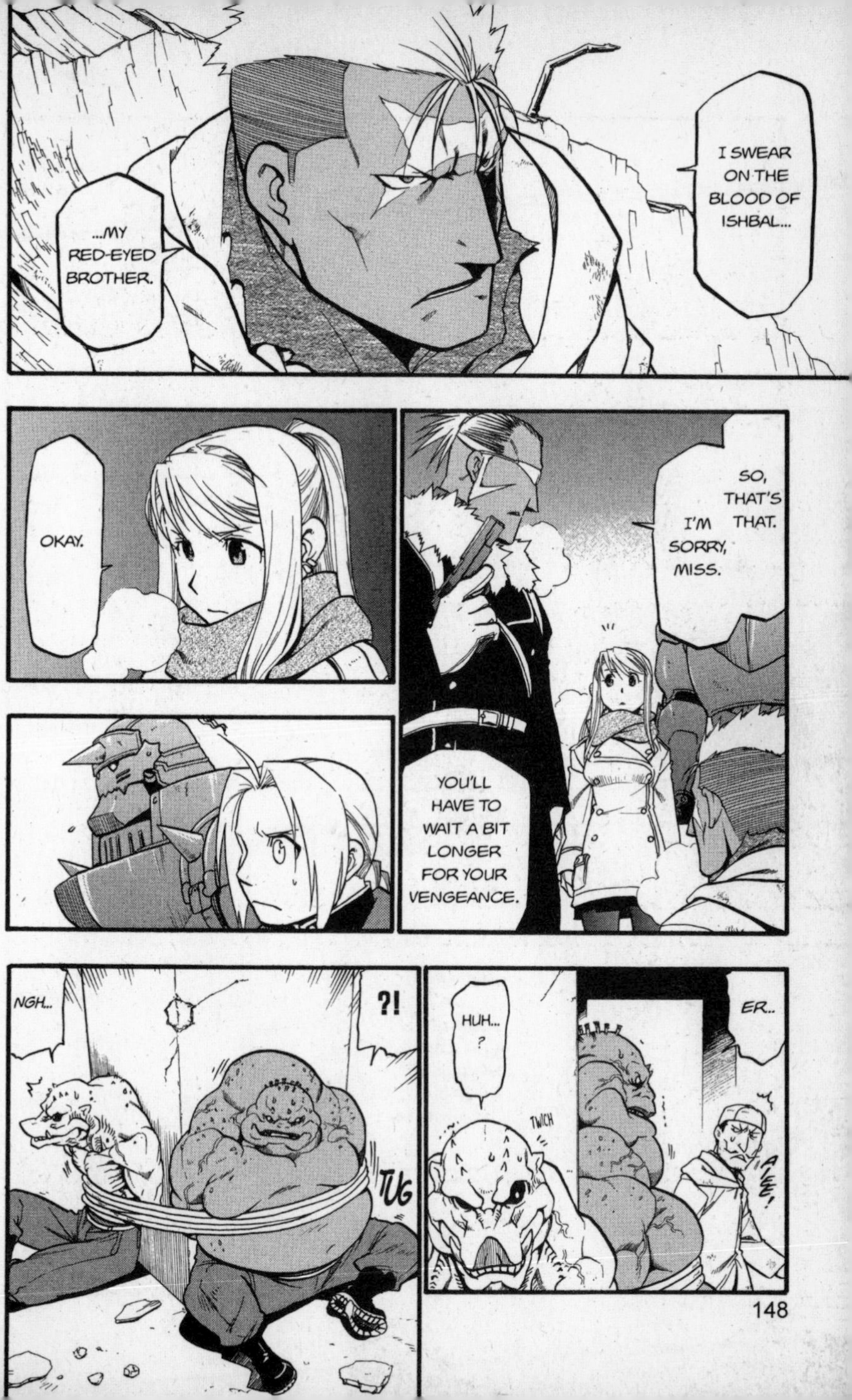
I SWEAR ON THE BLOOD OF ISHBAL...
...MY RED-EYED BROTHER.
SO, THAT'S THAT.
I'M SORRY, MISS.
YOU'LL HAVE TO WAIT A BIT LONGER FOR YOUR VENGEANCE.
OKAY.
ER..
HUH... ?
TWICH
?!
TUG
NGH..

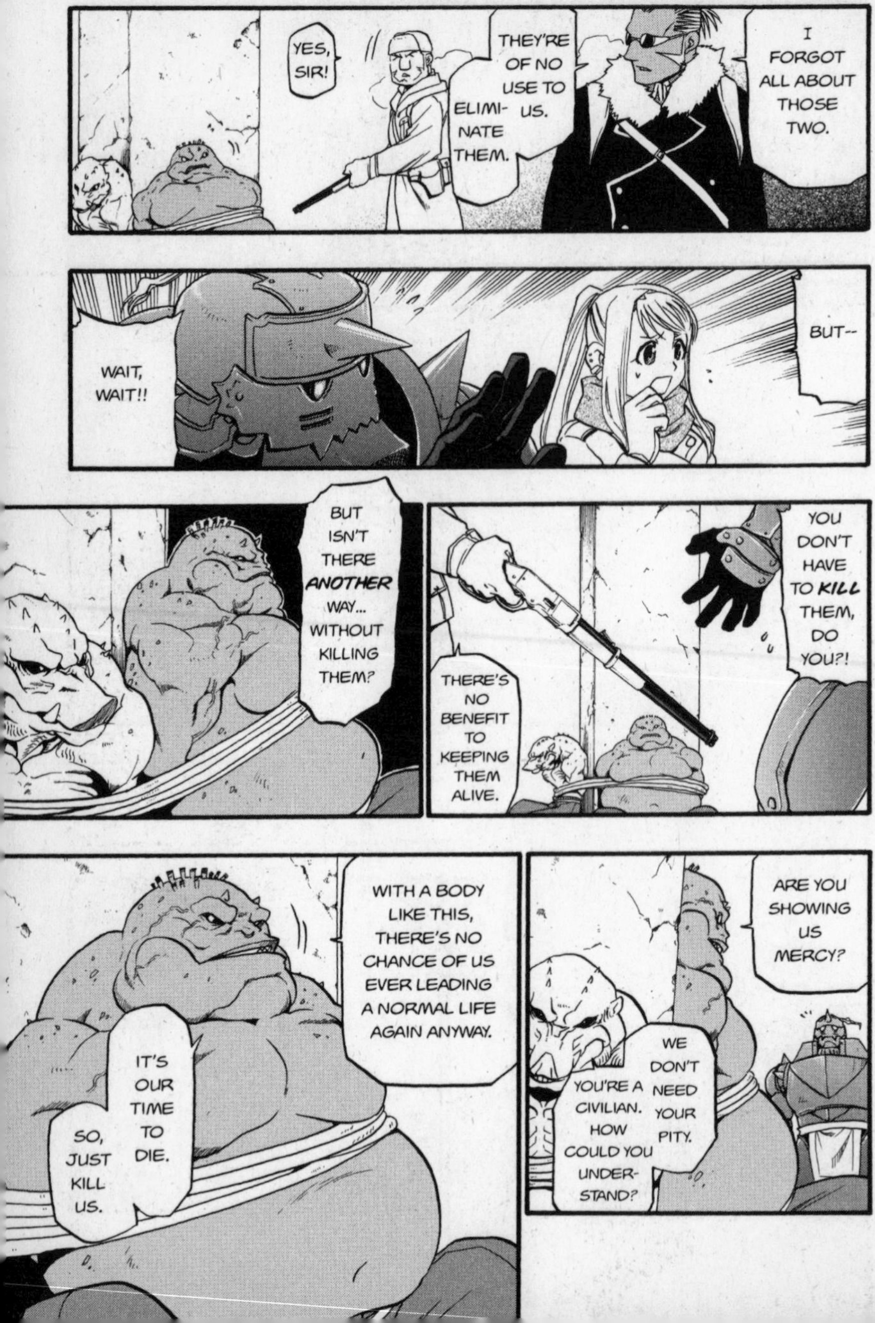
I FORGOT ALL ABOUT THOSE TWO.
THEY'RE OF NO USE TO US. ELIMINATE THEM.
YES, SIR!
BUT--
WAIT, WAIT!!
YOU DON'T HAVE TO KILL THEM, DO YOU?!
THERE'S NO BENEFIT TO KEEPING THEM ALIVE.
BUT ISN'T THERE ANOTHER WAY... WITHOUT KILLING THEM?
ARE YOU SHOWING US MERCY?
WE DON'T NEED YOUR PITY.
YOU'RE A CIVILIAN. HOW COULD YOU UNDERSTAND?
WITH A BODY LIKE THIS, THERE'S NO CHANCE OF US EVER LEADING A NORMAL LIFE AGAIN ANYWAY.
IT'S OUR TIME TO DIE.
SO, JUST KILL US.

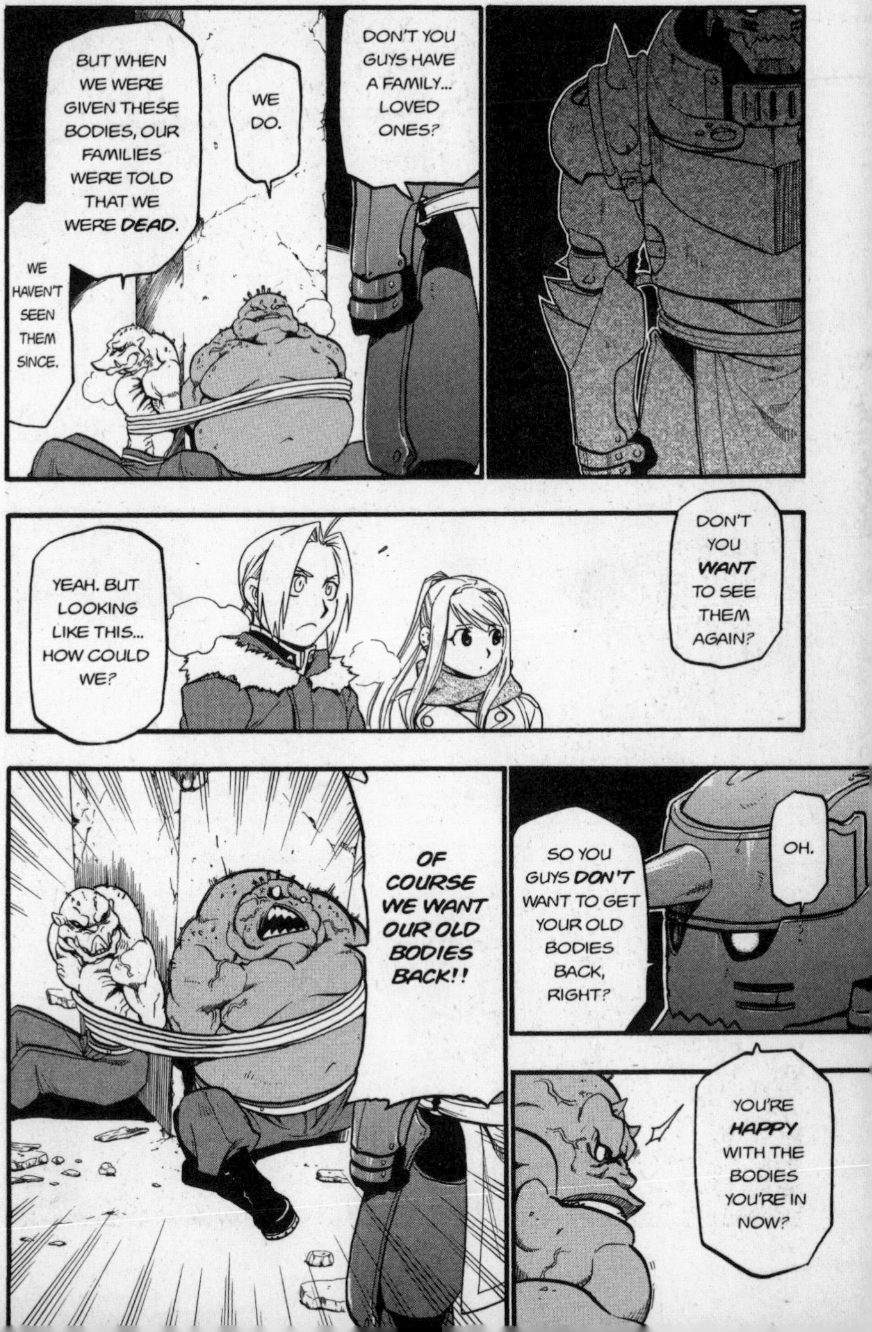

DON'T YOU GUYS HAVE A FAMILY... LOVED ONES?
WE DO.
BUT WHEN WE WERE GIVEN THESE BODIES, OUR FAMILIES WERE TOLD THAT WE WERE **DEAD**.
WE HAVEN'T SEEN THEM SINCE.
DON'T YOU **WANT** TO SEE THEM AGAIN?
YEAH. BUT LOOKING LIKE THIS... HOW COULD WE?
OH.
SO YOU GUYS **DON'T** WANT TO GET YOUR OLD BODIES BACK, RIGHT?
YOU'RE **HAPPY** WITH THE BODIES YOU'RE IN NOW?
OF COURSE WE WANT OUR OLD BODIES BACK!!

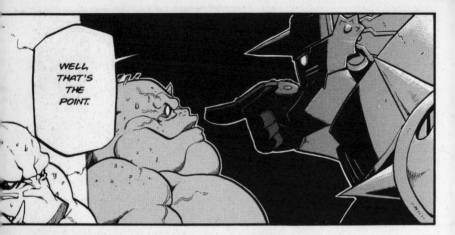

WELL, THAT'S THE POINT.
SO DON'T SAY IT'S HOPELESS AND JUST GIVE UP!
STOP BEING SO PESSIMISTIC!!
YOU HAVEN'T EVEN CONSIDERED THE POSSIBILITY THAT YOU MIGHT BE ABLE TO GET YOUR ORIGINAL BODIES BACK!!
HOW COULD YOU POSSIBLY UNDERSTAND...
...WHAT IT'S LIKE FOR US...?
I KNOW ALL ABOUT IT...
BECAUSE THIS IS MY BODY.

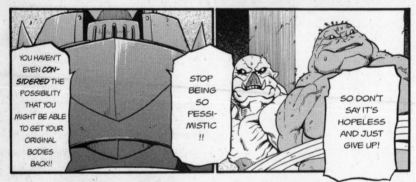

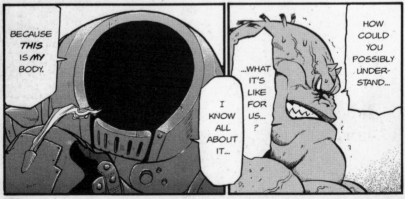

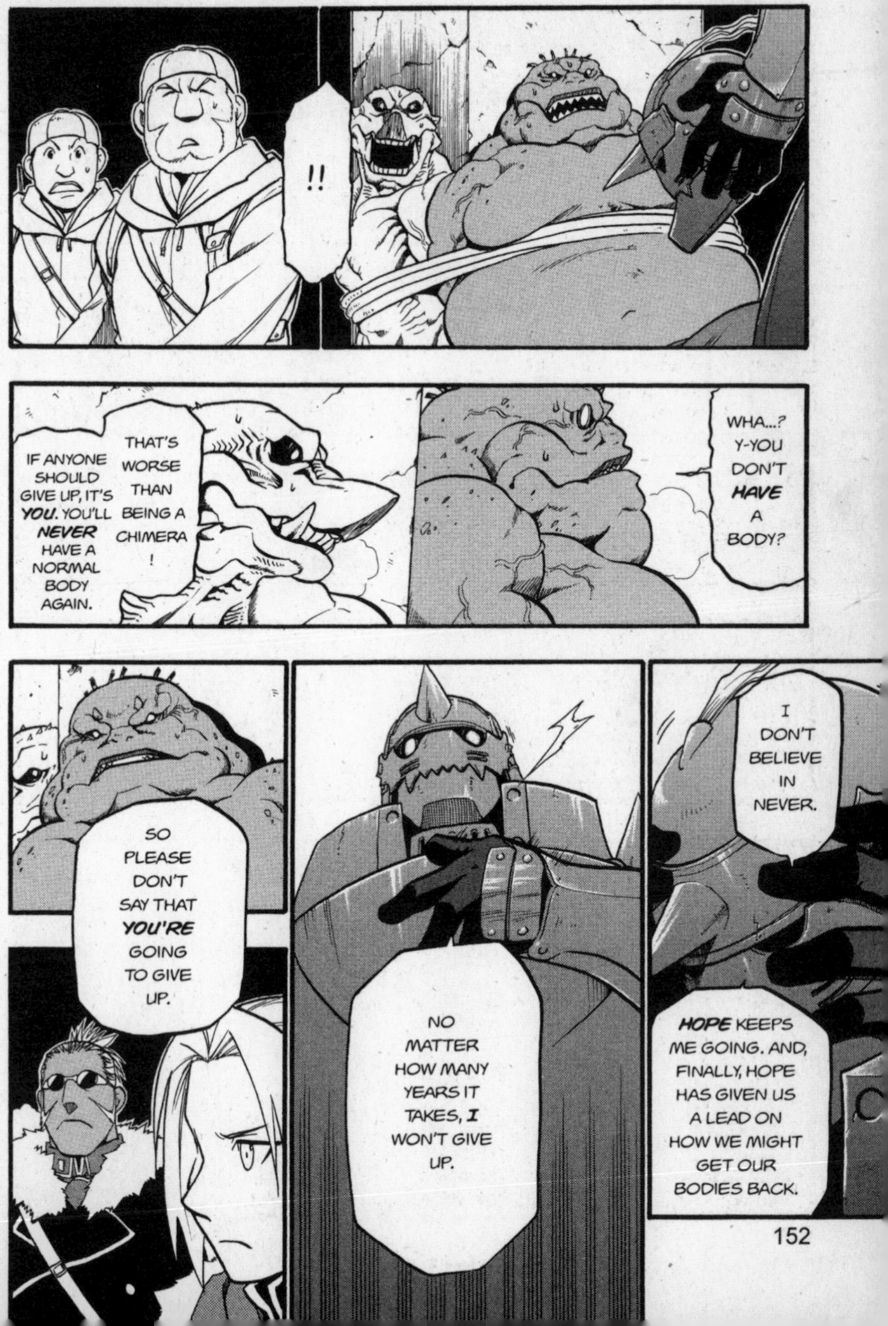
!!
WHA...? Y-YOU DON'T HAVE A BODY?
THAT'S WORSE THAN BEING A CHIMERA!
IF ANYONE SHOULD GIVE UP, IT'S YOU. YOU'LL NEVER HAVE A NORMAL BODY AGAIN.
I DON'T BELIEVE IN NEVER.
HOPE KEEPS ME GOING. AND, FINALLY, HOPE HAS GIVEN US A LEAD ON HOW WE MIGHT GET OUR BODIES BACK.
NO MATTER HOW MANY YEARS IT TAKES, I WON'T GIVE UP.
SO PLEASE DON'T SAY THAT YOU'RE GOING TO GIVE UP.

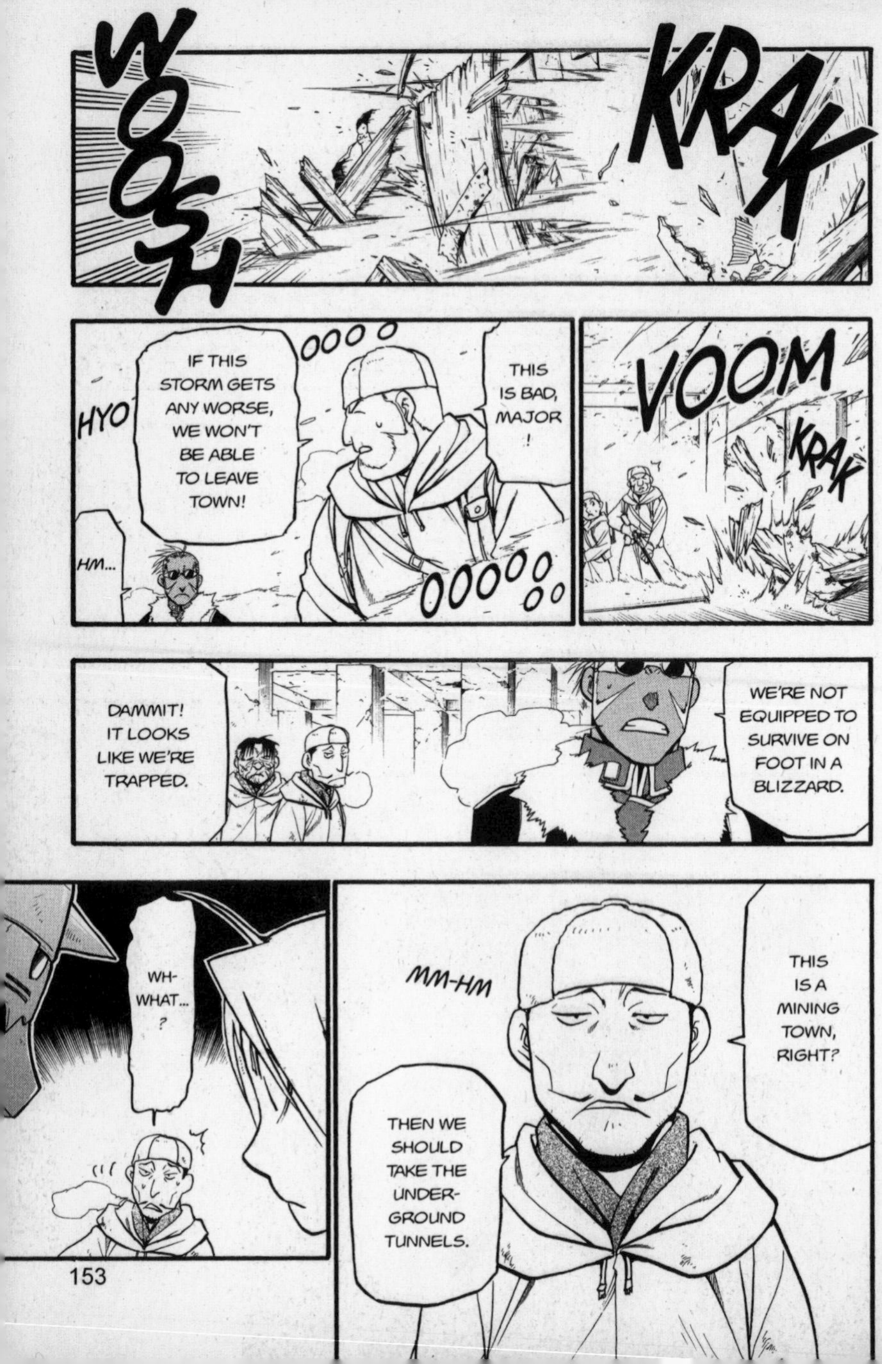

KRAK
WOOSH
VOOM
KRAK
THIS IS BAD, MAJOR!
OOOO
IF THIS STORM GETS ANY WORSE, WE WON'T BE ABLE TO LEAVE TOWN!
HYO
HM...
OOOOOOO
WE'RE NOT EQUIPPED TO SURVIVE ON FOOT IN A BLIZZARD.
DAMMIT! IT LOOKS LIKE WE'RE TRAPPED.
THIS IS A MINING TOWN, RIGHT?
MM-HM
THEN WE SHOULD TAKE THE UNDER-GROUND TUNNELS.
WH-WHAT... ?

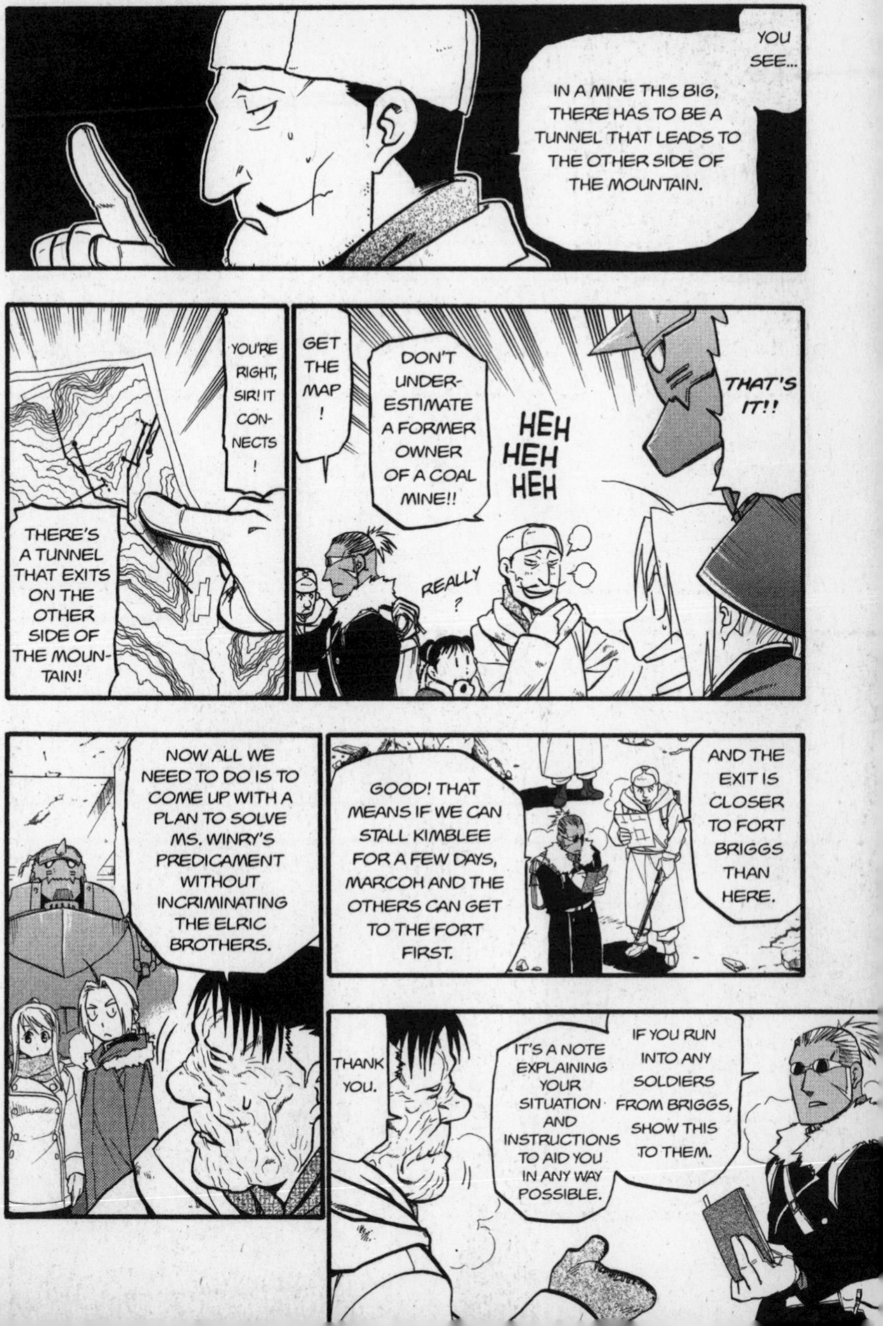
YOU SEE...
IN A MINE THIS BIG, THERE HAS TO BE A TUNNEL THAT LEADS TO THE OTHER SIDE OF THE MOUNTAIN.
THAT'S IT!!
DON'T UNDER-ESTIMATE A FORMER OWNER OF A COAL MINE!!
HEH HEH HEH
GET THE MAP!
REALLY?
YOU'RE RIGHT, SIR! IT CON-NECTS!
THERE'S A TUNNEL THAT EXITS ON THE OTHER SIDE OF THE MOUN-TAIN!
AND THE EXIT IS CLOSER TO FORT BRIGGS THAN HERE.
GOOD! THAT MEANS IF WE CAN STALL KIMBLEE FOR A FEW DAYS, MARCOH AND THE OTHERS CAN GET TO THE FORT FIRST.
IF YOU RUN INTO ANY SOLDIERS FROM BRIGGS, SHOW THIS TO THEM.
IT'S A NOTE EXPLAINING YOUR SITUATION AND INSTRUCTIONS TO AID YOU IN ANY WAY POSSIBLE.
THANK YOU.
NOW ALL WE NEED TO DO IS TO COME UP WITH A PLAN TO SOLVE MS. WINRY'S PREDICAMENT WITHOUT INCRIMINATING THE ELRIC BROTHERS.

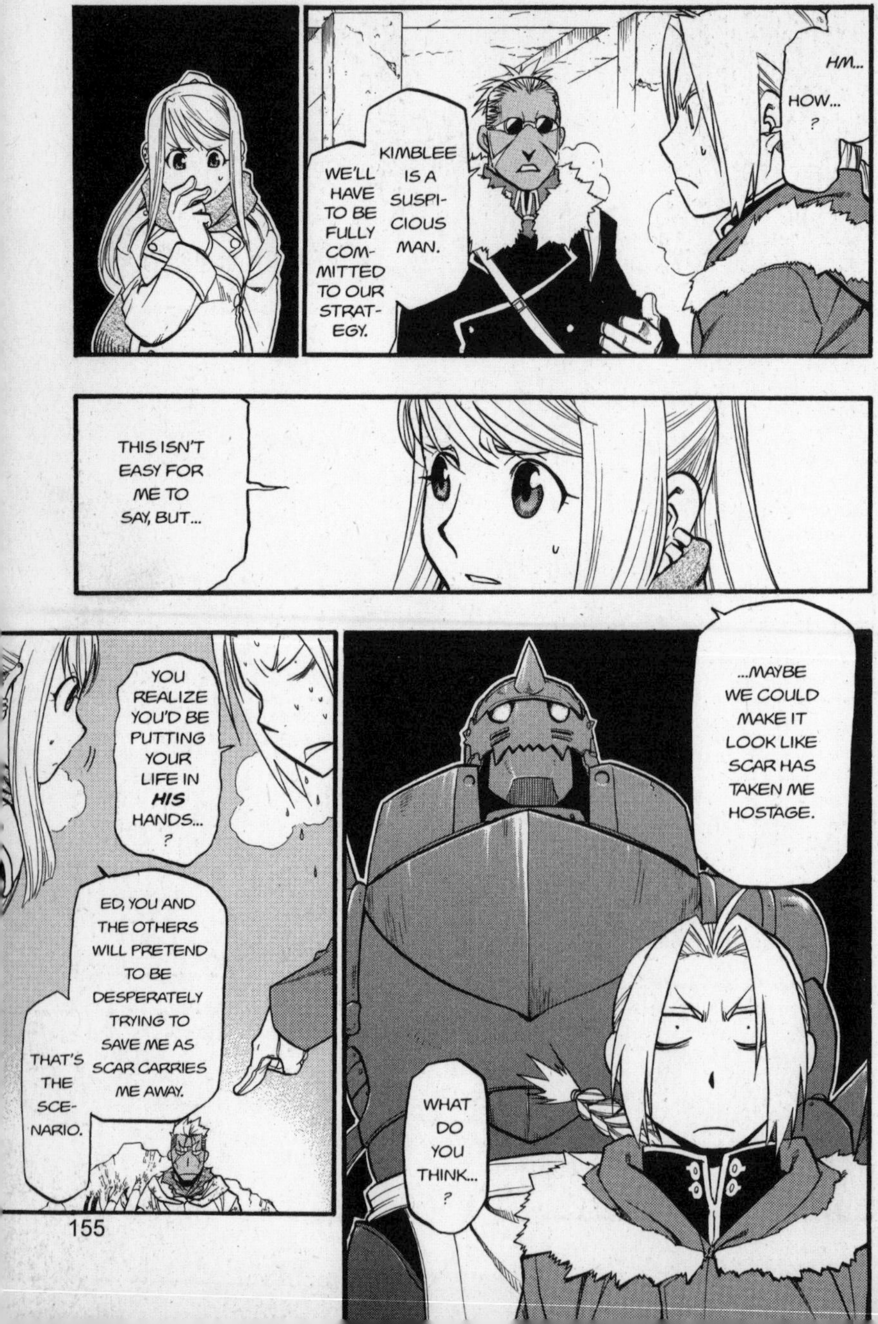
HM... HOW...?
KIMBLEE IS A SUSPICIOUS MAN.
WE'LL HAVE TO BE FULLY COMMITTED TO OUR STRATEGY.
THIS ISN'T EASY FOR ME TO SAY, BUT...
...MAYBE WE COULD MAKE IT LOOK LIKE SCAR HAS TAKEN ME HOSTAGE.
WHAT DO YOU THINK...?
YOU REALIZE YOU'D BE PUTTING YOUR LIFE IN ***HIS*** HANDS...?
ED, YOU AND THE OTHERS WILL PRETEND TO BE DESPERATELY TRYING TO SAVE ME AS SCAR CARRIES ME AWAY.
THAT'S THE SCENARIO.

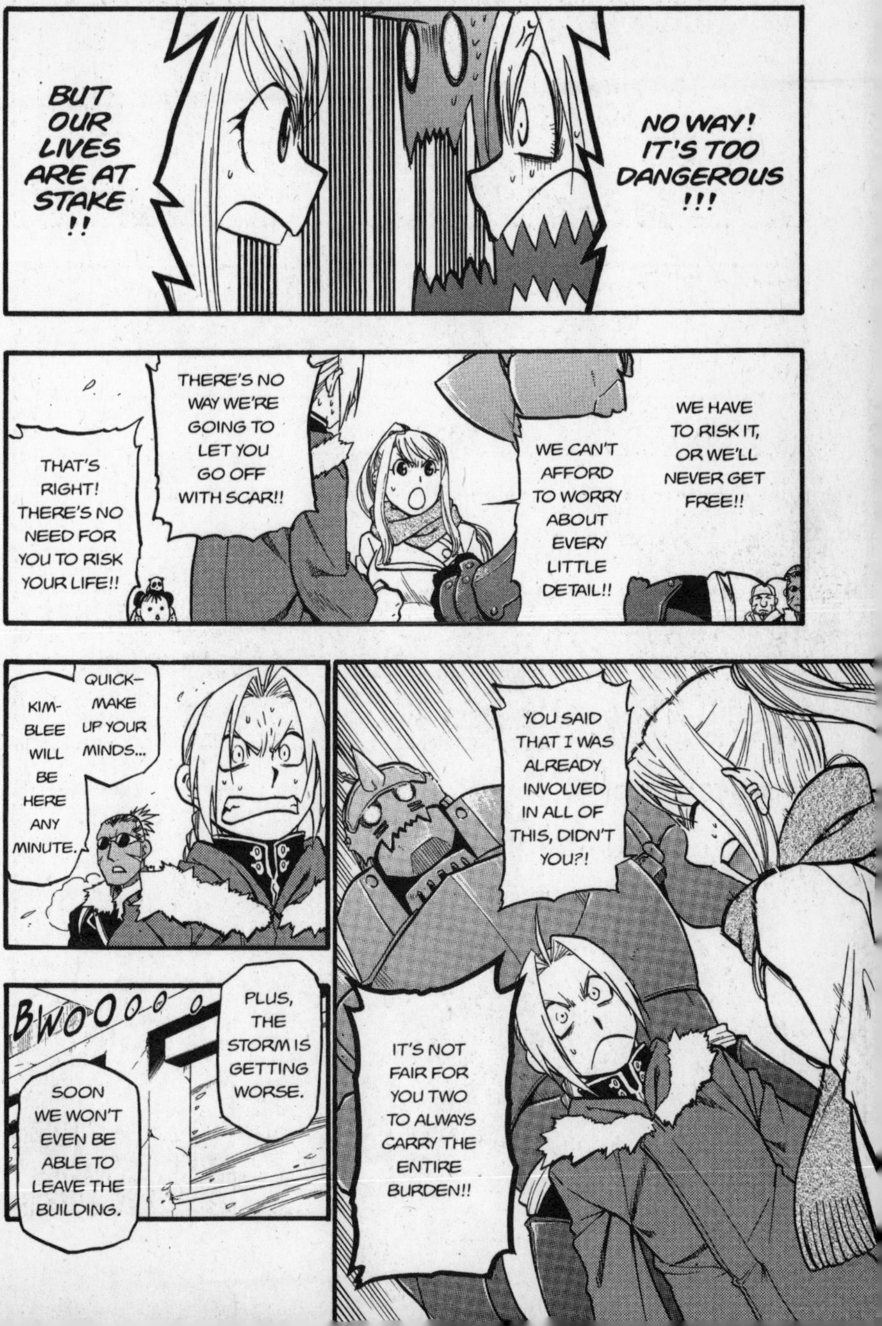
NO WAY! IT'S TOO DANGEROUS!!!
BUT OUR LIVES ARE AT STAKE!!
WE HAVE TO RISK IT, OR WE'LL NEVER GET FREE!!
WE CAN'T AFFORD TO WORRY ABOUT EVERY LITTLE DETAIL!!
THERE'S NO WAY WE'RE GOING TO LET YOU GO OFF WITH SCAR!!
THAT'S RIGHT! THERE'S NO NEED FOR YOU TO RISK YOUR LIFE!!
YOU SAID THAT I WAS ALREADY INVOLVED IN ALL OF THIS, DIDN'T YOU?!
IT'S NOT FAIR FOR YOU TWO TO ALWAYS CARRY THE ENTIRE BURDEN!!
QUICK—MAKE UP YOUR MINDS...
KIMBLEE WILL BE HERE ANY MINUTE.
BWOOOOO
PLUS, THE STORM IS GETTING WORSE.
SOON WE WON'T EVEN BE ABLE TO LEAVE THE BUILDING.

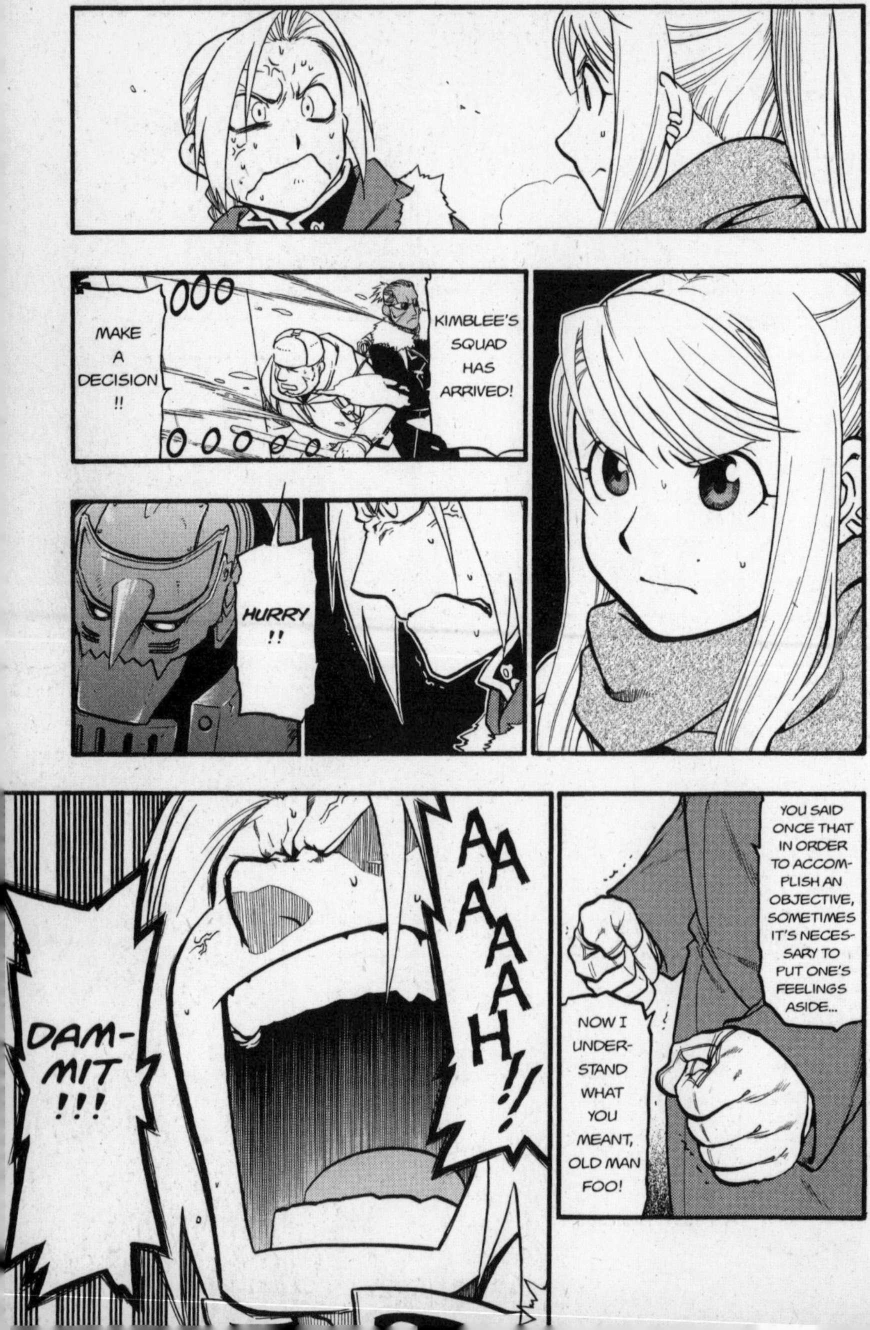
KIMBLEE'S SQUAD HAS ARRIVED!
MAKE A DECISION!!
HURRY!!
YOU SAID ONCE THAT IN ORDER TO ACCOMPLISH AN OBJECTIVE, SOMETIMES IT'S NECESSARY TO PUT ONE'S FEELINGS ASIDE...
NOW I UNDERSTAND WHAT YOU MEANT, OLD MAN FOO!
AAAAAH!!
DAM-MIT!!!

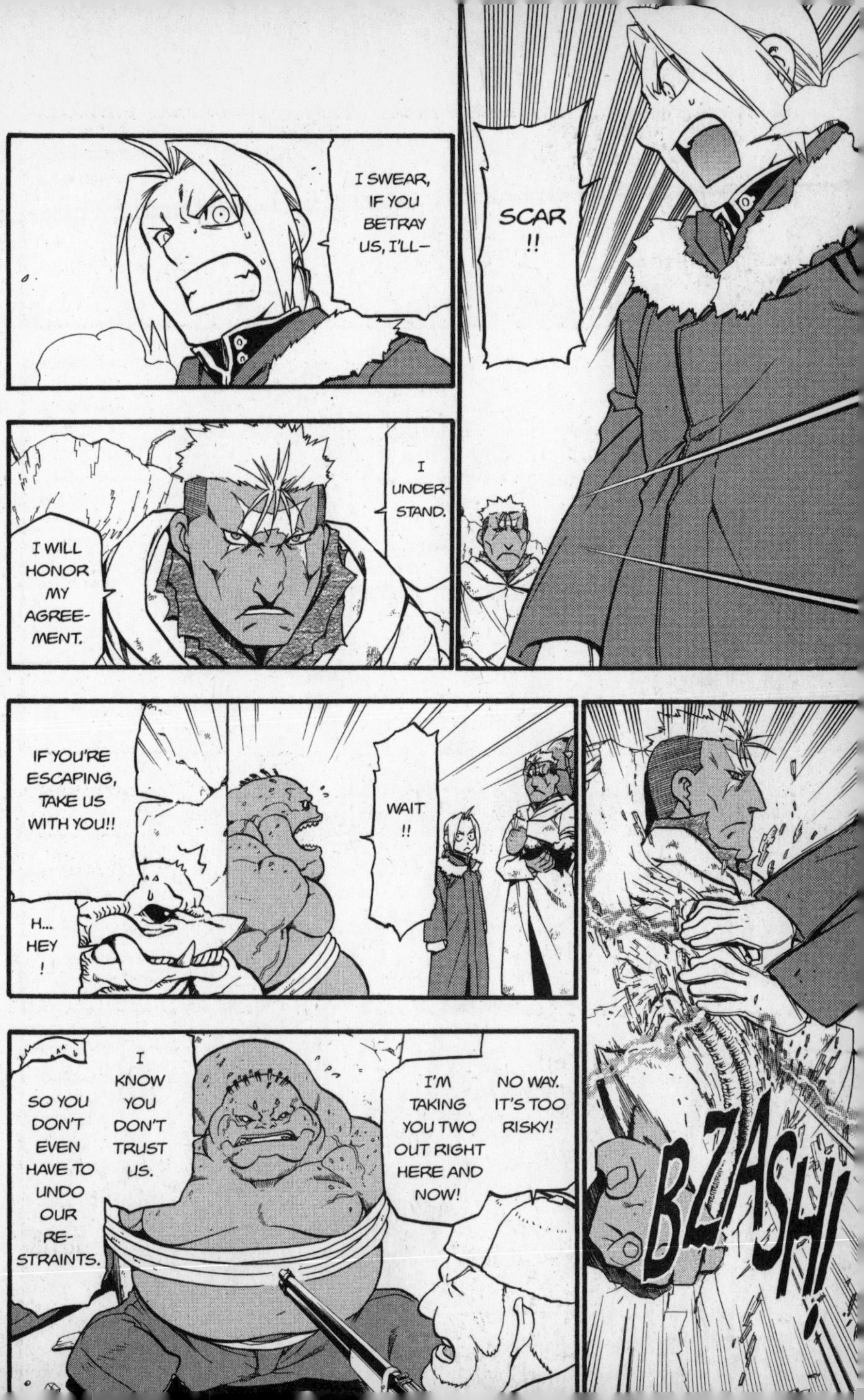
SCAR !!
I SWEAR, IF YOU BETRAY US, I'LL—
I UNDERSTAND.
I WILL HONOR MY AGREEMENT.
B-ZASH!!
WAIT !!
IF YOU'RE ESCAPING, TAKE US WITH YOU!!
H... HEY !
NO WAY. IT'S TOO RISKY!
I'M TAKING YOU TWO OUT RIGHT HERE AND NOW!
I KNOW YOU DON'T TRUST US.
SO YOU DON'T EVEN HAVE TO UNDO OUR RE-STRAINTS.

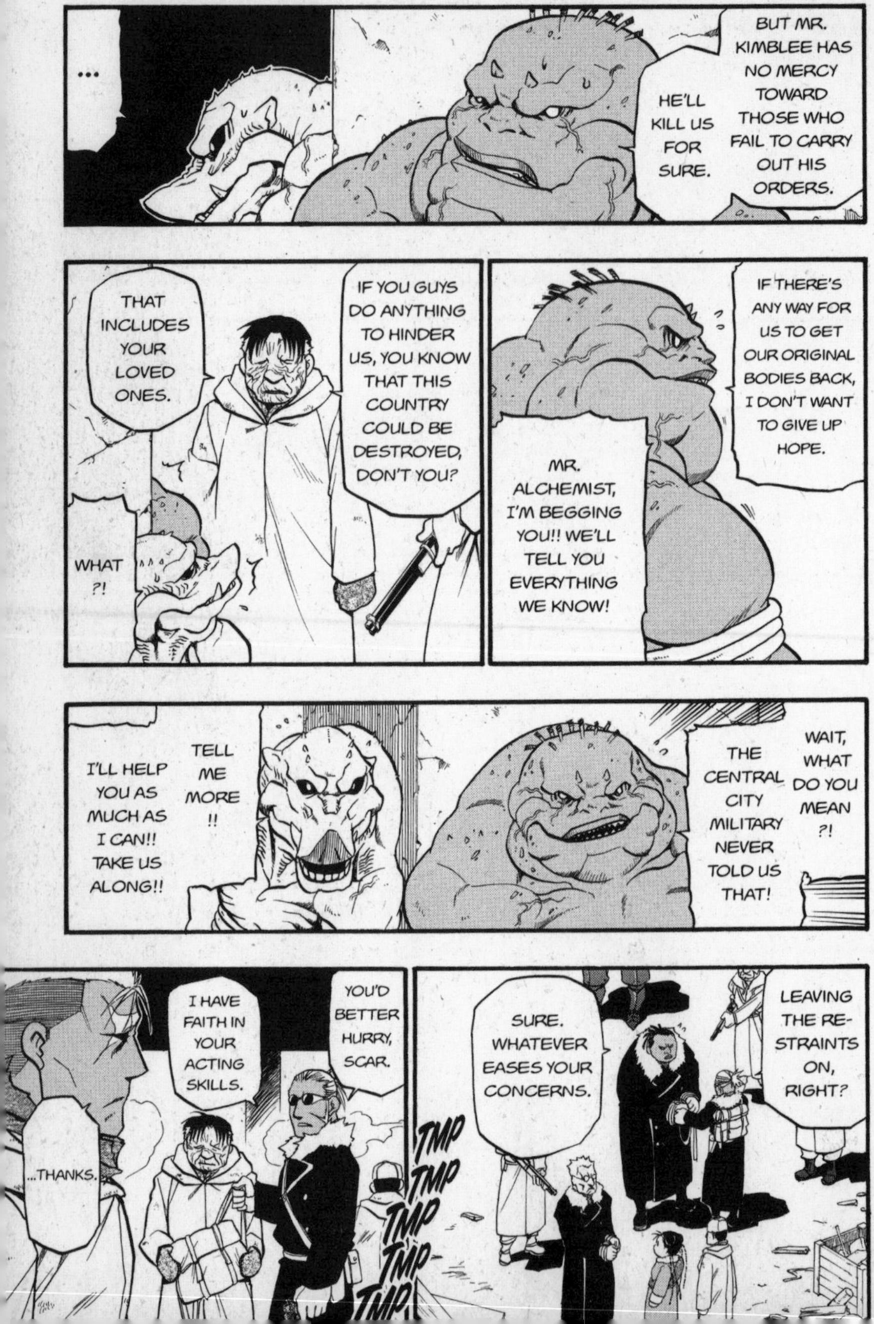
BUT MR. KIMBLEE HAS NO MERCY TOWARD THOSE WHO FAIL TO CARRY OUT HIS ORDERS.
HE'LL KILL US FOR SURE.
...
IF THERE'S ANY WAY FOR US TO GET OUR ORIGINAL BODIES BACK, I DON'T WANT TO GIVE UP HOPE.
MR. ALCHEMIST, I'M BEGGING YOU!! WE'LL TELL YOU EVERYTHING WE KNOW!
IF YOU GUYS DO ANYTHING TO HINDER US, YOU KNOW THAT THIS COUNTRY COULD BE DESTROYED, DON'T YOU?
THAT INCLUDES YOUR LOVED ONES.
WHAT ?!
WAIT, WHAT DO YOU MEAN ?!
THE CENTRAL CITY MILITARY NEVER TOLD US THAT!
TELL ME MORE !!
I'LL HELP YOU AS MUCH AS I CAN!! TAKE US ALONG!!
LEAVING THE RE-STRAINTS ON, RIGHT?
SURE. WHATEVER EASES YOUR CONCERNS.
TMP TMP TMP TMP TMP
YOU'D BETTER HURRY, SCAR.
I HAVE FAITH IN YOUR ACTING SKILLS.
...THANKS.

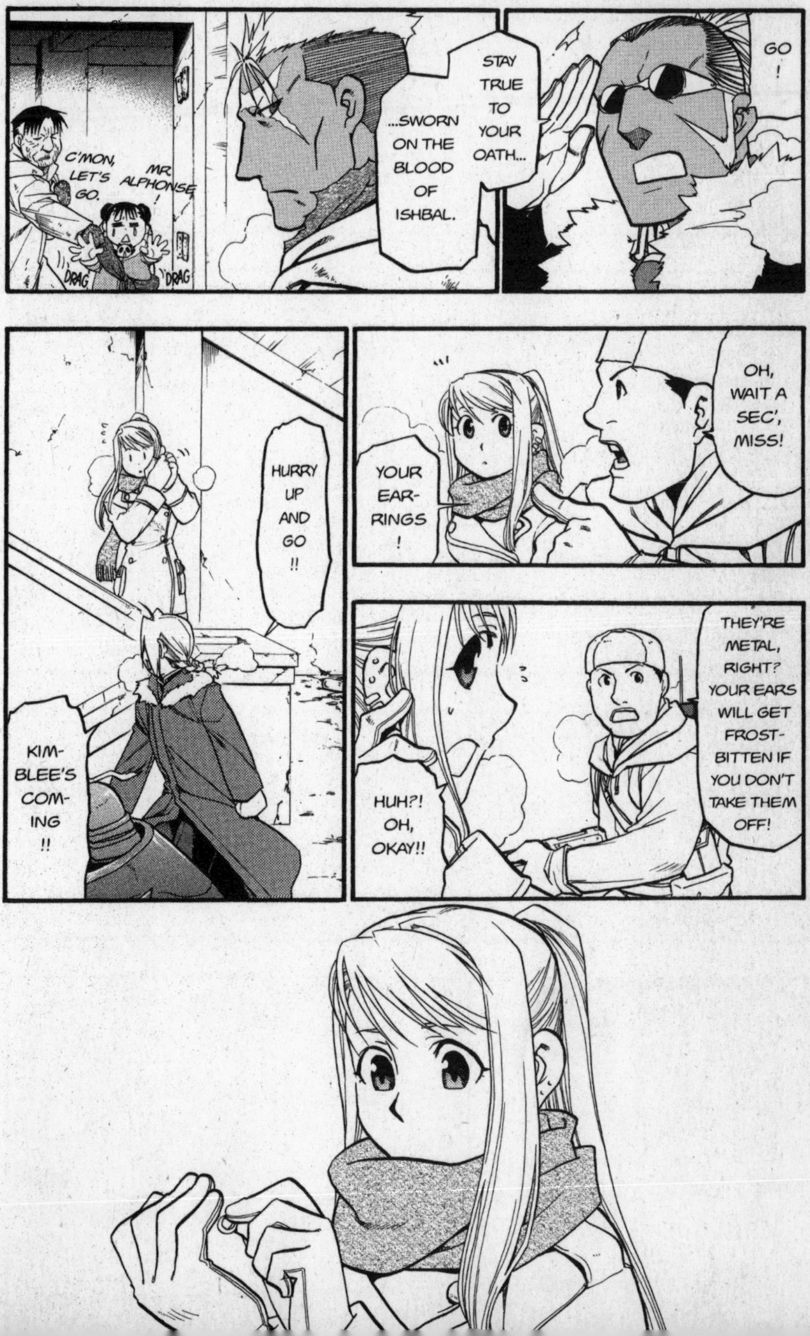
GO!
STAY TRUE TO YOUR OATH...
...SWORN ON THE BLOOD OF ISHBAL.
MR. ALPHONSE!
C'MON, LET'S GO.
DRAG
DRAG
OH, WAIT A SEC', MISS!
YOUR EAR-RINGS!
THEY'RE METAL, RIGHT? YOUR EARS WILL GET FROST-BITTEN IF YOU DON'T TAKE THEM OFF!
HUH?! OH, OKAY!!
HURRY UP AND GO!!
KIM-BLEE'S COM-ING!!

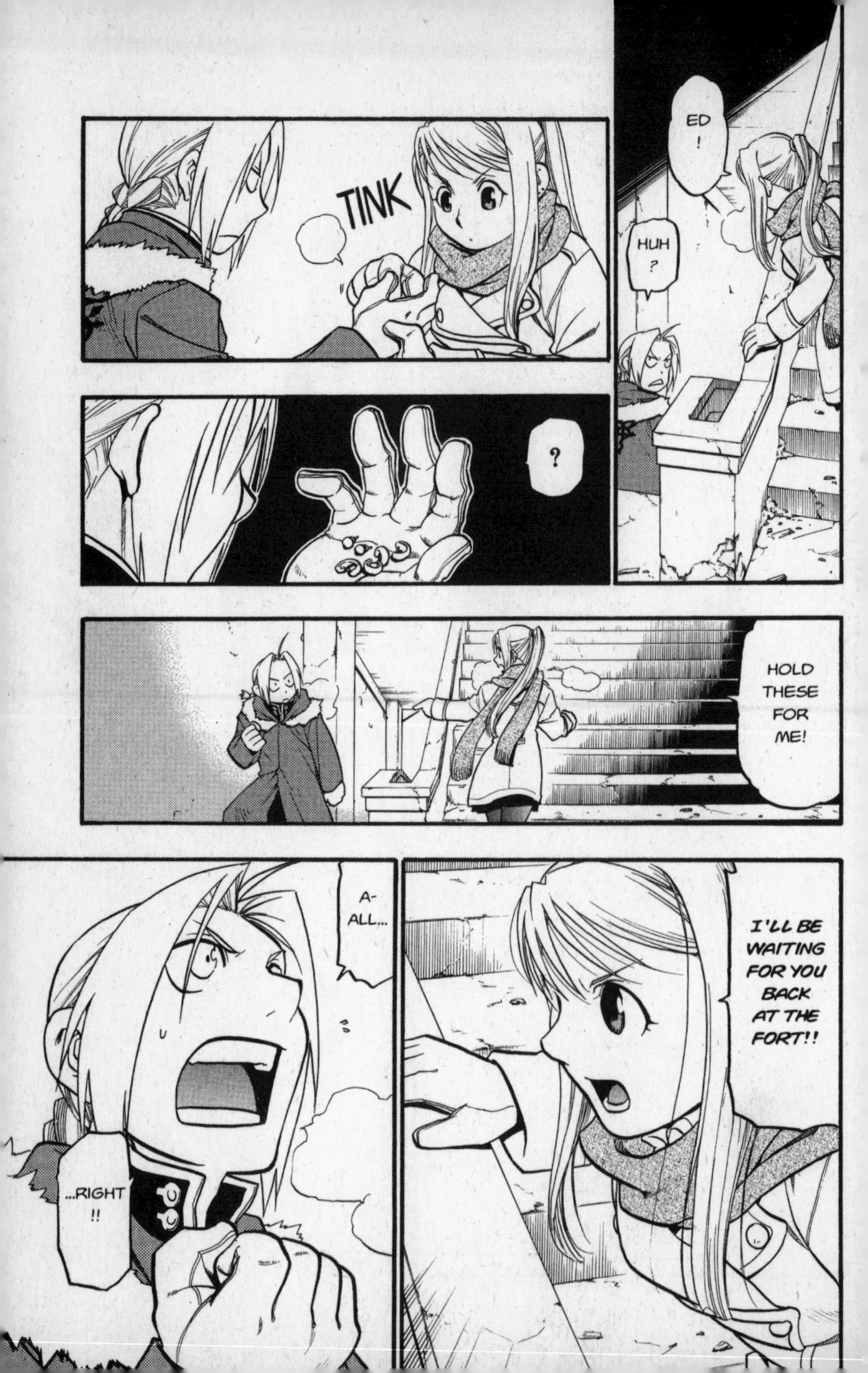
ED!
HUH?
TINK
?
HOLD THESE FOR ME!
I'LL BE WAITING FOR YOU BACK AT THE FORT!!
A-ALL...
...RIGHT!!

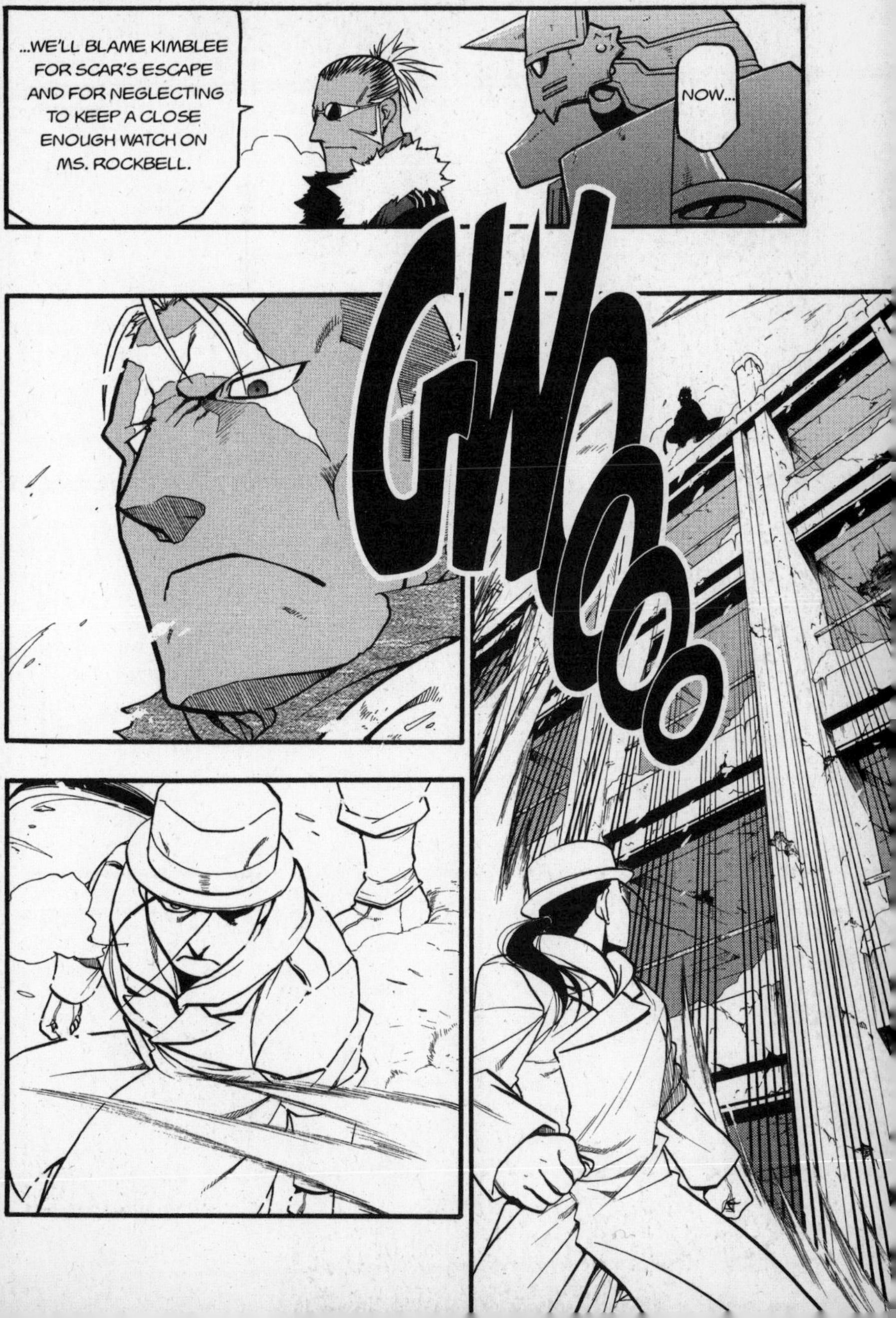
NOW...
...WE'LL BLAME KIMBLEE FOR SCAR'S ESCAPE AND FOR NEGLECTING TO KEEP A CLOSE ENOUGH WATCH ON MS. ROCKBELL.
GWOOOO

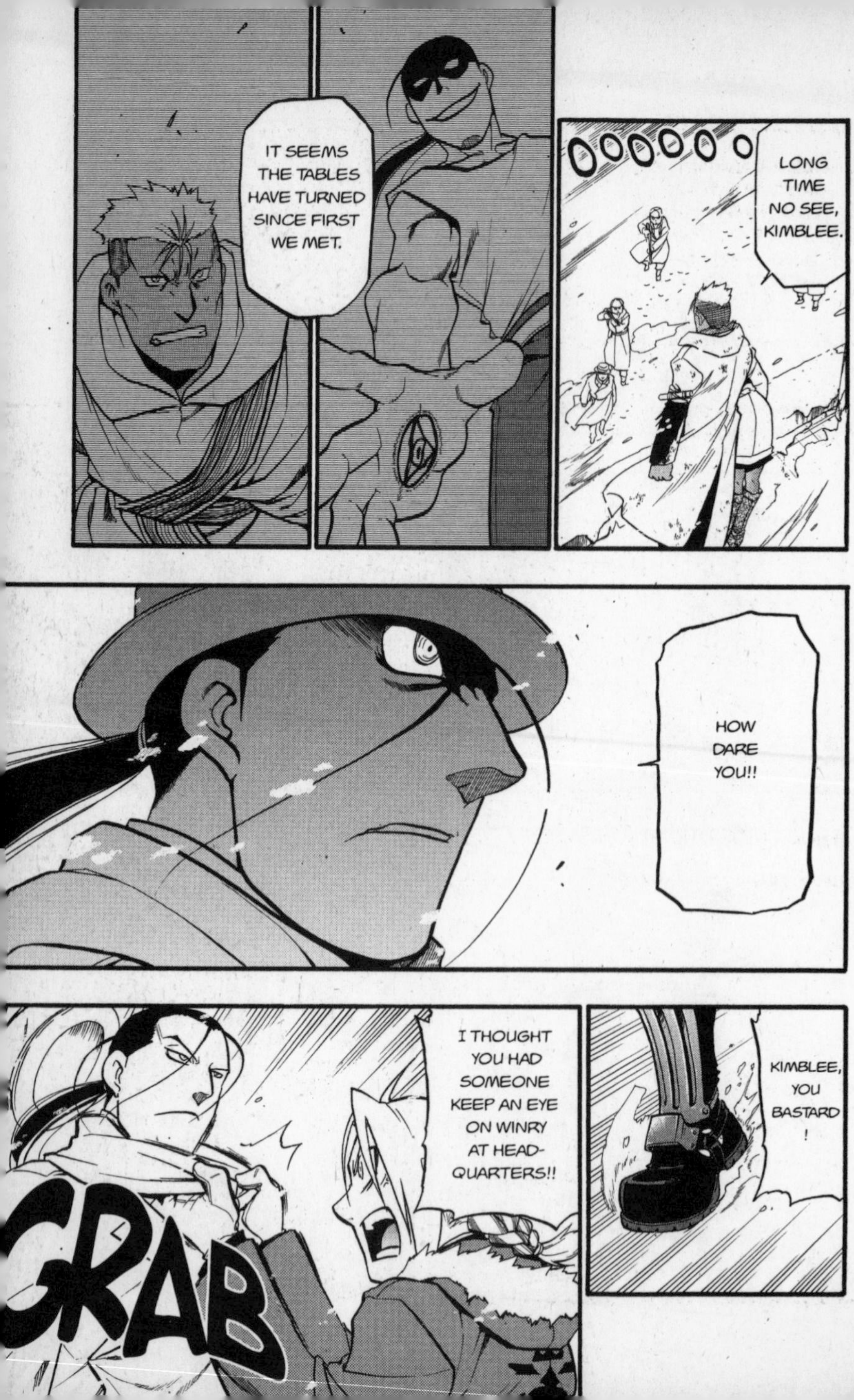
OOOOOO
LONG TIME NO SEE, KIMBLEE.
IT SEEMS THE TABLES HAVE TURNED SINCE FIRST WE MET.
HOW DARE YOU!!
KIMBLEE, YOU BASTARD!
I THOUGHT YOU HAD SOMEONE KEEP AN EYE ON WINRY AT HEAD-QUARTERS!!
GRAB

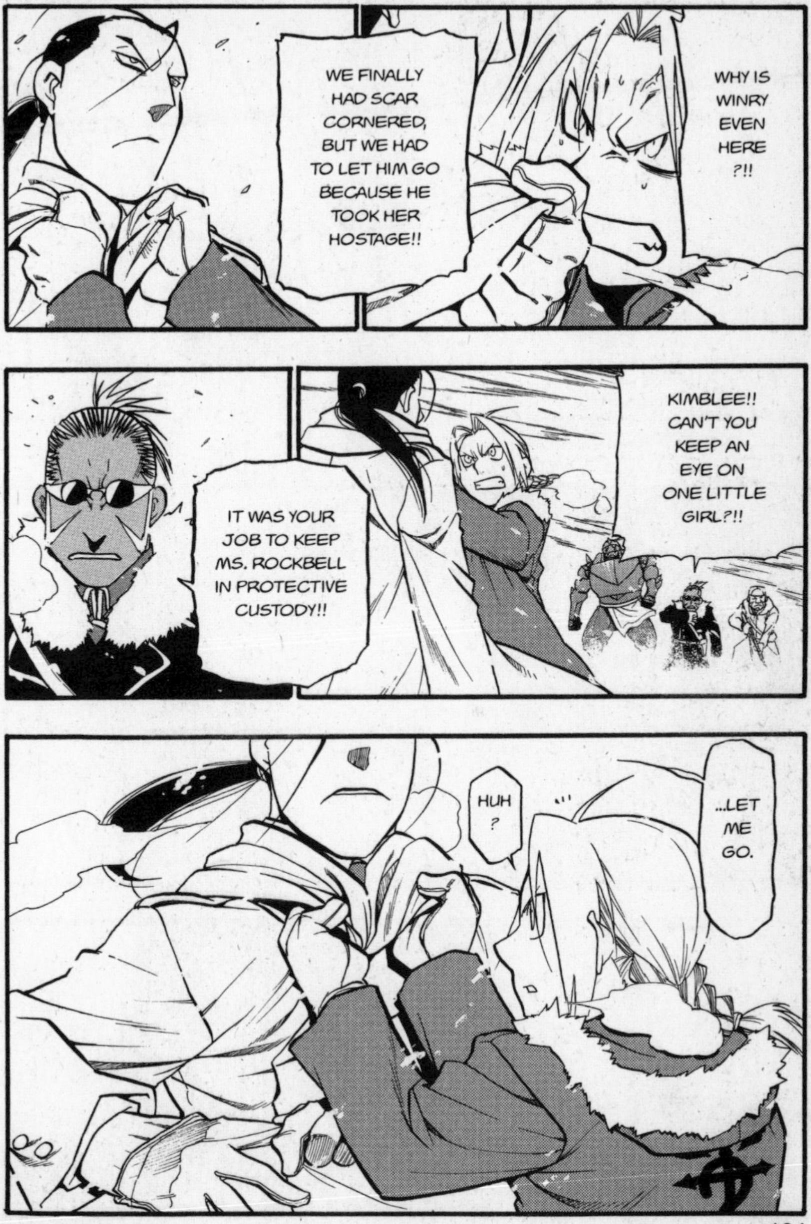
WHY IS WINRY EVEN HERE?!!
WE FINALLY HAD SCAR CORNERED, BUT WE HAD TO LET HIM GO BECAUSE HE TOOK HER HOSTAGE!!
KIMBLEE!! CAN'T YOU KEEP AN EYE ON ONE LITTLE GIRL?!!
IT WAS YOUR JOB TO KEEP MS. ROCKBELL IN PROTECTIVE CUSTODY!!
...LET ME GO.
HUH?

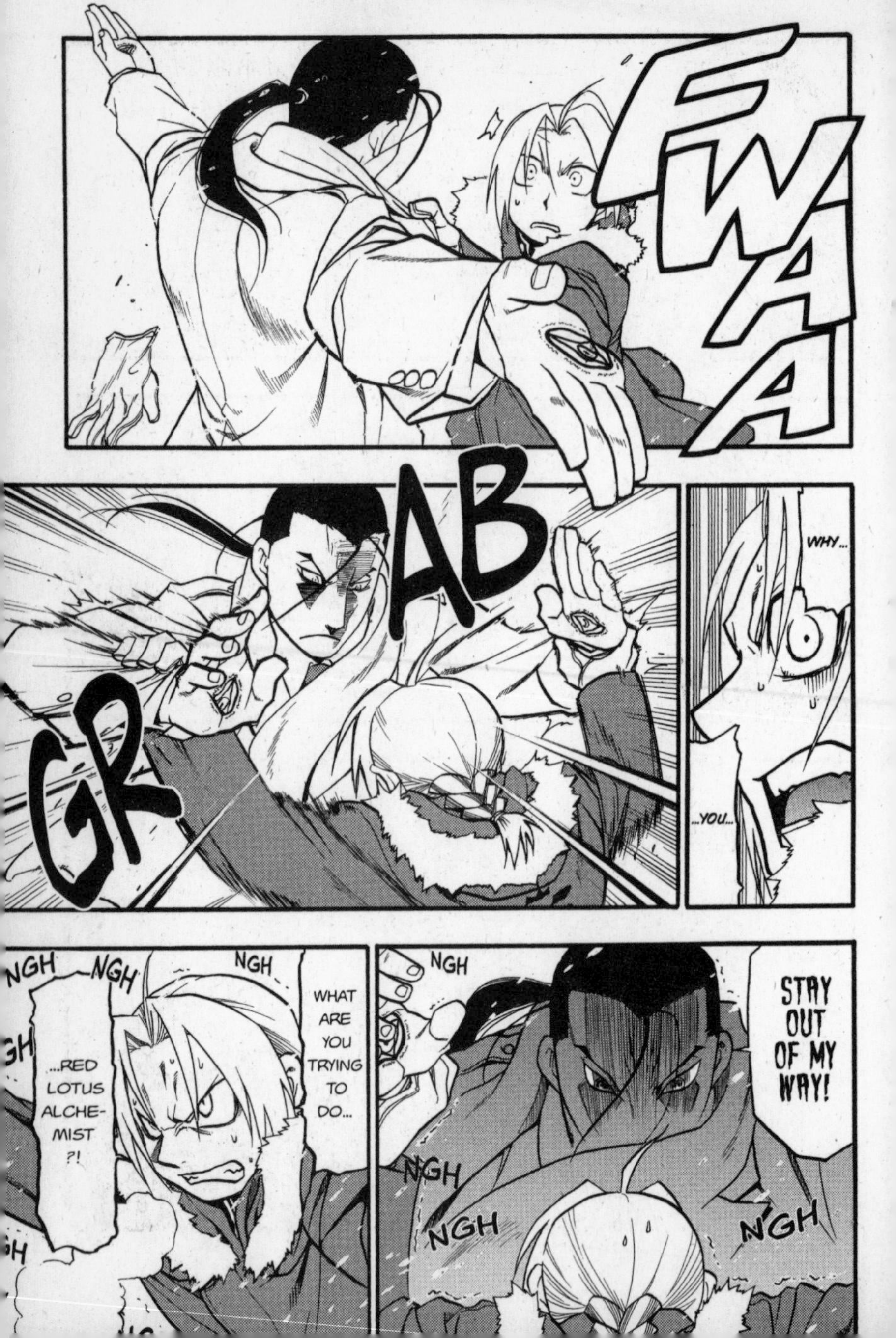

FWAAA
WHY...
...YOU...
GRAB
STAY OUT OF MY WAY!
NGH
NGH
NGH
NGH
WHAT ARE YOU TRYING TO DO...
...RED LOTUS ALCHEMIST ?!
NGH
NGH
NGH

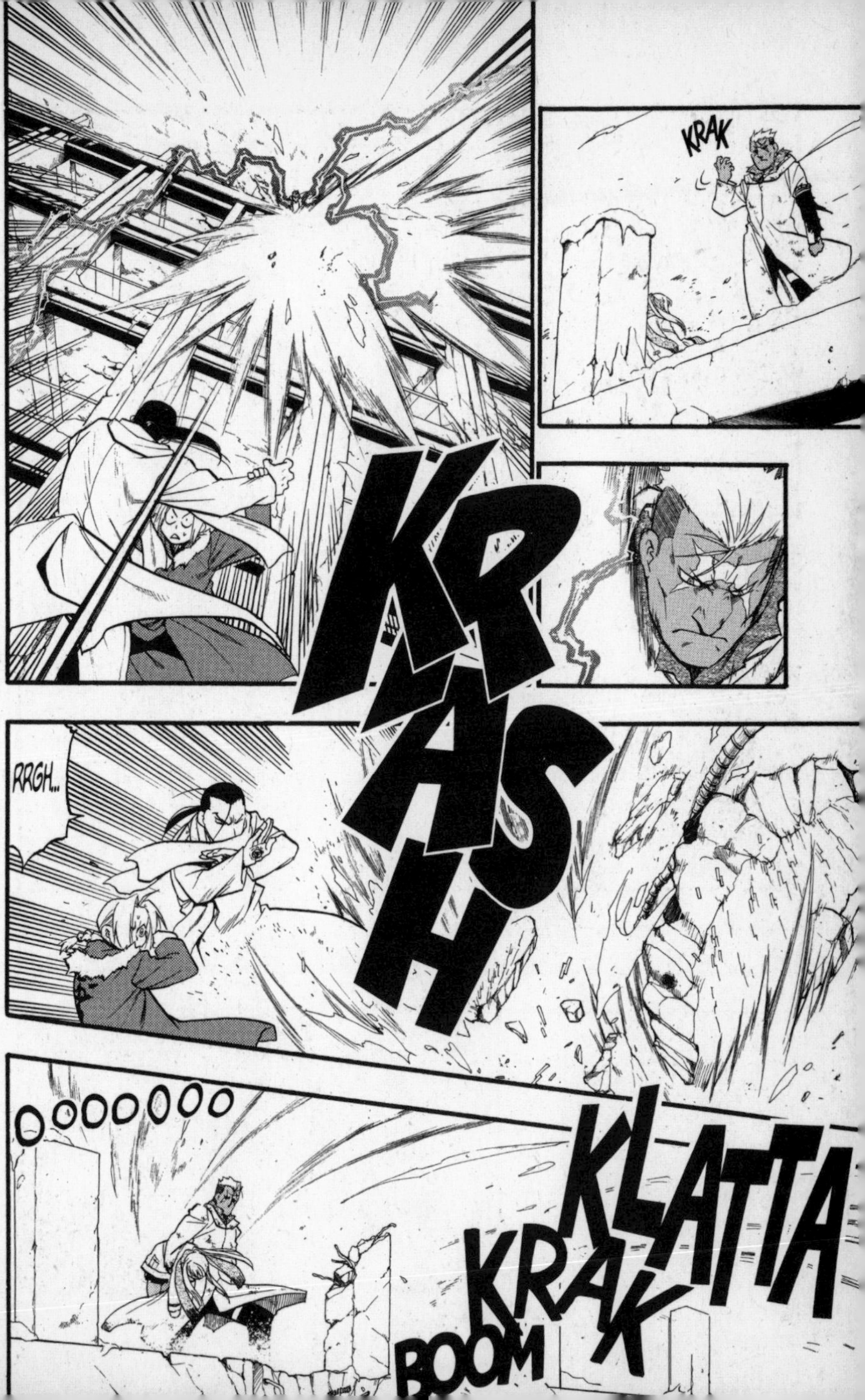
KRAK
KRASH
RRGH...
KLATTA
KRAK
BOOM
OOOOOOO

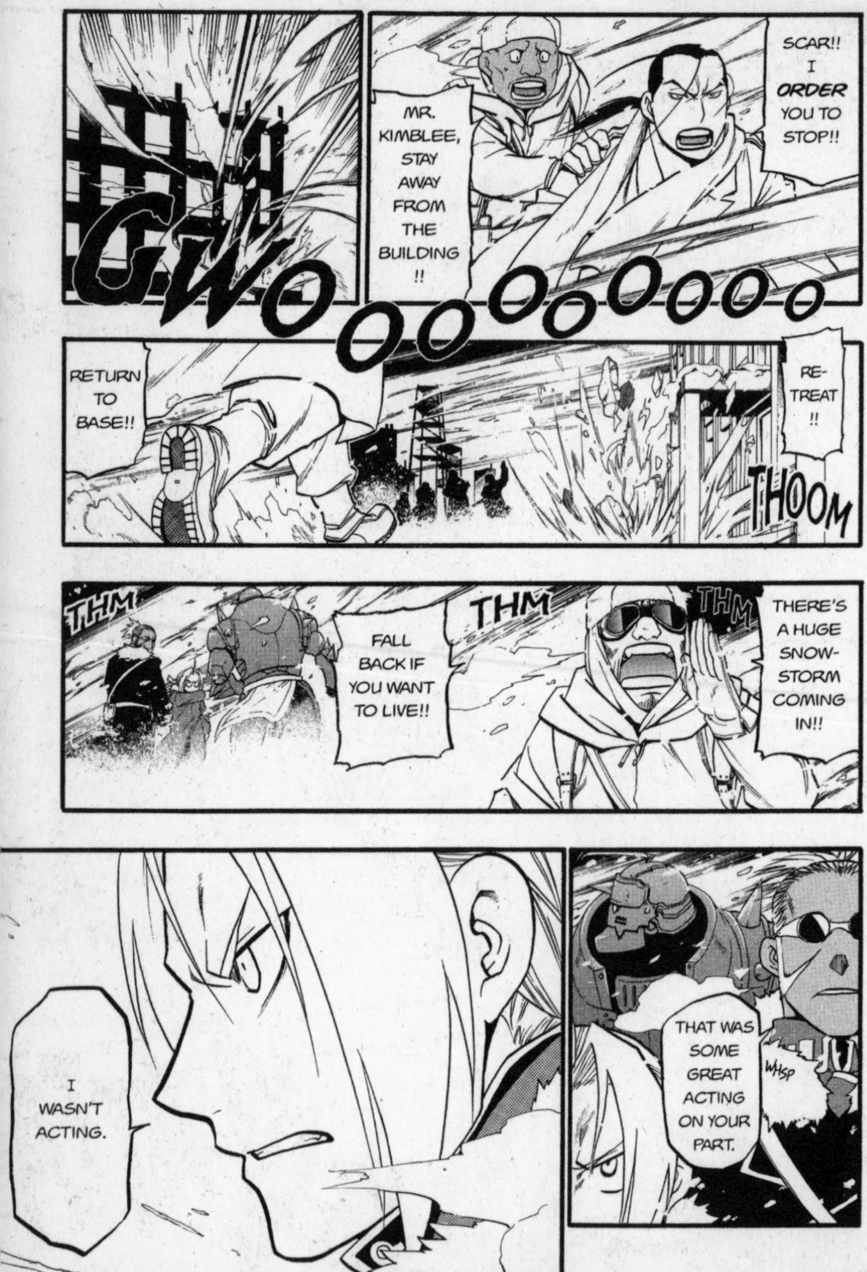
SCAR!! I ORDER YOU TO STOP!!
MR. KIMBLEE, STAY AWAY FROM THE BUILDING!!
GWOOOOOOOOOOOO
RE-TREAT!!
THOOM
RETURN TO BASE!!
THERE'S A HUGE SNOW-STORM COMING IN!!
THM
THM
FALL BACK IF YOU WANT TO LIVE!!
THM
THAT WAS SOME GREAT ACTING ON YOUR PART.
WHSP
I WASN'T ACTING.

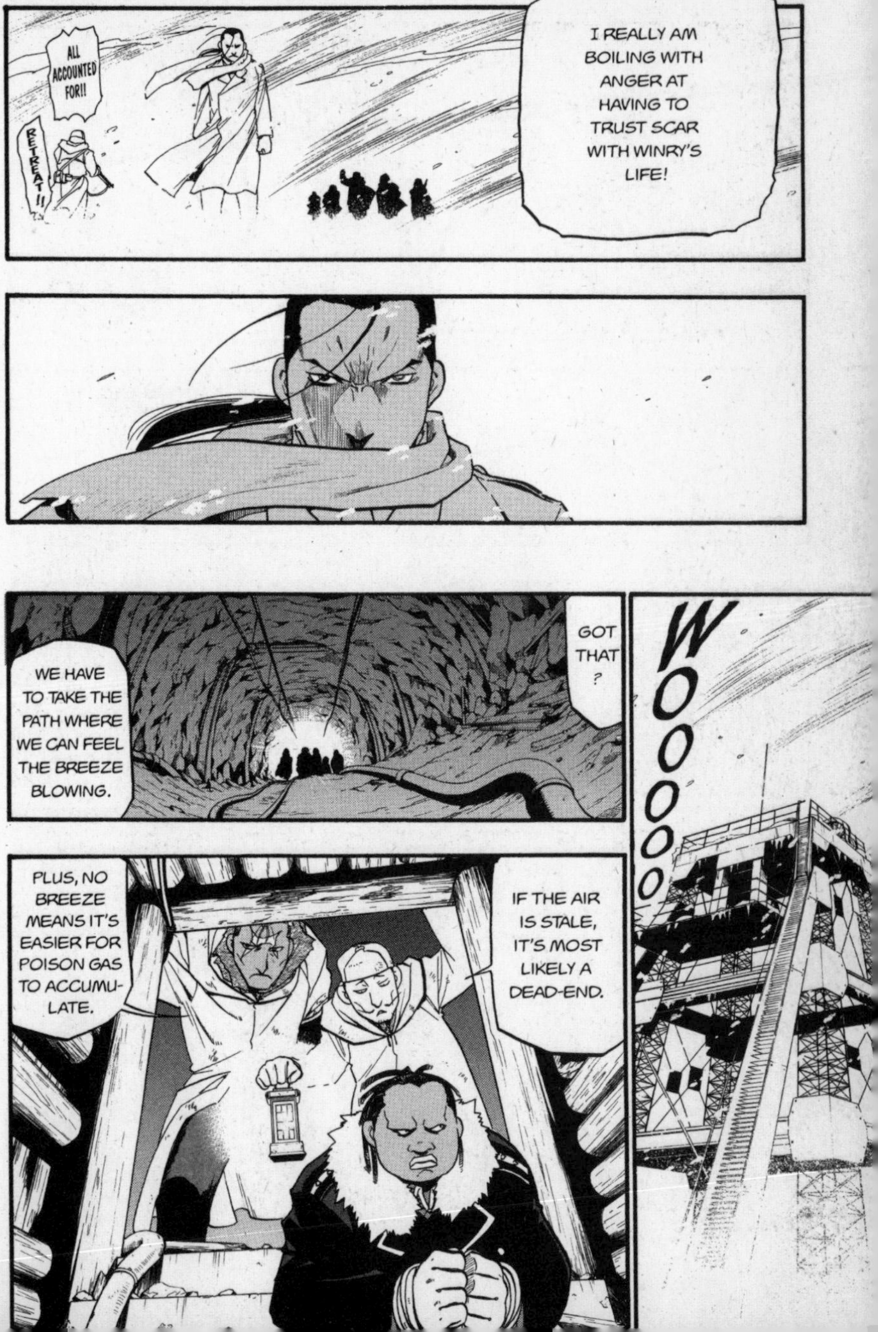
I REALLY AM BOILING WITH ANGER AT HAVING TO TRUST SCAR WITH WINRY'S LIFE!
ALL ACCOUNTED FOR!!
RETREAT!!
WOOOOOO
GOT THAT?
WE HAVE TO TAKE THE PATH WHERE WE CAN FEEL THE BREEZE BLOWING.
IF THE AIR IS STALE, IT'S MOST LIKELY A DEAD-END.
PLUS, NO BREEZE MEANS IT'S EASIER FOR POISON GAS TO ACCUMU-LATE.

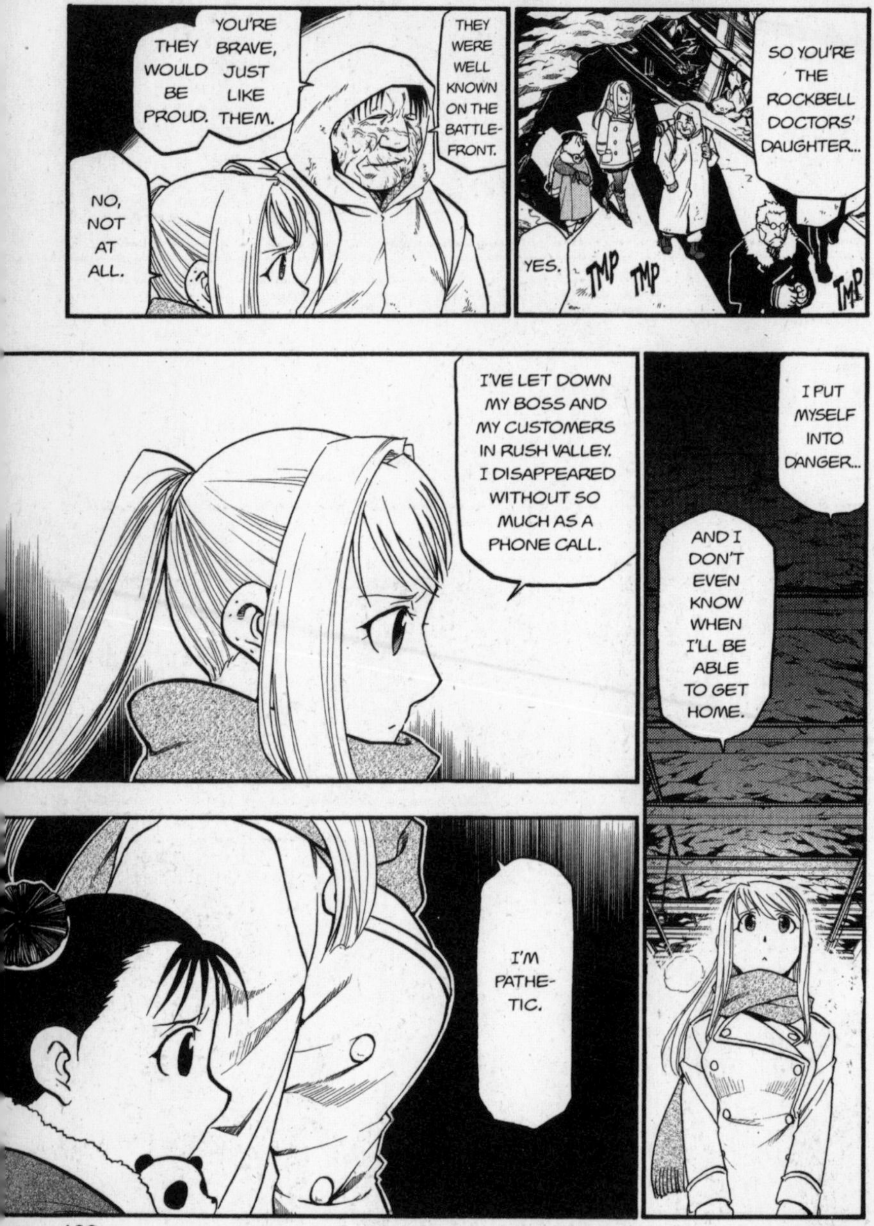
SO YOU'RE THE ROCKBELL DOCTORS' DAUGHTER...
YES.
TMP
TMP
TMP
THEY WERE WELL KNOWN ON THE BATTLEFRONT.
YOU'RE BRAVE, JUST LIKE THEM.
THEY WOULD BE PROUD.
NO, NOT AT ALL.
I PUT MYSELF INTO DANGER...
AND I DON'T EVEN KNOW WHEN I'LL BE ABLE TO GET HOME.
I'VE LET DOWN MY BOSS AND MY CUSTOMERS IN RUSH VALLEY. I DISAPPEARED WITHOUT SO MUCH AS A PHONE CALL.
I'M PATHETIC.

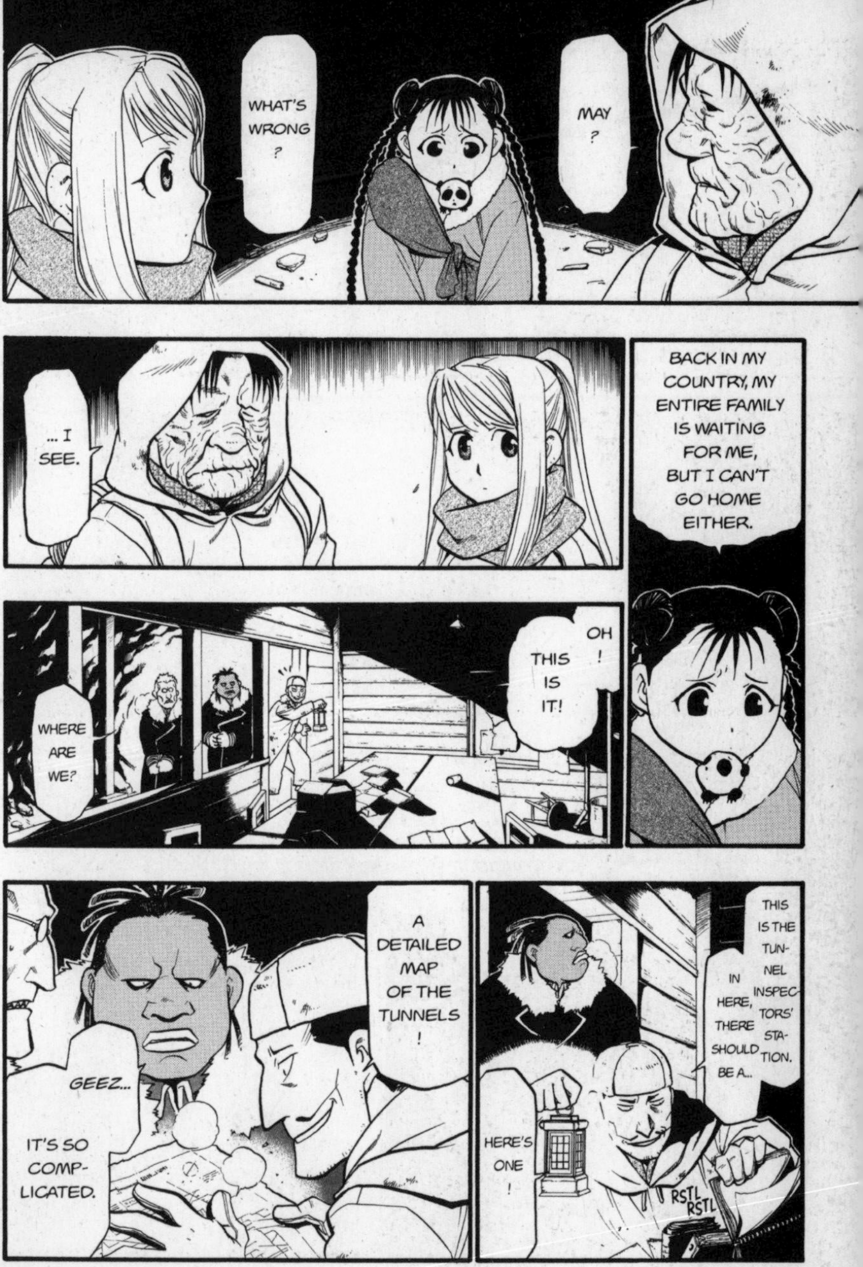
MAY ?
WHAT'S WRONG ?
BACK IN MY COUNTRY, MY ENTIRE FAMILY IS WAITING FOR ME, BUT I CAN'T GO HOME EITHER.
... I SEE.
OH !
THIS IS IT!
WHERE ARE WE?
THIS IS THE TUNNEL INSPECTORS' STATION.
IN HERE, THERE SHOULD BE A...
HERE'S ONE !
RSTL RSTL
A DETAILED MAP OF THE TUNNELS !
GEEZ...
IT'S SO COMPLICATED.

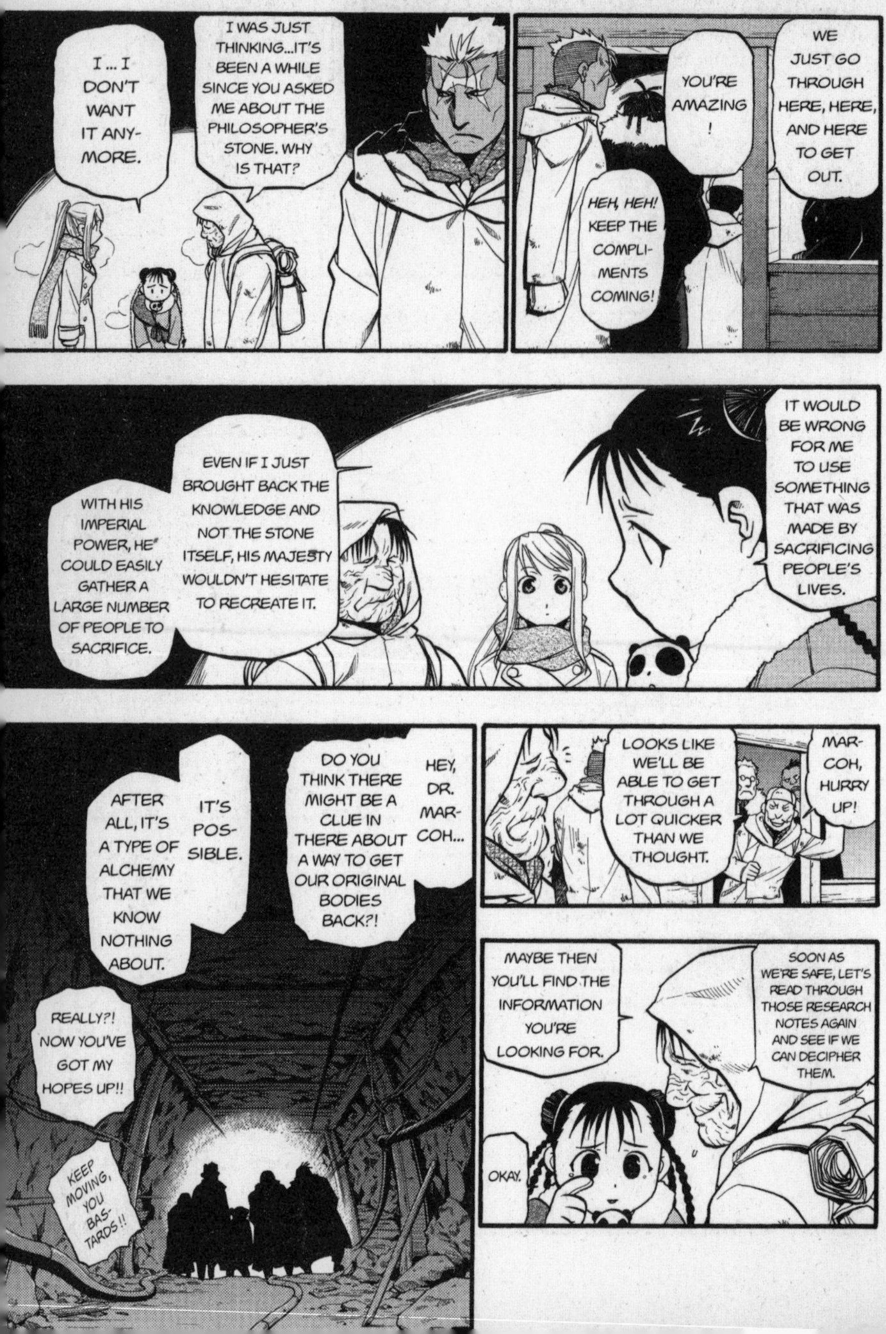
WE JUST GO THROUGH HERE, HERE, AND HERE TO GET OUT.
YOU'RE AMAZING!
HEH, HEH! KEEP THE COMPLIMENTS COMING!
I WAS JUST THINKING...IT'S BEEN A WHILE SINCE YOU ASKED ME ABOUT THE PHILOSOPHER'S STONE. WHY IS THAT?
I... I DON'T WANT IT ANYMORE.
IT WOULD BE WRONG FOR ME TO USE SOMETHING THAT WAS MADE BY SACRIFICING PEOPLE'S LIVES.
EVEN IF I JUST BROUGHT BACK THE KNOWLEDGE AND NOT THE STONE ITSELF, HIS MAJESTY WOULDN'T HESITATE TO RECREATE IT.
WITH HIS IMPERIAL POWER, HE COULD EASILY GATHER A LARGE NUMBER OF PEOPLE TO SACRIFICE.
MARCOH, HURRY UP!
LOOKS LIKE WE'LL BE ABLE TO GET THROUGH A LOT QUICKER THAN WE THOUGHT.
SOON AS WE'RE SAFE, LET'S READ THROUGH THOSE RESEARCH NOTES AGAIN AND SEE IF WE CAN DECIPHER THEM.
MAYBE THEN YOU'LL FIND THE INFORMATION YOU'RE LOOKING FOR.
OKAY.
HEY, DR. MARCOH...
DO YOU THINK THERE MIGHT BE A CLUE IN THERE ABOUT A WAY TO GET OUR ORIGINAL BODIES BACK?!
IT'S POSSIBLE.
AFTER ALL, IT'S A TYPE OF ALCHEMY THAT WE KNOW NOTHING ABOUT.
REALLY?! NOW YOU'VE GOT MY HOPES UP!!
KEEP MOVING, YOU BASTARDS!!

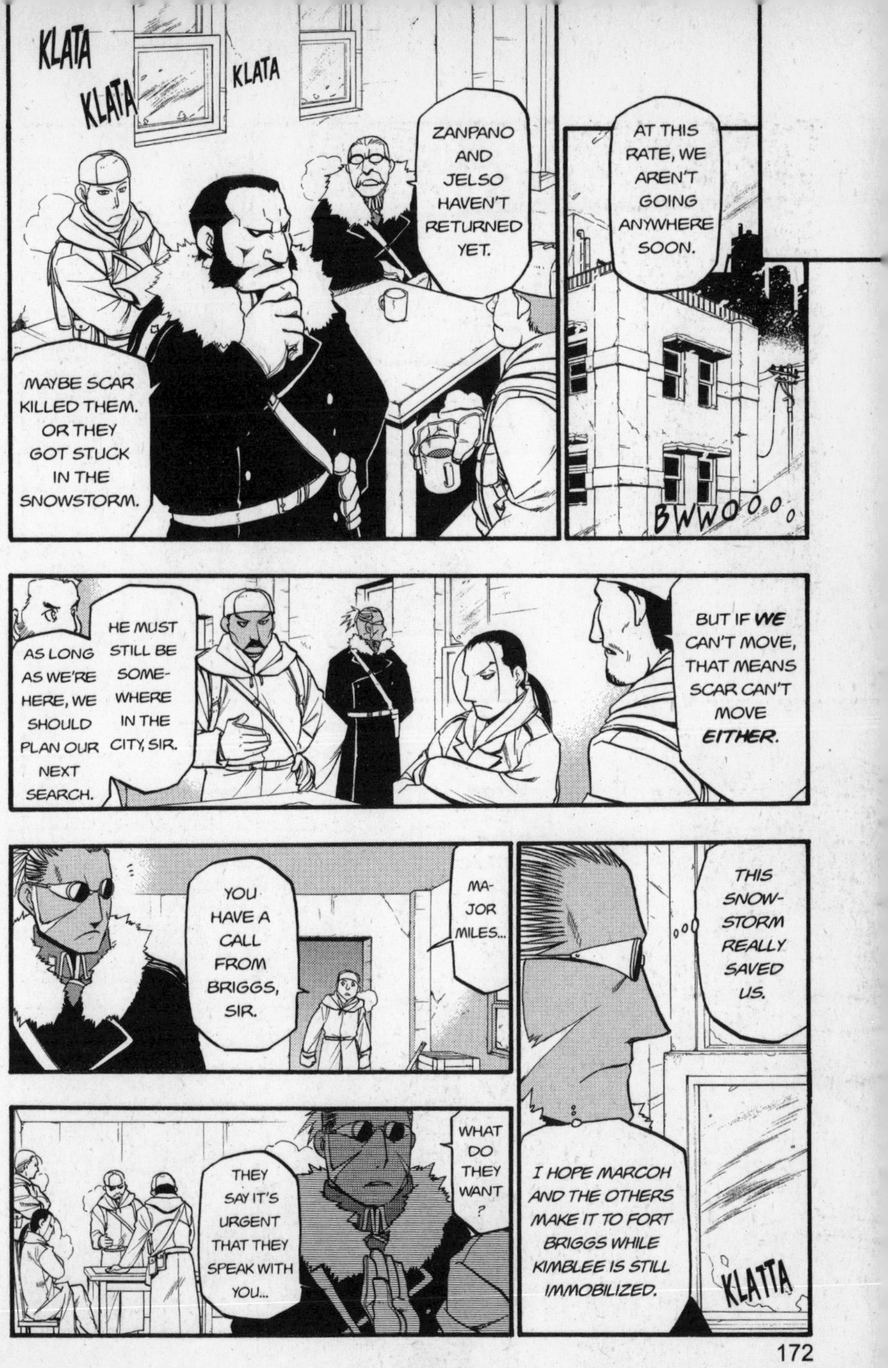
AT THIS RATE, WE AREN'T GOING ANYWHERE SOON.
BWWOOOO
ZANPANO AND JELSO HAVEN'T RETURNED YET.
KLATA
KLATA
KLATA
MAYBE SCAR KILLED THEM. OR THEY GOT STUCK IN THE SNOWSTORM.
BUT IF **WE** CAN'T MOVE, THAT MEANS SCAR CAN'T MOVE ***EITHER***.
HE MUST STILL BE SOMEWHERE IN THE CITY, SIR.
AS LONG AS WE'RE HERE, WE SHOULD PLAN OUR NEXT SEARCH.
THIS SNOWSTORM REALLY SAVED US.
I HOPE MARCOH AND THE OTHERS MAKE IT TO FORT BRIGGS WHILE KIMBLEE IS STILL IMMOBILIZED.
KLATTA
MAJOR MILES...
YOU HAVE A CALL FROM BRIGGS, SIR.
WHAT DO THEY WANT?
THEY SAY IT'S URGENT THAT THEY SPEAK WITH YOU...

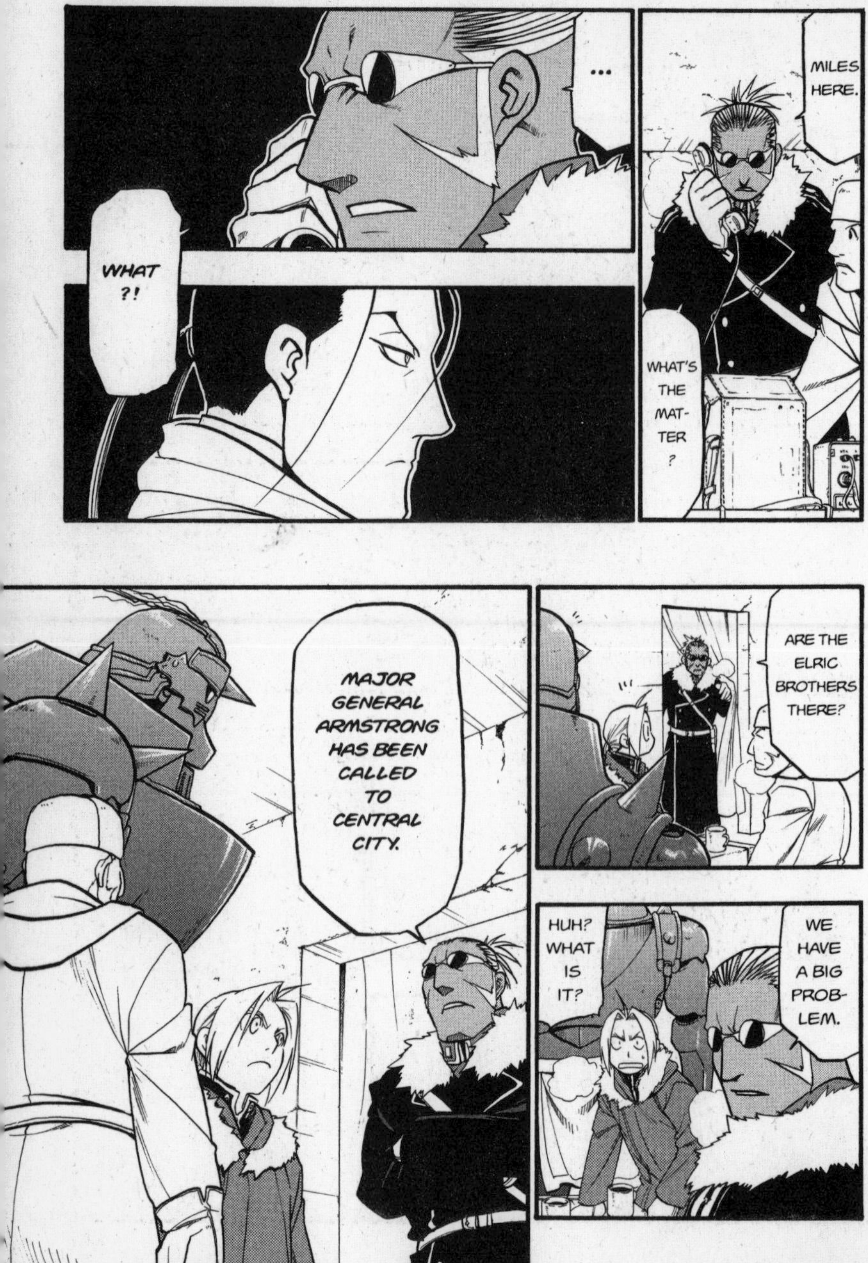
MILES HERE.
WHAT'S THE MATTER?
...
WHAT ?!
ARE THE ELRIC BROTHERS THERE?
WE HAVE A BIG PROBLEM.
HUH? WHAT IS IT?
MAJOR GENERAL ARMSTRONG HAS BEEN CALLED TO CENTRAL CITY.

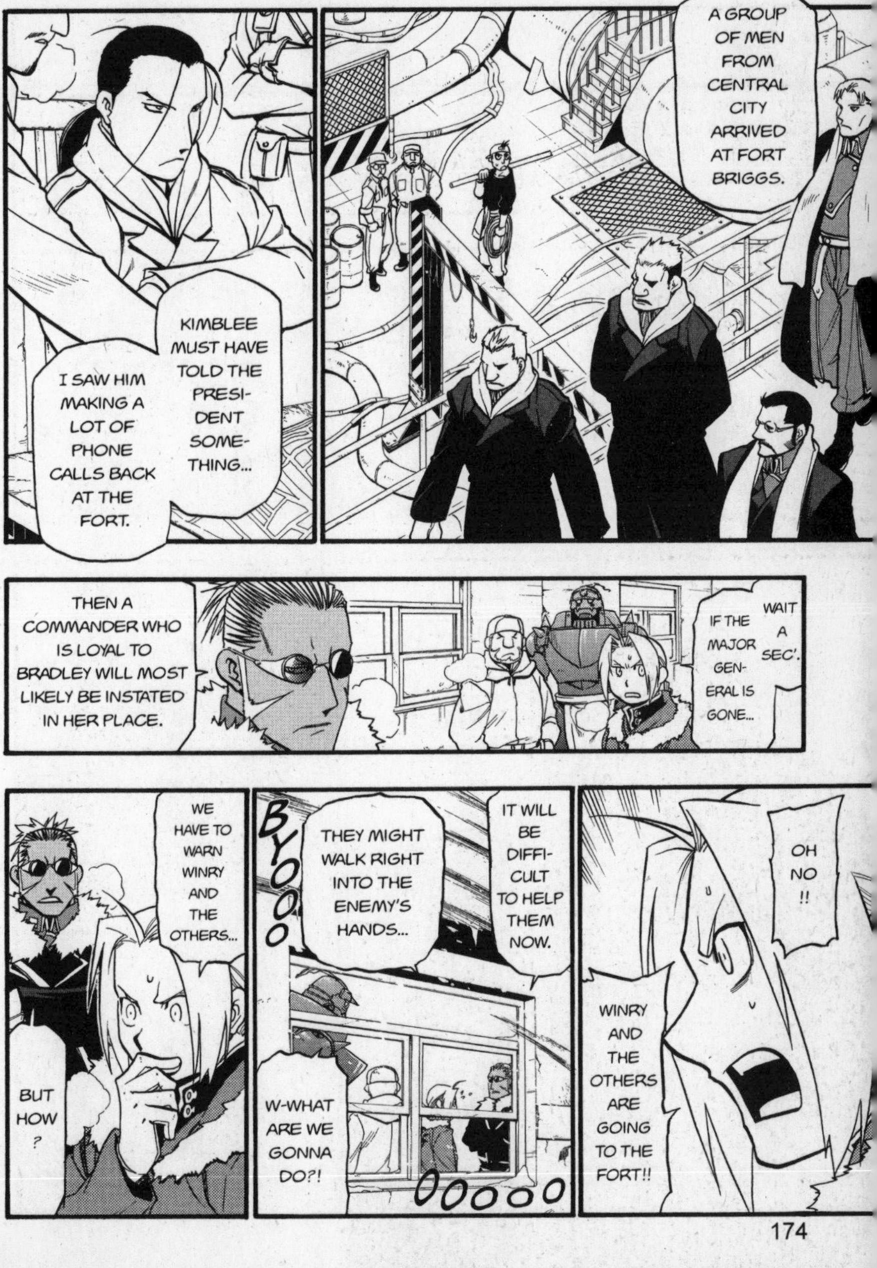
A GROUP OF MEN FROM CENTRAL CITY ARRIVED AT FORT BRIGGS.
KIMBLEE MUST HAVE TOLD THE PRESIDENT SOMETHING...
I SAW HIM MAKING A LOT OF PHONE CALLS BACK AT THE FORT.
WAIT A SEC'.
IF THE MAJOR GENERAL IS GONE...
THEN A COMMANDER WHO IS LOYAL TO BRADLEY WILL MOST LIKELY BE INSTATED IN HER PLACE.
OH NO!!
WINRY AND THE OTHERS ARE GOING TO THE FORT!!
IT WILL BE DIFFICULT TO HELP THEM NOW.
THEY MIGHT WALK RIGHT INTO THE ENEMY'S HANDS...
BYOOOOOOOOO
W-WHAT ARE WE GONNA DO?!
WE HAVE TO WARN WINRY AND THE OTHERS...
BUT HOW?

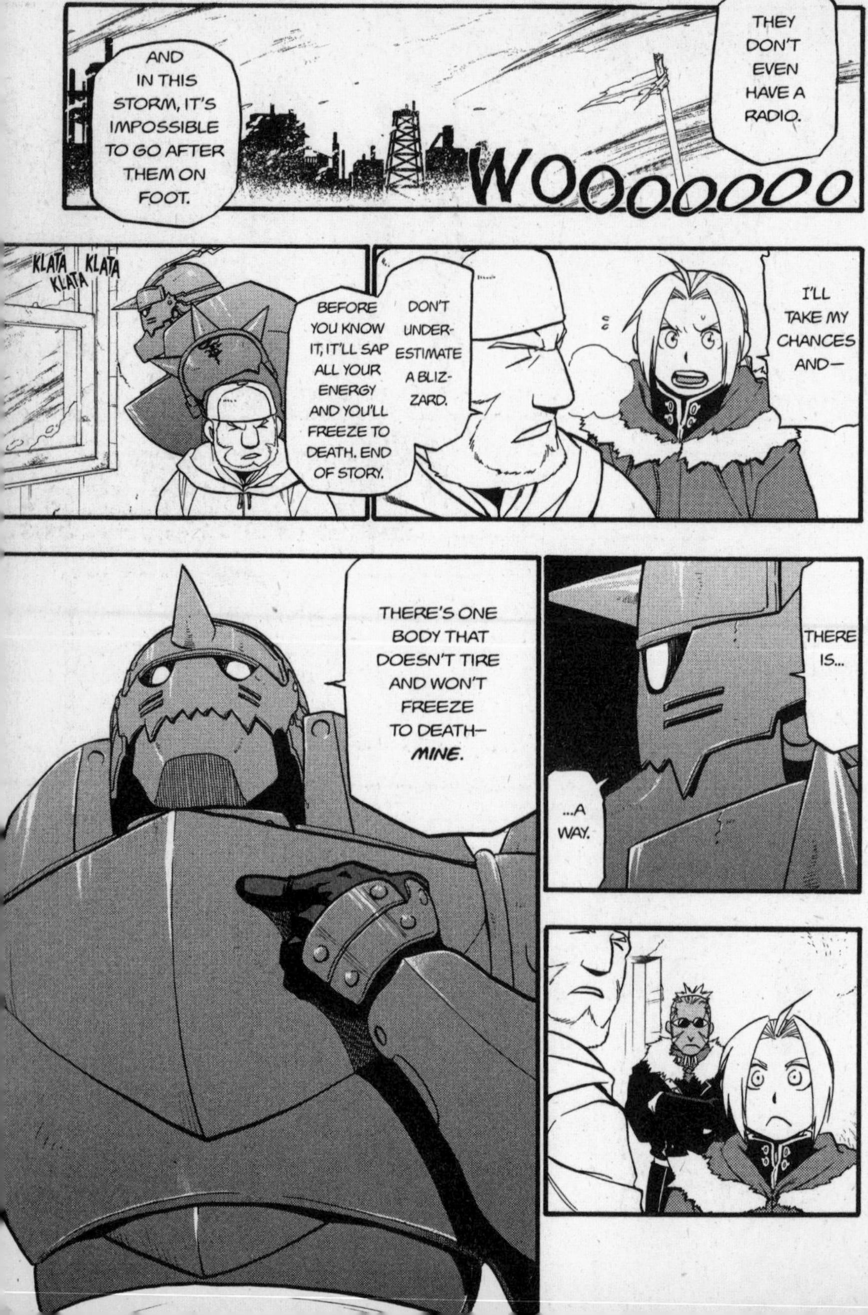
THEY DON'T EVEN HAVE A RADIO.
AND IN THIS STORM, IT'S IMPOSSIBLE TO GO AFTER THEM ON FOOT.
WOOOOOOOO
I'LL TAKE MY CHANCES AND—
DON'T UNDER-ESTIMATE A BLIZ-ZARD.
BEFORE YOU KNOW IT, IT'LL SAP ALL YOUR ENERGY AND YOU'LL FREEZE TO DEATH. END OF STORY.
KLATA KLATA KLATA
THERE IS...
...A WAY.
THERE'S ONE BODY THAT DOESN'T TIRE AND WON'T FREEZE TO DEATH— *MINE.*

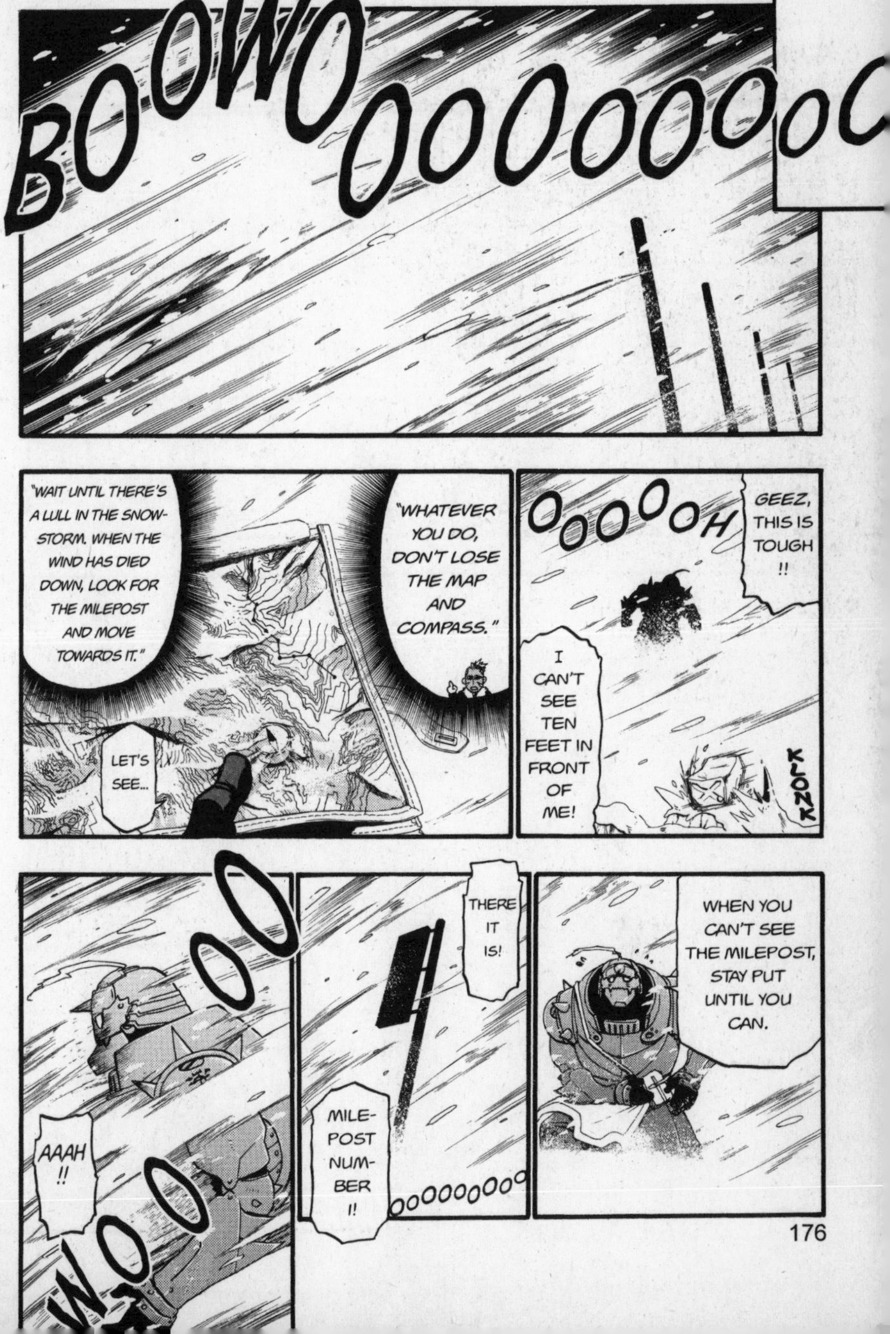
BOOWOOOOOOOOOO
GEEZ, THIS IS TOUGH!!
OOOOOOH
I CAN'T SEE TEN FEET IN FRONT OF ME!
KLONK
"WHATEVER YOU DO, DON'T LOSE THE MAP AND COMPASS."
"WAIT UNTIL THERE'S A LULL IN THE SNOW-STORM. WHEN THE WIND HAS DIED DOWN, LOOK FOR THE MILEPOST AND MOVE TOWARDS IT."
LET'S SEE...
WHEN YOU CAN'T SEE THE MILEPOST, STAY PUT UNTIL YOU CAN.
THERE IT IS!
MILE-POST NUM-BER!!
OOOOOOOO
WOOOOO
AAAH!!

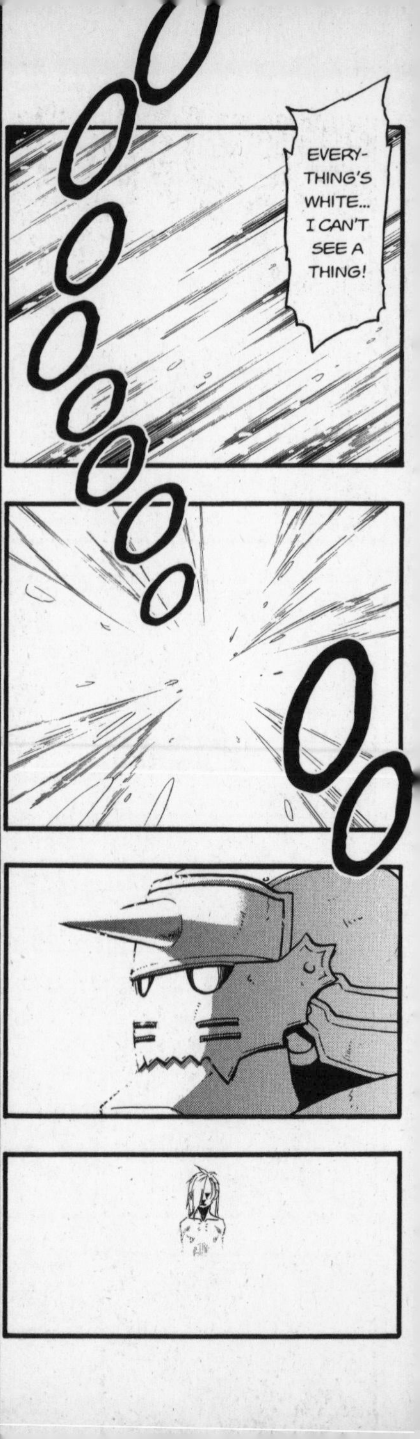
EVERY-THING'S WHITE... I CAN'T SEE A THING!

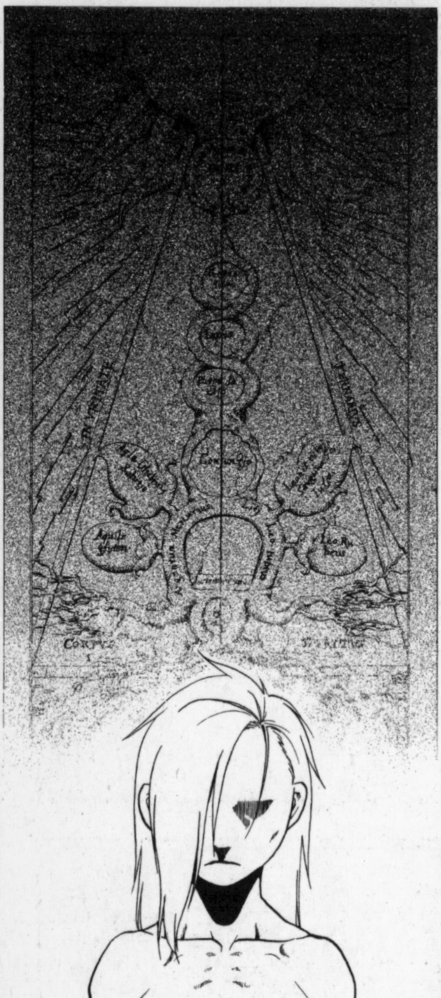

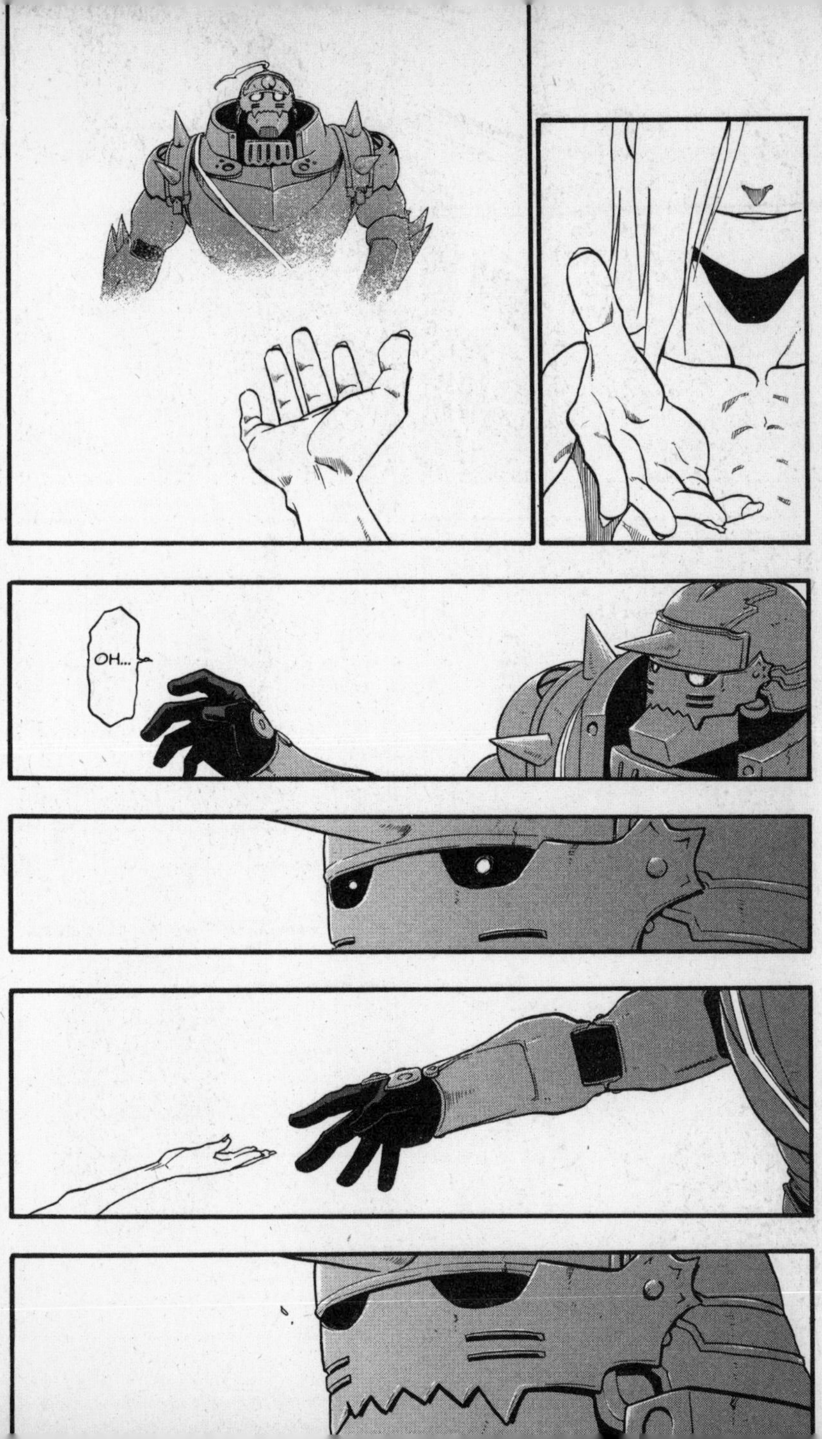
OH...

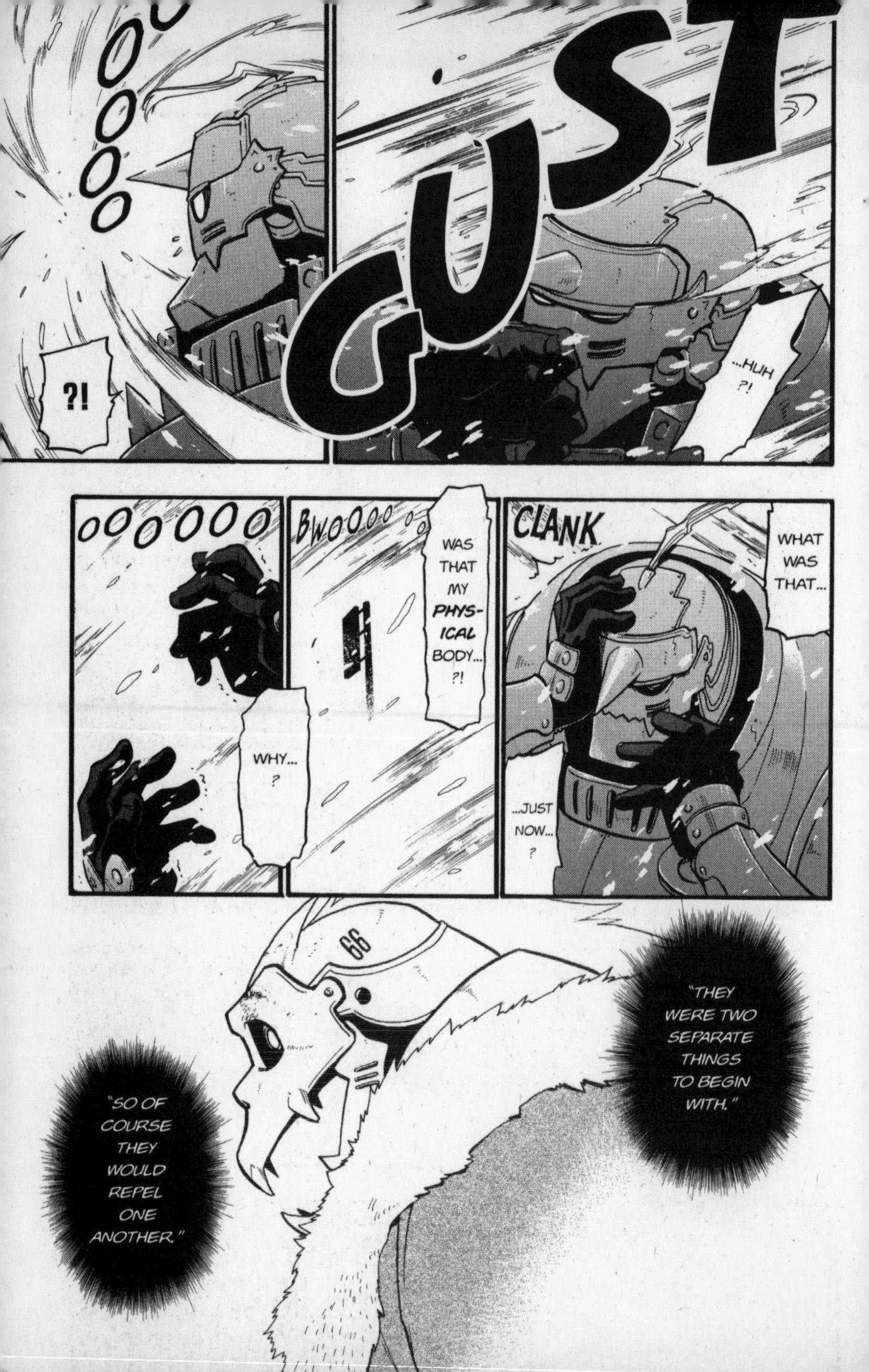
GUST
...HUH ?!
OOOOO
?!
CLANK
WHAT WAS THAT...
...JUST NOW... ?
BWOOOO
WAS THAT MY PHYSICAL BODY... ?!
WHY... ?
OOOOOO
"THEY WERE TWO SEPARATE THINGS TO BEGIN WITH."
"SO OF COURSE THEY WOULD REPEL ONE ANOTHER."

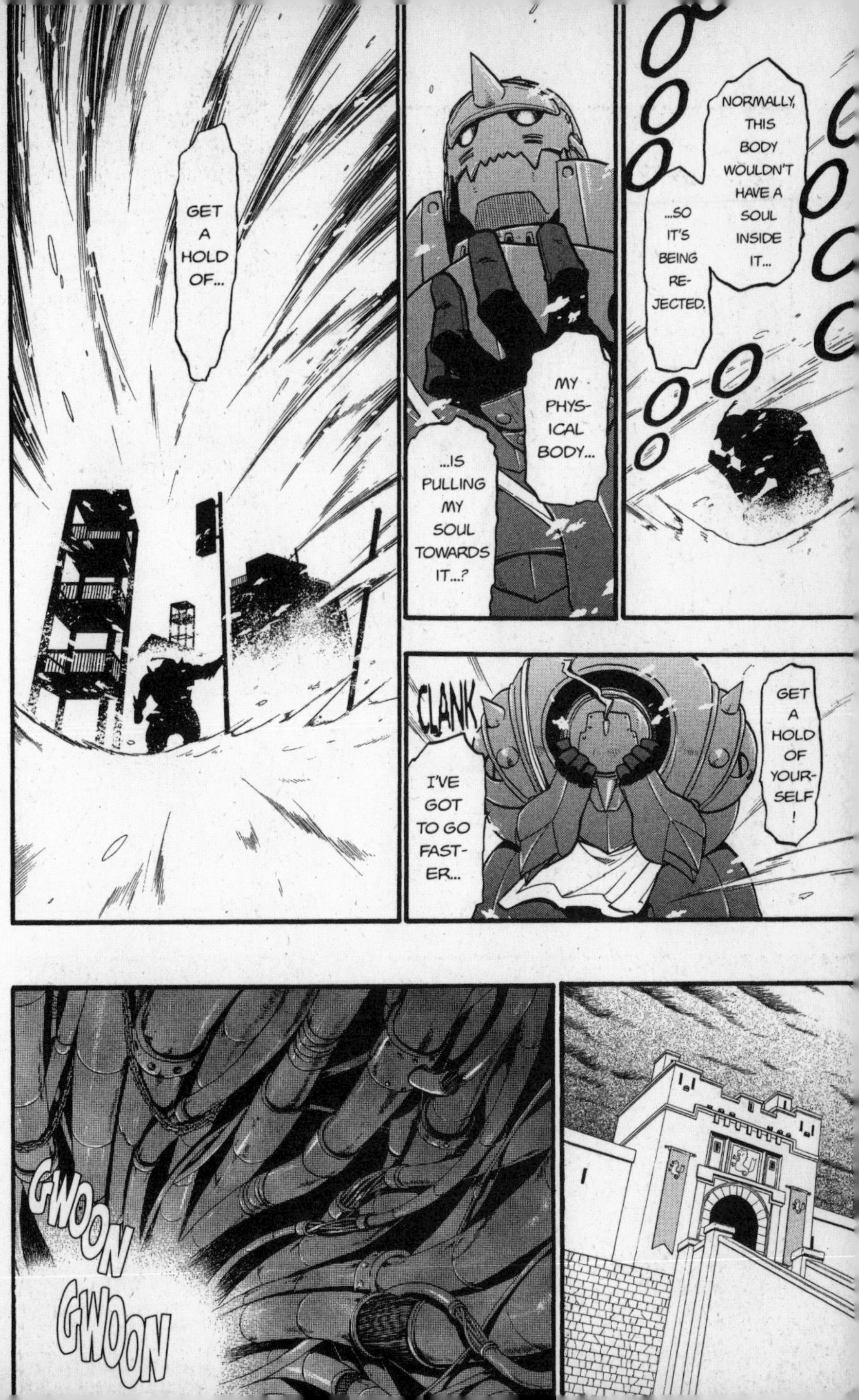
NORMALLY, THIS BODY WOULDN'T HAVE A SOUL INSIDE IT...
...SO IT'S BEING RE-JECTED.
MY PHYS-ICAL BODY...
...IS PULLING MY SOUL TOWARDS IT...?
GET A HOLD OF YOUR-SELF!
CLANK
I'VE GOT TO GO FAST-ER...
GET A HOLD OF...
GWOON
GWOON

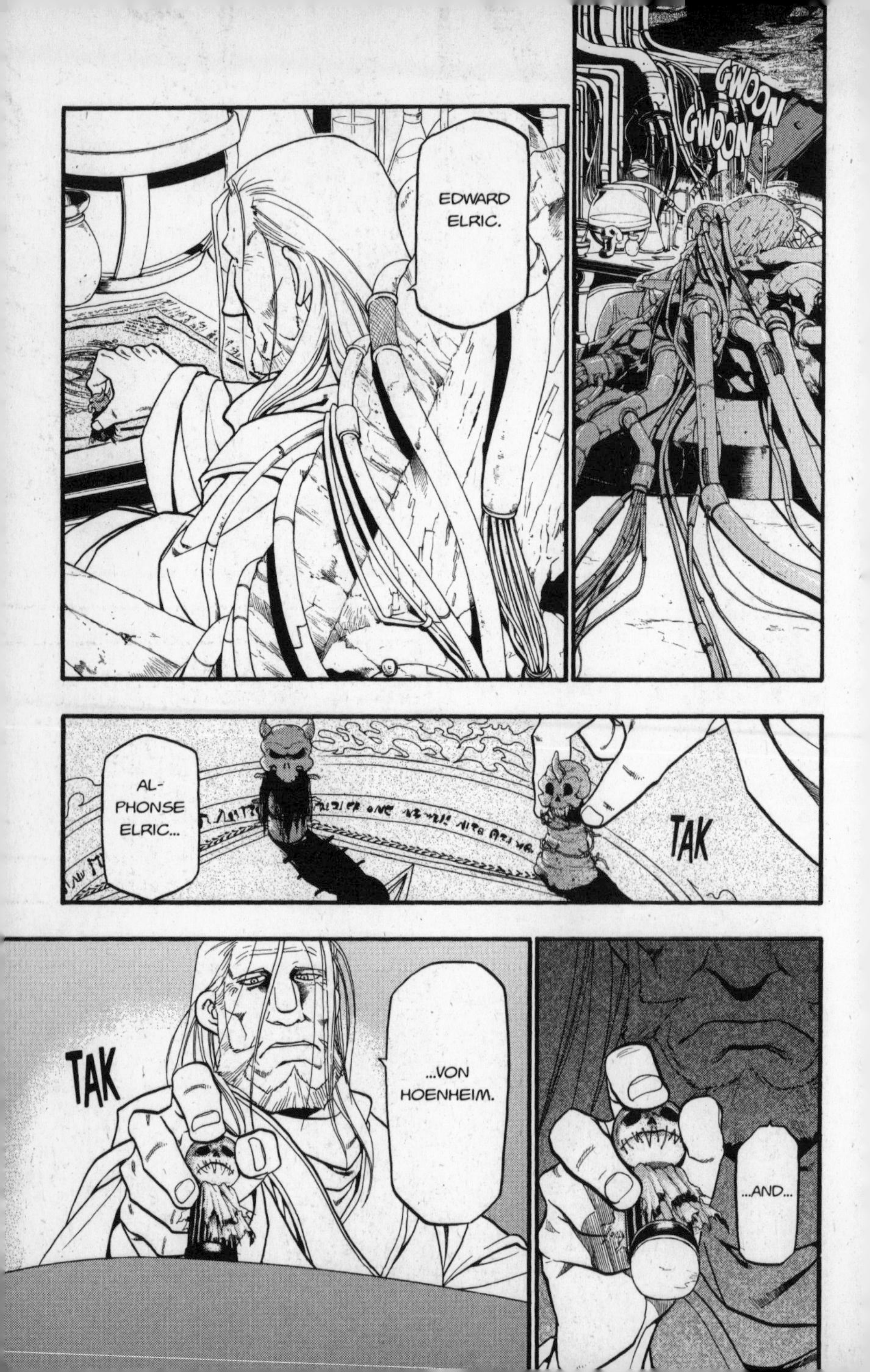
GWOON GWOON
EDWARD ELRIC.
TAK
AL-PHONSE ELRIC...
...AND...
TAK
...VON HOENHEIM.

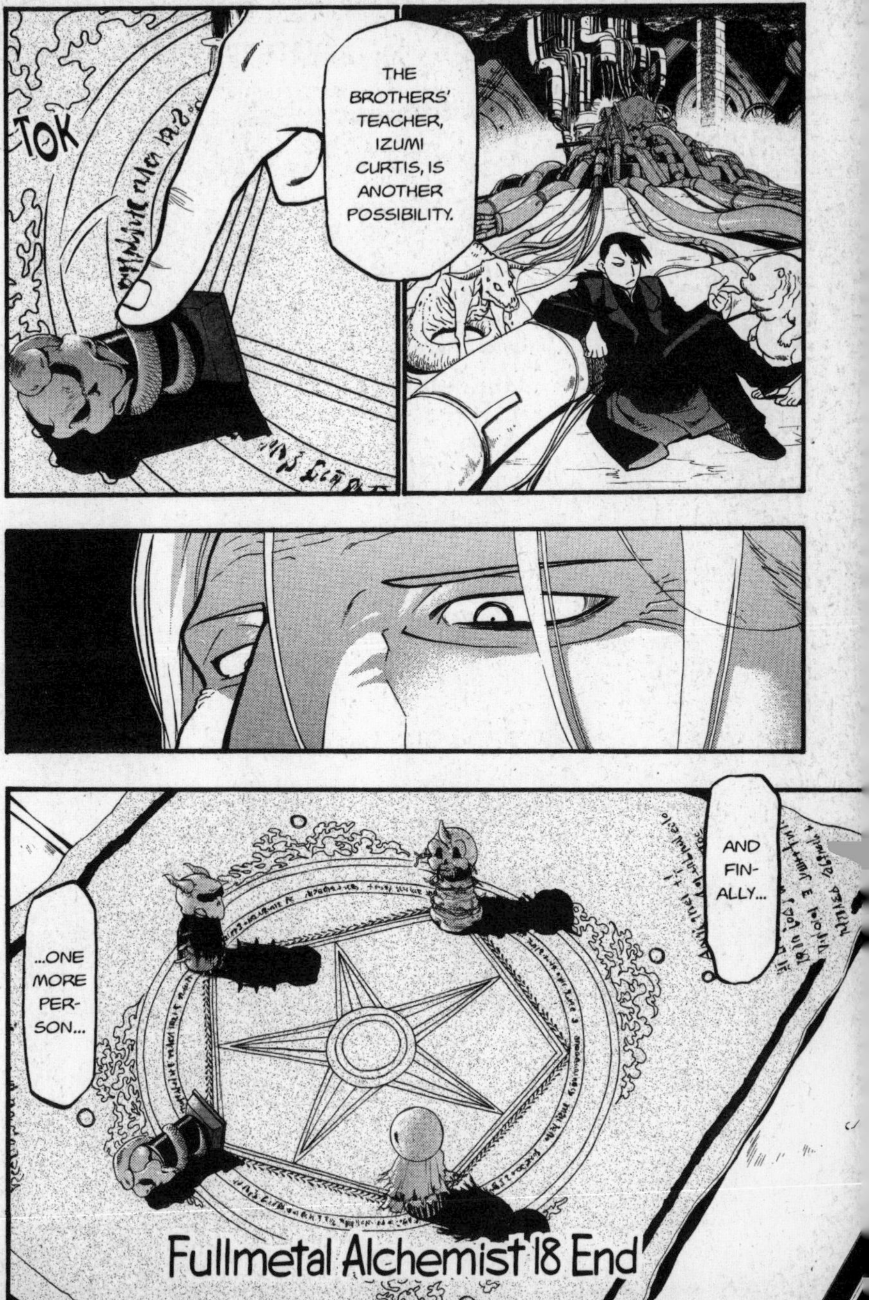
THE BROTHERS' TEACHER, IZUMI CURTIS, IS ANOTHER POSSIBILITY.
TOK
AND FIN-ALLY...
...ONE MORE PER-SON...
Fullmetal Alchemist 18 End

BAYATE THE FAITHFUL DOG

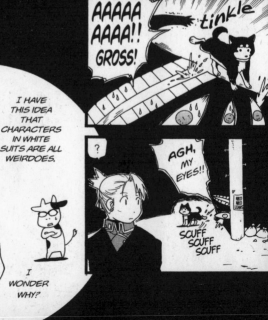

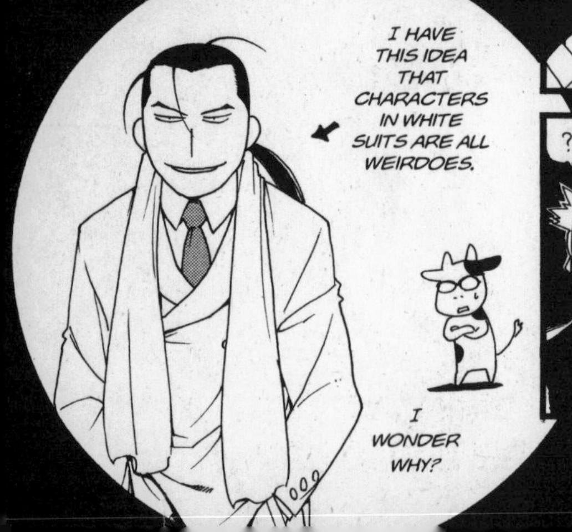

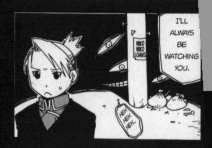

I'LL ALWAYS BE WATCHING YOU.
NIKO NIKO LOANS
HEH HEH HEH.
TUP TUP TUP TUP
HUH?
tinkle
AAAAA AAAA!! GROSS!
AGH, MY EYES!!
?
NIKO NIKO LOANS
SCUFF SCUFF SCUFF

FULLMETAL ALCHEMIST 18

SPECIAL THANKS to:

JUN TOHKO
AIYABALL
NONO
MASASHI MIZUTANI
COUPON
NORIKO TSUBOTA
HARUHI NAKAMURA
MICHIKO SHISHIDO
MASANARI YUZUKA sensei
Editor YUICHI SHIMOMURA

AND YOU!!

I HAVE THIS IDEA THAT CHARACTERS IN WHITE SUITS ARE ALL WEIRDOES.
I WONDER WHY?

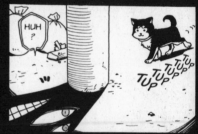

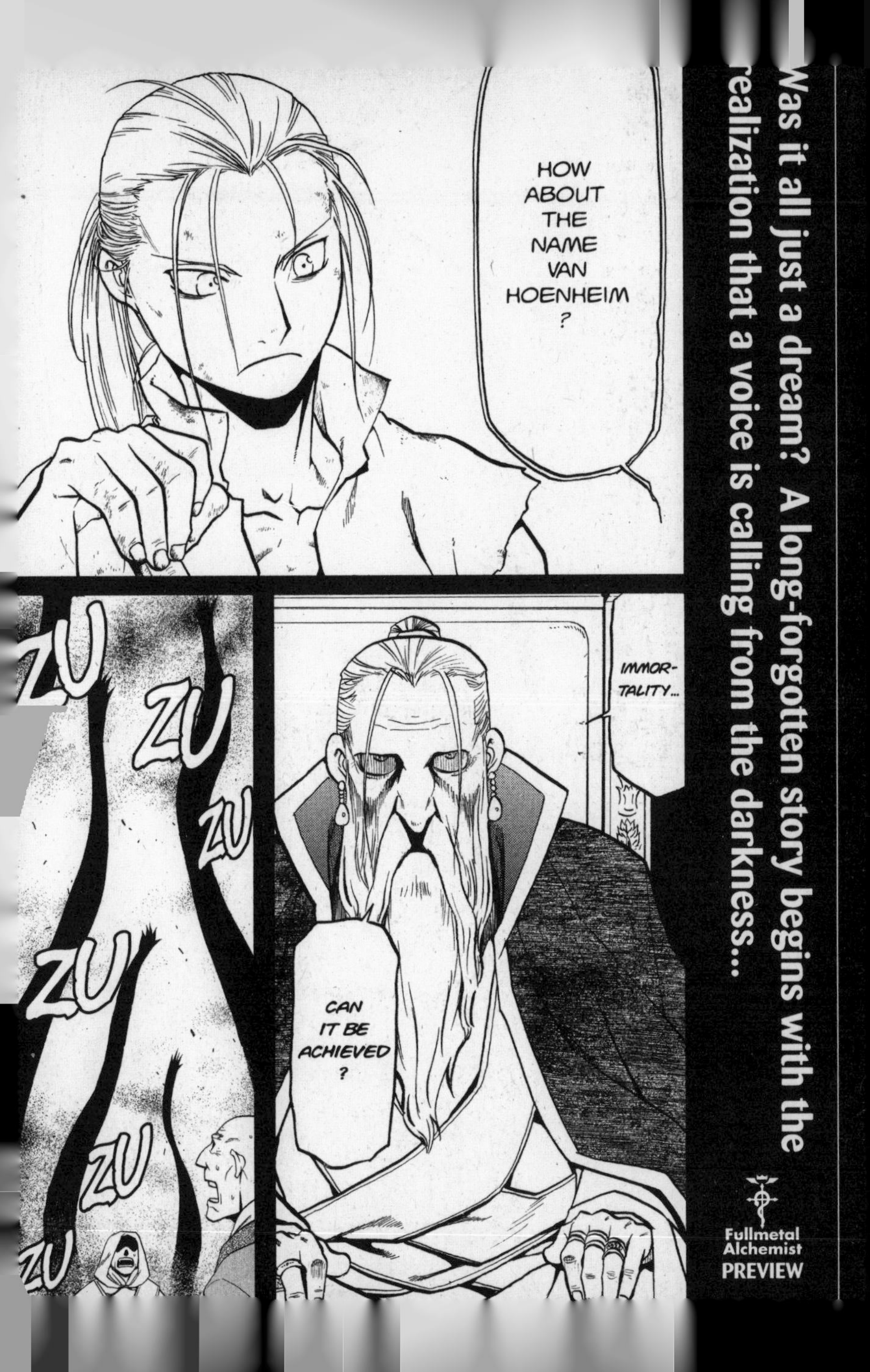
HOW ABOUT THE NAME VAN HOENHEIM?
IMMORTALITY...
CAN IT BE ACHIEVED?
ZU
ZU
ZU
ZU
ZU
ZU

Was it all just a dream? A long-forgotten story begins with the realization that a voice is calling from the darkness...

Fullmetal Alchemist
PREVIEW

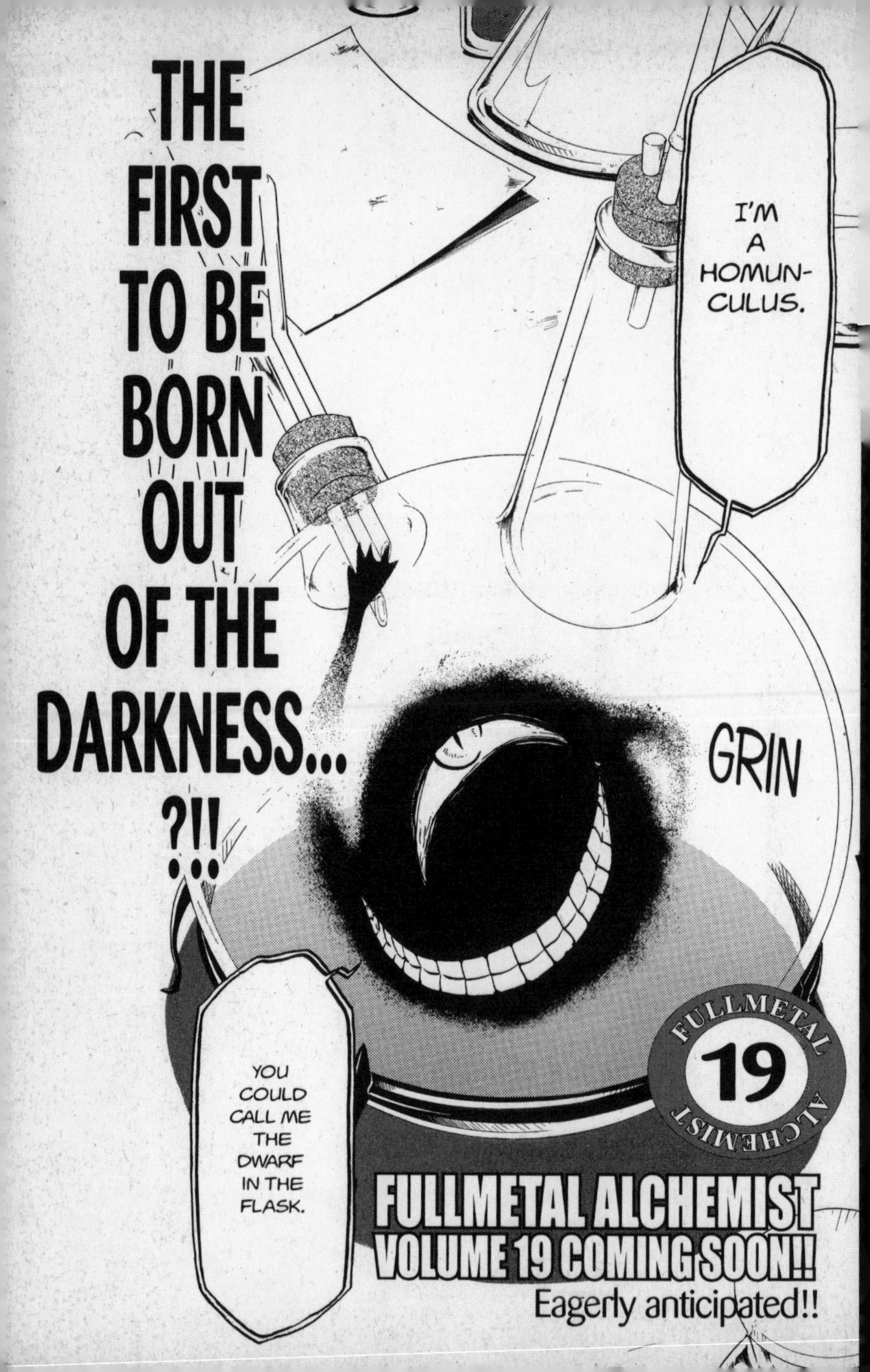
THE FIRST TO BE BORN OUT OF THE DARKNESS...?!!
I'M A HOMUN-CULUS.
GRIN
YOU COULD CALL ME THE DWARF IN THE FLASK.
FULLMETAL ALCHEMIST 19
FULLMETAL ALCHEMIST VOLUME 19 COMING SOON!!
Eagerly anticipated!!

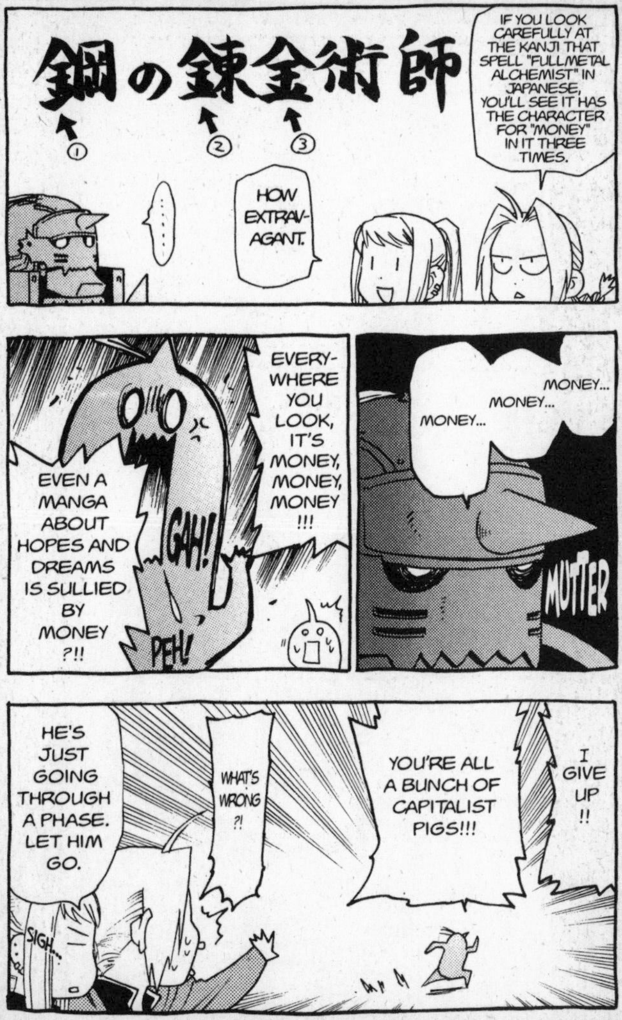
IF YOU LOOK CAREFULLY AT THE KANJI THAT SPELL "FULLMETAL ALCHEMIST" IN JAPANESE, YOU'LL SEE IT HAS THE CHARACTER FOR "MONEY" IN IT THREE TIMES.
鋼の錬金術師
①
②
③
HOW EXTRAV-AGANT.
......
MONEY...
MONEY...
MONEY...
MUTTER
EVERY-WHERE YOU LOOK, IT'S MONEY, MONEY, MONEY!!!
EVEN A MANGA ABOUT HOPES AND DREAMS IS SULLIED BY MONEY?!!
GAH!
PEH!
I GIVE UP!!
YOU'RE ALL A BUNCH OF CAPITALIST PIGS!!!
WHAT'S WRONG?!
HE'S JUST GOING THROUGH A PHASE. LET HIM GO.
SIGH...

IF MR. YOKI ATTEMPTED HUMAN TRANSMUTATION

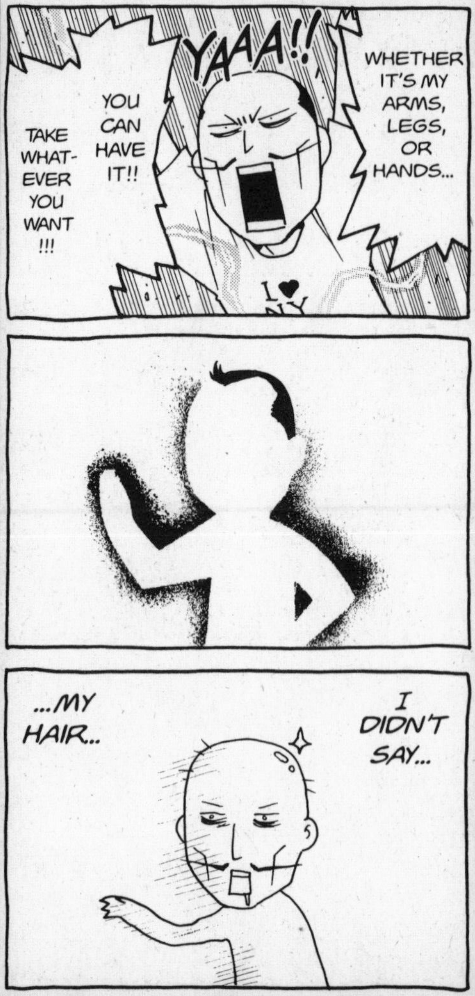
YAAA!!
WHETHER IT'S MY ARMS, LEGS, OR HANDS...
YOU CAN HAVE IT!!
TAKE WHAT-EVER YOU WANT !!!
I ♥ NY
I DIDN'T SAY...
...MY HAIR...

Fullmetal Alchemist Profiles

Get the background story and world history of the manga, plus:

- Character bios
- New, original artwork
- Interview with creator Hiromu Arakawa
- Bonus manga episode only available in this book

Fullmetal Alchemist Anime Profiles

Stay on top of your favorite episodes and characters with:

- Actual cel artwork from the TV series
- Summaries of all 51 TV episodes
- Definitive cast biographies
- Exclusive poster for your wall

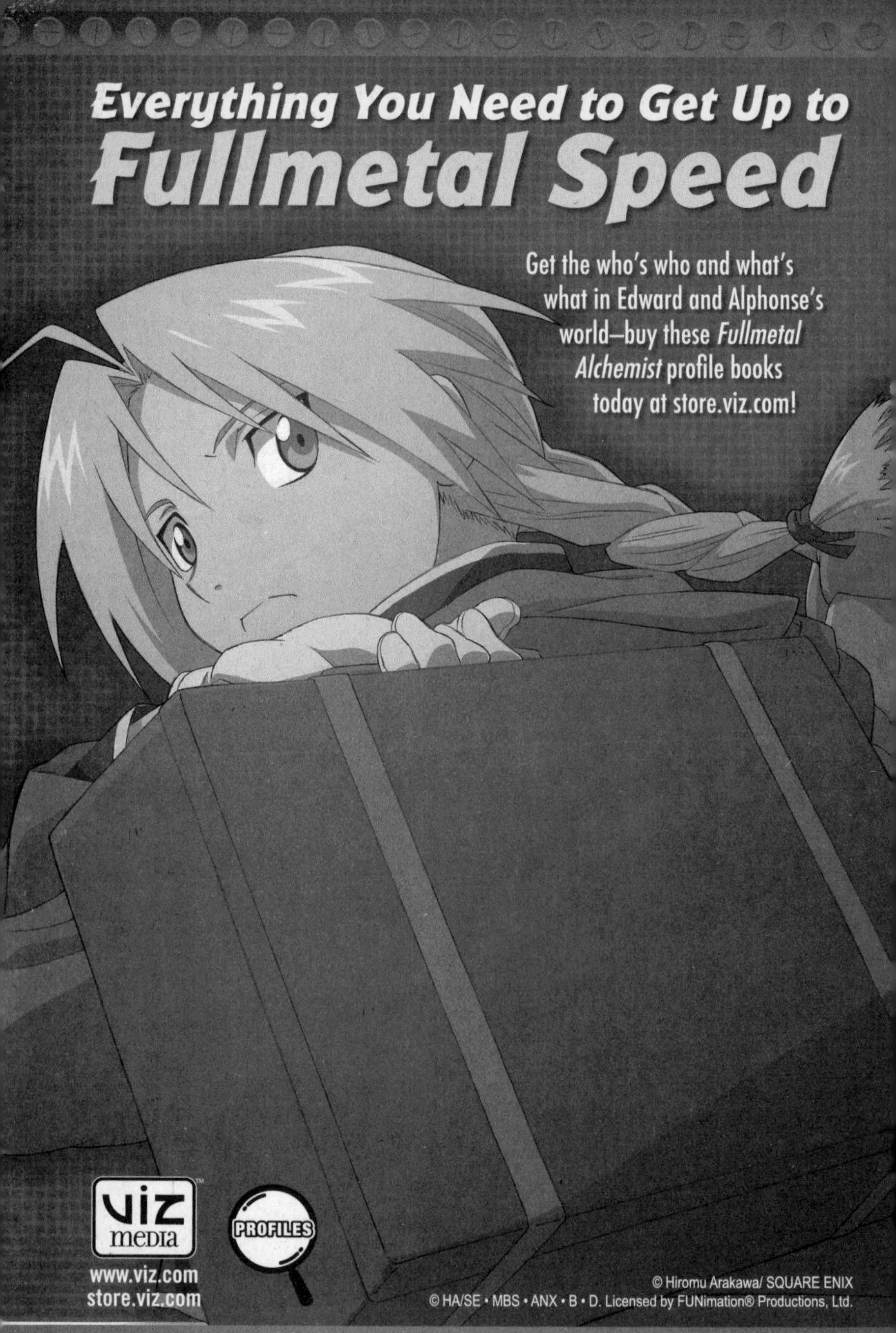

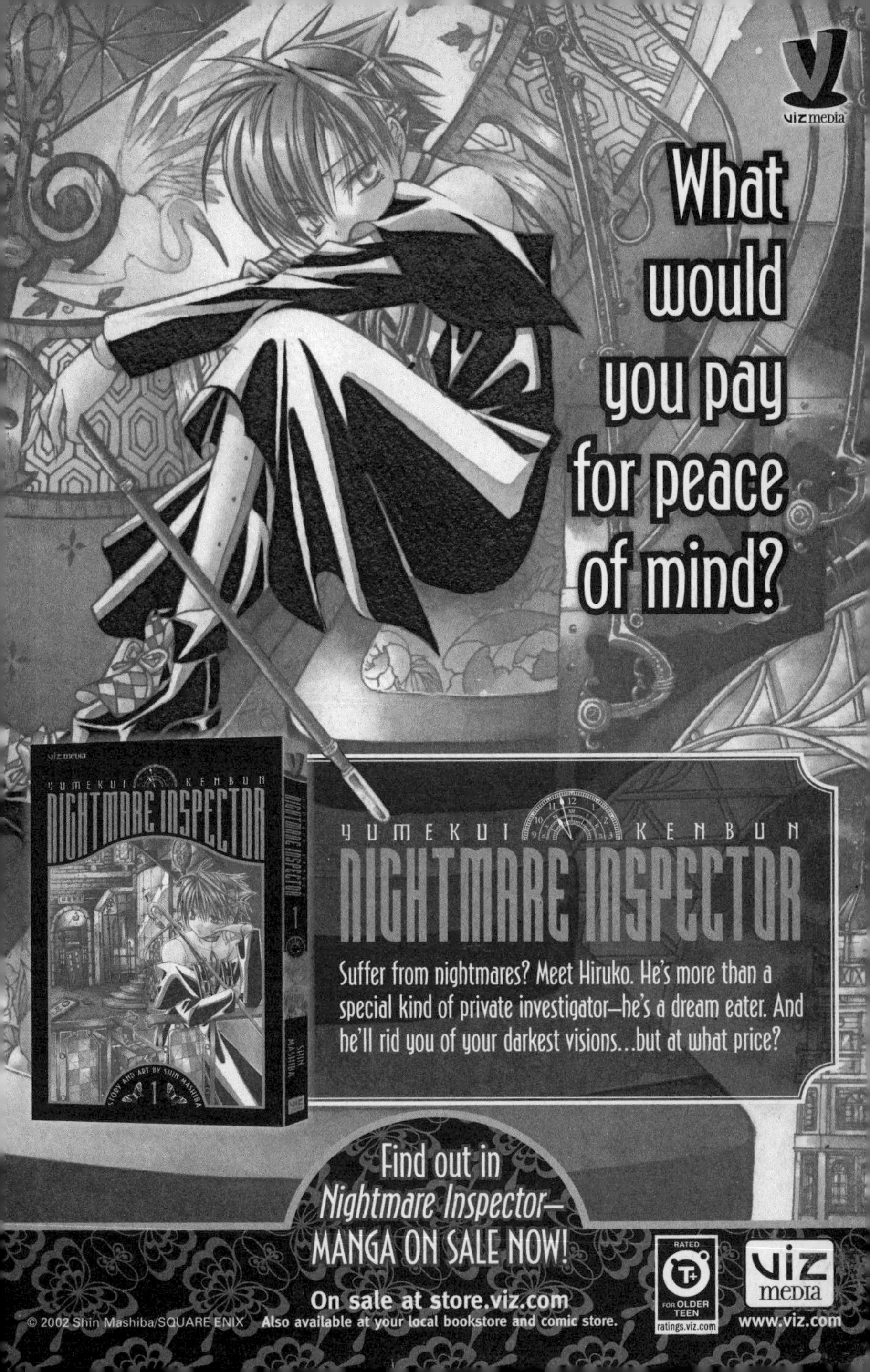

viz media
What would you pay for peace of mind?
viz media
YUMEKUI KENBUN
NIGHTMARE INSPECTOR
SHIN MASHIBA
1
STORY AND ART BY SHIN MASHIBA
YUMEKUI KENBUN
NIGHTMARE INSPECTOR
Suffer from nightmares? Meet Hiruko. He's more than a special kind of private investigator—he's a dream eater. And he'll rid you of your darkest visions...but at what price?
Find out in Nightmare Inspector—MANGA ON SALE NOW!
RATED T+ FOR OLDER TEEN
ratings.viz.com
viz media
On sale at store.viz.com
© 2002 Shin Mashiba/SQUARE ENIX
Also available at your local bookstore and comic store.
www.viz.com

LOVE MA

LET US KNOW WHAT YOU THINK!

OUR MANGA SURVEY IS NOW AVAILABLE ONLINE. PLEASE VISIT: VIZ.COM/MANGASURVEY

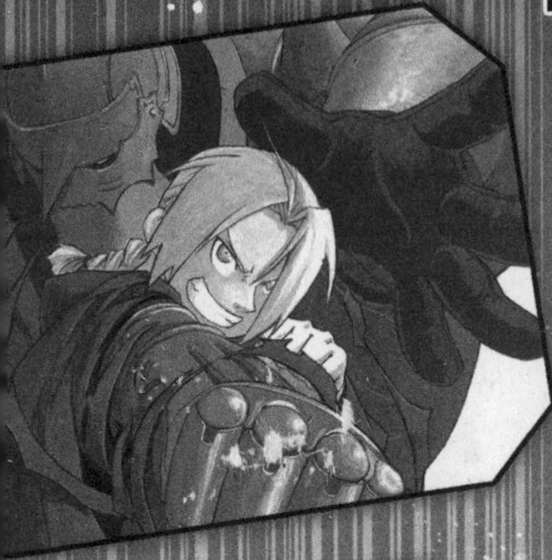
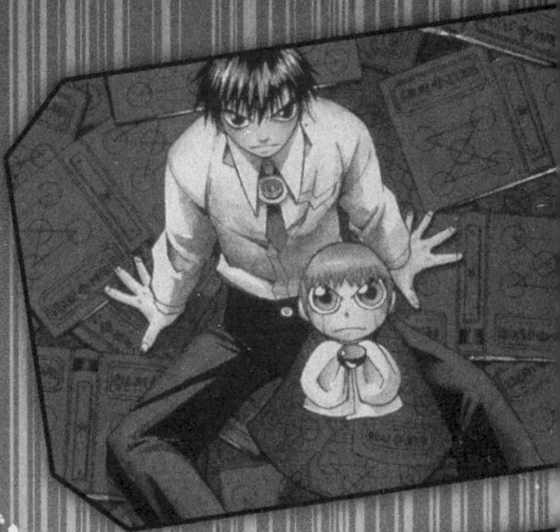
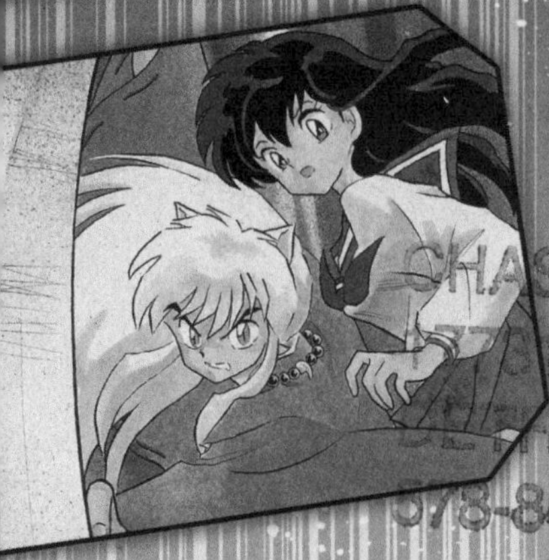
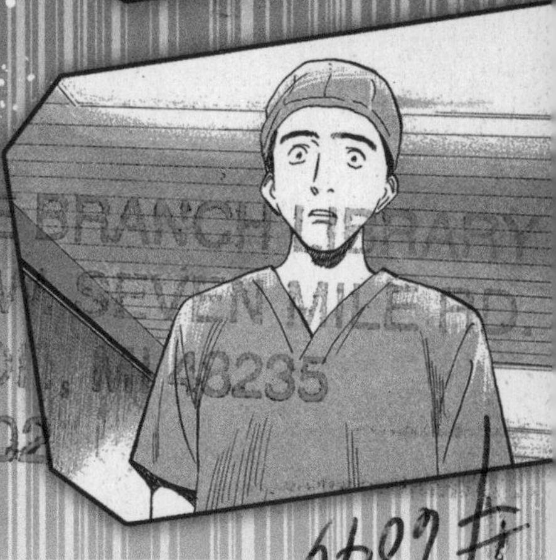

HELP US MAKE THE MANGA YOU LOVE BETTER!